Rule of Darkness

From James Montgomery, James Grahame, and E. Benger, *Poems on the Abolition of the Slave Trade* (1809).

Rule of Darkness

British Literature and
Imperialism, 1830–1914

Patrick Brantlinger

Cornell University Press
Ithaca and London

First published 1988 by Cornell University Press.

International Standard Book Number 0-8014-2090-3
Library of Congress Catalog Card Number 87-47823

Printed in the United States of America

Librarians: Library of Congress cataloging information appears on the last page of the book.

The paper in this book is acid-free and meets the guidelines for permanence and durability of the Committee on Production Guidelines for Book Longevity of the Council on Library Resources.

For Lavon, Leone, Rose, and Arnold

Contents

Preface

THE bibliography of studies of the British Empire in the nineteenth century is enormous. Controversies about the causes of imperial expansion, often focused on validating, qualifying, or refuting some version of the "economic theory of imperialism," are as live and unsettled today as they were in 1902 when John Hobson published *Imperialism: A Study.* Out of these controversies have arisen distinctions between various periods and kinds of imperialist expansion and domination, probably the most important of them the distinction between the era from the end of the Napoleonic Wars to the Berlin Conference of 1884–85 and the New Imperialism that began in the 1880s. This New Imperialism was characterized by intense rivalry among the European powers during the Scramble for Africa and large portions of Asia and the South Pacific.

As observers have concentrated their attention on the Scramble as a prelude to World War I, so developments in the early and mid-Victorian years have sometimes been overshadowed or ignored. Indeed, before the 1960s historians often treated those years with scant reference to imperialism, sometimes even viewing them as anti-imperialist. Although more recent historians have recognized that the expansion of the British Empire was continuous, albeit unsystematic, throughout the nineteenth century, they still sometimes deal with the period from 1830 to the 1880s as though imperialism was not yet an important issue.

The problem has been exacerbated by the ambiguity of the term "imperialism," itself a source of contention not only for historians and literary critics but for those politicians, journalists, colonists, social critics, and ordinary citizens who, during the nineteenth century, helped build the modern British Empire. Does imperialism refer only to formal acts of territorial aggrandizement by the state, or does it refer also to an ideology or range of ideological positions, from militant jingoism shading off into vaguer sentiments of patriotism and racial superiority? Even among those historians who treat empire-building as a continuous economic and political process, the idea still seems prevalent that the early and mid-Victorians were not imperialists in the ideological sense because they were not highly conscious of the Empire as a problem—in other words, because they were not jingoists. Such a conclusion overlooks the many forms that imperialist ideology took even without being highly self-conscious or militant. Indeed, the easy confidence about British world domination expressed in much Victorian writing prior to the 1880s can only be called imperialist, although it rarely boiled up into arguments for the military seizure of new territory. This was the era of "free trade imperialism," to adopt a phrase current, although still controversial, since the work of Ronald Robinson and John Gallagher. Historians following Robinson and Gallagher have mapped in great detail the actual expansion of the British Empire through the nineteenth century, but they have been less clear about the development of imperialist ideology. This book is an attempt to map the development of that ideology, especially from 1830 to the 1880s. It focuses on all forms of discourse but particularly on narrative forms—adventure tales, travelogues, histories—in which imperialist ideology was expressed, often with great energy and clarity. Its key point is that, though emphases and even theories about the Empire fluctuated greatly, imperialist discourse, like the actual expansion of the Empire, was continuous, informing all aspects of Victorian culture and society.

This is, then, a work of cultural history—not literary history or criticism in the traditional sense, nor political and social history. It assumes, with Michel Foucault, that discourse is a form of power, and that therefore what the Victorians thought, wrote, and read about their developing Empire mattered, even though what they thought, wrote, and read can now be critically understood as "ideology" (with that word's inevitable suggestion of error or mystification). Imperialist ideology was quite simply the chief enabling factor that made the political support for and expansion of the Empire possible. I have more to say about ideology, and especially about the ideological properties of various kinds of writing, in individual chapters. Here I note only that the retrospective critique of ideology cannot alter or improve upon the past, of course, but perhaps it can help change patterns of domination and racist thought in the present by revealing that the past is, for better or worse, our inheritance.

I explain my debts to various scholars—Martin Green, Fredric Jameson, Edward Said, Raymond Williams, and others—in the introduction. I am also indebted to students at Indiana University who have taken V611, my Victorian Studies seminar on imperialism, some of whom have written Ph.D. dissertations on related subjects. Samuel Olorounto on modern African novelists, Ling Mei Lim on V. S. Naipaul, Joan Corwin on Victorian and early modern travel literature, and Michael Harris on several colonial and postcolonial writers have all taught me a great deal, particularly about Victorian travel writing and about twentieth-century non-British responses to imperialism. Among my V611 students, I am especially indebted to Kimberly Koza, Paula Krebs, Jil Larson, Jeanne Laurel, Carolyn Redouty, and Keith Welsh. To the list I should add various names for various reasons: Richard Boyle, William Burgan, Donald Gray, Louis Hawes, Roger Henkle, Catherine Hoyser, Elizabeth Kalikoff, Jeanne Peterson, Thomas Prasch, John Reed, Allyn Roberts, David Slayden, William Thesing, and Martha Vicinus, as well as, in general, the Victorian Studies Club. Mary Burgan, chair of my department, and Deans Morton Lowengrub and Anya Royce have also been supportive, as has librarian Anthony Shipps. I also thank the John Simon Guggenheim Foundation and the National Endowment for the Humanities, whose fellowships helped support some of my research. And I am obligated to several journal editors and presses for permission to use revised versions of some earlier publications: to Thomas Mitchell, editor of *Critical Inquiry*, and the University of Chicago Press, to use the material in chapter 7; to Robert Langenfeld, editor of *English Literature in Transition*, to use some of the material in chapter 9; and to Arthur Marotti, editor of *Criticism*, and Wayne State University Press, to use, in revised form, the essay on *Heart of Darkness* that makes up chapter 10. Bernhard Kendler, Roger Haydon, and the Cornell University Press staff have been models of professional efficiency and kindness. And, of course, I am generally, always, grateful to Ellen, Andy, Susan, and Jeremy, all of whom helped somehow—as workers, wife, friends, students, teachers, inspirations, kids, distractions. This book is also for them.

PATRICK BRANTLINGER

Bloomington, Indiana

Rule of Darkness

"NEW CROWNS FOR OLD ONES!"

(Aladdin *adapted*.)

"Aladdin" Disraeli presenting Queen Victoria with the crown of the Empire of India. From *Punch*, 15 April 1876.

Introduction

The loyal to their crown
Are loyal to their own far sons, who love
Our ocean-empire with her boundless homes
For ever-broadening England, and her throne
In our vast Orient, and one isle, one isle,
That knows not her own greatness: if she knows
And dreads it we are fall'n.

—TENNYSON

In his review of my *Spirit of Reform: British Literature and Politics, 1832–1867*, George Woodcock noted that I had focused on domestic politics and said little about India, Canada, and the rest of the British Empire. But the era between the first two reform bills was, he noted, also "the age of . . . the Indian Mutiny, and its end is marked not only by the second Reform Act, but also by the British North America Act of the same year." Woodcock partially exonerated me on the ground that "early Victorian writers and journalists were for the most part unconscious Little Englanders. Only a few of them . . . were interested in the growing empire. By the end of the century all this had changed dramatically."[1] His is a familiar view, one to which I had indeed unconsciously subscribed. According to C. A. Bodelsen, in a book first published in 1925, "the part played by the colonies in mid-Victorian fiction is surprisingly small. A person dependent on [that] fiction . . . might be excused if he failed to discover that the Empire consisted of more than the islands of Great Britain and Ireland."[2] Sixty years later the same view still predominates. In his recent study of the British in India, for example, Karl de Schweinitz writes: "If one believes that the great Victorian novels reflected the critical problems of the society, one is forced to conclude that interest in imperialism was non-existent. At the most the colonies in that literature were far off-stage, a distant world to which the dramatis personae could be banished if it were convenient for the development of the novel. No one in Dickens, Thackeray, Eliot, or Trollope brooded about the imperial relationship."[3]

Woodcock's comments suggested to me a sequel to *The Spirit of Reform*, a book that would deal with Victorian literature and imperialism. But where to begin? If one accepts the traditional view, then the early and mid-Victorians were perhaps as oblivious to India and Canada as I had been when analyzing their responses to Chartism and the Anti-Corn Law League. In that case, a study of imperialist ideology might safely begin after the Second Reform Bill of 1867, when a self-conscious, drum-beating jingoism began to emerge in British culture. *The Spirit of Reform*, concerned with the first thirty years of Victoria's reign, might then be neatly followed by *The Spirit of Empire, 1867–1914*.

So tidy a chronological division, however, would clearly be much too tidy. The early and mid-Victorians were far from indifferent to "the colonies." On the contrary, colonial politics influenced all domestic issues and reform movements throughout the century. Although their attitudes and emphases often differed from those of later generations, many early Victorians took a keen interest in emigration, the "opening up" of Africa, the Eastern Question, and even the China trade. Only on the narrowest definition of imperialism as the explicit advocacy of the acquisition of new territory can it be said that any major early Victorian writer or politican was anti-imperialist.

In Thomas Carlyle, Bodelsen finds at least some of the ingredients of supposedly *later* imperialist ideology but views him as idiosyncratic, a prophet before his time, one moreover whose "influence on Imperialist thought and on the growth of the Imperialist movement is not striking" (24). Yet Bodelsen also quotes Carlyle himself in *Latter-Day Pamphlets* (1850): " 'Colonies excite more attention at present than any of our other interests' " (23). Similarly, among the four novelists whom Karl de Schweinitz thinks had little to say about "the imperial relationship," one—William Makepeace Thackeray—was born in India. Another—Anthony Trollope—wrote extensively about Ireland, Jamaica, Canada, Australia, and South Africa. Indeed, the colonies are the chief subject of Trollope's series of travelogues, which begins with *The West Indies and the Spanish Main* (1859), and he also wrote about them in several of his novels, as in the Australian setting of *John Caldigate* (1879).

Trollope is interesting in part because he wrote so much about the Empire even while he has seemed, at least to some critics, to have written little about it, and that from an anti- or at least a nonimperialist point of view. Of course to conclude that Trollope was not an imperialist, one must treat Ireland as a special case—not a colony, not imperialized territory—because Trollope often writes about it and always from a unionist or imperialist perspective. Moreover, Trollope offers a paradigm of the evolution from early to late Victorian Liberal attitudes toward the Empire. Trollope's "colonial thought passed through three phases," John Davidson contends, although he adds that, partly because the novelist was never a systematic thinker, these phases are not sharply distinct one from another. In the first phase Trollope expressed "separatist" views about some colonies, evident in *The West Indies* and in *North America* (1862). In the latter book Trollope contends, as Davidson puts it, that "colonial independence [is] not only inevitable, but desirable."[4]

Trollope thought of separation not as ending the imperial relationship, however, but as strengthening it. As he says about Canada in *North America*, colonies settled by British immigrants are like children whom the parent country should expect one day to grow up. It would be to repeat the blundering that caused the American Revolution not to grant the colonies freedom when they reach maturity. "It is very hard for a mother country to know when such a time has come; and hard also for the child-colony to recognize justly the period of its own maturity."[5] Of course Trollope excluded Ireland and India from his developmental paradigm, but Canada, South Africa, New South Wales—these colonies should all travel the route taken by the American colonies, though they should travel it nonviolently and with full encouragement from Britain. The ties of race, language, and trade would ensure their remaining within the imperial family—the sort of loose, supposedly voluntary structure still associated with the British Commonwealth of Nations.

In his next phase, roughly 1874–1880, the period of Disraeli's second administration, Trollope as Liberal propagandist attacked the trend toward imperializing new areas in the tropics (Davidson, 329). Here it would be easy again to construe Trollope's views as anti-imperialist. But as he had argued for greater independence for the colonies of white settlement, so Trollope objected to new territorial acquisitions in the tropics because he wished to strengthen the imperial relationship that already existed. First things first: he saw nothing to be gained by hoisting the Union Jack on Fiji. He believed that partitioning Africa would involve Britain in costly wars for parts of the globe apparently not suited to white colonization. In *South Africa* (1878) he expressed the fear that annexing Egypt would be a grave mistake, despising what he saw as Conservative opportunism. In October 1874, in one of his letters to the Liverpool *Mercury*, Trollope wrote: "There is, I think, a general opinion that Great

Britain possesses enough of the world . . . and that new territorial possessions must be regarded rather as increased burdens than increased strength. No doubt the power of the country and the prestige which belongs to its name are based on its colonial and Indian empire. Every Englishman sufficiently awake to be proud of England feels this; but there is at the same time a general conviction that . . . we have got all that can do us good, and that we should abstain from taking more, if it be possible to abstain."[6]

If we define imperialism narrowly, to include only the sort of opinion Trollope objected to—that is, the view that Britain has the right and duty to annex new territories whenever it seems in her interest to do so—of course we can describe Trollope as anti-imperialist. But Trollope objects to grabbing Fiji or Egypt because he has in mind the larger goal of defending and nurturing the Empire inherited from Britain's glorious past. Nowhere does he argue that India, the key to British power and glory, should be returned to the Indians, or that white settlers should relinquish the Cape to black Africans. On the contrary, he expresses the consistent, Carlylean view that non-European peoples—especially those of African descent, whether former slaves in Jamaica or Zulus in Natal—can progress toward civilization (without, perhaps, ever reaching it) only through white domination. Trollope thinks also, however, that through the mixing of races such groups as the "coloureds" or "mulattoes" he saw everywhere in Jamaica may combine the (white) intellectual ability and the (black) physical stamina necessary to plant civilization in the tropics.

Through the first two phases of his thinking about the colonies, Trollope believed that Britain must wisely govern the Empire it already possessed before thinking about conquering other parts of the globe. But during a third phase that Davidson labels "pessimistic," Trollope adopted views closer to the bellicose, conservative attitudes traditionally identified with imperialism. Davidson suggests that "troubles in Ireland, the Transvaal, and Egypt led him to break with the Liberal party, despair of the future, and embrace *machtpolitik* whenever the necessity arose" (329). In this last, brief phase Trollope came to believe that even the older colonies of white settlement should not be granted full independence, at least not in the near future. Britain would need to provide these colonies with continuing protection—both economic and military—and with "tutelage." And he tended also to be much more willing to countenance military solutions to Britain's overseas problems, particularly with regard to the Irish and the Boers.

To identify only this third phase of Trollope's opinions as imperialist is to overlook the consistent elements in his thinking, which corresponded closely to the developing attitudes of many Victorian Liberals. From the 1830s to the 1870s, public opinion generally seems to have favored granting partial independence to the colonies of white settlement (though not to India and other territories not settled by large numbers of British immigrants). With the Eastern and African crises of the seventies and early eighties, many Victorians veered toward the pessimism that Trollope expressed in his last phase. The earlier crises of the Indian Mutiny (1857) and the Jamaica Rebellion (1865), combined with almost continuous troubles in Ireland, helped trigger this shift, but no period in the nineteenth century can safely be called anti-imperialist or even indifferent to colonial issues. In fact, most early Victorians would have been mightily shocked by any suggestion that they took no interest in that glorious manifestation of "the genius of the race," the British Empire.

Whether one finds imperialism in a particular era depends largely on what one is looking for. By defining imperialism exclusively as an officially sanctioned policy of the direct military seizure and government of one nation or territory by another, historians sometimes come close to discovering that imperialism did not exist before about 1880; after that date the British Empire expanded greatly, but politicians at home were at most only "reluctant imperialists"—Gladstone is a prime example, unhappily agreeing to the invasion of Egypt in 1882. This narrow definition of imperialism may even make it appear that, time after time, Britain was reluctantly sucked into acquiring new territory. Nature apparently abhors weak societies as much as it abhors vacuums, and strong societies cannot help rushing in to occupy the weak. This historiographical approach hearks back to Sir John Seeley's famous, misleading dictum that "we seem, as it were, to have conquered and peopled half the world in a fit of absence of mind."[7] The politicians and taxpayers at home did not want more colonies to govern, goes this theory; even "the men on the spot," on the imperial frontiers, may not have wanted them; but the exigencies of the moment kept forcing Britain's hand.

If we take imperial expansion case by case—Afghanistan, the Transvaal, Egypt—such a view seems to have merit. Yet even the most reluctant imperialists were still imperialists, reluctantly opting to annex new territories because they believed that expansion was the best or at least the most expedient way to defend the Empire that already existed. As an ideology, moreover, imperialism bundles together different elements that more or less cohere, though these elements may also appear separately or in varying combinations, and with varying degrees of intensity.

Advocacy of territorial expansion by military force is one such element, no doubt the most obvious, but one could be, like Trollope, an imperialist without such advocacy. The other elements of imperialist ideology include, first and foremost, a chauvinism based on loyalty to the existing Empire, both to the ruling nation and to its colonies. Such chauvinism Trollope expressed in full measure throughout his career, and clearly it makes no sense to talk about imperialism without this element. Often a corollary to the advocacy of territorial annexation, though by no means a constant like imperial chauvinism, is advocacy of the use of military force to settle issues of foreign policy. The glorification of the military and of war frequently crops up as a subtheme of imperial chauvinism. Here Trollope, at least through the first two phases of his colonial thought, stops short: he is no praiser of war, and he frets about the expense new wars might entail, draining the national economy. But Trollope often expresses two further elements of imperialist ideology. He fully believes in the racial superiority of white Europeans (and of the English over all other Europeans). And he believes that, wherever the British flag flies, he and his compatriots have a responsibility to import the light of civilization (identified as especially English), thus illuminating the supposedly dark places of the world. In short, he believes in the "civilizing mission" of Britain, greatest nation in history. Like him, the majority of Victorian intellectuals and politicians, both early and late, expressed these ideas at one time or another, in varying combinations. The ideology was adaptable, shifting; its constituent parts, even though they are usually associated with various brands of conservatism, could just as easily consort with liberal and even radical political attitudes toward domestic issues.

One object of this book is to show how early and mid-Victorians expressed imperialist ideology in their writings, and a second object is to reassess, albeit briefly, late Victorian and Edwardian imperialist attitudes in light of earlier concerns. Imperialism, understood as an evolving but pervasive set of attitudes and ideas toward the rest of the world, influenced all aspects of Victorian and Edwardian culture. In some writers, attitudes that seem only loosely related and perhaps unconscious in early work crystallize into more consciously articulated positions later, following a path similar to Trollope's. Tennyson provides an obvious instance. It is common knowledge that as poet laureate he wrote occasional poems with imperialist themes, such as "The Revenge" (1878) and "The Defense of Lucknow" (1879), but neither the orientalism nor the patriotism expressed in many of his early poems has always been seen as connected with imperial issues. Thus W. D. Paden could analyze Tennyson's adolescent poems on oriental themes in relation to his reading, and to his "arrested" emotional development, without saying anything about their implicit politics.[8] Even the patriotic poems of the 1830s—"Love Thou Thy Land," "Of Old Sat Freedom on the Heights," and the rest—are often passed over as if merely occasional rather than expressions of an evolving, coherent ideology. But the political messages in Tennyson's early poetry are of a piece with those in his last writings:

> Hail Briton! in whatever zone
> Binds the broad earth beneath the blue,
> In ancient seasons or in new,
> No bolder front than thine is shone.[9]

Tennyson might have penned "Hail Briton!" at any time from the early 1830s on.

Furthermore, although the political values informing Tennyson's early oriental poems—"Persia," "The Ganges," and so forth—are not explicit, that fact itself suggests something about the evolution of what Edward Said calls orientalism. The "mysterious Orient" seems to the early Tennyson a daydream realm of ahistorical, exotic, and erotic pleasures, locked away in a charming past that bears no immediate relation to the concerns of modern, progressive, real Europe. But the political attitudes in these early poems, even if only unconscious, obviously relate to those consciously expressed in later poems, including "Akbar's Dream" (1892). There the great ruler of the Moghul Empire describes to his chief minister a prophetic dream in which he foresees the downfall of Moghul power and the coming of the British, bringing peace, justice, and civilizing reforms.

> I watched my son,
> And those that followed, loosen, stone from stone,
> All my fair work; and from the ruin arose
> The shriek and curse of trampled millions, even
> As in the time before; but while I groaned,
> From out the sunset poured an alien race,
> Who fitted stone to stone again, and Truth,
> Peace, Love and Justice came and dwelt therein,
> Nor in the field without were seen or heard
> Fires of Suttee, nor wail of baby-wife,
> Or Indian widow; and in sleep I said
> "All praise to Alla by whatever hands
> My mission be accomplished!"[10]

Akbar is an oriental King Arthur. The great work he has begun of civilizing the Indian wilderness will collapse, but the British will take it up again and complete it on a permanent basis.[11]

The examples of Carlyle, Trollope, and Tennyson could easily be multiplied. Yet some literary critics have tended to identify imperialism with only a handful of late Victorian and Edwardian writers; the usual list does not extend much beyond Rudyard Kipling, H. Rider Haggard, W. E. Henley, John Davidson, and a few others. Among some critics there is an evident desire to downplay politics altogether; my own view is closer to Fredric Jameson's. He contends that "the political perspective" is more than a theme and in terms of critical theory is also more than a mere "supplementary method . . . auxiliary to other interpretive methods current today"; such a perspective is rather "the absolute horizon of all reading and all interpretation."[12] This is true not because class consciousness or economic forces "determine" in some absolute, one-dimensional manner the ideas and values expressed in literature but simply because literature is inevitably social: it is written in society, by social beings, addressed to other social beings; it is written in language (to descend the obvious), and language as discourse inevitably both shapes and expresses social relationships—it is the very ground of their possibility.

Among recent analysts both Edward Said in *Orientalism* and Martin Green in *Dreams of Adventure, Deeds of Empire,* have treated imperialist ideology as informing all nineteenth-century European and American culture. Said defines orientalism as "a kind of Western projection onto and will to govern over the Orient" that manifests itself over the last two centuries in innumerable cultural productions, from the social sciences to the popular arts.[13] Applying Said's approach to French writing about Africa, Christopher L. Miller has analyzed an "Africanism" parallel to orientalism.[14] Previous forms of cultural history and criticism, particularly Marxist analyses of ideology, have not always paid adequate attention to racism, even while they have much to say about imperialism as a stage of capitalism ("the last") and as a form of false consciousness. But Frantz Fanon, Kwame Nkrumah, and other Third World writers have forged their own tradition of radical analysis, and recent feminist theorists have developed related accounts of the interplay between forms of domination, based on gender as well as on class and race.[15] Their work demonstrates the one-sidedness of imperialism's discourse with "difference," with its other or others—its deafness to alternative voices—and suggests how closely imperialism, racism, and sexism are interwoven, both with each other and with seemingly distinct systems of discourse, particularly those of social class, gender, and political reform.

Shakespeare's *Tempest* might be taken as the starting point for a full account of British imperialism in literature, Green suggests, but he starts instead with the Glorious Revolution of 1688 and Defoe's *Robinson Crusoe*, arguing: "There are reasons for dating the British empire's rise at the end of the seventeenth century, in fact at the Union of England with Scotland, in 1707; which is to say, at the very historical moment when the adventure tale began to be written, since *Robinson Crusoe* appeared in 1719. Defoe was one of the English government's agents in negotiating that union. And Defoe, rather than Shakespeare, is my candidate for the prototype of literary imperialism."[16] One essential point well established by Green, even with his rather late point of departure, is that the influence of imperial expansion on British culture has been continuous (it is not over yet, as the Falklands War showed). In the history of that influence the New Imperialism from the 1870s down to 1914 is only one of the more obvious chapters.

A second point Green makes is that "the adventure tales that formed the light reading of Englishmen for two hundred years and more after *Robinson Crusoe* were, in fact, the energizing myth of English imperialism. They were, collectively, the story England told itself as it went to sleep at night; and, in the form of its dreams, they charged England's will with the energy to go out into the world and explore, conquer, and rule" (3). I agree, and will have much to say about the structural and ideological properties of adventure tales, as well as the relations between such tales and other literary forms. Green notes that, in "the system of literature," pride of place has been given to the courtship or domestic novel; "the adventure novel was assigned less significance, and matched with more superficial responses" (54). But in political terms, Green suspects, imperialist adventure fiction has probably been "more influential than the serious novel" (49). This perception calls for an examination of the cultural dynamics that have caused this literary division of labor. In fiction the British Empire usually comes in second to domestic concerns, just as "natives" and "savages" are usually viewed as subhuman relative to Britons. Yet the "benighted" regions of the world, occupied by mere natives, offer brilliantly charismatic realms of adventure for white heroes, usually free from the complexities of relations with white women. Afterward, however, like Ulysses the heroes sail home, bank their treasures or invest their profits (provided the treasures do not disintegrate en route, like the radioactive "quap" in H. G. Wells's *Tono Bungay*), and settle into patriarchal, domestic routines.

Imperialism influenced not only the tradition of the adventure tale but the tradition of "serious" domestic realism as well. Adventure and domesticity, romance and realism, are the seemingly opposite poles of a single system of discourse, the literary equivalents of imperial domination abroad and liberal reform at home. In the middle of the most serious domestic concerns, often in the most unlikely texts, the Empire may intrude as a shadowy realm of escape, renewal, banishment, or return for characters who for one reason or another need to enter or exit from scenes of domestic conflict. As in Renaissance pastoral, so in the nineteenth-century English novel: a season of imperial adventure in an exotic setting can cure almost any moral disease. In *Sense and Sensibility*, India is only the place where Colonel Brandon has served, the land of "nabobs, gold mohrs, and palanquins," but the Antigua background in *Mansfield Park*, though not described, is obviously more significant. And while the India of *Jane Eyre* might be dismissed as incidental background, pertinent only to St. John Rivers, Mr. Rochester's West Indian ties, including his marriage to Bertha Mason, suggest the centrality of the imperial context, as Jean Rhys showed in her 1966 novel, *Wide Sargasso Sea*.

The Empire is something more than casual background in that quietest of domestic stories, *Cranford*, when the tedium of spinsterhood is disrupted by the return of Miss Matty's prodigal brother Peter from his military career in India. What he brings to Cranford is above all stories, tall tales, news of an exotic world of color and adventure which obviously contrasts with the unexciting routines of the elderly women who are the novel's main characters. "The ladies vied with each other who should admire him most; and no wonder; for their quiet lives were astonishingly stirred up by the arrival from India—especially as the person arrived told more wonderful stories than Sinbad the sailor; and, as Miss Pole said, was quite as good as an Arabian night any evening."[17]

Mr. Peter's yarn spinning offers a paradigm of the imperial adventure tale in Victorian society in general. As against the tame, monotonous realm of domestic routines and responsibilities emerges an alternative—daring, distant, charismatic, but somehow also irresponsible and immature. Elizabeth Gaskell treats the two realms as antithetical, and not least in terms of the kinds of storytelling which pertain to each, but the parts of the antithesis demand each other as ironically contrasting parts of a whole. Mr. Peter's stories, moreover, are not true or serious in the same way that *Cranford* can be called true and serious; their chief virtue is that they are exciting. As the narrator declares: "I found . . . that if we swallowed an anecdote of tolerable magnitude one week, we had the dose considerably increased the next, [and] I began to have my doubts. . . . I noticed also that when the Rector came to call, Mr. Peter talked in a different way about the countries he had been in. But I don't think the ladies in Cranford would have considered him such a wonderful traveller if they had only heard him talk in the quiet way he did to him. They liked him the better, indeed, for being what they called 'so very Oriental'" (153).

Here, as in Tennyson's early poetry, India is a realm of imaginative license (just as it was also a realm of moral and political license), a place where the fantastic becomes possible in ways that are carefully circumscribed at home. So little does truth or seriousness matter to Mr. Peter's storytelling that his masterpiece is also his least credible tale—the story he tells Mrs. Jamieson about a hunting trip that took him so high into the Himalayas, he exceeded the altitude of ordinary animals. "Firing one day at some flying creature, he was very much dismayed, when it fell, to find that he had shot a cherubim!" (159). Mrs. Jamieson responds in shocked tones that shooting an angel was surely an act of sacrilege, with which judgment Mr. Peter wryly agrees. (He might, however, have had to shoot Afghans or Nepalese in the course of duty; that would not have been sacrilege.) His tall tale offers a striking illustration of the relation between imperialist adventure fiction and the seemingly more serious tradition of domestic realism represented by *Cranford* itself. These apparently antithetical genres do not have separate histories, but influence and shade into each other in countless ways from the Renaissance onward.

The chapters of this book are arranged in roughly chronological order and further divided into three groups, "Dawn," "Noon," and "Dusk," representing the broad lineaments of a widespread, evolving ideology in British culture. Chapter 1 offers a brief overview of the subject, contrasting writings and attitudes from the beginning of the period—the 1830s and 1840s—with those from the end—the eighties and nineties. The second chapter deals primarily with a single writer, Captain Frederick Marryat. These two essays are intended to parallel the last two: chapter 8 also offers an overview, though it concentrates on the links between occultism and imperialism in late Victorian and Edwardian writing, and chapter 9 deals again with a single writer, Joseph Conrad (like Marryat a sailor, of course, and one who acknowledged Marryat's

[handwritten marginalia: notions of continuity + progress]

influence). Between these double bookends are five chapters focusing upon key texts written in the 1850s. After reviewing utilitarian and evangelical reformism in India in the 1830s and 1840s, chapter 3 focuses upon Thackeray's fiction, especially *The Newcomes* (1853–55). Chapter 4 deals with themes of emigration and the transportation of criminals to Australia in the fiction of Dickens, Bulwer-Lytton, Charles Reade, and Marcus Clarke, written mainly between the late 1840s and the 1860s. Chapter 5 addresses literary treatments of the Near East, ranging from Lord Byron to Sir Richard Burton's *Pilgrimage to Al-Medinah and Mecca* (1855). Chapter 6 offers a genealogy of the myth of the Dark Continent, looking backward to the antislavery movement but taking as a second point of departure the narratives of the great explorers of the fifties and sixties. The seventh chapter then turns to literary representations of the Indian Mutiny of 1857, extending to E. M. Forster's *Passage to India* in 1924. My emphasis on the 1850s is not accidental. The Australian gold rush, the search for the Nile's sources, the Crimean War, and the Mutiny made that decade a turning point for imperialist ideology, long before the New Imperialism manifested itself in the Scramble for Africa and all the other parts of the world that still remained to be overrun by European bearers of light and of Maxim guns.

Clearly my topic bears less directly on actual territorial aggrandizement than on the cultural expressions of that ideology which also goes by the name of imperialism. What is an ideology? The history of the idea of ideology is itself so laden with ideological baggage that it is perhaps impossible to hope for objectivity in dealing with it. Often ideology means false consciousness, or a view of the world which is false primarily because it contradicts the interests of the majority of those who adhere to it.[18] For many of its adherents, however, imperialism was a compelling set of beliefs precisely because it seemed to express their interests clearly and rationally. It was good to be British and on top of the world, a member of the most enlightened, progressive, civilized race in history, and to most Victorians and Edwardians it would have seemed crazy to deny it. The ways in which imperialism conflicted with the truer, deeper interests of the majority of Europeans were never easy to demonstrate, although J. A. Hobson attempted such a demonstration in *The Psychology of Jingoism* and *Imperialism: A Study*. We can now appreciate Hobson's arguments, but even so, contention about the nature of ideology seems an inevitable corollary of studies that deal with it. The hermeneutic dilemma that the very term ideology invokes is that which Karl Mannheim tried to address through his "sociology of knowledge" and which Wilhelm Dilthey's theory of the "cultural sciences" aimed to resolve. [19] As Raymond Williams points out, "there is an obvious need for a general term to describe not only the products but the processes of all signification, including the signification of values."[20] *Culture* is one such term, though it comes laden with connotations of sweetness and light, and of elitist exclusion, which may seem just as off-putting, and ultimately just as relativistic, as the pejorative or critical connotations of *ideology.* The "objective," "scientific" work of the anthropologists has lent culture a second, seemingly nonjudgmental definition. [21] Perhaps ideology needs to be treated in the same way, or perhaps the two terms culture and ideology need to be merged. This is the approach of the anthropologist Clifford Geertz, who attempts to extract ideology from its immediate ideological combat zones by defining it as "cultural system."[22]

If there has been any shortfall in Williams's amazingly comprehensive work, it is that he has not had much to say about imperialism and racism as factors in modern history. In the last two chapters of *The Country and the City,* however, he points out that "a model of city and country, in economic and political relationships, has gone beyond the boundaries of the nation-state, and is seen but also challenged as a model of the world":

> It is very significant that in its modern forms this [process] began in England. Much of the real history of city and country, within England itself, is from an early date a history of the extension of a dominant model of capitalist development to include other regions of the world. And this was not, as it is now sometimes seen, a case of "development" here, "failure to develop" elsewhere. What was happening in the "city," the "metropolitan" economy, determined and was determined by what was made to happen in the "country"; first the local hinterland and then the vast regions beyond it, in other people's lands. What happened in England has since been happening ever more widely, in new dependent relationships between all the industrialized nations and all the other "undeveloped" but economically important lands. Thus one of the last models of "city and country" is the system we now know as imperialism. [23]

Just as it is impossible to write an adequate history of British culture without attending to its social and political ramifications in country and city, in rural and urban experience at home, so it is impossible to understand that culture without looking abroad, to the colonies, the Empire, and the now independent nations of the Third World whose citizens remember the colonial phase of their histories as at best an aberration, at worst a nightmare of domination, exploitation, and slavery. For the white imperialists from the metropolis, by contrast, that phase was the chief glory and merit of modern history, the ever-rising pinnacle of progress and civilization. In *Facing Mount Kenya*, Jomo Kenyatta sums up this difference and offers a thoughtful assessment of it:

> There certainly are some progressive ideas among the Europeans. They include the ideas of material prosperity, of medicine, and hygiene, and literacy which enables people to take part in world culture. But so far the Europeans who visit Africa have not been conspicuously zealous in imparting these parts of their inheritance to the Africans, and seem to think that the only way to do it is by police discipline and armed force. They speak as if it was somehow beneficial to an African to work for them instead of for himself, and to make sure that he will receive this benefit they do their best to take away his land and leave him with no alternative. Along with his land they rob him of his government, condemn his religious ideas, and ignore his fundamental conceptions of justice and morals, all in the name of civilisation and progress.

As if this melancholy result were not enough, Kenyatta then adds: "If Africans were left in peace on their own lands, Europeans would have to offer them the benefits of white civilization in real earnest before they could obtain the African labour they want so much. They would have to let the African choose what parts of European culture could be beneficially transplanted, and how they could be adapted. He would probably not choose the gas bomb or the armed police force."[24] Maybe. At least it is good to express the vision of a nonexploitive, nonimperialist world. The unsung heroes of this book are those Victorian and Edwardian opponents of imperialism, such as Hobson, William Morris, and Olive Schreiner, who expressed a similar vision. They were always in the minority, though sometimes able to win local skirmishes. But before my own critique of the ideology of imperialism begins, it is worth noting that, even at the height of the rule of darkness, alternative, anti-imperialist visions of our common life together were available.

PART I DAWN

Dawn in the South Pacific. A typical missionary conversionist fantasy, from Rev. William Wyatt Gill, *Life in the Southern Isles* (1876).

1. From *Dawn Island* to *Heart of Darkness*

England cannot afford to be little.
—WILLIAM HUSKISSON, 1828

i

Studies of British imperialism as an ideological phenomenon have usually confined themselves to the period from the 1870s to World War I, in part because those years saw the development of a militantly expansionist New Imperialism. In the 1870s Germany, Belgium, and the United States began an intense imperial rivalry against the older colonial powers, above all Great Britain, for their own "place in the sun." Russia (like France) represented an older, more continuous threat to Britain's imperial hegemony, but the Bulgarian crisis of 1876 and the Second Afghan War of 1878–80 marked an intensification of that threat. Declining industrial growth and the "Great Depression" from 1873 to the 1890s also lent urgency to imperial issues in Britain, as did the increasingly divisive question of Irish Home Rule. Perhaps more than any other events before the Boer War, the invasion of Egypt in 1882 and the death of General Gordon at Khartoum three years later raised imperialist sentiment to a fever pitch that hardly abated even after the "revenge" for Gordon at Omdurman in 1898.

Literary historians have noted the jingoist trend in late Victorian and Edwardian writing, finding it most prominently expressed by Rudyard Kipling, H. Rider Haggard, and a few others, but for the most part they have tended to portray it as background or as one theme among many and to ignore it altogether before the 1880s. Such a narrowing of focus used to be encouraged by political and economic historians, who subscribed to a belief in a hiatus between the breakdown of the old Empire, signaled by the loss of the American colonies, and the emergence of the New

Imperialism after about 1880. Occasionally historians even claimed that this hiatus was anti-imperialist. The chief evidence offered for this view was the abolition of the slave trade and of slavery in all British territory by 1834; the establishment of partial self-government in the white settler colonies (Canada, Australia, New Zealand, the Cape of Good Hope); the alleged influence of the free trade arguments of John Bright, Richard Cobden, and the Manchester School; and the traditional reluctance of governments to pursue policies of imperial aggrandizement.[1] Lord Palmerston, for example, both as foreign secretary and as prime minister, was a frequent advocate of gunboat diplomacy, but also he was often reluctant to follow displays of naval power with military annexations. Palmerston and many of his contemporaries believed that British overseas interests should be secured whenever possible without formal imperialization.

Recent historians, however, following the work of John Gallagher and Ronald Robinson, have recognized that in the Victorian years down to 1880, British overseas expansion went on apace, even though the official attitude was frequently to resist that expansion.[2] British hegemony in India, dating from the Battle of Plassey in 1757, both grew and was consolidated up to the Indian Mutiny of 1857. The loss of the American colonies was partly offset during and immediately after the Napoleonic era by sizable gains in South Africa, Asia, the West Indies, and Canada. To designate patterns of political, economic, and cultural domination—patterns that involved annexation and the creation of new colonies only as a last resort—Robinson and Gallagher offer "informal empire" and "free trade imperialism," but they cite numerous instances from the early Victorian years of formal imperial expansion as well: "Consider the results of a decade of 'indifference' to empire. Between 1841 and 1851 Great Britain occupied or annexed New Zealand, the Gold Coast, Labuan, Natal, the Punjab, Sind, and Hong Kong. In the next twenty years British control was asserted over Berar, Oudh, Lower Burma, and Kowloon, over Lagos and the neighbourhood of Sierra Leone, over Basutoland, Griqualand, and the Transvaal; and new colonies were established in Queensland and British Columbia."[3] Furthermore, though the major areas of white settlement were granted partial self-government between 1840 and 1870, they remained tied to Britain in many ways. As Goldwin Smith argued in *The Empire* (1863), independence for the colonies of British settlement could lead to a stronger imperial alliance: "That connexion with the Colonies, which is really part of our greatness—the connexion of blood, sympathy and ideas—will not be affected by political separation. And when our Colonies are nations, something in the nature of a great Anglo-Saxon federation may, in substance if not in form, spontaneously arise out of affinity and mutual affection."[4] In contrast, especially after the Indian Mutiny of 1857, arguments for the independence of the largely nonwhite parts of the Empire grew scarce. The Mutiny was a key event, according to Francis Hutchins, in the emergence of an "illusion of permanence" about the British occupation of India.[5]

The word "imperialism," Richard Koebner concluded, was used through the 1860s only with reference to the French Second Empire and the autocratic policies of Napoleon III.[6] But between 1830 and the 1870s "the colonies" and "colonial interests" were familiar terms, and throughout the period there was frequent discussion in the press and in Parliament about the condition of the "British Empire."[7] For most Victorians, whether they lived early or late in the queen's reign, the British were inherently, by "blood," a conquering, governing, and civilizing "race"; the "dark races" whom they conquered were inherently incapable of governing and civilizing themselves. Racist theories of history were prevalent well before the development of social Darwinism, and these theories were often used to explain Britain's industrial and imperial preeminence.[8] In *The English and Their Origin* (1866), Luke Owen Pike declared: "There are probably few educated Englishmen living who have not in their infancy been taught that the English nation is a nation of almost pure Teutonic blood, that its political constitution, its social custom, its internal prosperity, the success of its arms, and the number of its colonies have all followed necessarily upon the arrival, in three vessels, of certain German warriors under the command of Hengist and Horsa."[9]

Sixteen years earlier, in *The Races of Men* (1850), Robert Knox had set forth a pseudo-scientific theory of race which explained why some peoples were the imperialists and others the imperialized in history. Knox is cynical about war, empires, and genocide; he is no patriotic praiser of everything British:

See how a company of London merchants lord it over a hundred millions of coloured men in Hindostan . . . the fact is astounding. Whilst I now write, the Celtic [French] race is preparing to seize Northern Africa by the same right as we seized Hindostan—that is, might, physical force—the only real right is physical force; whilst we, not to be behind in the grasp for more acres, annex New Zealand and all its dependencies to the British dominions, to be wrested from us by-and-by by our sons and descendants as the United States were and Canada will be, for no Saxon race can ever hold a colony long. The coolness with which this act of appropriation has been done is, I think, quite unparalleled in the history of aggressions.[10]

It is not clear whether the Saxon race as rulers are unable to hold their empires for long or whether, as colonists and pioneers, they are too energetic and ruthless to remain under home rule. In any case, Knox goes on to excoriate "that den of all abuses, the office of the Colonial Secretary," for "declaring New Zealand to be a colony of Britain." He speaks of "organized hypocrisy" as the source of the idea that "the aborigines are to be protected"—he recognizes, apparently, that they will be not protected, but robbed and murdered. Yet he equivocates; he is no humanitarian. Although he seems to disapprove of organized robbery and murder, might makes right, and what happens to the dark races of men around the world is simply their racial destiny. "Why is it," he asks, "that destiny seems to have marked them for destruction?" They are physically and mentally inferior, he answers, doomed to perish while "feebly contending against the stronger races for a corner of [the] earth" (147).

Knox appears to argue that Saxons—his own race, as he is fond of pointing out—should keep out of other parts of the world and desist from robbing and murdering the dark races of men. Actually, however, he argues that European colonial expansion and the demise of the "weak races" are inevitable. "Since the earliest times . . . the dark races have been the slaves of their fairer brethren." Nothing has changed in the nineteenth century except that genocide is now masked in terms of "protecting the aborigines." Perhaps it is only hypocrisy that Knox objects to—not imperialism, not even genocide. Knox speculates that the Colonial Office has greedily wanted to establish "another India in Central Africa," so that "the wealth, the product of the labour of many millions of Africans, in reality slaves, as the natives of Hindostan, but held to be free by a legal fiction, might be poured into the coffers of the office." He rejoices, however, that "climate interfered" with this scheme, at least as attempted by the Niger Expedition of 1841, and "exterminated the crews of their ships" (150: Knox's apparent satisfaction with this disaster is of a piece with his view of history as a vast charnel house of race war and racial extinction).

Knox rails against humanitarian efforts to protect the aborigines: "How

I have laughed at the mock philanthropy of England!" (161). Genocide is the way of history, and the Saxon race, though closely followed in its murderous proclivities by other European breeds, is better at it than any other. "What a field of extermination lies before the Saxon Celtic and Sarmatian races! The Saxon will not mingle with any dark race, nor will he allow him to hold an acre of land in the country occupied by him; this, at least, is the law of Anglo-Saxon America. The fate . . . of the Mexicans, Peruvians, and Chilians, is in no shape doubtful. Extinction of the race—sure extinction—it is not even denied" (153). Certain races—the dark, nonprogressive ones (but what can "progress" mean to Knox?)—seem to have been produced by nature simply to be liquidated, swept aside by the Saxons and other white, progressive races. And there is nothing to be done about it; "hence the folly of the war carried on by the philanthropists of Britain against nature" (153). No late Victorian social Darwinist could have stated this racist theory of history in more explicit, more dismal terms.

Knox's extreme cynicism was quite idiosyncratic for mid-century, however, though both his racism and his thesis that might makes right seem partly to echo Carlyle. Nevertheless, racist theories of history quite similar to his, though more positively expressed, were just as common in those years as in the eighties and nineties. That the early and mid-Victorians did not call themselves imperialists, moreover, suggests merely that they did not feel self-conscious or anxious about their world domination. They could be imperialists without subscribing to any formal doctrine, so thoroughly were the patterns of expansion and hegemony established at home and abroad. Freedom and free trade were for equals; John Stuart Mill assumed quite readily that the liberal theses he expounded in *On Liberty* (1859) and *Representative Government* (1861) did not apply to Indians or to other "lesser peoples." And although James Mill believed that colonies in general were a bad idea, emigration and the founding of new, independent communities were another matter, as was the governance of India.[11] Like his son after him, James Mill did not believe that freedom and democracy made any sense as categories in the context of India, or that they should be applied to other nonwhite peoples. In *The Colonies of England* (1849), J. A. Roebuck, Benthamite radical and parliamentary ally of the Mills, could write: "I say, that for the mass, the sum of human enjoyment to be derived from this globe which God has given to us, it is requisite for us to pass over the original tribes that we find existing in the separate lands which we colonize. . . . When the European comes in contact with any other type of man, that other type disappears. . . . Let us not shade our eyes, and pretend not to see this result."[12]

Imperialism may not have had a name before 1870, but though nameless it did more than provide mere background in the writings of the early and mid-Victorians. India was important for Macaulay, the Mills, and Thackeray as well as for Kipling, and certainly it was just as central to the greatest Anglo-Indian writer before Kipling, Philip Meadows Taylor, who published his bestselling *Confessions of a Thug* in 1839. Though he had never been to India, Sir Walter Scott tried his hand at an oriental novel in *The Surgeon's Daughter* (1827), and both Robert Southey in *The Curse of Kehama* (1810) and Thomas Moore in *Lalla Rookh* (1817) contributed to the growing stock of stereotypic images of India. Standard histories of the Romantic movement either ignore these works or treat them as examples of literary exoticism, a minor trend compared to the major themes pursued by "great" writing. Such histories have also downplayed the eastern travels of Byron's Childe Harold and Don Juan, and the orientalism of such poems as "The Giaour."

When we turn from poetic to economic discourse, emigration to the colonies had been urged as a solution to unemployment and depression as early as the end of the Napoleonic Wars. Thomas Malthus thought that emigration could never be more than a temporary palliative to the problem of "redundant population," but Wilmot Horton and other theorists disagreed. In the early 1820s Horton proposed to alleviate pauperism through government-subsidized emigration to the colonies, and later emigration schemes such as Edward Gibbon Wakefield's also aimed at improving the economic situation at home while simultaneously developing the colonies.[13] Responding in *Chartism* (1839) to these issues, Carlyle wrote: "How thick stands your population in the Pampas and Savannahs of America . . . ? Alas, where now are the Hengsts and Alarics of our still growing, still expanding Europe; who, when their home is grown too narrow, will enlist and like firepillars guide onwards those superfluous masses of indomitable living valour; equipped, not now with the battle-axe and war-chariot, but with the steam-engine and plough-share?"[14] This sort of *Lebensraum* argument was not invented by German propagandists in the twentieth century; it echoes throughout the era of industrial and imperial expansion.

Emigration as an urgent national issue was an idea shared by many writers from about 1815 onward. Coleridge believed that colonies were the answer to Malthus: "Colonization is not only a manifest expedient for, but an imperative duty on, Great Britain. God seems to hold out his finger to us over the sea."[15] Coleridge understood that not only surplus population but surplus capital needed to be exported: "I think this country is now suffering grievously under an excessive accumulation of capital, which, having no field for profitable operation, is in a state of fierce civil war with itself" (216). The colonies and most other parts of the world, even when populated by "natives," Romantic and early Victorian writers often perceived as virtually empty—"waste places"—if not exactly profitable areas for investing surplus capital then an almost infinite dumping ground for the increasingly dangerous army of the poor and unemployed at home. "We have Canada with all its territory," wrote Robert Southey; "we have Surinam, the Cape Colony, Australasia . . . countries which are collectively more than fifty-fold the area of the British isles, and which a thousand years of uninterrupted prosperity would scarcely suffice to people. It is time that Britain should become the hive of nations, and cast her swarms; and here are lands to receive them. What is required of government is to encourage emigration by founding settlements, and facilitating the means of transportation."[16]

There were only a few "blanks" left on the map by 1830, the largest in Africa, and by the end of the century these had been filled in by the last major European explorers. But in the 1830s there seemed to be innumerable desert islands, even a desert continent or two, waiting to be developed for civilization by white colonists. If the colonists discovered footprints in the sand, there was little in that to impede the progress of civilization. "Savages" who did not "develop" the land and its resources were often viewed as having no right of possession, and the task of "civilizing" them—provided it was deemed possible—was defined in terms of their conversion both to Christianity and to "productive labor" or "industry." In an 1856 review of a book on Paraguay and Brazil, Charles Kingsley wrote: "Each people should either develop the capabilities of their own country, or make room for those who will develop them. If they accept that duty, they have their reward in the renovation of blood, which commerce, and its companion, colonization, are certain to bring."[17] Commerce and colonization are for Kingsley almost identical forms of social redemption and progress. Wherever there are barbarians and backward peoples, like the Indians of Paraguay (whose only help toward civilization has been, Kingsley believes, the evil guidance of Jesuit missionaries), a social vacuum exists into which the energies of progressive, industrious, white and preferably Protestant races can and should flow.

Macaulay's work in India in the 1830s aimed at the progress and civilizing of that vast empire; so, too, felt the Mills, did their work for the East India Company. Both Charles Lamb and Thomas Love Peacock, friend of Bentham and Shelley and father-in-law of George Meredith, also worked for the East India Company. Peacock succeeded James Mill as chief examiner of correspondence and, on his retirement in 1856, was succeeded in turn by John Stuart Mill. The connection may seem fortuitous, but the author of *Nightmare Abbey* and *Crotchet Castle* was the designer of the first armored steamboats employed by the Royal navy. These were used on the Irrawaddy in the First Burmese War (1824–26), in which Captain Frederick Marryat participated, and again on the Yangtze during the First Opium War (1840–42).[18] Peacock, lover and satirist of the intellectual foibles of his age, was thus a pioneer of gunboat diplomacy. His involvement with the East India Company, and with armored steamboats, seems offhand, perhaps disconnected from his literary career. Imperialism, moreover, is not a pressing concern that he examines in detail in his novels—which suggests only that he sees nothing controversial or problematic about it. But Peacock clearly takes pride in British hegemony in India and around the globe. In an outline of his early poem "The Genius of the Thames" (1812), one of whose themes is "the mutability of empire," Peacock stresses "the naval domination of Britain and extent of her commerce and navigation."[19] In the poem itself he praises the superiority of the Thames over all other rivers, because it has been the chief thoroughfare for British naval power, commerce, and imperial glory. All previous empires have declined and fallen, Peacock says, but "if skill and courage true" continue to energize it, the empire of the Thames will last as long as the world:

> Still shall thine empire's fabric stand,
> Admired and feared from land to land,
> Through every circling age renewed,
> Unchanged, unshaken, unsubdued;
> As rocks resist the wildest breeze,
> That sweeps thy tributary seas. (6:15)

Though never a doctrinaire utilitarian or radical, Peacock belongs somewhere on the liberal end of the spectrum in regard to domestic politics, but he no more sensed a contradiction between domestic liberalism and the imperialism of his India House career than did the Mills. Throughout most of the nineteenth century, in fact, there was often no sharp division between liberals and conservatives concerning colonial issues. At times those who adopted liberal positions on domestic issues could be even more "hawkish" about foreign affairs than their conservative opponents. Thus the First Opium War, opposed by the Tories in Parliament, was defended by Whigs and Radicals as a means of forcing supposedly free trade on the reluctant Chinese.

The development of modern India was greatly influenced by Benthamite radicalism and by other Liberal reform impulses emanating from Britain. According to Eric Stokes: "The whole transformation of English mind and society, as it expressed itself in liberalism, was brought to bear on the Indian connexion. And it was brought to bear—it is this which makes Indian history important for the most insular of English historians—by its most distinguished representatives, James and John Stuart Mill, Bentham and Macaulay. One has only to add Maine, Fitzjames Stephen, and Morley for later Indian history, to enumerate most of the important figures in the intellectual history of English liberalism in the nineteenth century."[20] Stokes demonstrates that the articulation between Indian history and the liberal attitudes and movements concerned with domestic reform was both intricate and powerful. Similarly, the movement for the abolition of slavery was also a precursor to the European partitioning of Africa. So the connections between reform at home and empire abroad proliferate. Indeed, it was largely out of the liberal, reform-minded optimism of the early Victorians that the apparently more conservative, social Darwinian, jingoist imperialism of the late Victorians evolved.

Peacock's connections with imperial issues might almost be dismissed as irrelevant to an understanding of his novels. The same view cannot be taken of the dual career of Captain Marryat, forerunner of G. A. Henty, W. H. G. Kingston, Dr. Gordon Stables, and the many other writers of imperialist adventure fiction for boys who flourished from the 1880s on. And it would also be inappropriate for another highly popular early Victorian novelist, Edward Bulwer-Lytton, who underwent a political metamorphosis similar to that of his friend Benjamin Disraeli, from radical to conservative; he became secretary for the colonies in the Derby-Disraeli cabinet in 1858. According to his biographer, T. H. S. Escott, "the true cult of the colonies . . . was founded by Bulwer-Lytton in the *Caxtons* [1850] eight years before, in the Derby Cabinet, he began to educate his colleague Disraeli into considering the upholding of England's empire to be the great object of Conservative policy."[21] Escott's claims are exaggerated: Disraeli needed no such education, and anyway there was plenty of public interest in colonial issues prior to *The Caxtons*. But Bulwer's stance toward the Empire was aggressively expansionist. So was that of his son, who while viceroy of India from 1876 to 1880 was responsible for precipitating the Second Afghan War.[22]

Just as India serves as a focus of humanitarian concern for the evangelicals and utilitarians in the 1820s and 1830s, so Australasia looms large in the imaginative worlds of Bulwer, Dickens, Trollope, Clough, Henry Kingsley, Charles Reade, and Samuel Butler, not just as a convict depot, an erewhon, or a convenient destination for the Micawbers and Peggotties and other characters who need to be given happy endings but as an ideal standard against which to measure life at home.[23] If imperialism often served as an ideological counterweight to domestic liberalism, providing conservative ballast even for forms of radical opinion, it also served as a reservoir of utopian images and alternatives that helped energize reform impulses at home. Emigration for Carlyle, for example, is always double-edged: the colonies offer hope to the poor and unemployed in Britain, a hope that emerges from a radical awareness of the failure of home politics to provide a good life for all.

The Scramble for Africa may have occurred largely in the last two decades of the nineteenth century, but intense public interest in the "penetration" and "opening up" of the supposedly Dark Continent began seven or eight decades earlier with the abolitionist movement and culminated in Thomas Fowell Buxton's ill-fated Niger Expedition of 1841. Sir Richard Burton and John Hanning Speke's expedition to find the sources of the White Nile in 1856–58 and the publication of David Livingstone's bestselling *Missionary Travels* in 1857 initiated the final era of African exploration, which led to a carving up of the entire continent into European-ruled colonies and protectorates. Similarly, in the mid-1850s both the Crimean War and the Indian Mutiny evoked jingoist sentiments in literature and the press long before the word "jingo" was coined in the music halls. Carlyle, Dickens, Kingsley, Ruskin, and Tennyson all supported the Governor Eyre Defense Committee, jingoist in all but name (Eyre was in their view the hero rather than villain of the Jamaica Rebellion of 1865). They were opposed by Mill, Huxley, Darwin, Tom Hughes, and other liberal intellectuals who wanted Eyre to stand trial for murder. In some respects the Jamaica controversy was as much a turning point in the history of reformist political attitudes as the Second Reform Bill.[24]

The early and mid-Victorians were far from being "unconscious Little Englanders." But the imperialism of the early and mid-Victorian decades differed from that of the later era, partly because informal kinds of political domination were more possible between 1830 and the 1860s, producing an easy confidence that rarely saw anything problematic about such domination. What was good for Britain was good for the world. Even in the Hungry Forties, Marryat's novels of warfare and shipwreck floated on seas of optimism. Hero and celebrator of Admiral Nelson's navy, Marryat for a time fancied himself a liberal reformer. He made two unsuccessful election bids for Parliament on a platform consisting chiefly of naval reform and especially his pet project, abolishing the press gang— a more sensible sort of reform, Marryat felt, than the foolishness about abolishing slavery. Despite the author's brief stint as a liberal politican, Marryat's attitude toward the colonies, apparent in all of his seagoing novels, can be described only as imperialist. In *Masterman Ready* (1841), for example, young William Seagrave and his family, together with the loyal old sailor Ready, are marooned on a desert island; their industry and resourcefulness turn it into a thriving miniature colony. This is the right way to go about subduing and planting the entire world, Marryat suggests. At one point William asks his father to explain "the nature of a colony," and Mr. Seagrave responds with a brief history of the ascendancy of the British Empire, triumphing over its French, Spanish, Portuguese, and Dutch rivals until "the sun is said, and very truly, never to set upon . . . English possessions; for, as the world turns round to it, the sun shines either upon one portion or another of the globe which is a colony to our country."[25]

Late Victorian and Edwardian defenders of the Empire, made nervous by overseas rivals and threats of national decadence, often gave this expression a temporal as well as a geographical meaning—the sun would never set on an empire that would be, unlike all its predecessors, everlasting. But brimming with a social optimism that quickly evaporated after the Victorian boom years, Mr. Seagrave thinks of the Empire as a nursery for new, independent nations that will one day replace it. As soon as a colony grows "strong and powerful enough to take care of itself, it throws off the yoke of subjection, and declares itself independent; just as a son who has grown up to manhood leaves his father's house and takes up a business to gain his own livelihood" (141). The United States is an example, and even black Africans, even "barbarians and savages," may one day form "a great nation." This idea leads William to ask whether, if "nations rise and fall," England will "ever fall, and be of no more importance than Portugal is now?" (141). Mr. Seagrave replies: "History tells us that such is the fate of all nations. We must, therefore, expect that it will one day be the fate of our dear country." As Trollope would later reiterate in *The New Zealander*, Seagrave optimistically adds: "At present we see no appearance of it, any more than we perceive the latent seeds of death in our own bodies; but still the time arrives when man must die, and so it must be with nations" (141).

The reform optimism of the early Victorians, dissected so thoroughly in *Middlemarch*, spills over into numerous civilizing projects and stories about converting the savages which too often foreshadow Kurtz's pamphlet for the Society for the Suppression of Savage Customs in *Heart of Darkness*. Macaulay, advocate of the Anglicization not just of Indian education but ultimately of all things Indian, believed that the greatness of British imperialism would be shown not in its ability to conquer and govern the dark races of the world but in its work of conversion: "To have found a great people sunk in the lowest depths of slavery and superstition, to have so ruled them as to have made them desirous and capable of all the privileges of citizens, would indeed be a title to glory all our own. The sceptre may pass away from us. . . . Victory may be inconstant to our arms. But there are triumphs which are followed by no reverse. There is an empire exempt from all natural causes of decay. Those triumphs are the pacific triumphs of reason over barbarism; that empire is the imperishable empire of our arts and our morals, our literature and our laws."[26]

In her exemplary tale *Dawn Island*, written for the national Anti-Corn Law Bazaar in 1845, Harriet Martineau offers an optimistic fable of the conversion of the savages which dispenses with military and political domination and almost with Christian proselytizing. On an island in the South Seas which, Martineau says, ought to have been peaceful and edenic, the islanders are thwarted from attaining social harmony and progress by their savage customs. They make constant war on each other, offer up human sacrifices, and practice cannibalism and infanticide. Small wonder, then, the prophecy that haunts the old priest Miava seems to be coming true: "The forest-tree shall grow; the coral shall spread and branch out; but man shall cease."[27] Miava himself is called out of retirement to preside over sacrificial and cannibal rites in preparation for a war that decimates the island's already much-depleted population. Savagery, a kind of collective suicide, seems to involve the Malthusian principle in reverse. With such very savage behavior, Martineau suggests, it is a wonder any savages are left in the world.

One day, however, there comes to Dawn Island the "Higher Disclosure" of civilization, in the form of a great "outrigger-less canoe," navigated by celestial-seeming white men. Where there was barbarism, there shall be reason; where there was infanticide, there shall be happy families; where there was war and no "industry," there shall be commercial relations. The "Higher Disclosure" is, in fact, the gospel of free trade, and the benevolent Captain proceeds to teach the savages "the best lesson any one ever taught them," which is "to trade—honestly" (71). White sailors unpack the miraculous commodities they have brought along, products of British industry and ingenuity. "The strongest desire was excited in the minds of Miava and his companions to obtain more of the precious articles brought by the strangers" (74).

> The exchanges of food and foreign goods were carried on with more order than is usual on the first occasion of a newly-discovered people being one of the parties; and when even the most fortunate sellers found that, much as they gained, there were many other desirable things which they could not have till they could offer commodities less perishable and more valuable than food, it was not difficult to bring them to a purpose of preparation for a better traffic, if the Europeans would promise to come again. (87)

This is "the advent of Commerce" to Dawn Island, the only true dawn as far as Martineau is concerned. The unprogressive fetishism of the islanders is supplanted by the commodity fetishism of the British. Finding that they can acquire spectacles, knives, mirrors, axes, and bolts of cloth from the godlike white men if they produce goods to exchange, the islanders miraculously shed their savage ways and take their first steps on the path of progress and civilization. As the ship sails away from this scene of unmitigated commercial benevolence, good Dr. Symons, whose eyeglasses had been stolen by a thievish savage, says to the equally good Captain: "You were like a preacher or a prophet to these poor people. . . . Were my spectacles your text? If so, they are highly honoured." The Captain replies: "Every thing is honoured, be it what it may . . . which is an instrument for introducing the principles and incitements of

civilization among a puerile people." And about his own role as missionary of the free trade gospel, the Captain adds: "Yes,—I was their preacher
and prophet just now . . . I thought of nothing less, when I landed, than
giving such a discourse; but it warmed my heart and filled my head to see
how these children of nature were clearly destined to be carried on some
way towards becoming men and Christians by my bringing Commerce to
their shores" (94).

The early Victorians felt they could expand naturally, with trade goods
and Bibles as easily as with guns. They could sail to the far corners of the
world as explorers, missionaries, abolitionists, traders, and immigrants,
opening new fields for the expansive wonders of their industrial revolution, their special forms of religious, political, and economic grace, and
their bourgeois-heroic values of self-help and upward mobility. They had
no need to worry about decline or degeneration, nor did they try in any
systematic way to rationalize imperial expansion by recourse either to
philosophical idealism or to the biological sciences. At the same time free
trade theory, central to both liberal and radical thought, was itself often
linked to the need for colonization to open new markets and to make the
"nonproductive" areas of the globe "productive." Though a kind of anti-
imperialist ideology held sway in the thirties and forties, Bernard Semmel
writes, it was directed against "the old colonial system of mercantilism."
Its proponents were also "the spokesmen, and, in some cases, the theorists of a new free trade imperialism which, they held, would prove
more effective and profitable," given England's progressive and increasingly dominant economic power.[28] For writers as various as Macaulay, Carlyle, Martineau, and Dickens, free trade was the dawn that
would bring the full light of day to the dark places of the world.

ii

In contrast to Martineau's and Marryat's quite typical early Victorian
optimism about the colonies and the civilizing mission of British commerce are numerous examples of late Victorian and Edwardian pessimism. At the Great Durbar of 1903, for example, Lord Curzon would
not permit the singing of "Onward Christian Soldiers" because it contains the line "Crowns and Thrones may perish, / Kingdoms rise and
wane."[29] In a 1907 speech at Birmingham, Curzon, while insisting that
the Empire would be everlasting if only it maintained its high ideals,

presented it as a field of escape and endeavor away from "the sordid controversies and . . . depressing gloom of our insular existence." Throughout his speech Curzon unintentionally expressed the "craven fears" of decadence against which he warned his audience. "If it is extinguished or allowed to die our Empire will have no more life than a corpse from which the spirit has lately fled, and like a corpse will moulder."[30] That image, imperial corpse, is ultimately more vivid and persuasive than the image Curzon intended to substitute for it, empire everlasting.

The confident era of free trade doctrine gave way only gradually to the defensiveness, self-doubt, and worries about "fitness," "national efficiency," and racial and cultural decadence which characterize the end of the century. Of the Edwardian age Samuel Hynes writes that "the idea of decline and fall haunted imaginations of the time."[31] This was especially true following the Boer War, but decadence had become a theme as early as Tennyson's "Locksley Hall Sixty Years After" (1886) and Haggard's *Allan Quatermain* (1887). Tennyson's aging, disgruntled narrator foresees nation and empire crumbling, "Demos working its own doom," and the old "cry of 'Forward, Forward,' lost within a growing gloom."[32] Haggard's aging hero declares: "Civilisation is only savagery silver-gilt. A vainglory is it, and, like a northern light, comes but to fade and leave the sky more dark."[33]

Social doubt emerges in many ways from the 1870s onward—in, for example, the fad for "invasion scare" novels which commenced with Sir George Chesney's *The Battle of Dorking in* 1871 and led to the rise of the entire anxious genre of spy fiction; in the popularity of neoromantic and adolescent literary modes as vehicles for jingoist values; in the emergence of dogmatic, warmongering forms of social Darwinism and neo-Hegelianism; and in the decadent movement, with its "decline and fall" motifs. "'Imperialism,' as the word is generally understood, was for Britain," according to Bernard Porter, "a symptom and an effect of her decline in the world, and not of strength."[34] Although the equation is far from exact, imperialism as an element in British culture grew increasingly noisy, racist, and self-conscious as faith in free trade and liberal reformism declined. The militant imperialism of the late Victorian and Edwardian years thus represents a national (indeed, international) political and cultural regression, a social atavism to use Joseph Schumpeter's term, but an atavism with more dimensions, both economic and cultural, than Schumpeter recognized.

Empire involved military conquest and rapacious economic exploitation, but it also involved the enactment of often idealistic although
nonetheless authoritarian schemes of cultural domination. The goal of
imperialist discourse is always to weld these seeming opposites together or
to disguise their contradiction. Missionary zeal, utilitarian reformism in
India in the 1830s, the utopianism of imperial "federation," the "service"
ideal expressed by Kipling and others, and the justification of empire and
war in neo-Hegelian terms were ideas ordinarily held sincerely, but they
were also placed on the defensive as much by the brutal facts of genocide
and exploitation as by anti-imperialist criticism. Toward the end of the
century the war correspondent George W. Steevens found that he had to
talk down "the new humanitarianism" and defend brutality as the truly
humane course of action: "We became an Imperial race by dealing
necessary pain to other men. . . . Civilisation is making it too easy to
live. . . . A wiser humanitarianism would make it easy for the lower
quality of life to die. It sounds brutal, but why not? We have let brutality
die out too much."[35] Just as pointedly, the neo-Hegelian philosopher of
empire J. A. Cramb could write that "the battlefield is an altar" and that
"in the light of History, universal peace appears less as a dream than as a
nightmare."[36]

The "social imperialism" of Joseph Chamberlain emerged in the 1890s
as the direct rival of socialism and the nascent Labour party for the
allegiance of the working class. In a speech Cecil Rhodes suggested how
imperialism could serve as an alternative to socialism at home: "My
cherished idea is a solution for the social problem, i.e., in order to save
the 40,000,000 inhabitants of the United Kingdom from a bloody civil
war, we colonial statesmen must acquire new lands to settle the surplus
population, to provide new markets for the goods produced by them in
the factories and mines. The Empire, as I have always said, is a bread and
butter question. If you want to avoid civil war, you must become imperialists." Lenin later quoted this speech in his 1916 pamphlet on imperialism and, of course, did not disagree with Rhodes's argument.[37] Neither
did that other great critic of imperialism, J. A. Hobson, who also recognized that the Empire was a political safety valve and a substitute for
reform at home. "It has become a commonplace of history," wrote
Hobson in 1902, "how Governments use national animosities, foreign
wars and the glamour of empire-making, in order to bemuse the popular
mind and divert rising resentment against domestic abuses." Through
imperial fanfare and exploitation abroad, "the vested interests," accord-

ing to Hobson, "at the same time protect their economic and political supremacy at home against movements of popular reform."[38]

Even in the earlier period of high social confidence, imperialist ideology had preserved and nurtured various conservative fantasies, chief among them the mythology of the English gentleman, against the corrosive effects of popular reform and democratization at home. This is one of the reasons why Schumpeter's term "atavism" is appropriate; his argument against economic imperialism may be untenable, but not his perception that the late Victorian expansion and defense of empire involved regressive social and cultural patterns. The themes of nineteenth-century culture gradually shift, John MacKenzie has noted, away from domestic class conflict toward racial and international conflict, suggesting how imperialism functioned as an ideological safety valve, deflecting both working-class radicalism and middle-class reformism into noncritical paths while preserving fantasies of aristocratic authority at home and abroad. In his analysis of Victorian popular theatre MacKenzie points out that, although many early nineteenth-century melodramas expressed "class tensions," by the end of the century "such class antagonism had disappeared": "By then, imperial subjects offered a perfect opportunity to externalise the villain, who increasingly became the corrupt rajah, the ludicrous Chinese or Japanese nobleman, the barbarous 'fuzzy-wuzzy' or black, facing a cross-class brotherhood of heroism, British officer and ranker together. Thus imperialism was depicted as a great struggle with dark and evil forces, in which white heroes and heroines could triumph over black barbarism, and the moral stereotyping of melodrama was given a powerful racial twist."[39] A similar shift is apparent in other forms of cultural expression. The history of fiction between the 1830s and 1900, for example, is characterized by a general movement from domestic realism and concern with social reform, through the craze of the 1860s for sensation novels, to the various forms of romance writing of the eighties and nineties which include imperialist adventure stories for adolescents and adults alike.

Imperialism grew particularly racist and aggressive from the 1870s on, partly because the social class domination of both the bourgeoisie and the aristocracy was perceived to be eroding. Inscribed in the adventure narratives of many late Victorian and Edwardian writers is the desire to revitalize not only heroism but aristocracy. The narrator of "Locksley Hall Sixty Years After" rails against "Demos working its own doom" and mourns his chivalrous "forefather":

Yonder in that chapel, slowly sinking now into the ground,
Lies the warrior, my forefather, with his feet upon the hound.

Crossed! for once he sailed the sea to crush the Moslem in his pride;
Dead the warrior, dead his glory, dead the cause in which he died.

(ll. 27–30)

Tennyson links the desire for a rebirth of the aristocracy with a "cause" many felt was not really dead, completing what the medieval crusaders began. The myth of the second coming of King Arthur, in "Merlin and the Gleam" and elsewhere, though perhaps in a less direct way, expresses the same set of conservative values.

The nineteenth century experienced an "eclipse" and numerous attempts at resurrection of the hero, attempts that became increasingly militant in the era of the New Imperialism. An eclipse of the hero characterizes one sort of Victorian fiction—Thackeray's "novel without a hero," for example, or the impossibility of leading "epic lives" expressed in *Middlemarch*. But there was a resurgence of heroes and hero-worship in another sort—in, for example, Charles Kingsley's *Westward Ho!* (1853) and the burgeoning new industry of boys' adventure tales, started by Captain Marryat. Throughout the history of the imperializing West, domesticity seeks and finds its antithesis in adventure, in charismatic quests and voyages that disrupt and rejuvenate. "I cannot rest from travel," declares Tennyson's aging Ulysses, and he expresses not a little submerged contempt for Telemachus, to whom he leaves the homebody task of subduing " a rugged people . . . to the useful and the good": "He works his work, I mine." Heroes (and imperialist writing often translates experience into epic terms) are made "to strive, to seek, to find, and not to yield" to the blandishments of home. The domestic, as in *Middlemarch*, is often associated with issues of democratic reform and with the difficulties involved in personal and political compromise. Against these complexities, which often call for submission to social norms treated as "laws" of evolution, imperialism offers a swashbuckling politics and a world in which neither epic heroism nor chivalry is dead. Both are to be rediscovered in crusading and conquering abroad.

Such a contrast also suggests that peace and prosperity, feminine wiles and domestic tranquillity, are dangerous to the high ideals of England's past. Tennyson's Ulysses craves action, a field for heroic endeavor as large as it is unspecified. In much of his poetry Tennyson juxtaposes peace and war in ways that frequently associate the former with cowardice and greed, the latter with the highest virtues. Worried about the possibility of a French invasion, Tennyson in the early 1850s penned some of his most bellicose patriotic verse, calling for the "noble blood" of Britain to awake and "arm, arm, arm!"

> Peace is thirty-seven years old,
> Sweet Peace can no man blame,
> But Peace of sloth or of avarice born,
> Her olive is her shame.[40]

Perhaps even more than a French invasion, Tennyson feared the degeneration of heroism, chivalry, adventure—reversion (or progress) toward domesticity in one direction, and loss of political influence for such ideals in another. Viewed thus, "Sweet Peace" was only a prostitute.

From 1815 to the Crimean War and Indian Mutiny of the 1850s, and from then to the Boer War, the British engaged only in "little wars" against poorly armed "barbarians" and "savages." Industrial technology made those wars lopsided, and in such circumstances journalists and historians frequently had to manufacture heroism out of quite flimsy materials. Winston Churchill remarks in his autobiography that his military studies at Sandhurst were "thrilling," but also that "it did seem such a pity that it all had to be make-believe, and that the age of wars between civilised nations had come to an end forever. If it had only been one hundred years earlier . . .! Fancy being nineteen in 1793 with more than twenty years of war against Napoleon in front of one! However, all that was finished."[41] Here Churchill expresses a typical late Victorian view of the epic past as more glorious than the domesticated, peaceful present. "The British Army had never fired on white troops since the Crimea, and now that the world was growing so sensible and pacific— and so democratic too—the great days were over." But the little wars of imperial expansion still offered some scope for action: "Luckily . . . there were still savages and barbarous peoples. There were Zulus and Afghans, also the Dervishes of the Soudan. Some of these might, if they were well-disposed, 'put up a show' some day. There might even be a [new] mutiny or a revolt in India. . . . These thoughts were only partially consoling, for after all fighting the poor Indians, compared with taking part in a real European war, was only like riding in a paper-chase instead of in the Grand National" (44–45).

Similarly, despite or perhaps because of the greatness of the major Victorian explorers, exploration after the 1870s rapidly declined into mere travel, Cook's Tours came into vogue, and the "penetration" of

Africa and Asia turned into a sordid spectacle of tourism and commercial exploitation. In *Oceana; or, England and Her Colonies* (1886), James Anthony Froude describes the disappearance of adventure from the modern world as he observed it during a steamer voyage from the Cape to Australia: "We had no adventures. We passed St. Paul's Island and Kerguelen Island . . . but saw neither. The great ocean steamers are not driven into port by stress of weather, but go straight upon their way. Voyages have thus lost their romance. No Odyssey is possible now, no 'Sinbad the Sailor,' no 'Robinson Crusoe,' not even a 'Gulliver's Travels,' only a Lady Brassey's Travels."[42] For Martineau, commerce was the gospel, the source of progress, the bearer of the seeds of civilization, and free trade meant equal trade. How profits were made she could explain without blinking, in terms of work or industry that produced "desirable things" from raw materials. But for many late Victorians the knowledge that trade was usually unequal and unfree seemed unavoidable, and commerce generally seemed antithetical to heroism and high ideals. Instead of thriving and becoming civilized through contact with Europeans, moreover, the savages of places like Dawn Island just as often died out, failing to comprehend or appreciate their white conquerors even when those conquerors tried also to be their benefactors. The Indian Mutiny and the Jamaica Rebellion proved to many Victorians that the "dark races" were destined to remain forever dark until they perished from the face of the earth. For a few racial purists, the sooner they perished, the better.

But what would an empire be worth without savages to civilize? Because late Victorian imperialism had little utilitarian or evangelical optimism about converting the heathen, its fanfare often seems compensatory, an attempt to reclaim a waning heroism or an adolescent romanticism before the frontiers shut down. In Arthur Conan Doyle's 1911 fantasy *The Lost World*, a newspaper editor tells the hero: "The big blank spaces in the map are all being filled in, and there's no room for romance anywhere."[43] Doyle seems to agree, but in defiance of this fact of modern life he writes a wild romance about the discovery of an Amazonian region where dinosaurs still exist and where the savages are more apelike than human. Civilization itself could stultify; the search for adventure for Doyle was a way back through layers of artifice and taboo to the raw edges of primitive life, the jungle, the originary wilderness.

Parallel to the waning of adventure is another theme, the decline of the noble savage. Haggard's great Zulu warriors are exceptions in late Victorian literature, figures in a partly Rousseauistic, partly sanguinary daydream. As Victorian social and political confidence waned, respect for "savagery" seems also to have waned. If the world's "aborigines" were not to be completely decimated by those seemingly inevitable accompaniments of commerce and Christianity, disease, infertility, and genocide, their fate was to be tamed, converted, harnessed to the great wheel of industry like the emaciated chain gang Marlow sees at the Outer Station in *Heart of Darkness*. The relatively naive racism of the early decades of the century often found room for the noble savage, as in several of Marryat's novels; increasingly it gave way to depictions of Africans and Asians in terms of a pseudo-scientific racism similar to Robert Knox's, based on reductive versions of social Darwinism which did not mourn and sometimes explicitly advocated the elimination of "inferior races."

Imperialist discourse is inseparable from racism. Both express economic, political, and cultural domination (or at least wishes for domination), and both grew more virulent and dogmatic as those forms of domination, threatened by rivals for empire and by nascent independence movements (the Indian National Congress, for example), began gradually to crumble in the waning decades of the century. Not only do stereotypes of natives and savages degenerate toward the ignoble and the bestial in late Victorian thinking, however; so do the seemingly contrasting images of European explorers, traders, and colonizers. In early Victorian literature the numerous offspring of Robinson Crusoe, such as Marryat's seafaring heroes, hold out manfully against the cannibals, some of whom they usually manage to convert; late Victorian literature is filled with backsliders like Conrad's Kurtz who themselves become white savages.

The opposite of Martineau's conversion daydream is the nightmare of "going native." Conrad's *Heart of Darkness* has sometimes been treated as atypical because it criticizes imperialism during the heyday of empire, but many late Victorian stories pursue similar themes. In *The Beach of Falesá* and *The Ebb Tide*, for example, Robert Louis Stevenson produced accounts of the contemporary results of empire quite at odds with his romances of historical adventure. His South Seas stories are as skeptical about the influence of white civilization on primitive societies as anything Conrad wrote. The narrator of *Falesá*, John Wiltshire, is himself no explorer or rugged pioneer but a semi-educated trader sent to the island to operate a trading station. He discovers that he has competitors: two

Englishmen, Captain Randall and Case, and their sidekick Black Jack. "Trade and station belonged both to Randall," says Wiltshire; "Case and the negro were parasites."[44] But Randall is a degenerate, boozy representative of that usually noble species the British sea captain, and Case and Black Jack "crawled and fed upon him like the flies, he none the wiser" (10). The imagery of parasitism rubs off on Wiltshire; trade itself—the very white presence on the island, with the one exception of the Protestant missionary Tarleton—seems diseased, parasitic, close to what Hobson says about "economic parasitism" in *Imperialism* (1902). The full description of Captain Randall offers as powerful a suggestion of the decadence of the imperial adventure as anything in Conrad: "In the back room was old Captain Randall, squatting on the floor native fashion, fat and pale, naked to the waist, grey as a badger, and his eyes set with drink. His body was covered with grey hair and crawled over by flies; one was in the corner of his eye—he never heeded; and the mosquitoes hummed about the man like bees. Any clean-minded man would have had the creature out at once and buried him; and to see him, and think he was seventy, and remember he had once commanded a ship, and come ashore in his smart togs, and talked big in bars and consulates, and sat in club verandahs, turned me sick and sober" (9). Nothing could be farther from Marryat's heroic, hardworking sailors. Masterman Ready, for example, is "a hale and active man," though he has been at sea for more than fifty years. He has sailed everywhere and seen everything, weathering all the storms of life bravely and humbly, and, though he is full of exciting yarns, "he might be believed even when his stories were strange, for he would not tell an untruth." He is no scholar, but he is a great reader of the Bible. "The name of Ready was very well suited to him, for he was seldom at a loss . . . in cases of difficulty and danger" (*Masterman Ready*, 13–14).

In *Falesá*, adventure has given way to trade (although it sneaks in through the back door because trade gives way to crime). A felt contradiction between trade and the heroic, aristocratic significance of adventure results in a narrative that links together imperial domination, the profit motive, moral degeneracy, parasitism, and ultimately murder or attempted murder. Case is the main villain. In his attempt to corner the copra market he has killed or driven away Wiltshire's predecessors; Wiltshire is next on his list. While snooping in the jungle, Wiltshire learns that Case has rigged up a kind of puppet theatre of fake devils and "Tyrolean harps" to play upon the superstitions of the natives. He demolishes this source of Case's power in a spectacular finale, dynamiting his rival's handiwork just before Case shoots him in the leg. Wiltshire cuts the villain's throat as the jungle flares up around them.

This violent demystification of the island, and the apparent elimination of European villainy from it, leads to an ironically happy ending for Wiltshire. When he learns that Uma, the Kanaka girl whom Case persuaded him to marry by a fake marriage ceremony, has been declared taboo, he must choose between rescuing his business by jilting her or being declared taboo himself. He chooses the latter, both because he is stubborn and because "I never had anything so near me as this little brown bit of a girl" (36). In his own rough way he falls in love and has the missionary unite him with Uma in a legal ceremony. Having rid the island of fake devils and real criminals, Wiltshire can settle down to a life of peaceful business and domestic contentment. Here, then, is another way Stevenson's story marks the end of the innocent, heroic adventurousness of Marryat and early Victorian imperialism: the conclusion transforms ironic adventure tale into domestic problem story, with Wiltshire worrying about his children's futures:

> My public house? Not a bit of it, nor ever likely. [He has been hoping to return to England and open a pub with his savings.] I'm stuck here, I fancy. I don't like to leave the kids, you see: and—there's no use talking— they're better here than what they would be in a white man's country, though Ben took the eldest up the Auckland, where he's been schooled with the best. But what bothers me is the girls. They're only half-castes, of course; I know that as well as you do, and there's nobody thinks less of half-castes than I do; but they're mine, and about all I've got. I can't reconcile my mind to their taking up with Kanakas, and I'd like to know where I'm going to find the whites? (89).

By the end of his story Wiltshire is, like Conrad's Almayer, beyond adventure, a figure stranded in the backwaters of the Empire with nowhere to go. Both traders are marooned, but not in ways that resemble Robinson Crusoe or any of Marryat's characters. Instead they are marooned in plenty of company, surrounded by natives, half-castes, and Europeans whom they (and apparently their authors) consider their inferiors, racially in the first two cases and socially or morally in the third. And yet Wiltshire and Almayer are half-sunk into savagedom themselves, modern versions of Tennyson's Lotos-Eaters. Almayer has been beached by his own extravagant daydreams of wealth and a new life with his racially mixed daughter in Europe. She prefers savagedom, or at least life with Dain Maroola, and leaves her father high and dry in Borneo with death his only prospect. Wiltshire is almost a comic version of Almayer, both simpler and more sensible, and the domesticated end of his narrative suggests that his future life will be a series of essentially unheroic but honest compromises with his situation, his children, and his loving wife. "I'm stuck here, I fancy"—thus Stevenson's modern Crusoe, mildly complaining, settles down among the Kanakas to make the best of his island life, giving up the struggle either to bring civilization to the wilderness or to return to Britain.

Falesá suggests how issues of social class and racial domination can simultaneously conflict and merge in imperialist writing. Wiltshire's dilemma arises in part because his petit bourgeois status lets him feel at best only a slight superiority over the Kanakas, while they in turn are not so savage as he at first thinks. He is an appealing character because, although he continues to believe in the racial superiority of whites, he allows experience to produce a rough equality in his own half-"civilized," half-"savage" family. Miscegenation thus parallels the decay of adventure and imperial domination generally—the white man is losing his grip racially as well as politically. Almayer, however, in contrast to Wiltshire, cannot accommodate himself to the native world in which he has lived most of his life. Continuing to dream about wealth and high social standing "at home" in Europe, he is destroyed by his inflexibility.

Much late Victorian and Edwardian writing, perhaps especially when it is most aggressively imperialist, has an elegiac quality about it, mourning the loss of adventure, heroism, true nobility. At the margins, on the shrinking frontiers, the forces of nature or of savagery might still be untamed and an "epic life" might still be possible; but most of the world, for many observers writing between the 1880s and 1914, seemed to be collapsing into a bland, not quite honorable or even respectable domesticity, like Wiltshire's family life at the end of *Falesá*. Although they sometimes criticize the violence, exploitation, and racism of imperialism, Conrad's stories more consistently express the diminution of chances for heroism in the modern world, the decline of adventure. In *An Outcast of the Islands*, Conrad describes the modern degeneration of the ocean itself, rather like Froude's lament about the lack of adventure on modern voyages. The sea as "mistress," once mated with the "strong men" of the past, has been prostituted to modern commerce and technology:

> Like a beautiful and unscrupulous woman, the sea of the past was glorious. . . . It cast a spell . . . its cruelty was redeemed by the charm of

its inscrutable mystery, by the immensity of its promise, by the supreme witchery of its possible favour. Strong men with childlike hearts were faithful to it, were content to live by its grace—to die by its will. That was the sea before the time when the French mind set the Egyptian muscle in motion and produced a dismal but profitable ditch. Then a great pall of smoke sent out by countless steamboats was spread over the restless mirror of the Infinite. The hand of the engineer tore down the veil of the terrible beauty in order that greedy and faithless landlubbers might pocket dividends. The mystery was destroyed. . . . The sea of the past was an incomparably beautiful mistress. . . . The sea of today is a used-up drudge, wrinkled and defaced by the churned-up wakes of brutal propellers, robbed of the enslaving charm of its vastness. [45]

Earlier in the century, for Captain Marryat and Harriet Martineau, free trade and heroic adventuring among the barbarians and savages of the world had gone hand in hand. Now, like Stevenson, Conrad contrasts a past of innocent adventure and a present of commercial money-grubbing.

To Stevenson's and Conrad's sense of the decadence of the imperial adventure we might compare another passage from Churchill's autobiography, one that deplores the mechanized combat of World War I. As a young cadet at Sandhurst, Churchill regretted the recent absence of warfare among the European powers (though he later found the Battle of Omdurman glorious enough). But rather than renew the possibility of military glory, World War I spelled its ultimate demise. Just as technology was undermining the glamor of the sea for Conrad, so

war, which used to be cruel and magnificent, has now become cruel and squalid. In fact it has been completely spoilt. It is all the fault of Democracy and Science. From the moment that either of these meddlers and muddlers was allowed to take part in actual fighting, the doom of War was sealed. Instead of a small number of well-trained professionals championing their country's cause with ancient weapons and a beautiful intricacy of archaic manoeuvre, sustained at every moment by the applause of their nation, we now have entire populations, including even women and children, pitted against one another in brutish mutual extermination, and only a set of blear-eyed clerks left to add up the butcher's bill. From the moment Democracy was admitted to, or rather forced itself upon the battlefield, War ceased to be a gentleman's game. To Hell with it! Hence the League of Nations. (65)

The vanishing of frontiers, the industrialization of travel and warfare, the diminishing chances for heroism, the disillusionment with civilization and the civilizing mission—these late Victorian and early modern themes point insistently toward another: the decline of Britain's position in the world as an industrial, military, and imperial power.

In British literature from about 1830 to the 1870s, white heroes rarely doubt their ability to tame various geopolitical mistresses—Africa, the sea, the world—and to bring civilized order out of the chaos of savage life. Early Victorians did not call themselves imperialists or bang the drum for territorial expansion—they traversed the world as advocates of free trade, commerce and Christianity, and the benefits of being British. Only later, as doubts multiplied, would imperialism develop into a self-conscious ideology. As Carlyle understood, "the unconscious is the alone complete"; what has to be consciously calculated is necessarily problematic, already diseased or dying. Charles Kingsley says of Amyas Leigh, hero of *Westward Ho!*, that he "never thought about thinking, or felt about feeling."[46] He and the other Elizabethan sea dogs, apparently in "a fit of absence of mind," sailed forth to beat the Spaniards and conquer the world—and did so because they were Englishmen, with Anglo-Saxon blood in their veins.

In the 1850s, at least, Kingsley was able to believe that no further explanation of Britain's imperial greatness was necessary. His historical adventure novel (he called it an epic) offers as its central theme the racist and sexist tautology that informs much writing about the Empire throughout the nineteenth century: the English are on top of the world because they are English. With that nonexplanation of their prowess perhaps most Victorians agreed. In his speech for the Ladies' Sanitary Association in 1859, Kingsley stressed the anti-Malthusian role that domesticity played in subduing the rest of the world. He assumed his audience shared his belief that "the English race is probably the finest, and that it gives not the slightest sign whatever of exhaustion; that it seems to be on the whole a young race, and to have very great capabilities in it which have not yet been developed, and above all, the most marvellous capability of adapting itself to every sort of climate and every form of life, which any race, except the old Roman, ever has had in the world."[47] Kingsley then suggested that, if the ladies of the audience were truly interested in sanitary reform, they could do no better than do their duty for the Empire. About "four-fifths of the globe cannot be said as yet to be in anywise inhabited or cultivated," he declared, "or in the state into which men could put it by a fair supply of population, and industry, and human intellect." Thus he believed that the chief duty of the ladies of the audience, "one of the noblest duties," was simply "to help the increase of the English race as much as possible." The rest of history—including sanitary reform—would presumably take care of itself.

Title page to George Cruikshank, *The Progress of a Midshipman, Exemplified in the Career of Master Blockhead* (1821).

2. Bringing Up the Empire: Captain Marryat's Midshipmen

i

Dec. 25 [1806]: Engaged a battery, and received a shot in the counter.
Jan. 2 [1807]: Stove the cutter, and Henry Christian drowned.
Jan. 4: Anchored, and stormed a battery.
Jan. 6: Took a galliot; blew up ditto.
Jan. 8: Trying to get a prize off that was ashore, lost five men.[1]

T HESE entries from the log of a British midshipman during the Napo-leonic Wars are also part of the juvenilia of the "seafaring Dickens," Captain Frederick Marryat. He began his naval career at age fourteen, in 1806, the year after the Battle of Trafalgar. When he retired from the navy twenty-seven years later, he had served in the Mediterranean, Canada, and the West Indies, and with the naval flotilla that sailed up the Irrawaddy in the Burmese War of 1824–26. He had also published three of his twenty novels, beginning with *Frank Mildmay; or, The Naval Officer* in 1829.

"Every high-spirited boy wishes to go to sea . . . but if the most of them were to speak the truth, it is not that they . . . want to go to sea, [but] that they want to go from school or from home."[2] So says old Masterman Ready in the 1841 novel of that name; Marryat himself had to run away from school repeatedly before his father would consent to ship him off (literally) to the navy. As a member of Parliament, an executive of Lloyd's marine insurance company, colonial agent for Trin-idad and Grenada, and owner of plantations on those islands, Joseph Marryat had strong ties to the Royal Navy. These enabled him to find an ideal situation for his unruly second son as a first-class volunteer on the frigate *Impérieuse*, under the command of Lord Cochrane, later earl of Dundonald.[3] Following Nelson's victory at Trafalgar the British fleet blockaded French ports, and ships like Cochrane's engaged in single actions closer to privateering than to full-scale battles between fleets. During the three years Marryat served on the *Impérieuse*, "he was witness to more than fifty engagements" (1:20). He was wounded three times, nearly left for dead once, and commended twice for gallantry. On one occasion he helped steer an "explosion vessel" close to enemy ships and lit the fuse, barely escaping before it blew up. On another, he jumped overboard to rescue a drowning midshipman, Henry Cobbett, son of the radical journalist. Altogether during his two-and-a-half decades of service, he received over two dozen citations for saving lives, usually those of drowning shipmates.

Marryat's laconic log does not suggest how much his midshipman years meant to him, but he later wrote:

> The cruises of the *Impérieuse* were periods of continual excitement, from the hour in which she hove up her anchor till she dropped it again in port. . . . The expedition with which parties were formed for service; the rapidity of the frigate's movements, night and day; the hasty sleep, snatched at all hours; the waking up at the report of the guns, which seemed the only key-note to the hearts of those on board: the beautiful precision of our fire, obtained by constant practice; the coolness and courage of our captain, inoculating the whole of the ship's company; the suddenness of our attacks, the gathering after the combat, the killed lamented, the wounded almost envied; the powder so burnt into our faces that years could not remove it; the proved character of every man and officer on board, the implicit trust and the adoration we felt for our commander . . . the hair-breadth escapes, and the indifference to life shown by all—when memory sweeps along those years of excitement even now, my pulse beats more quickly with the reminiscence. (1:19–20)

Marryat's midshipman novels recreate his years of excitement. *Frank Mildmay* is the most directly autobiographical, but *The King's Own, Newton Forster, Peter Simple,* and *Mr. Midshipman Easy* also look back nostalgically to an age of youthful adventure when heroic action was almost routine. They imply that the peace and national prestige enjoyed by their first readers in the 1830s and 1840s are founded upon valiant deeds that comprise the glory of British history. "Let the author, a sailor himself," says Marryat in *The King's Own*, "take this favourable opportunity of appealing to you in behalf of a service at once your protection and your pride."[4] So deeply ingrained in his fiction are the themes of patriotism and martial valor, however, that such an explicit appeal seems unnecessary. Typical of Marryat's approach is the heading to chapter 46 of *Peter Simple*: "O'Brien tells his crew that one Englishman is as good as three Frenchmen on salt water—They prove it."[5]

Marryat's novels set the pattern for the imperialist adventure fiction that flourished from the seafaring writers who emulated him in the 1830s (Frederick Chamier, Edward Howard, Michael Scott, and others), through the Mexican westerns of Captain Mayne Reid, the "Robinsonades" of R. M. Ballantyne, and the historical romances of Charles Kingsley, down to Haggard, Stevenson, Kipling, and Conrad. The maritime tales of the 1830s, of which Marryat's are only the best known, portray the adventures of boy-heroes—usually midshipmen, usually during the Napoleonic Wars—providing a nostalgic, swashbuckling, but also conservative contrast to the literature of social reform which explored slums and workhouses and criticized corn laws and game laws. Whether written by Marryat or one of his seagoing cronies, who together made the *Metropolitan Magazine* (edited for a time by Marryat) an organ of military, naval, and patriotic sentiment in an era of peace abroad but political turmoil in Britain, these stories are alike in their essential features. Chamier's *Ben Brace* (1836), *Jack Adams* (1838), and *Tom Bowling* (1841) might have been the focus of this chapter, except that Marryat wrote much more and was both original and influential in ways Chamier and the others were not.[6]

At least one aspect of the maritime fictional pattern can be seen in Marryat's log, which he kept as part of his midshipman's training.

> July 25 [1808]: Burning bridges and dismantling batteries. (1:46)

The log enumerates actions but not actors, and that this pattern was typical of naval journals can be seen from Cochrane's log. A storm nearly wrecked the *Impérieuse* in November 1806, on Marryat's first cruise. He later wrote of "the cry of terror which ran through the lower decks . . . the enormous waves which again bore her up and carried her clean over the reef will never be effaced from my memory" (quoted in Lloyd, 32). In contrast, Cochrane's log records this near-disaster without emotion, in so reticent a style that it is impossible to tell how close the *Impérieuse* came to going down:

> Nov. 19th: Fresh breezes and cloudy. 5:15 a.m. ship struck and beat over a shoal. Clewed up and came to. Struck top gallant masts.
> Nov. 20th: Weighed and made sail 4:30 p.m. off Ushant. Squalls and fresh gales. Joseph Bennett fell overboard and was drownded. (Lloyd, 32)

Terror, emotion, self-expression of any kind has no place in ships' logs. Even the captain goes unnamed; only the drowned are identified. Starting with verbs or participles, the subjectless phrases speak only a staccato language of events. Though Marryat's novels express various, mostly adolescent emotions, they are picaresque narrations of one adventure after another which subordinate both emotion and character to action. "As far as I can see," says Lieutenant O'Brien to midshipman Peter Simple, "the life of a man consists in getting into scrapes, and getting out of them" (PS, 157). Marryat peoples his stories with numerous Smollett-like characters whose grotesque or unique foibles suggest a rich proliferation of individuality, but character and plot are oddly disconnected. Except insofar as courage or cunning helps one survive violence or get out of scrapes, personal foibles have no bearing on a character's destiny, which is in any case qualified, in a sense predestined, by the reader's awareness of the British triumph over the French.

"There certainly is a peculiar providence in favor of midshipmen," says the narrator of *Mr. Midshipman Easy*; "they have more lives than a cat—always in the greatest danger, but always escaping from it."7 Stories of heroic action in which survival is a matter of luck or providence make individual character seem beside the point. The character who survives many scrapes winds up with little or no character at all, in the sense of complex, deeply rooted personal identity. Stereotypes—the commonest alleged traits of groups—take the place of individuality. The thieving Italian, the volatile Frenchman, the lazy Barbadian complement by contrast the courageous, rollicking British tar. Character shrinks to a semaphore, a signal code of stereotypic traits, while action becomes paramount: the hero is he who can swim with the tide of events, which threatens at every moment to overwhelm mere selfhood.

As Stein tells Joseph Conrad's Jim, "The way is to the destructive element submit yourself, and with the exertions of your hands and feet in the water make the deep, deep sea keep you up."8 Like Jim, the imperialist adventurer must lose himself to find himself. Tennyson expresses the impulse in "Locksley Hall": "I must mix myself with action, lest I wither by despair."9 The domestic *Bildungsroman* records the slow, complex evolution of the protagonist's identity, but adventure-initiation stories, by contrast, jettison psychological complexity and maturation alike. The hero is thrown into do-or-die situations that render his previous upbringing almost irrelevant. Of course it helps that he is the son of a gentleman, that he has the Anglo-Saxon racial traits of pluck and absolute integrity. Nevertheless, the imperialist hero's education is, in a sense, complete in the moment of his first storm or battle. Though in reality a midshipman had to acquire much technical knowledge before he could be promoted to lieutenant, in Marryat's fictional world the education of a Jack Easy or a Peter Simple has more to do with "getting into scrapes and getting out them" than with navigational training. Apart from the abrupt, unforgettable lessons of courage and survival, what midshipmen need to know is ironically summed up by the drunken sailor whom Peter meets on the coach to Portsmouth: "You must larn to chaw baccy, drink grog, and call the cat [o'-nine-tails] a beggar, and then you know all a midshipman's expected to know nowadays" (PS, 23).

Not only does action diminish the importance of individual identity; so too does the authoritarian structure of naval hierarchy. Foreshadowing the boy-heroes of Henty and Kipling, Marryat's midshipmen escape from home and school into realms of adventure which promise freedom but instead place them on a lowly rung of a complex pecking order of sailors, officers, and gentlemen—at the pinnacle of which stand family, country, and God. In *The Settlers in Canada*, Alfred Campbell says that "a midshipman's ideas of independence are very great," but the navy is the wrong place to realize those ideas: "I had rather range the wilds of America free and independent," he tells his family, "than remain in service, and have to touch my hat to every junior lieutenant."[10] Alfred's discontent is, however, not quite typical, and he is happy enough when later promoted. Though there is usually a moment when Marryat's heroes regret what they have left behind, it passes quickly. When Frank Mildmay first comes on board, the filthy, claustrophobic midshipmen's berth repels him: "'Good Heaven!' thought I . . . 'and is this to be my future residence? —better go back to school; there, at least, [are] fresh air and clean linen.'"[11] But for the glory-bound there is no turning back. Mildmay's fate is to survive claustrophobia, bullying, and arbitrary orders and to be thrust abruptly into action at Trafalgar. "It would be difficult to describe my feelings on this occasion," he says. "Not six weeks before, I was the robber of hen-roosts and gardens—the hero of a horse-pond . . . now suddenly, and almost without any previous warning or reflection, placed in the midst of carnage, and an actor of one of those grand events by which the fate of the civilized world was to be decided" (FM, 43). The homesickness Frank earlier felt is swept away in the high drama of combat.

Despite their moments of regret, then, Marryat's prodigal sons are glad to be rid of home and school. They nevertheless discover rigorous substitutes for home and school on shipboard. School on shore is usually an unpleasant affair in his fiction, but Marryat often points out that the public schools were tame compared to shipboard education of the brutal sort. Older midshipmen bully the younger ones without stint; as Jack Easy puts it, "the weak go to the wall." As far as home is concerned, several Marryat heroes have bizarre or insane fathers, but whereas naval life provides an escape from these erratic fathers, it nonetheless thrusts the sons into a realm of hierarchy and discipline enforced by a multitude of surrogate father and brother figures. The worst of these are tyrants like the diabolical Lieutenant Vanslyperken in *Snarleyyow; or, The Dog Fiend*, who mercilessly torments Smallbones much as Wackford Squeers torments Smike in *Nicholas Nickleby*. (Vanslyperken is Dutch, however; no British officer, at least in a Marryat novel, is ever quite so diabolical.) But the best officers prove, like Captain Cochrane, to be far better role models than the real fathers whom the midshipmen leave behind. Toward the end of their adventures together, Captain O'Brien says to Peter Simple: "Haven't I brought you up myself, and made a man of you, as I promised I would, when you were a little shalpeen, with a sniffling nose, and legs in the shape of two carrots?" (PS, 384). In contrast, Peter's father goes mad from worrying about who will inherit the estate of their aristocratic relative, Lord Privilege: "He . . . fancied himself a jackass, and . . . brayed for a week, kicking the old nurse in the stomach, so as to double her up like a hedgehog. He had taken it into his head that he was a pump; and, with one arm held out as a spout, he . . . obliged the old nurse to work the other up and down for hours together" (PS, 449).

Marryat's prodigal sons find their own sanity in patriotism, action, and naval discipline. Their surrogate fathers on shipboard teach them the machismo wisdom of submitting themselves "to the destructive element." The prodigal sons sail toward glory, not freedom. On such a voyage the moment of combat is always the high point, the meaningful danger, to which the rest of the tale, no matter how colorfully and energetically contrived, serves merely as backdrop. Such a peak moment would of course find its place in a midshipman's log, provided he lived through it; all other moments leading up to and away from it are troughs, blank periods of toil and discipline though relieved by highjinks and foibles—but not worth noting in a log. In Marryat's world, life splits into two sorts of time: periods of routine stretching between peak and peak— and the peaks themselves, nearly timeless climaxes of violence. Perhaps adventure fiction always takes this form: if the troughs between the crests of high action are shortened or entirely omitted, as in Marryat's log, then adventure narratives approximate pornography, with moments of violence replacing moments of orgasm until violence itself becomes routine.

There was nothing routine about Trafalgar, but Frank Mildmay describes how he quickly became inured to carnage. At first, he says, he felt both afraid and ashamed to be afraid. "But when we had once got fairly into action, I felt no more of this, and beheld a poor creature cut in two by a shot with the same indifference that at any other time I should have seen a butcher kill an ox." Frank wonders about his transformation: "Whether my heart was bad or not, I cannot say; but I certainly felt my curiosity was gratified more than my feelings were shocked, when a raking shot killed seven and wounded three more." (FM, 43). After the battle Frank helps the surgeon, "and [I] saw all the amputations performed, without flinching. . . . I am afraid I almost took a pleasure in observing the operations, without once reflecting on the pain suffered by the patient. Habit had now begun to corrupt my mind. I was not cruel by nature; [but] I loved the deep investigation of hidden things; and this day's action gave me a clear insight into the anatomy of the human frame, which I had seen cut in two by shot, lacerated by splinters, carved out with knives, and separated with saws!" (FM, 45).

Though young Frank may not be "cruel by nature," Marryat's good-humored novels are certainly sadistic by nature. As representations of war they record the reactions of those thrust into war's midst, but they express little or no regret about the tragic consequences of violence. Peter Simple says that "the very idea of going into action is a source of joy to an English sailor, and more jokes are made, more merriment excited, at that time than at any other" (PS, 280). As in fairy tales and Disney cartoons, violence and slapstick merge. Death becomes the biggest joke of all, the ultimate form of comic relief, but with none of the bitterness of, say, Joseph Heller's Catch-22. The cartoon-like natures of Peter Simple, Jack Easy, and their brave, rollicking mates suggest that character itself in Marryat's world has been prematurely blown to bits; what takes its place is only the noses, fingers, arms, legs, the shreds of selfhood. Marryat's comic-heroic stereotyping thus prefigures the twin goals of death and glory.

Writing of the "simultaneous appearance at the end of the eighteenth century of the works of Sade and the tales of terror," Michel Foucault might also be describing the emergence of the imperialist adventure romance, of which Marryat's and Chamier's are the originals. "It is not their common predilection for cruelty which concerns us here; nor is it the discovery of the link between literature and evil, but something more obscure and paradoxical at first sight: these languages which are constantly drawn out of themselves by the overwhelming, the unspeakable, by thrills, stupefaction, ecstasy, dumbness, pure violence, wordless gestures, and which are calculated . . . to . . . make themselves as transparent as possible at this limit of language toward which they hurry, erasing themselves in their writing for the exclusive sovereignty of that which they wish to say and which lies outside of words . . . these languages very strangely represent themselves in a slow, meticulous, and infinitely extended ceremony."[12] If by ceremony Foucault means both the repetition and the celebration of pure act, "pure violence," the unlikely generic similarity between Sadean pornography and "tale of terror" or Gothic romance on the one hand and the imperialist adventure romance on the other becomes evident in the impulse each shares to submerge language, reason, selfhood in "the destructive element" of death. Despite their naive, hearty good cheer, or perhaps because of it, Marryat's novels are informed by a spirit of "altruistic suicide"—of an ultimate self-sacrifice ending in silence.[13]

Before he began to write novels, Marryat recorded his basic story in several drawings upon which his friend George Cruikshank based a series of engravings, entitled *The Progress of a Midshipman, Exemplified in the Career of Master Blockhead* (1821).[14] Cruikshank's frontispiece captures the imperialist adventure formula: through seas strewn with wrecked boats and drowning fellow aspirants, Blockhead steers toward the summit of his ambition—promotion, and a place in the officers' Valhalla at the top of the rock. In several of the engravings Blockhead, a caricature of Marryat, has a shocked or frightened look on his face as he plunges forward into action. Even the successful midshipman's voyage is a suicide mission through "the destructive element" with both glory and death as its goal: Blockhead, like Tennyson's Ulysses, sails toward a version of the Happy Isles.

Cruikshank illustrated many nautical and patriotic works besides Marryat's, including the 1841 edition of *Songs Naval and National*, mainly by Charles Dibdin. Alongside James Thomson's "Rule Britannia" and William Garrick's "Hearts of Oak," one finds such "comic" ballads as Dibdin's "Well It's No Worse," in which a jolly old tar, a sort of seafaring Rabbi Ben Ezra, recollects how

> I went to sea all so fearlessly,
> Broach'd my grog all so carelessly,

> By and by, in a brush, I lost my arm,
> Tol de rol, de rol de ri![15]

The sailor supposes there is little "harm" in this loss, because now he has no arm to "lift . . . 'gainst a friend." In the second stanza he recollects the loss of his leg; in the third, of his eyesight; and in the fourth, of his wife. Thus much reduced and symbolically castrated, the old tar concludes:

> Being old, I've lost all but my tongue:
> Tol de rol, de rol de ri!
> So, says I,
> 'Twas not so when I was young;
> But, then, says I again, you dunce!
> Be fear afar
> From every tar;
> Damme, a man can die but once!

Marryat's midshipmen are never so thoroughly demolished as Dibdin's merry amputee, though occasionally they are wounded, left for dead, and later resurrected. Discipline and violence nevertheless reduce them also to figures of heroic slapstick, odd yet expendable cells of the body politic for whose health and happiness they would cheerfully sacrifice limbs, eyes, wives, lives.

Of course Marryat's boy-heroes survive all scrapes: they generally receive their promotions, marry their sweethearts, and inherit fortunes by the end of their adventures. But the love interest in Marryat's fiction, in common with other features that might involve some complexity or subtlety of characterization, is always secondary to the moments of action. In his admiring essay on Marryat, Conrad declares that the midshipman novels, "like amphibious creatures, live on the sea" but "flounder deplorably" when they "frequent the shore."[16] They flounder in part because their portrayals of parents, schoolmasters, and women are, if anything, even more stilted and stereotypic than their portrayals of sailors and foreigners. Marryat obviously felt that the representation of domestic life was tangential to his main concern; perhaps he hurried through the writing of onshore scenes. "Mme. de Staël has pronounced love to be an episode in a man's life," says Frank Mildmay; "and so far it is true. There are as many episodes in life as there are in novels and romances; but in neither case do they destroy the general plot of the history, although they may, for the time, distract or divert our attention" (FM, 214). This odd bit of reasoning suggests both that love is tangential to the important aspects of the story and that the various scrapes or episodes, seemingly the smaller units of the plot, are themselves diversions from "the general plot of the history." Perhaps there is some overarching story—fate, everyman's voyage through the "destructive element," the history of England—which neither individual character nor specific scrapes can alter.

Like the irrelevance of individual identity, the idea that specific scrapes or events have no important bearing on the overarching story or metanarrative of history fits Marryat's authoritarian politics. In the totalitarian world of a British warship, where the Captain names only the drowned in his log, the living must obey their superiors and wait to be named in turn. The political lesson is obvious. Under the watchful eyes of various surrogate fathers, Jack Easy sheds his insane father's ideas about equality. Poor Nicodemus Easy is the victim of his liberal madness; at the end of the story, he accidentally hangs himself in his bizarre phrenological machine, designed to equalize people's brains. Shortly before this piece of tragic slapstick, Jack confronts his father: "Your principles are all confounded nonsense. . . . The most lasting and imperishable form of building is . . . the pyramid . . . and to that may the most perfect form of society be compared. It is based upon the many, and rising by degrees, it becomes less as wealth, talent, and rank increase in the individual, until it ends at the apex or monarch, above all. Yet each several stone from the apex to the base is necessary for the preservation of the structure, and fulfils its duty in its allotted place" (ME, 382). Jack adds: "If all were equal, there would be no arts, no manufactures, no industry, no employment. As it is, the inequality of the distribution of wealth [in society] may be compared to the heart, pouring forth the blood like a steam-engine through the human frame, the same blood returning from the extremities by the veins, to be again propelled, and keep up a healthy and vigorous circulation" (ME, 383).

Though Marryat twice ran unsuccessfully for Parliament, the second time on what he considered to be principles of liberal reform, he was always a Tory and his political attitudes can be described only as imperialist and antidemocratic.[17] In his 1832 election bid he declared that he represented the "Ships, Colonies, and Commerce" interest (1:200). His reforming impulse did not extend much beyond his pet project of eliminating "the degrading, unjust, oppressive system of the impressment of seamen" (1:201). Nevertheless, on losing the election, "he challenged his enemies to say if they could point out one page [of his writings] in which he advocated anti-Liberal notions" (1:202). But Marryat's liberalism was a very thin veneer over a much more fundamental set of reactionary assumptions. Just two years after the election, while touring the Continent, Marryat wrote to Lady Blessington:

I . . . see the English papers, and I am very much disgusted. Nothing but duels and blackguardism. Surely we are extremely altered by this Reform [Bill]. Our House of Lords was the *beau ideal* of all that was aristocratical and elegant. Now we have language that would disgrace the hustings. In the House of Commons it is the same, or even worse. The gentleman's repartee, the quiet sarcasm, the playful hit, where are they? all gone; and, in exchange for them, we have—you lie, and you lie. This is very bad, and it appears to me, strongly smacking of revolution; for if the language of the lower classes is to take the precedence, will not they also soon do the same? I am becoming more Conservative every day; I cannot help it; I feel it a duty as a lover of my country. (Quoted by Warner, 105)

As in countless conservative diagnoses of social evils so in Marryat's, language is a key source of symptoms—the words other people use, quite apart from what they have to say, express the inner rot at the heart of the body politic. Marryat's opinion of the reformed Parliament thus looks forward to Thomas Carlyle's condemnations of the "National Palaver," while it also recalls Edmund Burke's analysis of the French Revolution as insane ideological and linguistic froth subverting traditional institutions—"the polluted nonsense of . . . licentious and giddy coffee-houses" undoing the silent "work of ages."[18] At the heart of all authoritarian politics lies the desire to abolish dialogue (particularly the language of others), to use words strictly in the imperative mode, to call forth acts of heroism and devotion. This desire seeks to subject "every possible language, every future language, to the actual sovereignty of [a] unique Discourse which no one, perhaps, will be able to hear."[19]

ii

Marryat's conservatism in regard to Parliament and the lower classes at home carries over to his attitudes toward the colonies and the various races of human beings found in them. His father's West Indian connections obviously influenced what Marryat thought about the slave trade, slavery, and their abolition. Furthermore, although the French are the main enemy in the midshipman novels, Africans, American Indians, and other dark-skinned characters often appear in Marryat's fiction in "sidekick" roles, as the loyal satellites—virtually personified colonies—of the imperialist heroes. The black sidekick speaks the hero's language, assists him in his work, and in general does his bidding.[20]

In his argument against his father's insane egalitarianism, Jack Easy is supported by his friend Mesty (short for Mephistopheles), a freed slave turned ship's cook and then promoted to corporal. As Jack elaborates upon the social pyramid and the circulation of wealth, his versions of the great chain of being and the social organism, his father points to Mesty and asks: "Can he forget the horrors of slavery? Can he forget the base unfeeling lash? No, sir, he has suffered, and he can estimate the divine right of equality" (ME, 384). But when Jack asks Mesty to state his opinion of equality, the African shows his filed teeth and replies: "I say d—n equality, now I major-domo" or ship's corporal. Nicodemus then ludicrously undercuts the egalitarianism he has always espoused by blurting out: "The rascal deserves to be a slave all his life" (ME, 384).

Mesty is to Midshipman Jack Easy as Friday is to Robinson Crusoe, Chingachgook to Natty Bumppo, and Umslopagaas to Allan Quatermain: the noble savage in partnership with the conquering hero. In each case the white hero shares some of the qualities of the savage sidekick, but the doubling or mirroring process is lopsided: white always overshadows black. A contradictory irony arises in Marryat, partly because the bond between Jack and Mesty seems to involve the very principle of equality that Jack learns to reject. But the apparent equality that obtains between Jack and Mesty is based instead on mutual respect for each other's different, quite unequal, racial and social identities. Like the many other white/black, civilized/savage doubles in imperialist adventure fiction, Jack and Mesty form a harmoniously unbalanced antithesis; there is never any doubt who is the dominant and who the inferior member of the pair.

Mesty, once an Ashanti "prince," was sold into slavery, later escaping thanks to the Royal Navy. "But he found that the universal feeling was strong against his colour, and that on board of a man-of-war he was condemned, although free, to the humblest of offices" (ME, 83). Hearing Jack expound the doctrine of equality, Mesty "immediately took a fondness for our hero, and in a hundred ways showed his attachment. Jack also liked Mesty, and . . . every evening . . . they . . . generally met in the forecastle to discuss the principles of equality and the rights of man" (ME, 83). Mesty demonstrates his courage and resourcefulness on numerous occasions, often rescuing Jack from scrapes. Because of his valor, he is promoted to corporal and is overjoyed to lord it over the common deckhands. Equality is not the message of Jack and Mesty's bond, but power and the highly unequal though respectful sharing of power. Equality, Jack tells his father, "can and does exist nowhere. We are told that it does not exist in heaven itself—how can it exist upon earth?" (ME, 381)

When Mesty tells Jack his history in chapter 15, what Marryat offers is essentially a slave narrative, similar to many written for the abolitionist cause. But Mesty's is not a narrative that leads to the conclusion slavery should be abolished. Marryat dignifies Mesty's story by "translating" the comic dialect the Ashanti prince ordinarily speaks "into good English" (ME, 140). As a royal child, Mesty says, "I lived happy. I did nothing but shoot my arrows, and I had a little sword which I was taught to handle, and the great captains who were about my father showed me how to kill my enemies . . . sometimes I . . . played with the skulls, and repeated the names of those to whom they had belonged, for in our country, when we kill our enemies, we keep their skulls as trophies" (ME, 141). Mesty grows to be a great hunter, and one day, after killing a panther which has wounded him, he is declared "a hero and a great captain. I filed my teeth, and I became a man" (ME, 141).

Mesty's life as a warrior prince follows the noble savage pattern of Aphra Behn's Oroonoko (1688) and of numerous eighteenth- and nineteenth-century abolitionist tracts.[21] When Mesty goes to war, however, he brings back not only the skulls of slain enemies but also prisoners for sale on the coast—he is both a prince and a "caboceer" or slave-trader (ME, 141). Like Oroonoko's, Mesty's aristocratic status in Africa undergoes a complete, tragic reversal when he himself is sold into slavery. The moral Marryat attaches to Mesty's narrative is not that slavery is wrong and emancipation right, however, but that both slavery and aristocracy are products of society in its most primitive or natural condition.

Just as a rigid hierarchy governs sailors and officers on shipboard in Marryat's novels, so a rigid hierarchy of races and perhaps also of stages of social development governs history. In Barbados, Peter Simple is amused by the fine distinctions of race and racial mixtures that the islanders make. He attends a fancy dress ball at which he observes:

The progeny of a white and a negro is a mulatto, or half and half—of a white and a mulatto, a quadroon, or one-quarter black, and of this class the company were chiefly composed. I believe a quadroon and white make the mustee or one-eighth black, and the mustee and white the mustafina, or one-sixteenth black. After that, they are whitewashed, and considered as Europeans. The pride of colour is very great in the West Indies, and they have as many quarterings as a German prince in his coat of arms; a quadroon looks down upon a mulatto, while a mulatto looks down upon a *sambo*, that is, half mulatto half negro, while a *sambo* in turn looks down upon a *nigger*. The quadroons are certainly the handsomest race of the whole; some of the women are really beautiful. (*PS*, 260)

In this and other descriptions of the West Indies, Marryat treats Caribbean society as aping its European betters. The Barbadian hierarchy of color mimics what are implicitly much more fundamental hierarchies of race in nature and of aristocracy and social class in Britain.

Marryat is not troubled by the widespread miscegenation evident in Barbadian society, but neither does he question the idea that whites are racially superior to blacks. Indeed, in their very mimicry of European social distinctions, using the superficial gauge of skin coloration, the Barbadians show their inferiority. A similar message underlies Mesty's comic black dialect and all other instances of minstrelese in imperialist fiction, in which blacks are held to have a wonderful facility for imitation. No matter how astonishing their apings of white ways, the message runs, they can never become the genuine article. Ironically, the imperialist work of converting the savages undercuts itself at this point: the idea of imitation makes a mockery of the idea of conversion. In Mesty's case, he is warlike, dignified, a noble savage or child of nature in Africa; but as a ship's cook and corporal, he is half-buffoon—still a great warrior but in matters of civilization, like talking plain English, able only to mimic his betters.

Nor does Marryat, despite Mesty's narrative, ever suggest that slavery is an evil institution that should be abolished. On the contrary, in *Newton Forster* (1832), written during the antislavery debates of the early 1830s, Marryat paints a vivid picture of the happy life on a slave plantation. When Newton asks his host at Barbados "many . . . questions relative to the slave-trade," Mr. Kingston takes him and Captain Berecroft for a visit to a plantation so they can judge for themselves "as to the truth of the reports so industriously circulated by those . . . inimical to the employment of a slave population."[22] The first thing Newton learns is that the planter treats his happy slave children with great kindness, as if they were household pets, almost family. The children are raised comfortably, with plenty to eat, in the "nursery-yard" where the "breeding women" reside. These women, also contented, receive careful medical attention and are again treated by the master almost like family (though the master, Marryat makes clear, does not serve as the stud). "Now these are all my *breeding* women," the planter tells his visitors; "they do no work, only take care of the children, who remain here until they are eight or nine years old. We have a surgeon on the estate, who attends them as well as the other slaves when they are sick" (NF, 93). Far from housing the master's harem, the nursery-yard is a pleasant, sanitary child-care facility; the planter points out that his slaves marry and form families that are not broken up by sale. He also points out that his slaves work only "eight hours a day—except in crop-time, and then we are very busy" (NF, 94). As they stroll about the estate, Newton observes comfortable slave cottages surrounded by flourishing gardens, with poultry and pigs in abundance.

When Captain Berecroft asks whether the slaves are able to "lay up much money," the planter responds: "Very often enough to purchase their freedom, if they wished it" (NF, 94). That slaves could purchase their freedom but might not wish to comes as a surprise to Newton and Berecroft, whose visit to the plantation reverses most of their previous notions about slavery. Those notions, Marryat believes, are mainly attributable to the false propaganda of the abolitionists. Toward the end of the tour the planter asks his visitors: "Now you have witnessed what is termed slavery, what is your opinion? Are your philanthropists justified in their invectives against us?" (NF, 95). Captain Berecroft wishes to be assured that all plantations are as "well regulated" as the one they have just toured, and the planter's reply is again intended to be surprising: though not all plantations are so well regulated as his own, he says, "they soon will be: it is to the interest of all the planters that they should" (NF, 95).

Part of the reason that all planters will soon operate their plantations on benevolent principles is that the slave trade has been abolished. Most of the cruelty associated with slavery, according to Marryat's kindly planter, derives from the slave trade, both because of the horrors of the middle passage and because, as long as planters could import new slaves from Africa, they treated the slaves they already owned as expendable. "The abolition of the slave-trade was an act of humanity" worthy of a great country like Britain, says the planter. Now, however, the foolish philanthropists are trying to abolish slavery as well, which will lead "to the extermination of their own countrymen" in the West Indies (NF, 95). Perhaps by extermination the planter has in mind the slave rebellion that overthrew slavery in Haiti—a threat that obviously contradicts the rosy picture given of slavery on his estate. Or perhaps he means merely that the plantation economy of West Indian whites will be ruined by the abolition of slavery. Whatever the case, Marryat draws a sharp distinction between abolition of the slave trade, which he approves on humanitarian grounds (it had been outlawed as long ago as 1808), and abolition of slavery, which he thinks would be unnecessary and destructive.

Not all of the views expressed by the planter are necessarily Marryat's. After their visit, Newton is still not convinced that slavery is a good thing: "Even the shadow of liberty is to be venerated by an Englishman" (*NF*, 99). Against Newton's lingering skepticism, however, Captain Berecroft poses a religious counterpoint. The Captain agrees with Newton that liberty should be "venerated by an Englishman": the planter's "discourse did, however, bring one idea into my head; which is, that there is a remarkable connection between religion and slavery. It was in a state of bondage that the Jews were prepared to receive the promised land . . . and who knows but that this traffic [in slaves], so offensive to humanity, has been permitted by an Allwise Power, with the intent that some day it shall be the means of introducing Christianity into the vast regions of African idolatry? . . . He worketh by his own means, which are inscrutable" (*NF*, 99–100).

In other writings Marryat shows himself to be more ambivalent toward slavery than he is in *Newton Forster*. In his *Diary in America* (1839), Marryat attacks the northern white hypocrisy that discriminates against supposedly free blacks: "In the United States, a negro, from his colour, and I believe his colour alone, is a degraded being. Is not this extraordinary, in a land which professes universal liberty, equality, and the rights of man?"[23] Marryat goes to some length to show that "the African race," while on the whole inferior to the white race, is not *very* inferior, and also that individual blacks can often prove superior to individual whites. In stating his case, Marryat indicates that his opinion has changed since the writing of *Newton Forster*:

> It was not until I had been some time in Philadelphia that I became convinced how very superior the free coloured people were in intelligence and education, to what, from my knowledge of them in our West-India Islands, I had ever imagined them capable of. Not that I mean to imply that they will ever attain to the same powers of intellect as the white man, for I really believe that the race are not formed for it by the Almighty. I do not mean to say that there *never* will be great men among the African race, but that such instances will always be very *rare*, compared to the numbers produced among the white. But this is certain, that in Philadelphia the free coloured people are a very respectable class, and, in my opinion, quite as intelligent as the more humble of the free whites. (*D*, 175–76)

Marryat's change of opinion is salutary and may help to explain his highly favorable (albeit comic and stereotypic) portrayal of Mesty. Certainly the West Indian life depicted in *Peter Simple* (1834), written immediately after *Newton Forster*, is more buffoonish than anything in Marryat's latter novels. But it also seems likely that, intent on debunking abolitionist philanthropy in *Newton Forster*, Marryat produced its rosy picture of West Indian slavery; intent on debunking democratic institutions in America, however, he produced his favorable portrait of the free coloured people of Philadelphia and his attack on the hypocrisy of supposedly liberal northern whites. In both cases, in other words, Marryat was more concerned to undermine democratic, liberal, or reformist views than he was to present a consistent theory either of slavery or of race.

Though critical of white hypocrisy, Marryat's responses to slavery and freed blacks in his *Diary in America* bear little resemblance to Charles Dickens's angry diatribe against slavery in *American Notes* (1844) or to Harriet Martineau's fiercely abolitionist stance in *Demerara* (1833) and *Society in America* (1839). Despite his sympathetic rendering of Mesty, Marryat remained in his attitudes toward slavery and Africans at best equivocal. The same is true of his portrayals of members of other "dark races." Though one of the shrewdest, ablest, bravest characters in *Mr. Midshipman Easy*, Mesty reaches his upper limit with his promotion to corporal—his ultimate locus on the great chain of being. Ashanti princedom in the English naval hierarchy translates to corporal—not captain, lieutenant, or even boatswain.

Marryat's world consists of interlocking hierarchies: social classes, naval and military ranks, Ashanti royalty, the dark-to-light pecking order of Barbados, the species of plants and animals in nature. The social pyramid is thus a series of pyramids; at any given moment Marryat's characters always belong to several hierarchies. A person's positions on two social ladders may be quite unequal, as in the case of Mesty's double status, as African prince and as shipboard cook and corporal. Shipboard resembles the social realm: everything and everyone has a definite place (or several places). Only the corrosive nature of revolutionary principles and democratic reform, Marryat seems to feel, causes confusion to arise. His least sympathetic characters are usually those who do not accept their place in at least one of the hierarchies to which he assigns them. A contrast to loyal Corporal Mesty is the purser's steward on board the *Harpy*, a cockney named Easthupp with a criminal background upon whom Conrad may have modeled Donkin in *The Nigger of the "Narcissus."* When he hears Jack spouting the egalitarianism Jack later rejects, Easthupp declares that he too is "a *hout-and-hout* radical" and tries to curry favor with him. Jack immediately dislikes the impudent fellow and kicks him down "the after-lower-deck hatchway," about where Easthupp belongs on the social ladder. "Jack knew a gentleman when he met one, and did not choose to be a companion to a man beneath him in every way" (ME, 96).

Just as he sees no contradiction in situating Mesty as a prince in savagedom and a cook and corporal in civilization, so, in his *Diary in America*, Marryat depicts American Indians as noble savages as long as they remain wild but as drunken, dissolute buffoons when they become half-civilized. Nevertheless, Indians rank higher than most other races on Marryat's totem pole of social worth. In *The Settlers in Canada*, the Campbell family, immigrants from Britain, learn that "even in its un-enlightened state" the "character" of the Indian "has in it much to be admired" (SC, 58). It proves difficult to convert Indians to Christianity, because their monotheistic beliefs are "so near what is right" that it is hard to convince them they need to cross over the gulf between darkness and light (SC, 194). But although conversion of the heathen seems to several of the characters—and to Marryat himself—to be an important goal, possible if pursued patiently enough, their conversion will also entail the destruction of what is most savage, warlike, and therefore admirable about them. In *Diary in America*, Marryat describes a Sioux village near Fort Snelling where a white missionary had taken up the good work of conversion. Marryat's ambivalence surfaces: "Although from demi-civilization, the people have lost much of their native gran-deur, still they are a fine race, and well disposed. But the majority of the Sioux tribe remain in their native state"—where Marryat clearly thinks they are happiest and most admirable (D, 229). The goal of converting the Ashanti prince or the Sioux warrior is always shadowed by the dismal prospect of liquidating the warlike virtues of human nature in its primi-tive state. And Marryat, war hero himself, values nothing more highly than the warlike virtues. Hence his admiration for the Ashanti, the Zulus, the Sioux, the Burmese, and other martial societies—all those savage groups who were best able to defend themselves against the imperialist encroachments of white civilization. In contrast to the charis-matic, warlike world of the savage, the completely civilized world of the future will unfortunately be tame, unexciting, barren, and somehow unnatural.

Furthermore, though to civilize savages and convert the heathen seems a work of humanitarian progress, there is always the threat that the children of light may revert to darkness. Conversion operates in both directions in *The Settlers in Canada*. There, and also in *Diary in America*, Marryat treats the threat of "going native" in fairly positive terms. In the travelogue he describes "half breds [*sic*]" who combine some of the best Indian traits with the ways of the white man. "Monsieur Rainville" or "*de* Rainville," for example, is "descended from one of the best families in France" on his father's side, and from the Sioux on his mother's. Rainville proves to be a better civilizer than white missionaries, because he knows and follows many Sioux customs (*D*, 231). And in *Settlers*, both the old hunter Malachi Bone and young Martin Super are whites who are "almost Indian," able to outwit and outfight their adversaries because they know all that the Indians know and more (*SC*, 39). The illiterate Martin signs himself with a picture of his totem animal, "the painter" or cougar, and says: "I am almost an Indian myself" (*SC*, 42). And Malachi, who lives "entirely by the chase," is so "browned and weather-beaten—indeed so dark, that it [would be] difficult to say if he were of the Indian race or not" (*SC*, 67). These two Natty Bumppo figures help the Campbell family, acting as mediators between the wilderness and civilization.

Malachi takes young John Campbell under his wing and converts him into a skilled hunter and woodsman, expert in Indian ways. And when John's older brother Percival is kidnaped by an Indian band, *Settlers* approximates the many captivity narratives that characterize early American frontier literature.[24] When Percival is rescued after nearly two years of captivity, he too is "almost an Indian." He has been well-treated by Angry Snake, even though his captor is otherwise a "bad Indian," but it was Angry Snake's "intention to adopt the boy, as he was very partial to him" (*SC*, 258). After this education in Indian and forest lore, the released Percival must be "awakened from his Indian dream" and reconverted to civilized life (*SC*, 271). So thoroughly has Percival taken on an Indian identity that he speaks only "the Indian tongue" and must be tied up by his white rescuers to prevent his escaping back to the Indians. "His sojourn of nearly two years in the woods with the Indians," says the narrator, "without seeing the face of a white man had . . . wholly obliterated, for the time, his recollections of his former life—so rapid is our falling off to the savage state." Malachi Bone reiterates the point: "It's wonderful how soon we return to a state of nature when once we are in the woods" (*SC*, 263).

Though Percival's reconversion occurs fairly rapidly, it is neither easy nor entirely happy. Soon, however, "Percival was . . . reconciled to his removal from an Indian life, and appeared most anxious to rejoin his father and mother, of whom he talked incessantly; for he had again recovered his English, which, strange to say, although he perfectly understood it when spoken to, he had almost forgotten to pronounce, and at first spoke with difficulty" (SC, 272). In a narrative about social identity, in which transactions and transformations between civilization and savagery are central and frequent, the loss of the ability to speak one's native tongue represents a symbolic outer limit of regression or "social death."[25] But in this instance the victim of social death can be resurrected, his life changed for the better. When Percival's cousin Mary, who has also been held hostage though for a much shorter time, is asked whether she thinks that "his residency among the Indians has made a great change in Percival," she replies: "A very great one; he is more manly and more taciturn; he appears to think more and talk less" (SC, 280). So the loss of language is finally not a social death for Percival, but a gain, perhaps a doubling, of "taciturn" cultural authority. This wish-fulfilment pattern informs many imperialist adventure romances, in which the civilized hero acquires a savage identity and yet remains civilized. In most cases the culturally hybrid character proves to be superior to both the merely civilized and the merely savage characters whom he aids, outwits, or defeats. Natty Bumppo is again an obvious example, as is Haggard's Allan Quatermain.

Both because he admires Indian ways and because of his ultimate faith in the blessings of civilization and the truths of Christianity, Marryat can treat "going native" or reverse conversion as a romantic adventure, daydream more than nightmare, uniting the best of both worlds, civilized and savage. In contrast, in his last completed novel for children, *The Mission; or, Scenes in Africa* (1846), Marryat portrays a potential regression to African savagery as a far more monstrous threat than Percival's Indian metamorphosis. Sir Charles Wilmot's daughter, returning from India, has been shipwrecked on the east coast of South Africa. Several years after the accident Sir Charles learns that she may have survived and be "living with the savages."[26] Sir Charles tells his grandnephew, Alexander: "What a pang it gives me when I . . . reflect that my poor girl . . . may at this moment be alive, may have returned to a state of barbarism, the seeds of faith long dead in her bosom, now changed to a wild untutored savage, knowing no God" (M, 9). Worse yet, she may have had children. "The idea of my grandchildren having returned to a state of barbarism is painful enough," says Sir Charles, but the worst of all is not knowing. Alexander therefore sets out on "the mission" to learn the truth about his aunt's fate.

Most of Marryat's South African novel takes the form of a travelogue, not quite an explorer's journal, in which Alexander learns the history of the Cape Colony, the ethnology of its "natives," its geography, and the strange, colorful facts of its flora and fauna. During his numerous adventures Alexander receives highly favorable impressions of several African "races," including, for instance, "the Caffres, a fine warlike race" (M, 22). From the missionary Mr. Swinton, he also learns about the "mixed race" of the Griquas:

> By the Dutch colonial law, these people could not hold possession of any land in the colony; and this act of injustice and folly has deprived us of a very valuable race of men, who might have added much to the prosperity of the colony. Brave and intelligent, industrious to a great degree, they, finding themselves despised on account of the Hottentot blood in their veins, have migrated from the colony and settled beyond the boundaries. Being tolerably provided with firearms, those who are peaceably inclined can protect themselves, while those who are otherwise, commit great depredations upon the poor savages, following the example shown them by the colonists. (M, 161)

The Dutch in Marryat's novel, as in many later British accounts of South Africa, come off worse than the Africans whom Alexander encounters. Swinton's description of the Griquas also suggests that in their case Marryat is not troubled by the idea of miscegenation which forms part of Sir Charles's nightmare—his horror of having half-black, heathen grand-children. In any case, Alexander's quest ends successfully somewhere near the Zambezi River. When he first meets the partly white chief Daaka, he is afraid Daaka may be his first cousin. But Alexander is led to the scene of the shipwreck and there discovers that his aunt must have died with everyone else on board. "You don't know," Alexander later tells Swinton, "what a load has been removed from my mind. . . . My poor uncle! God grant that he may live till my return with . . . the assurance that he has no grandchildren living the life of a heathen and knowing no God" (M, 142).

Perhaps Marryat's attitudes toward the dark races of the world were more influenced by Christianity than by racism, though the two are impossible to separate. Certain it is, however, that his portrayals of Africans, Indians, and other nonwhite peoples are usually more sympathetic—and often more knowledgeable—than those by many of his imitators. Like Cooper and Melville, Marryat sees many of the virtues of savagery and at least some of the vices of civilization. Nevertheless, the social pyramid is clear and unalterable. The English are at the pinnacle of the hierarchy of races and nations, just as the monarch is at the pinnacle of the English hierarchy of class and power. No doubt because his faith in this authoritarian social structure was secure, Marryat felt little difficulty about treating non-European races and nations with a generosity that became increasingly rare in later Victorian and Edwardian writing. And of all his comparatively favorable descriptions of dark, supposedly inferior humanity, none is more favorable than his account of the Burmese, whom Marryat helped to defeat in the 1824–26 Rangoon War.

Marryat gives an account of the Burmese campaign in his *Diary on the Continent*. As all good warriors should, he salutes "the Burmahs" for their valiant resistance. They are, he says, "a very powerful race . . . possessing great strength and energy," and because they are surrounded "by the Cochin Chinese, the Chinese, and the Hindoos, all races of inferior stature and effeminate in person, with little or no beard," they could conceivably compete with the British in imperializing the rest of Asia.[27] The East India Company had thus better be on its guard; mere Hindu sepoys will not be able to protect the British Empire in India if the Burmese mount an invasion (*DC*, 95). Besides their manly, warlike virtues, moreover, the Burmese are only "semi-barbarous," and even this term "must be used in the most favourable light; because, surrounded on every side by people who are wedded to their own customs, the Burmahs have a liberality and a desire to improve, which is very remarkable" (*DC*, 96). The "good tempered" Burmese "work very hard, and with the greatest cheerfulness." But should their desire to improve manifest itself in the acquisition of up-to-date military technology, then the British in India will be in for a struggle. "They have a high respect for the English, or the white faces, as they call us; and the superiority of our warlike instruments, and our ships. . . . They perceive how far they are behind us, and are most anxious to improve" (*DC*, 99). Marryat here describes some powerful inducements toward a social conversion—improvement or, as it is now called, development—which may work against British hegemony.

Marryat, however, is not really troubled by the threat of a Burmese invasion of India. For one thing, he was of course on the victorious side when he sailed up the Irrawaddy in 1824—the British soundly defeated the Burmese. For another, the Burmese, for all their anxiety to improve, are still mired in the retarding superstitions and customs of the Orient. Their government is "most despotic" (doubly so, after the British take-over) (*DC*, 98). And despite their semibarbarism, they are still "very superstitious" (*DC*, 92). Marryat describes their custom of carrying precious stones as charms about their persons, hidden by their making "an incision in the flesh, generally the arm or leg," where they insert the gem "and allow the skin to heal over it, so that the stone remains there." He then adds: "Soldiers and sailors in search of plunder will find out anything, and this practice of the Burmahs was soon discovered; and after the assault and carrying of a stockade, you would see the men passing their hands over the bodies, and immediately they felt a rising in the limb, out with their knives and cut in for the rubies" (*DC*, 92).

Marryat himself brought back some two hundred valuable stones carved out of Burmese corpses by the sailors under his command, part of his large collection of booty from the Empire. "After the Rangoon war," according to his daughter Florence, "his chambers became quite a museum of Burmese and Indian antiquities. The statue of the King of Ava, now in the Ethnological Museum of Leyden, belonged to him, and was one of his greatest treasures. It is encrusted with gold and precious stones, of more or less value" (2:85–86). There was, she says, "scarcely a room . . . that was not decorated with some of the spoils which Captain Marryat had collected in his travels round the world." Marryat's spoils are emblematic of the spoils of imperialism in general, gems prised from the heart of darkness: "A Burmese shrine with silver idols, rifled from a pagoda; the carved tusks of a sacred elephant; opossum skins from Canada, embroidered with porcupine quills and coloured beads; toys in tortoise shell ivory, with precious stones and curious shells, were scattered everywhere, recalling memories of the Rangoon war, America, India, and the Celestial Empire" (2:85). It is perhaps some satisfaction for the modern reader that Marryat donated the jewel-encrusted statue of the king of Ava to an ethnological museum (much to his children's chagrin), and that, although he insisted that they were *not* infested, his flea-infested collection of Canadian pelts caused some of his guests to go away "irritated" (2:80).

Marryat's chief legacy, however, was neither actual loot from the Empire nor contributions to ethnology. Though remarking that the novels "flounder deplorably" when they venture on shore, Conrad never-theless says that Marryat's "greatness is undeniable." His characters form "an endless variety of types, all surfaces, with hard edges, with memorable eccentricities of outline, with a childish and heroic effect in the drawing." They somehow "do not belong to life," Conrad thinks; "they belong exclusively to the Service. . . . And yet they have life . . . a headlong, reckless audacity, an intimacy with violence . . . and an exuberance . . . which only years of war and victories can give. His adventures are enthralling" ("Tales of the Sea," 47–48). In his "Humble Remonstrance" to Henry James, Robert Louis Stevenson speaks of "the literature of conduct," and that phrase can serve for imperialist adventure fantasy in general. The initiator of the Victorian literature of conduct was Captain Marryat, recalling his own days of youthful heroism when he, like many prodigal sons, found his identity by losing it, countless times, in action. "The way is to the destructive element submit yourself, and with your hands and feet in the water make the deep, deep sea keep you up." The captain's memories of staying afloat—his midshipman novels, above all—are his imaginary spoils of war. And through them, Conrad says, Marryat became "the enslaver of youth" ("Tales of the Sea," 47).

During his own midshipman years Marryat learned how to stay afloat on "the deep, deep sea" perhaps better than how to lead a sedentary life on land. His recollections of adolescent courage and violence may have served him as life-preservers after his retirement from the navy. During his second life on shore, in any case, the successful novelist and less successful family man never seemed quite at ease. "I can only compare the world of authors to so many rats drowning in a tub," he once wrote, "forcing each other down to raise themselves, and keep their own heads above water" (quoted by Warner, 112). Life on shipboard was perhaps safer after all; at least there everyone and everything had its place. But just before he died on 9 August 1848, at his country estate in Norfolk two miles from the sea, he dictated to his daughter and to posterity the final entry in his hero's log: "I am happy. . . . After years of casual, and, latterly, months of intense thought, I feel convinced that Christianity is true . . . and that God is love. . . . It is now half-past nine o'clock. World, adieu!"[28]

Part II NOON

The Temple of Juggernaut. From Edward H. Nolan, *The History of the British Empire in India and the East*, vol. 2 (ca. 1859).

3. Thackeray's India

Englishmen are as great fanatics in politics as Ma-
homedans in religion. They suppose no country can be
saved without English institutions.
—SIR THOMAS MUNRO, 1818

In a decade of domestic reform Captain Marryat's fiction nostalgically recalled an era of military triumph. Between the Burmese campaign of 1824–26 and the Afghan and Opium wars that commenced in 1839, there was little contemporary military action for British writers and politicians to celebrate or deplore. Yet starting in February 1838 the *New Monthly Magazine* published an autobiographical account of the martial exploits of one Major Goliah O'Grady Gahagan, who fought in India "in all Wellesley's brilliant campaigns" and also "by the side of Lord Lake at Laswaree, Deeg, Furruckabad, Futtyghur, and Bhurtpore."[1] These Indian conflicts took place not in the 1830s but even earlier than Marryat's first naval engagements; Gahagan saw action in the Second Maratha War of 1803–5, so to his story there is a nostalgic cast also.

The comic invention of the young writer and artist William Makepeace Thackeray, Major Gahagan places himself in a category distinctly higher than Marryat's: "The writers of marine novels have so exhausted the subject of storms, shipwrecks, mutinies, engagements, seasickness, and so forth, that (although I have experienced each of these in many varieties) I think it quite unnecessary to recount such trifling adventures" (312). Gahagan is referring to his own voyage out to India in 1802 as "a raw cornet of seventeen, with blazing red hair, six feet seven in height"; the only events during the voyage worth mentioning concern his flirtation with Julia Jowler, daughter of his commander. But in contrast to the tired adventures to be found in marine novels, Gahagan's adventures in India are of "no ordinary interest," because "I have led a more remarkable life than any man in the service—I have been at more pitched battles, led more forlorn hopes, had more success among the fair sex, drunk harder, read more, and been a handsomer man than any officer now serving her Majesty." These are large claims, of course, especially in light of the Major's further claim that "I will not boast of my actions" (311).

In the tall-tale narration of *The Tremendous Adventures of Major Gahagan*, Thackeray parodies Marryat and other military novelists, as he was later to parody Disraeli, Bulwer-Lytton, and Fenimore Cooper in his series for *Punch*, "Novels by Eminent Hands." As George Levine says, "Thackeray's career begins in deflating every kind of social pretension, every sort of rhetorical falsification," and parody and satire are his normal modes.[2] At the same time Thackeray takes revenge upon some of his closest and most revered family members, including his step-father, Major Henry Carmichael-Smyth, and his brother-in-law, Lt.-Col. Merrick Shawe, both of whom served in India. From them Thackeray undoubtedly heard many "tremendous adventures" as well as much tedious military gossip.

Thackeray was born in Calcutta in 1811 and sent to England to be educated at the age of six. Gordon N. Ray writes: "The boy was a seven months baby; and the doctor . . . informed his mother that . . . she could bear no further children, [so] she lavished all her love on William [and] he was brought up like a little prince. Two native attendants were devoted to his exclusive service; and he passed his time playing in the large, high-ceilinged rooms of his father's great house or seeing the sights of Calcutta—the carriages on the Esplanade or the crocodiles in the Ganges—from the neat oxen-drawn carriage in which he rode with his black nurse."[3] The abrupt, traumatic end to Thackeray's oriental boyhood, when like numerous Anglo-Indian children he was shipped "home" both for health and for schooling, begs comparison with Rudyard Kipling's early life. Whereas Kipling returned to India as a teenager and there commenced his life's work as a journalist and author, however, Thackeray never returned to the scenes of his earliest childhood. Yet Thackeray and his relations in Britain continued to be deeply influenced by India, just as James and John Stuart Mill, without ever traveling to Asia, were affected in incalculable ways by their work for the East India Company.

"The indirect effect of Thackeray's Indian heritage and experience was immense," Ray declares.[4] Similarly, according to Henry James, Thackeray's "birth at Calcutta" in some mysterious way made "for his distinction" as a novelist. "Is it only a vain imagination," James wonders, "or is there in [Thackeray's] large and easy genius an echo of those masteries and dominations which sometimes straightened and sometimes broke the backs of so many of his ancestors and collaterals? Even if we treat it as a mere . . . background to his image, we rejoice for him in this ghostly company of actors in a vast drama."5 Certain it is that, besides spoofing British military power and glory in *Major Gahagan*, Thackeray has a good deal to say about India in several of his later novels, especially *The Newcomes*. India is the scene also of Jos Sedley's tax collecting and of a portion of William Dobbin's service after Waterloo in *Vanity Fair*. Pen's uncle, the Major, served in India before returning to England in 1806, and the Claverings and Colonel Altamont have important Indian ties in *Pendennis*. Nevertheless, significant though it is, India remained *background* for Thackeray in both biographical and fictional terms. From the vantage point of the rulers, the Empire was in some sense always mere background, the periphery not the center of attention.

Despite the importance of India in *Vanity Fair* and in his two most autobiographical novels, Thackeray made it the main setting for no story other than *Major Gahagan*. Perhaps that comic tale can be interpreted not merely as a mock-epic spoof upon military and marine novels but also to some extent as Thackeray's unconscious rejection of one aspect of his Anglo-Indian heritage. Major Gahagan's braggadocio calls into question the chief message of Marryat's fiction—that military service and heroism are supreme values, the absolute bedrock of Britain's imperial greatness. This is not to suggest that Thackeray was either a pacifist or an anti-imperialist. But he realized that the theme of "the indomitable majesty of BRITISH VALOUR" could be taken to ridiculous extremes— which is exactly where Goliah Gahagan, "Lord of the Elephants," takes it. The military history of the British in India may have suggested mock epic instead of epic to Thackeray because Indians themselves (as Gahagan describes them) made such unequal combatants. By the 1830s the army of the East India Company, consisting mostly of sepoys or native troops, had swept aside most resistance. The Napoleonic age of military adventure appeared to have given way to a much more stable, serious age of reforming, converting, and civilizing. Thackeray says little, however, either in *Major Gahagan* or in the great novels of the late forties and the fifties, to suggest that he was much concerned with the reformist tendencies of the 1830s. To understand the significance of Thackeray's treatment of India in *Vanity Fair*, *Pendennis*, and *The Newcomes*, I first examine main themes in other British writing about India from the 1830s to the time of the Mutiny in 1857. Thackeray's attitudes can then be seen as in part a reaction against those themes, just as the mock-epic *Major*

Gahagan expresses the author's reaction against marine novels and military vainglory.

i

From the time of the Battle of Plassey in 1757 down to the commencement of Warren Hastings's impeachment in 1788, the extension and exploitation of the East India Company's holdings went on with little supervision by Parliament or other branches of British government. Though the eastern adventures and enrichment of various "nabobs," including Robert Clive, made segments of the British public uneasy, only with Hastings's trial did the idea become widespread that the British government had important obligations toward its growing Indian empire. Edmund Burke's attacks on Hastings pointed the way to the concept of trusteeship in the relations between Britain and all of its overseas dominions. "All political power which is set over men," Burke declared, "being wholly artificial, and . . . in derogation from the natural equality of mankind at large, ought to be . . . exercised ultimately for their benefit . . . such [power is] in the strictest sense a *trust*; and it is of the very essence of every trust to be rendered *accountable*."[6]

Burke's emphasis on trusteeship contributed to reshape the East India Company from a trading concern with its own military force into a virtual branch of government, following rules of supposedly responsible behavior laid down by Parliament. From the late 1700s to its demise in 1858, the East India Company was in effect one arm of a dual control over India; the home government was the other. By the time the company ceased to function as a trading concern in 1833, the idea had become paramount that Britain had acquired a special trust or obligation for civilizing India. The decade of reform at home—the 1830s—was also a decade of reform in India. And the chief reformers at home—the utilitarians and evangelicals—were also the chief reformers in India. As governor-general of India from 1828 to 1835, Lord William Bentinck helped to make the 1830s the heyday of Benthamism in India.[7] At the same time missionary activity was on the rise. The East India Company had discouraged the strenuous efforts of a few missionaries before 1813. But in that year the curtailing of the company's trading monopoly removed the chief obstacles to missionary work, and for the first time government funds were earmarked for educational purposes in India.

Neither utilitarians nor evangelicals respected Indian customs, beliefs, and patterns of social organization. Evangelical responses to Indian religions varied from the implacably hostile to the opinion that, given patience and enough missionaries, Indians would soon see the light. Charles Grant believed that "we cannot avoid recognizing in the people of Hindostan, a race of men lamentably degenerate and base . . . gov-erned by malevolent and licentious passions, strongly exemplifying the effects produced on society by a great and general corruption of manners, and sunk in misery by their vices."[8] Similarly, William Wilberforce declared that the Hindu deities are "absolute monsters of lust, injustice, wickedness and cruelty." Arguing before Parliament in 1813 for help with missionary and educational work, Wilberforce asked: "Are we so little aware of the vast superiority . . . of British institutions, over those of Asia, as not to be prepared to predict with confidence, that the Indian community which should have exchanged its dark and bloody supersti-tions for the genial influence of Christian light and truth, would . . . be bound . . . by the ties of gratitude to those who have been the honoured instruments of communicating them?"[9] Here indeed was a national calling; Britain itself was to be the divine instrument for bringing Chris-tian light and truth to Asia.

More generous were the opinions of Reginald Heber, bishop of Cal-cutta in the mid-1820s. Heber traveled extensively in northern India and developed some respect for most of the people he encountered. If Indians were benighted, it was not because they were morally or racially inferior to Europeans. "Of the natural disposition of the Hindoo, I see abundant reason to think highly," Heber wrote in his *Journal*; "they are constitu-tionally kind-hearted, industrious, sober, and peaceable, at the same time that they show themselves on proper occasions, a manly and courageous people."[10] The chief force deflecting Indians from the path of genuine civilization was false religion, particularly Hinduism. "All that is bad about them appears to arise either from the defective motives which their religion supplies, or the wicked actions which it records of their gods, or encourages in their own practice" (128). Heber was not prepared to say that God's mercy and salvation would be withheld from Hindus and Muslims if their lives were virtuous. All the same, he worried about the more sensational, retrograde aspects of Hindu religious practices—infan-ticide, human sacrifice, and suttee or widow-burning. Suttee especially, as a contemporary practice that seemed to be on the increase and that Heber witnessed on more than one occasion, horrified him as it did every reformer, whether evangelical, utilitarian, or merely humanitarian, and whether British or Indian (57–58, 126–28).

Though their truths were secular and rationalist, the utilitarians did not lag behind the evangelicals in reforming zeal. The chief point is registered by James Mill in his influential *History of British India* (1817): "In looking at the pursuits of any nation, with a view to draw from them indications of the state of civilization, no mark is so important, as the nature of the *End* to which they are directed. Exactly in proportion as *Utility* is the object of every pursuit, may we regard a nation as civilized. Exactly in proportion as its ingenuity is wasted on contemptible or mischievous objects . . . the nation may safely be denominated barbarous."[11] As Mill goes on to say of the condition of "the astronomical and mathematical sciences" among the Hindus, Indian astrology offers nothing that is not merely irrational, antiutilitarian, and therefore "barbarous." In comparison with *any* European society, Mill believes, the Hindus fall short. Perhaps they approximate the social development of medieval Europe, a view frequently offered by sympathetic British observers; Mill still finds Indians inferior to Europeans. "Should we say that the civilization of the people of Hindostan, and that of the people of Europe, during the feudal ages, is not far from equal, we shall find upon a close inspection, that the Europeans were superior" in religion, philosophy, government, poetry, warfare, manufactures, and most of the arts and architecture with the exception of a few handicrafts such as "the fabrication . . . of trinkets" (247). To this survey of the inferiority of India to medieval Europe, Mill adds that "in point of manners and character, the manliness and courage of our ancestors, compared with the slavish and dastardly spirit of the Hindus, place them in an elevated rank" (247). This claim leads Mill to a characteristic assertion about the general dishonesty of Indians: "Our ancestors . . . though rough, were sincere; but, under the glosing exterior of the Hindu, lies a general disposition to deceit and perfidy" (247).

Mill thinks of Indian society and history as entirely dominated by—and "petrified" into a "stationary state" by—oriental despotism and Hindu priestcraft: "We have . . . seen, in reviewing the Hindu form of government, that . . . despotism and priestcraft taken together, the Hindus, in mind and body, were the most enslaved portion of the human race" (236–37). It is the responsibility of the British imperializers of India to liberate Indians from the slavery of their own making. Yet despite his negative assessment of Indian society and the positive role he assigned to British influence, Mill was no mere British chauvinist. As Eric Stokes points out, Mill's "astonishing arraignment of the entire populations of India and China shows the fantastic authority which he was prepared to grant to the philosophic intelligence" (Stokes, 53). That intelligence understood that European customs and institutions were comparatively more rational than oriental ones but still far below the absolute standard of utility.

Mill in any case makes clear that the imperialist aggrandizement of the East India Company in the eighteenth century was largely motivated by the greed and ambition of its leaders, particularly Clive. Beyond company jurisdiction "the English themselves were not amenable to . . . British laws; and the Company had no power of coercion except by sending persons out of the country. . . . The natural consequence was that the crimes of the English and their agents were in a great measure secured from punishment, and the unhappy natives lay prostrate at their feet" (378). Mill does not ask how citizens of a morally and legally superior nation can find themselves engaging in deceitful, rapacious, indeed criminal activities in other, supposedly inferior parts of the world. Instead, he offers what had already become the standard view of Clive's career: his crimes were great, but so were his temptations; his actions, though sometimes immoral by European standards, were consonant with oriental standards; and "though never inattentive to his own interests," he never acted against the interests of the East India Company (406).

Similar views can be found in Thomas Babington Macaulay's essays on Clive and Warren Hastings. If the origins of the British empire in India are tainted by Clive's criminality, they are also marked by his greatness. "Like most men who are born with strong passions and tried by strong temptations," Macaulay says, Clive "committed great faults."[12] On the other hand, "every person who takes a fair and enlightened view of his whole career must admit that our island, so fertile in heroes and statesmen, has scarcely ever produced a man more truly great either in arms or in council." For Macaulay, the story of Clive and the East India Company is above all an imperialist epic, showing "how a handful of [Englishmen], separated from their home by an immense ocean, subjugated, in the course of a few years, one of the greatest empires in the world" (307). If we keep such heroism in mind, "great faults" can be forgiven. Besides, what Clive and his colleagues did was no worse than what oriental despots had been doing for ages. Like Mill, Macaulay operates with a double standard; he excuses Clive, Hastings, and other Europeans as merely behaving like Indians when they commit their greediest, most violent, or most deceitful acts.

"What the horns are to the buffalo, what the paw is to the tiger, what the sting is to the bee, what beauty, according to the old Greek song, is to woman, deceit is to the Bengalee" (386). In contrast to the naturally perfidious Bengalis whom he conquered, Clive, according to Macaulay, was "constitutionally the very opposite of a knave, bold even to temerity" and without "any signs of a propensity to cunning" (334). But Clive "considered Oriental politics as a game in which nothing was unfair"; like Hastings after him, he therefore learned to fight "Asiatic mendacity" with "Asiatic mendacity" (400). Clive

> knew that the standard of morality among the natives of India differed widely from that established in England. He . . . had to deal with men destitute of what in Europe is called honour . . . who would un-scrupulously employ corruption, perjury, forgery, to compass their ends. . . . Accordingly this man, in the other parts of his life an honour-able English gentleman and soldier, was no sooner matched against an Indian intriguer, than he became himself an Indian intriguer, and de-scended, without scruple, to falsehood, to hypocritical caresses, to the substitution of documents, and to the counterfeiting of hands. (334)

Here is the typically circular pattern of racist thought. Clive's great faults are projected onto Indians, whose supposedly perfidious nature is then used to excuse those faults in Clive. Macaulay's account of Clive, and to a lesser extent of Hastings, offers a variation on the theme of "going native." To compass the higher ends of civilization, Clive and Hastings both stooped to the means of oriental despotism. But their adoption of the presumably lower, dishonorable, moral and legal standards of Indians was only temporary, whereas oriental despots themselves "are perhaps the worst class of human beings" (329).

For Macaulay, the ultimate justification for the behavior of Clive and Hastings—and thus for the British imperialization of India—is quite simple: Indians, because of the baseness of their own social character and moral standards, deserved and needed to be imperialized. This need was especially great for the Bengalis, whose territories the East India Com-pany first came to dominate. By their racial nature, Macaulay believes, the Bengalis are a people who almost begged to be conquered and ruled; their weaknesses created a power vacuum into which the bold East India Company adventurers inevitably rushed.

> The race by whom this rich tract [Bengal] was peopled, enervated by a soft climate and accustomed to peaceful avocations, bore the same relation to other Asiatics which the Asiatics generally bear to the bold and energetic children of Europe. The Castilians have a proverb, that in Valencia the earth is water and the men women; and the description is at least equally applicable to the vast plain of the lower Ganges. Whatever the Bengalee

does he does languidly . . . singularly pertinacious in the war of chicane, he seldom . . . enlists as a soldier. We doubt whether there be a hundred genuine Bengalees in the whole army of the East India Company. There never, perhaps, existed a people so thoroughly fitted by nature and by habit for a foreign yoke. (329)

This is, no doubt, Whig history at its most self-indulgent. But it is also typical of much British writing and thinking about how a mere handful of Englishmen conquered a worldwide empire upon which, indeed, the sun never set. Macaulay's examination of Clive's career offers two typical answers to this question, or really what amount to the two parts of a single answer: British greatness (heroism, energy, morality, intelligence), and Indian or other non-European inferiority (cowardice, laziness, dishonesty, stupidity). It is, of course, not far from such chauvinistic thinking to complete exoneration of Clive, as in Thomas Carlyle's scorn for the pettiness of Clive's accusers. Worshiper of force and heroes, Carlyle lacks even the minor reservations of Mill and Macaulay about Clive: "Not fit for book-keeping alone, the man was found fit for conquering Nawaubs, founding kingdoms, Indian Empires!"[13]

Whether tainted by criminality or not, the heroic image of Clive gives an individualistic slant to the history of the British in India. For this slant, the work of imperializing Asia was not at first something officially planned or even condoned by the home government; it was instead the natural—almost accidental—result of the virtues of individual British adventurers. The history of the Empire becomes a moral allegory or melodrama, pitting white heroes, the representatives of Anglo-Saxon courage, integrity, and industry, against black villains and cowards. Such an allegorization had the double advantage of transferring guilt for violence and rapacity from the home government or the British people as a whole to aggressive individuals acting at the periphery, and then from these individuals to the peoples they conquered. Of course it also turned violence and rapacity into virtues, treating acts of aggression as acts of necessity and self-defense.

As a corollary of this individualistic perspective, for liberal historians from Mill and Macaulay forward, "it was a matter almost of dogma that the English conquest of India was unpremeditated" (Chamberlain, 37). Later this notion was memorably applied to the entire British Empire by Sir John Seeley, in The Expansion of England: "We seem . . . to have conquered and peopled half the world in a fit of absence of mind."[14] Specifically of India, Seeley wrote: "Nothing great that has ever been done by Englishmen was done so unintentionally, so accidentally, as the conquest of India" (143). This perspective led him to speak of "the general law of expansion which prevails in the modern part of English history" as virtually a force of nature, making inevitably for the progress of all nations (143). In India what the first British imperializers, Clive among them, found was "a state of wild anarchy" into which the naturally expansive, progressive, order-bringing energies of the British flowed irresistibly, to the ultimate benefit of both Britain and India. Indeed for Seeley, as for many other Victorians, "a condition of anarchy seems almost to have been chronic in India since Mahmoud," allayed only temporarily in the north by the first Mogul emperors. Thus India was "of all countries that which is least capable of evolving out of itself a stable Government" (155); if such an evolution was ever to take place, the British had first to rule India and reform it.

John Stuart Mill, who entered East India House under his father's sponsorship in 1822 and served until the company's demise in 1858, was in general less dogmatic and ethnocentric in his opinions about India than his father or Macaulay, and of course far more liberal than Carlyle. Nevertheless, the younger Mill believed that, having acquired an oriental empire largely by "accidental" means, it was now the duty of Britain to govern that empire with benevolent despotism.[15] In *On Liberty*, Mill argued that "the despotism of custom is everywhere the standing hindrance to human advancement," and among Indians and other orientals custom is especially tyrannical. "The greater part of the world has, properly speaking, no history, because the despotism of custom is complete. This is the case over the whole East."[16] To break that despotism in India—that is, to make India progressive and eventually independent of foreign domination—the best instrument available, Mill believed, was the counterdespotism of the East India Company.

Mill understood that racism, oppression, and exploitation were possible in all colonial settings. And "among a people like that of India the utmost efforts of the public authorities are not enough for the effectual protection of the weak against the strong"—that is, especially for the protection of Indians against "European settlers."[17] Europeans in India, Mill declared, tend to "think the people of the country mere dirt under their feet; it seems to them monstrous that any rights of the natives should stand in the way of their smallest pretensions; the simplest act of protection to the inhabitants against any act of power on their part which they may consider useful to their commercial objects, they denounce . . . as an injury" (261). Against the illegitimate exercise of power by Europeans, as well as against the ancient "despotism of custom," Mill contended, the slowly, haphazardly evolved institutions of the East India Company offered the best protection and hope for progress. This view was paradoxical, to say the least. From its early days as a peaceful, mercantilist trading concern through its eighteenth-century military aggrandizement, nothing in the company's history suggested the role of benevolent despot. But the changed outlook that derived partly from Hastings's impeachment, reinforced by the humanitarian—albeit authoritarian—concerns of the evangelical and utilitarian reformers, had transformed the company from a mere business into a unique sort of government, still insulated from Parliament and the Colonial Office. The company had become a civil service administration carried on largely by Anglo-Indian experts—in many respects the very government by educated authority of which the Benthamites most clearly approved.

Mill was aware, moreover, that from the 1830s onward the achievements of the reformers were considerable. Among those achievements, none were more striking than the educational and legal reforms of Macaulay during his term as law member of the Supreme Council in India between 1834 and 1838. In the debate between orientalists and westernizers, Macaulay's Minute on Indian Education (1835) helped win the day for those who insisted that higher education for Indians should be conducted in English rather than in Sanskrit, Persian, or Arabic. "A single shelf of a good European library," Macaulay declared, is "worth the whole native literature of India and Arabia."[18] It did not matter that Macaulay had read almost no Indian or Arabic literature and learned no Indian language fluently. He was as convinced he was right as James Mill, and he was in a position to enforce his authority. Whenever the British government of India contemplated new educational facilities after the 1830s, its aim was Macaulay's, to teach "what is best worth knowing"—and "English is better worth knowing than Sanscrit or Arabic" (729).

Equally influential was Macaulay's work in drawing up a uniform penal code, still the basis of modern Indian law. Bentham had earlier expressed the desire to be the Solon of India; not without reason did Macaulay think of himself as its Lycurgus.[19] According to K. M. Panikkar:

> The legal system under which India has lived for a hundred years and within whose steel frame her social, political and economic development has taken place is the work of Macaulay. . . . The establishment of the great principle of equality of all before law in a country where under the

Hindu doctrines a Brahmin could not be punished on the evidence of a Sudra . . . and where, according to Muslim law, testimony could not be accepted against a Muslim was itself a legal revolution of the first importance. Few, indeed, who compare Macaulay's code with its great predecessors, whether those of Manu, Justinian or Napoleon, will cavil at the claim that the Indian penal code was a great improvement on the previous systems.[20]

Panikkar adds that "the imposing and truly magnificent legal structure, under which not only 360 million people of India but the millions in Pakistan and Burma have lived during the last 100 years, has changed the basis of society" in profound and mainly liberating ways.

To this positive assessment should be contrasted the criticisms of other Indian analysts. Jawaharlal Nehru, for example, argued that though "the tyranny of old custom is often a terrible thing," still it tended to be more flexible than British reformers acknowledged, whereas British law was applied ruthlessly and uniformly to the entire subcontinent in ways that failed to respect local customs and beliefs. Furthermore, the Victorian legal reform of India, according to Nehru, was as much in the interest of conservative elements as it was liberating in its effects.[21] Nevertheless, Macaulay and other Victorian reformers, for better or worse, helped westernize at least the upper classes and many of the institutions of India. Seldom has the exercise of "philosophic intelligence" in politics been more powerful; reform in India in the 1830s was in many ways far more thoroughgoing than reform in Britain.

To a large extent, as Karl Marx noted, modern Indian political, legal, and educational structures are the products of an occidental tyranny superimposed upon an oriental tyranny. "European despotism, planted upon Asiatic despotism, by the British East India Company, [has formed] a more monstrous combination than any of the divine monsters startling us in the Temple of Salsette."[22] In all of his articles about the British in India, Marx emphasized the destructive impact of British rule: the breakdown of older, indigenous institutions; the often total disrespect for native customs, opinions, religions; the neglect of public works; the subversion of native handicraft industries for the benefit of British mass production industries; the economic exploitation of India, Burma, and China. Such negative results must weigh against positive benefits that came from the work of Macaulay, the Mills, and other British reformers. But however much Marx himself was inclined to emphasize the destructive side of British rule, he was insistent that the wheels of the Juggernaut of history must grind forward: "England, it is true, in causing a social revolution in Hindustan, was actuated only by the vilest interests, and was stupid in her manner of enforcing them. But that is not the question. The question is, can mankind fulfill its destiny without a fundamental revolution in the social state of Asia? If not, whatever may have been the crimes of England she was the unconscious tool of history in bringing about that revolution."[23] No matter how one chooses to answer it, Marx's question goes to the heart of all modern considerations of European imperialism. It will be answered by the futures of India and the other "developing" countries of the world.

ii

From Marlowe's *Tamburlaine the Great* through Dryden's *Aurung-Zebe* to Beckford's *Vathek*, portrayals of the orient and of India in particular as a realm of fabulous riches and cruel potentates helped establish the nineteenth-century stereotype offered in such Romantic works as Southey's *Curse of Kehama* (1810) and Moore's *Lalla Rookh* (1817). Milton's descriptions of Satan in *Paradise Lost* as something of an oriental despot, seated "High on a throne of royal state, which far / Outshone the wealth of Ormuz and of Ind" suggests the infernal connotations of the stereotype.[24] Even at its most positive, English literature represented India as only a false Eden, a sensual paradise of luxury, tyranny, and erotic decadence, suggesting the Freudian infantile fantasy of omnipotence projected onto peoples living on the other side of the world.

This self-indulgent, erotic India is lavishly and for the most part positively presented in Moore's popular updating of the *Arabian Nights*. In Southey's poem, however, perhaps in response to criticism of his comparatively favorable treatment of Islam in earlier works, the image of India is dark, destructive, and as fantasically negative as any drawn by Charles Grant or James Mill. Indeed, as Southey declared in his "Original Preface," he wished to illustrate his belief that Hinduism "of all false religions is the most monstrous in its fables and the most fatal in its effects."[25] *The Curse of Kehama* is therefore full of lurid details of Hindu religious practices; it begins, for example, with a long tirade against the suttee that occurs at the funeral of Kehama's murdered son Arvalan. As one wife stoically submits to her fate, another struggles vainly against the crowd who "force her on" and "bind her to the dead" (19). With the insanely ecstatic crowd chanting and howling around the funeral pyre, the wicked Brahmin priests set their torches to it, and the poor wives of Arvalan go up in flames.

Just as fearsome in intent is Southey's portrayal of the infamous Juggernaut:

> Prone fall the frantic votaries in its road,
>   And, calling on the God,
> Their self-devoted bodies there they lay
>   To pave his chariot-way.
>   On Jaga-Naut they call:
> The ponderous Car rolls on, and crushes all.
> Through flesh and bones it ploughs its dreadful path.

Southey thus emphasizes two of the most spectacular topics in evangelical and utilitarian attacks upon Hinduism, as he does also in his "Ode on the Portrait of Bishop Heber," where the reader learns that Britain's debt to "Heathendom" is particularly great in India. This is because "Providence" has given Britain its "dominion there in trust" and thus has also given it much civilizing work to do, Britain's divine calling:

> Yea, at this hour the cry of blood
> Riseth against thee from beneath the wheels
> Of that seven-headed Idol's car accurst;
> Against thee, from the widow's funeral pile,
>   The smoke of human sacrifice
>   Ascends even now to Heaven. [26]

According to Southey's version of the "white man's burden," it will take an army of Bishop Hebers to stamp out the worst abominations of Hinduism.

Juggernaut and suttee provided focuses for British literature about India well into the Victorian period. It was hardly tempting to write novels or plays about the reformers' debates over Indian education or the new penal code, but suicidal zeal and widow burning were naturally melodramatic subjects. In the late 1830s, moreover, new revelations about a destructive offshoot of Hinduism provided another sensational focus for reformist writing and served as the subject of the first bestselling Anglo-Indian novel, Philip Meadows Taylor's *Confessions of a Thug* (1839). If one defines Anglo-Indian as any Briton who spent a large portion of his or her adult life in India—thus excluding Macaulay and Thackeray—then Taylor was without doubt the greatest Anglo-Indian writer before Kipling. Shipped out to India in 1824 at age fifteen, Taylor wound up in the service of the Nizam of Hyderabad, one of the (ostensibly) independent "native princes." He married a Eurasian woman whose grandmother had been a princess of Delhi; his close, sympathetic identity with Indians and Indian social patterns gave him a perspective often critical of British racism and misgovernment. Nevertheless, in *Confessions of a Thug*, Taylor wrote one of the great Victorian crime novels—and the criminal element was the product not of the workhouse or the London slums but of Hinduism. Like several of the Newgate novels written in the 1830s and early 1840s, Taylor's story has a definite reformist purpose: the suppression of Thuggee, the secret cult of professional murderers and robbers who worshiped Kali, Hindu goddess of destruction.

As a superintendant of police in part of the Nizam's territories in the late 1820s, Taylor came close to detecting Thuggee himself, but a reassignment of duties curtailed his investigation of mysterious murders of strangers traveling through his district. Taylor believed that had he been able to continue his detective work, he would have been "the first to disclose the horrible crime of Thuggee to the world, but it fell to the good fortune of Major [William] Sleeman to do so afterwards."[27] Taylor was nevertheless instrumental in suppressing Thuggee in his district in the early 1830s, gathering testimony from captured Thugs which became the source of his novel. As Taylor explained in his autobiography: "Day after day I recorded tales of murder, which, though horribly monotonous, possessed an intense interest; and as fast as new approvers [witnesses] came in, new mysteries were unravelled and new crimes confessed" (1:112).

Out of Thug confessions Taylor constructed his slightly fictionalized horror story, which from the viewpoint of the "confessor" is ironically a success story. The narrative almost takes the shape of a dramatic monologue in which the speaker—a captured Thug whom Taylor names Ameer Ali—"confesses" to a Sahib, a British police official like Taylor himself. To escape the worst punishments (transportation to a penal colony or death), Ameer Ali has turned witness against both himself and his former confederates; he is therefore completely forthcoming. But he is also forthcoming because, like James Hogg's "Justified Sinner," he feels no guilt, only pride—both in his former deeds as a ritual murderer and in his present service to his British captors: "You ask me, Sahib, for an account of my life; my relation of it will be understood by you, as you are acquainted with the peculiar habits of my countrymen; and if, as you say, you intend it for the information of your own, I have no hesitation in relating the whole; for though I have accepted the service of Europeans, in my case one of bondage, I cannot help looking back with pride and exultation on the many daring feats I have performed."[28]

Ameer Ali is a thoroughly convincing fanatic who believes that, despite the efforts to suppress it, Thuggee "cannot be annihilated." In response to this assertion, the listening Sahib offers one of his few comments: "It is indeed too true, Ameer Ali, said I, [that] your old vocation seems to be as flourishing as ever, but it cannot last. Men will get tired of exposing themselves to the chance of being hunted down like wild beasts, and hung when they are caught; or what is perhaps worse to many, of being sent over the Kala-Panee [ocean]; and so heartily does the Government pursue Thugs wherever they are known to exist, that there will no longer be a spot of ground in India where your profession can be practised" (1). The Sahib says little else to interrupt Ameer Ali's gruesomely detailed narration, which runs from his initiation into Thuggee by his father, through his commission of dozens of murders and robberies, his capture and confession. On one level, his narration forms a perverse adventure story, the mirror opposite to Marryat's midshipman tales: the reader understands that, instead of the glorious bravery and patriotism of Jack Easy or Peter Simple, Ameer Ali has a pride in his murderous deeds that is both childish and hideously diabolical. Taylor's Sahib does little moralizing, because he does not have to: his power is absolute; the situation is totally clear to the reader; and Ameer Ali can be given more than enough narrative rope to hang himself.

The structure of Taylor's novel reproduces the dominative relationship of its imperial context in a uniquely transparent way. In most British writing about the Empire, English discourse and authority are imposed on imperialized peoples, often to the extent of denying them even imaginary voices (and what voices are occasionally granted support imperialism). But in *Confessions of a Thug* the Sahib is nearly silent while the self-convicting Ameer Ali speaks on for three hundred pages. The patiently listening and recording Sahib is the perfect Benthamite policeman, an ideal figure of imperial discipline and surveillance, or "panopticism," to use Foucault's term.[29] Authoritarian silence wraps a steel cage of implicit rationality around Ameer Ali's irrational discourse. In turn, the Thug is the perfect Benthamite prisoner: both his situation and his willingness—indeed, eagerness—to confess strip him of all privacy, all mystery, all power. Indeed, other Thug witnesses have already convicted Ameer Ali by reconstructing his life story in detail and in advance of his own redundant narration. Toward the end of the novel

Ameer Ali tells how he came to be captured and brought before "the officer who was employed by the English Government to apprehend Thugs" (presumably Sleeman). This figure of authority orders "an attendant munshi" to read the accusations against him: "The man unfolded a roll of paper written in Persian, and read a catalogue of crime, of murders, every one of which I knew to be true; a faithful record it was of my past life, with but few omissions. Allah defend me! thought I, there is no hope" (330).

When every detail of one's supposedly secret life can be penetrated, known from a myriad hidden sources by the imperial authorities, there seems no alternative but to cooperate and confess, even though one's confessions merely repeat what the authorities already know. It is as if he—the confessant without freedom or privacy—is trapped in a hall of mirrors he cannot see and of accusatory voices he cannot hear, rather like Joseph K. in Kafka's *The Trial*. In no way, however, is Ameer Ali's situation as a prisoner overtly marked by injustice. The legal rigmarole and courts in Kafka's novel are characterized by their nightmarish irrationality and inaccessibility, but the Sahib's attitude is knowing, patient, apparently even sympathetic, though also rendered secure by absolute authority. British justice in Taylor's India is as thorough and even-handed as any justice anywhere. Ultimately Ameer Ali is also subject to the judgment of a presumably rational authority thousands of miles across the ocean, an authority far more powerful than Kali: the British reading public. He ends his confessions on a note of unconscious irony: "I fear that I have often wearied you by the minute relation of my history; but I have told all. . . . Possibly you may have recorded what may prove fearfully interesting to your friends. If it be so, your end is answered; you have given a faithful portrait of a Thug's life, his ceremonies, and his acts; whilst I am proud that the world will know of the deeds and adventures of Ameer Ali, the Thug" (338).

If Thuggee showed the worst side of Hinduism to British readers, its suppression seemed to show the greatest benefits of British rule and civilization. Charles Trevelyan believed that "nothing which the missionaries have ever alleged against Hinduism is half so damning as the evidence" gathered from captured Thugs, and he concluded that "if we were to form a graduated scale of religions, that of Christ and that of Kalee would be the opposite extremes."[30] Although over the short run the application of force could provide a "partial remedy for Thuggee, and the other evils which spring from a false belief," Trevelyan thought that the long-term solution could come only from the diffusion of "a liberal

English education." This was the ultimate panacea for utilitarian reformers, as conversion was for evangelicals. "Minds which have been imbued
from childhood with the literature and science of Europe," said Trevelyan, "cannot return to the absurdities" of Hinduism. The conclusion
of his 1837 *Quarterly Review* essay on Thuggee echoes Macaulay's
optimism about progress in India through European instruction: "May
we not look forward with confidence to that national regeneration which
the gradual infusion of English literature, English science, and English
morals into the mass of Indian society, must produce at no distant
period?" (395).

Taylor's novel is a paradigm of Benthamite reformism in the imperialist
setting; in one fashion or another most British writing about India
between the 1830s and 1858 expresses utilitarian or evangelical concerns.
But no reformist themes ruffle the comic surface of *The Tremendous
Adventures of Major Gahagan*, which Thackeray published just a year
prior to the *Confessions*. The difference is of course partly that Thackeray
was writing a parody, with no serious intention of depicting either India
or the British in India. But the same difference is evident in his major
novels in which India figures at least as significant background: *Vanity
Fair*, *Pendennis*, and *The Newcomes*. Thackeray rarely touches upon
themes that other British writers about India find urgent. In Taylor's
novel, moreover, framed by the silent authority of the imperial police an
Indian character—albeit criminal—is permitted to tell his entire life story
and is given a careful hearing. In Thackeray's novels, in contrast, even in
chapters set in India, Indian characters are few in number, usually minor
in significance, and almost entirely silent. Taylor's listening Sahib records
(presumably with complete fidelity) the voice of superstitious, boastful,
homicidal fanaticism. Thackeray's boastful Major Gahagan, on the other
hand, is all comic palaver about his own tall-tale bravery and deeds. In
context, Gahagan's estimate that he is worth at least a thousand Indian
combatants seems almost true: although his Irish bluster renders his self-
proclaimed superiority to all other *British* soldiers incredible, the Maratha warriors he mows down seem almost nonexistent. Various Maratha
chieftains—Scindia and Holkar, for example—are named, and Gahagan
in disguise is nearly mated to a Maratha harem. But the Indians are
essentially noncharacters, shadows without voice or substance, blown
away as easily by Gahagan's boasting as by British firepower: "I sheared off
three hundred and nine heads in the course of that single campaign"
(320) and so forth.

If Thackeray believed that the British had a mission to reform, convert, or civilize India, he did not express that belief through Gahagan, nor through any of the Anglo-Indian characters of his later novels. Indeed, with the exception of the corrupt, shadowy Indian banker Rummun Loll in *The Newcomes*, Indian characters—apart from a few servants—are even less in evidence later than in Gahagan's tale. Neither in the Indian nor in the British context, moreover, did Thackeray translate moral turpitude and criminality into political terms as subjects for social correction or reform. The pattern in his fiction is almost always the contrary one of translating politics into the terms of individual morality: Vanity Fair is just how the world is, and in such a fallen comic world political activity and politicians—the younger Pitt Crawley, for example, or Sir Francis Clavering in *Pendennis*—inevitably seem corrupt or ludicrous or both.

Thackeray's closest approach to the reform themes of utilitarians and evangelicals comes in his mention of suttee in *The Newcomes*. The point is not reform of the Hindu practice of widow burning, however, but of the British marriage market. The allusion to suttee by the narrator (Arthur Pendennis) suggests how barbaric certain British practices still are—but the barbarism seems to pertain naturally and perhaps inevitably to Indians: "For though I would like to go into an Indian Brahmin's house and see the punkahs and the purdahs and tattys, and the pretty brown maidens with great eyes, and great nose-rings, and painted foreheads, and slim waists in Cashmere shawls . . . and have the mystery of Eastern existence revealed to me . . . yet I would not choose the moment when the Brahmin of the house was dead, his women howling, his priests doctoring the child of a widow, now frightening her with sermons, now drugging her with bang, so as to push her on his funeral pile at last, and into the arms of that carcase, stupefied, but obedient and decorous."[31] Far better, Pen thinks, is the independence of Ethel Newcome, able to make choices for herself even if they are the wrong choices. The analogy points in an obvious way to the superiority of British over Indian customs. But what of British aristocrats who offer "their daughter for sale," ready to sacrifice her at the altar of wealth or social station? In such cases the Anglican priest who performs the wedding ceremony will be no better than "the Lord Arch-Brahmin of Benares"; and the marriage itself, between sacrificial daughter and her corpse of a wealthy groom, no better than a suttee—"yonder the [funeral] pile is waiting on four wheels with four horses, the crowd hurrahs, and the deed is done" (1:301).

Pen also mentions Juggernaut, but as a metaphor for the self-sacrificing behavior of Colonel Newcome rather than as an instance of India's need for reform. Despite the significance of India as background in *The Newcomes*, Thackeray pays no attention to Indian customs, religions, or politics. Similarly, most of what is said about India in *Vanity Fair* centers on Jos Sedley, whose "name appeared . . . in the Bengal division of the East India Register, as collector of Boggley Wollah, an honourable and lucrative post, as everybody knows."[32] Jos is about as despicable as a character can be without being criminal; if Thackeray intended his portrayal to typify East India Company rule in India, the criticism would be devastating. But just as Thackeray's depiction of Major Gahagan does not indict British military action in India, so his fat collector of Boggley Wollah represents no more than individual foibles and weaknesses. Jos is a type in moral terms but not in Georg Lukács's sense of typifying a social class or movement.[33]

Perhaps the most significant fact about Boggley Wollah is its isolation from British and even Anglo-Indian society. It is as far away as Jos Sedley can go without vanishing off the face of the earth: "Boggley Wollah is situated in a fine, lonely, marshy, jungly district. . . . Ramgunge, where there is a magistrate, is only forty miles off, and there is a cavalry station about thirty miles farther; so Joseph wrote home to his parents, when he took possession of his collectorship. He had lived for about eight years of his life, quite alone, at this charming place, scarcely seeing a Christian face except twice a year, when the detachment arrived to carry off the revenues which he had collected, to Calcutta" (28). This oriental dead-end is a safe place for Jos to flee to when the pressures of life at home—especially women (that is, Becky Sharp) and his cowardly behavior at Brussels during Waterloo—become too much for him. But Jos is also a civilian version of Goliah Gahagan: at London, in Becky's company, he fabricates tall tales about his adventures in India; at Calcutta, in the company of Anglo-Indians, he fabricates tall tales about his adventures in Europe and "was called Waterloo Sedley during the whole of his subsequent stay in Bengal" (373). The returned prodigal Peter Brown entertains the old ladies of Cranford with his oriental tales; Jos fabricates accounts of tiger hunting and helping conquer the French; the reader perceives both as stretchers of truth. Whereas Gaskell implies something genuinely charismatic about Peter, however, few characters in literature are more anticharismatic than Jos, who flees back to Boggley Wollah because "he dreaded to meet any witnesses of his Waterloo flight" (372). There, on the opposite side of the world, rather like an inept, obese, comic Lord Jim, Jos is able to vegetate, feed, and grow fatter—and also ironically grow rich and successful—away from the sight of his own kind.

Thackeray may not mean his Jos Sedley to typify British rule in India, but he surely does see in Jos one sort of imperial parasite—exactly the wrong sort of individual to conquer and tame a wilderness. There is something at least ironic about a boastful coward like Jos making good in the Indian setting when he probably could not make good at home. Jos is the Wilkins Micawber of *Vanity Fair*, but with none of Micawber's redeeming qualities. When his father's financial affairs come tumbling down after Waterloo, moreover, Jos's career with the East India Company is rising. Thus Jos is in a position to be appalled when his impoverished father seeks his help to start a new wine export business to India. By that time Jos has been "promoted to a seat at the Revenue Board at Calcutta," and he is "wild with rage" when he receives his father's letter of request and "a bundle of . . . bacchanalian prospectuses" (381).

Meanwhile, in chapter 43, "the reader has to double the Cape" to follow the fortunes of good Major Dobbin and "our gallant old friends of the —th regiment . . . under the command of the brave colonel, Sir Michael O'Dowd." After Waterloo, Dobbin's regiment is shipped off "ten thousand miles to the military station of Bundlegunge, in the Madras division of our Indian empire" (418). India thus becomes the locale of Dobbin's exile from Amelia, though all we learn about his experiences at Madras concerns Glorvina O'Dowd's attempts to "fascinate" him. When he eventually hears from his sister that Amelia is about to remarry, Dobbin applies for home leave and returns from his oriental exile, though a bout of illness nearly kills him during the voyage. Coincidentally Dobbin sails home on the same East Indiaman, the "Ramchunder, Captain Bragg," with Jos. Meanwhile the —th regiment, without Dobbin, proceed to "distinguish" themselves in the Burmese campaign of 1824–26.

Thackeray's India—created by the battles in which Gahagan, Major Pendennis, and Colonel Newcome fought but seemingly untouched by the controversies of utilitarian and evangelical reformers—makes an appropriate dumping ground for a man of Jos Sedley's nonexistent talents, just as Coventry Island is appropriate for Rawdon Crawley's exile. There, Crawley is set up as governor and "praised with immense enthusiasm" by the *Swamp Town Gazette*, pilloried just as enthusiastically by the *Swamp Town Sentinel*, and ultimately doomed to die when he contracts Swamp Town fever, thus widowing Becky (538). But the principal setting of Thackeray's "comic history"—the fictional as well as actual metropole— is of course "home," England; India, Burma, Coventry Island, and all other parts of the Empire are distinctly "away," distant places of exile at the margins of Thackeray's vision of social reality. Perhaps what the narrator says about *not* describing the Battle of Waterloo applies also to his apparent disinterest in the doings of characters in colonial exile: "We do not claim to rank among the military novelists. Our place is with the non-combatants. When the decks are cleared for action we go below and wait meekly [with] the ladies and the baggage" (282).

Thackeray, uninterested in political issues, is equally uninterested in military and imperialist adventure. Despite Waterloo and the military careers of Dobbin, George Osborne, and the —th regiment, *Vanity Fair* is a "novel without a hero," a domestic realist antithesis to an imperialist romance like *Mr. Midshipman Easy.* Yet war is not insignificant to Thackeray's concerns: even though it occurs offstage, Waterloo is an absolutely crucial event. In much the same way the condition of exile to the periphery, to India or the colonies, takes on a paradoxical prominence as the exotic offstage of Thackeray's domestic puppet theatre. Paradoxically, too, "India" is almost more significant in London than it is at Boggley Wollah, Calcutta, or Madras, and especially after Jos's final return, when he joins the Oriental Club and Amelia begins entertaining his "brother Indians": "From these she heard how soon Smith would be in Council; how many lacs [of rupees] Jones had brought home with him; how Thomson's House in London had refused the bills drawn by Thomson, Kibobjee and Co., the Bombay House, and how it was thought the Calcutta House must go too; how very imprudent, to say the least of it, Mrs. Brown's conduct (wife of Brown of the Ahmednuggar Irregulars) had been with young Swankey of the Body Guard" (581). The topics of Anglo-Indian gossip to which Amelia listens are the chief topics also in Thackeray's representations of India—business, military assignments, love making. Nowhere in the novel is there a suggestion that the business and military connections are in any way controversial, matters for political debate and possible reform, change, or revolution. Jos Sedley's colleagues—and Thackeray—express no interest in Britain's divine calling or utilitarian aims. In the extensive treatments of India in both *Pendennis* and *The Newcomes*, moreover, the only issue even remotely to call into question Britain's dealings with Indians concerns the affairs of the great Bundelcund Bank in which Colonel Newcome invests his fortune. What happens to the bank Thackeray blames on oriental chicanery; while its victims are innocent Englishmen like the Colonel.

iii

Though several of Thackeray's Anglo-Indian characters are soldiers, warfare for them is largely a thing of the past. Dobbin's regiment goes off to the Burmese War, but only after Dobbin himself goes home; Major Pendennis and Colonel Newcome are veterans of the Maratha campaigns, like Goliah Gahagan. In the unromantic India of the full-scale novels, business—as with Jos Sedley's tax collecting—predominates, though always with the suggestion that it is somehow ignoble or dishonorable, a fallen condition compared to the military glories of the past. In *Pendennis* both Colonel Altamont (alias Amory, alias Armstrong) and Lady Clavering's father Mr. Snell, "a disreputable old lawyer and indigo smuggler," mix business with crime in India, and when Altamont surfaces in England to blackmail Sir Francis Clavering, he is both a bigamist and a returned convict who has murdered to escape from New South Wales.[34] Their criminality, and the "disreputable" origins of Lady Clavering's fortune, contrast with Major Pendennis's martial integrity. A similar contrast is evident in *The Newcomes*, between Col. Thomas Newcome's blunt military bearing and innocence and the Bundelcund Bank speculation in which he becomes entangled.

Upon his final return to London Jos Sedley rents a house on the fringes of "the comfortable Anglo-Indian district of which Moira Place is the centre" (*Vanity Fair*, 578). He purchases furnishings for it from "the assignees of Mr. Scape, lately admitted partner into the great Calcutta House of Fogle, Fake, and Cracksman, in which poor Scape had embarked seventy thousand pounds, the earnings of a long and honourable life" (579). Thackeray goes into some detail about how Scape's investment leads to his ruin—it is an oriental version of John Sedley's bankruptcy. The shady dealings of Fogle, Fake, and Cracksman, moreover, foreshadow the great Bundlecund Bank through which Colonel Newcome will first make and then lose a fortune. Both shady businesses are examples of the Indian agency house or private investment firm, through which Thackeray's own considerable fortune was lost in the early 1830s. As Gordon Ray explains:

Until the last months of 1833 Thackeray was a young gentleman of substantial prospects . . . worth between £15,000 and £20,000. . . . Though the nature of the catastrophe that overtook him is not altogether clear, it seems reasonable to suppose that the bulk of Richmond Thackeray's estate was lost in the collapse of the great Indian agency-houses. . . . The cycle began with the failure of Palmer and Company for £5,000,000 in 1830, and ended with the failure of Cruttenden and Company for £1,350,000 in 1834. Both Thackeray and Major Carmichael-Smyth were particularly interested in Cruttenden . . . and it may have been the Major's obstinate adherence to this firm, like the loyalty of Colonel Newcome to the Bundelcund Bank . . . which brought

Thackeray to disaster. A hint in a letter to his mother suggests that the sum
which he lost totalled £11,325.[35]

The fate of Scape and his family in *Vanity Fair* thus resembles that of
the Thackerays in the early 1830s. Having invested his fortune and
become a partner in the agency house, Scape replaces Fake, who retires
"to a princely park in Sussex (the Fogles have been long out of the firm,
and Sir Horace Fogle is about to be raised to the Peerage as Baron
Bandana)" (579). Shortly after Scape's investment the business "failed for
a million, and plunged half the Indian public into misery and ruin" (and
by Indian Thackeray of course means Anglo-Indian; there was evidently
no oriental public in his estimation). "Scape, ruined, honest and broken-
hearted at sixty-five years of age, went out to Calcutta to wind up the
affairs of the house. Walter Scape was withdrawn from Eton, and put into
a merchant's house. Florence Scape, Fanny Scape, and their mother,
faded away to Boulogne, and will be heard of no more. To be brief, Jos
stepped in and bought their carpets and sideboards, and admired himself
in the mirrors which had reflected their kind handsome faces" (579).
How disaster overtakes the Scape family, together with half the Indian
public, is not explained, although the names of two of the partners, Fake
and Cracksman, suggest financial skulduggery. But poor Scape himself is
"honest," just as Colonel Newcome will later be presented as the soul of
honor and good intentions.

Scape's bankruptcy is a mere passing allusion in *Vanity Fair*, contrasting once again the unworthy Jos Sedley's prosperity to someone else's
misfortune, but the treatment of the Bundelcund Bank in *The Newcomes*
is far more elaborate than that of Scape's firm. The bank's rise and fall is
the source of—and corresponds precisely to—the rising and falling prosperity of the Colonel and his son Clive, the novel's protagonists. Pen the
narrator even says that "this Bundelcund Banking Company, in the
Colonel's eyes, was in reality his son Clive" (2:141), an identification that
implies the simultaneously unselfish selfishness of the Colonel. Thomas
Newcome would do anything to make his son happy, wealthy, and a
gentleman; he would even "have put his head under Juggernaut's chariot-
wheel—have sacrificed any ease, comfort, or pleasure for the youngster's
business" (2:262). Were it not for Clive, the good Colonel, "who had
plenty of money for his own wants, would never have thought of speculation. [But his] desire was to see his boy endowed with all the possible gifts
of fortune" (2:141). The Colonel's self-sacrificing urge to make Clive's
fortune adumbrates Abel Magwitch's desire to make a gentleman out of

Pip in *Great Expectations*. Of course Clive does not start from below the middle class on the social ladder, nor does the Colonel do anything criminal—on the contrary, he becomes the victim of the wily speculators who run the Bundelcund Bank. But nevertheless the good-selfish Colonel is unable to recognize that money cannot buy Clive's happiness—a Midas-like blindness evident in his identification of the bank with Clive (or at least, of the welfare of the bank with Clive's welfare).

As in much Victorian fiction, honest investment is one thing, speculation another. According to John Vernon, "In Balzac, Dickens, Eliot, Melville, Flaubert, Dostoevsky, and James . . . we repeatedly see the giddy excitement of an unstable social and economic world of booms and busts, of speculative bubbles swelling and bursting, of the gambling mentality—the sense of life out on a limb or about to soar or crash—as well as the disgust all this shades into and becomes mired in."[36] Yet the distinction between gambling or speculation and sound investment is fuzzy; it seems often to depend merely on whether a business venture succeeds or fails. The Bundelcund Bank is in any case similar to numerous other shady investment firms that make and break characters' fortunes in the novels of Thackeray's contemporaries—the "United Metropolitan Improved Hot Muffin . . . Company" in *Nicholas Nickleby*, for example, or, closer to Thackeray's interests, the "Anglo-Bengalese Disinterested Loan and Life Insurance Company" in *Martin Chuzzlewit*. But Dickens presents such businesses as totally fraudulent from the outset, whereas the Bundelcund Bank in *The Newcomes* seems both prosperous and legitimate through much of the novel.

At several points in his narration, Pen describes the Bundelcund Bank's business as it grows into "one of the most flourishing commercial institutions in Bengal" (2:119).

Founded . . . at a time when all private credit was shaken by the failure of the great Agency Houses, of which the downfall had carried dismay and ruin throughout the presidency, the B.B. had been established on the *only* sound principle of commercial prosperity—that of association. The native capitalists, headed by the great firm of Rummun Loll and Co. . . . had largely embarked in the B.B., and the officers of the two services and the European mercantile body of Calcutta had been invited to take shares in an institution which to merchants, native and English, civilians and military men, was alike advantageous and indispensable. How many young men of the latter services had been crippled for life by the ruinous cost of agencies, of which the profits to the agents themselves were so enormous! The shareholders of the B.B. were their own agents. (2:119)

So the Bundelcund Bank is initially presented as a legitimate improvement over the sort of agency house whose failure caused Thackeray's loss of fortune. The bank has apparently lawful dealings throughout the orient, doing "an immense opium trade" with China, for example, while also carrying on "a vast trade in wool" with New South Wales (2:119). Later Clive's friend Fred Bayham, expert in "the affairs of the Bundelcund Banking Company . . . talked of cotton, wool, copper, opium, indigo, Singapore, Manilla, China, Calcutta, Australia, with prodigious eloquence and fluency. His conversation was about millions" (2:267). Fred, Clive, and Pen attend the annual dinners of the bank directors at Blackwall, where there is much celebrating the success of the firm, and where—by this time in the story—Colonel Newcome presides as "the kindly old chairman" while "the Prince, his son," sits with Fred and Pen and takes "but a modest part in the ceremonies" (2:267). Though the reader suspects from the beginning that the bank is unsound, in part because it is identified with speculation, even at this late stage in the novel all that is overtly amiss is that Clive's apparent good fortune has deflected him from his artistic career. Clive's painter friend J. J. Ridley fears that the success of the bank has spoiled Clive for painting (2:114), and Clive himself tells Pen that "I hate banks, bankers, Bundelcund, indigo, cotton"—"I would rather be at home in my painting-room" than at board meetings (2:294). Thackeray's moral seems perfectly clear: too much money undermines both the work ethic and dedication to the arts; success spoils Clive Newcome and his father.

Through most of *The Newcomes*, passages about the Bundelcund Bank might be taken as merely illustrating this moral. They might be interpreted even more loosely, as incidental allusions like the paragraph about the Scape family in *Vanity Fair*, were it not that business matters occupy so much of the story. Upon the London banking concern of the Colonel's half-brothers as well as the Bundelcund Bank in Calcutta depend the fortunes of the entire Newcome family, whose history involves a rise from working-class origins into the *nouveau riche* bourgeoisie and then, through Sir Brian Newcome, into the lower fringes of the aristocracy. As a historical novel chronicling the rise of a family, moreover, *The Newcomes* is structured in terms of several contrasting social levels, from the most private, intimate, sympathetic circle—Clive, his father, and his friends (including Pen the narrator)—to the extended Newcome family consisting of the Colonel's selfish half-brothers, their wives, and children, to the larger society encompassing Britain and British India. As the focus moves outward from private to public, Thackeray's treatment of characters and themes grows less sympathetic. What is at the periphery of the novel's concentric social circles—India—is treated least sympathetically of all, as the ultimate source of the fortunes and the misfortunes of the novel's most central, most sympathetic figures, Clive and the Colonel.

Quite late in the novel the affairs of the Bundelcund Bank—and hence the affairs of Clive and his father—appear to be prospering. Their fortunes (money but also destinies) are identified with the bank's just as, Pen says, the Colonel conflates bank and Clive. Colonel Newcome now rivals his half-brothers in wealth and influence. Clive, though not interested in business, takes "a seat in the assembly of East India shareholders, and a voice in the election of directors of that famous Company" (2:284), while his father applies for the directorship of the company itself on the basis of his position with the bank. To make himself a better candidate for that high post, the Colonel runs for Parliament on the Liberal side, defeating his treacherous nephew Barnes Newcome, who runs as a Conservative. But before his political and business ambitions are realized, the bubble bursts, the Bundelcund Bank fails, and the fortunes of the Colonel and his son come crashing down.

Speculation is the general disease that explains the failure of the Bundelcund Bank, just as it supposedly accounts for Scape's ruin in *Vanity Fair.* But behind most instances of speculation in Victorian fiction lurks the shady speculator—a Fake, a Cracksman—who reaps profits while leaving the unwary but honest investor in the lurch. Dickens's phony businesses are always run by such dishonest financiers, from Ralph Nickleby to Mr. Merdle in *Little Dorrit*, and Augustus Melmotte in Trollope's *The Way We Live Now* is another example. In *The Newcomes* the individual who eventually seems to have most power over bank affairs is Colonel Newcome himself—he is certainly its London chief—and yet he is also a babe in the woods when it comes to business matters. Who then is the swindling traitor who finally scuttles the good ship of the Bundelcund Bank?

Pen receives an early warning that the affairs of the bank are shaky from Fred Bayham, who accosts him one day with the news that "the good ship . . . has narrowly escaped a great danger . . . there was a traitor in her crew—she has weathered the storm nobly—who would have sent her on the rocks, sir, who would have scuttled her at midnight" (2:275). Of course the traitor cannot be the Colonel, that incarnation of honesty and good intentions who—as Pen declares on several occasions—is not really suited to business anyway. He is an old soldier, representing honor and glory; business is for the less-than-honorable, and his engagement in business does not tarnish his sterling character. In much the same way Clive's interest in painting is antagonistic to the world of business. Art and war, Clive and the Colonel, are separate, pure, higher than the money-grubbing world of commerce; yet as the plot records, the diseases of the lower world infect the higher, the periphery invades the center, India corrupts England.

The immediate traitor who brings down the bank is the vindictive Barnes Newcome. As partner in his father's and uncle's London firm, Barnes causes a "temporary panic" by refusing "acceptance of thirty thousand pounds' worth of bills" from the Bundelcund Bank (2:276). The action leads to complete rupture between the two businesses, after which the Colonel "vowed that his brother and his nephew were traitors alike, and would have no further dealings with them" (2:276). But Barnes is only a partial traitor compared to Rummun Loll, a treacherous figure from the farthest social periphery. Despite Bayham's assurance to Pen that the Bundelcund ship has been saved, the temporary panic induced by Barnes is merely prelude to the shipwreck that follows. And the chief blame for catastrophe falls upon "the great Indian millionaire," the only oriental character that Thackeray portrays in any detail in his major novels. From the outset Thackeray's attitude toward Rummun Loll is quite obviously that expressed by Bayham at the time of the bank's failure—the Indian tycoon is a "confounded old mahogany-coloured heathen humbug" (2:331).

The failure of the Bundelcund Bank, as Pen notes, is perfectly predictable for anyone who has the prescience to distrust the deceitful Bengali from his first appearance early in the story. Then even generous-hearted Colonel Newcome finds him detestable. The dark, sinister figure from the periphery shows up first at an evening party thrown by Clive's aunt, Mrs. Hobson Newcome—much too close to the social center as far as the Colonel is concerned. Pen describes him as "the celebrated Indian merchant, otherwise his Excellency Rummun Loll, otherwise his Highness Rummun Loll, the chief proprietor of the diamond mines in Golconda, with a claim of three millions and a half upon the East India Company" (1:81)—harmless enough, unless it is understood that great wealth is always suspect in Thackeray's fiction. But the Colonel's reaction to "the Rummun," and his reaction to the Colonel, offer quite transparently, and at the very opening of the novel, a contrast between white hero and mahogany-colored villain. "As soon as his Excellency saw the Colonel, whom he perfectly well knew, his Highness's princely air was exchanged for one of the deepest humility. He bowed his head and put his two hands before his eyes, and came creeping towards him submissively. . . . The Rummun, still bending and holding his hands before him, uttered a number of rapid sentences in the Hindustani language, which Colonel Newcome received twirling his mustachios with much hauteur. He turned on his heel rather abruptly, and began to speak to Mrs. Newcome" (1:81). When Mrs. Newcome says that "the Indian Prince was so intelligent," Colonel Newcome's response is unequivocal: "The Indian what?" he asks, obviously aware that Rummun Loll is a humbug and no prince.

The "heathen gentleman," however, has the effrontery to seat himself "by one of the handsomest young women in the room, whose fair face was turned towards him, whose blonde ringlets touched his shoulder, and who was listening to him as eagerly as Desdemona listened to Othello" (1:81–82). For the old soldier, the situation is nearly intolerable: "The Colonel's rage was excited as he saw the Indian's behaviour. He curled his mustachios up to his eyes in his wrath. 'You don't mean that that man calls himself a Prince? That a fellow who wouldn't sit down in an officer's presence is . . .'" but his sister-in-law interrupts him before he can complete his remark. Meanwhile the fraudulent prince flirts with other young ladies at the party, much to the Colonel's, and supposedly the reader's, discomfort. Barnes, showing his own traitorous qualities, asks the Colonel: "Is there anybody you would like to meet? Not our friend the Rummun? How the girls crowd around him! By Gad, a fellow who's rich in London may have the pick of any gal . . . I've seen the old dowagers crowdin' round that fellow, and the girls snugglin' up to his indiarubber face. He's known to have two wives already in India; but, by Gad for a settlement, I believe some of 'em here would marry" (1:83).

After Colonel Newcome's hostile reaction to the heathen humbug, it seems scarcely credible when the Colonel does an about-face and goes into business with him. The reason for the reversal, according to the Colonel, is that Rummun Loll has helped him avoid losing money through an agency house:

Do you know, [writes the Colonel from India to Clive,] I narrowly missed losing half a lakh of rupees which I had at an agent's here? And who do you think warned me about him? Our friend Rummun Loll . . . with whom I made the voyage from Southamptom. He is a man of wonderful tact and observation. I used to think meanly of the honesty of natives, and treat them haughtily, as I recollect doing this very gentleman at your uncle Newcome's. . . . He heaped coals of fire on my head by saving my money for me: and I have placed it at interest in his house. . . . He talks to me

> about the establishment of a bank of which the profits are so enormous and
> the scheme so (seemingly) clear that I don't know whether I mayn't be
> tempted to take a few shares. (2:10–11)

"I used to think meanly of the honesty of natives"—the Colonel has
apparently learned a salutary lesson about racial stereotyping. But the
lesson is just beginning. Thackeray believes he knows better; and the
entire scheme of the Bundelcund Bank rests ultimately on the quicksand
of that "Asiatic mendacity" which Macaulay, Charles Grant, James Mill,
and Thackeray all identified particularly with the Bengali race.

The plots of both *Pendennis* and *The Newcomes* are series of more or
less successful maneuvers to keep the central characters uncontaminated
by lower, peripheral social realms. In both novels, immorality, crime,
and disease emanate in part from India, the farthest periphery. In *Pendennis* the criminal element, represented most fully by Colonel Altamont, is European, though with Indian and colonial links. In *The
Newcomes* the chief villain is Rummun Loll, who bears ultimate blame
for both the fortune and the misfortune of the British protagonists, father
and son. (Indeed, the fortune the Colonel makes from the bank is a kind
of misfortune, as is its loss.) On to Rummun Loll's unsavory character
Thackeray projects all his own resentment for the loss of his Indian-based
fortune in 1833. The Bengali tycoon serves also as a scapegoat for any
lingering guilt Thackeray and his readers may have that the British do not
really belong in India—that they conquered an empire there by unlawful
force, and by force they have been extracting fortunes from that empire
ever since. Thackeray's treatment of the Bengali businessman offers an
especially clear instance of blaming the victim, a racist pattern that
underwrites all imperialist ideology.

For Thackeray the age of piratical nabobs like Robert Clive was over,
succeeded by an age of peaceful, legitimate commerce (*The Newcomes*,
1:88). Yet the Bundelcund Bank is illegitimate. Although the Colonel's
character remains free from taint, the portrait of Rummun Loll seems to
accumulate all of Pen's—and Thackeray's—misgivings about speculation
and about commerce in general. Native capitalists and aristocrats may
have invested in the Calcutta agency houses in which Thackeray lost his
fortune, but no one besides Anglo-Indians—Fakes, Fogles, Scapes—
seems to have managed such houses or played anything like the control-
ling part that Rummun Loll plays in *The Newcomes*. But what exactly is
that role? Thackeray is especially weasely on the extent of Rummun Loll's
involvement in the bank and its failure. The ambiguity of the text opens
an ever-widening gap between the innocence of the Colonel and the

criminality of the Indian pseudo-prince. Apart from advising the Colonel to invest in the bank, however, at first Rummun Loll seems to be merely another investor. When Pen says that "the native capitalists, headed by the great firm of Rummun Loll and Co., of Calcutta, had largely embarked in the B.B.," the only extraordinary note is the idea that there *are* native capitalists (2:119). But the native investors are doing only what all the European investors do. Later, when the Colonel is described as the London director of the bank and Rummun Loll as its Calcutta director, there seems little to choose between them. But after the great Bundelcund bubble bursts, the person most obviously responsible is the inevitably deceitful Bengali tycoon: "When the accounts of that ghastly bankruptcy arrived from Calcutta, it was found, of course, that the merchant prince Rummun Loll owed the B.B.C. twenty-five lakhs of rupees, the value of which was scarcely ever represented by his respectable signature" (2:333). Pen's "of course" captures the inevitability of this outcome; readers attuned to Thackeray's racist categories will have known all along what to expect.

In the meantime the Bengali swindler has been living like a prince, throwing lavish parties attended by "the greatest and proudest personages of that aristocratic city," Calcutta (2:332). "The fairest Calcutta beauties had danced in his halls" (2:332)—the sexual innuendo makes it all the more imperative, from Thackeray's perspective, that on the eve of the most splendid of his parties, which is also the eve of the collapse of the bank, Rummun Loll should have the further effrontery to be "seized in the grip" of cholera and die (2:332). At the farthest periphery, in the imperial Hades of Calcutta, disease like crime and sexual transgression has its abode. Of course, some European investors in the bank appear to have engaged in sharp practices as well—"the reverend Baptist Bellman," for example, the "Chief Registrar of the Calcutta Tape and Sealing-Wax Office (a most valuable and powerful amateur preacher who had converted two natives . . .)." This enthusiastic missionary had "helped himself to £73,000 . . . for which he settled in the Bankruptcy Court" (2:333). Bellman, like the Rev. Charles Honeyman, suggests Thackeray's antipathy toward the missionary project of evangelizing India; but when it comes to embezzlement and running up debts, the Europeans are mere tyros compared to the shadiest con man in the story.

Meanwhile, back at Clive's establishment in London, "bills are up in the fine new house. Swarms of Hebrew gentlemen with their hats on are walking about the drawing rooms, peering into the bedrooms . . . inspecting ottomans, mirrors, and a hundred articles of splendid trumpery"

(2:333–34). The hint of antisemitism is further evidence that Thackeray thinks persistently in racial stereotypes. The hint has its own auto-biographical twist, moreover. Shortly before the collapse of his Indian fortune, the young Thackeray himself worked for "a bill-discounting firm in Birchin Lane" (Ray, 159). He experienced the world of indebtedness and bankruptcy as both agent and victim; he acted much as the Hebrew gentlemen act in *The Newcomes*. Later, to his chagrin, a fellow writer in *Fraser's Magazine* for 1843 would refer to a "Bill Crackaway," sharp about shady business practices in London (Ray, 159). Thackeray was apparently eager to wish away his involvement in such practices; there-fore, in standard antisemitic fashion, he projected something he did not like about himself onto Hebrew gentlemen.

In the same manner Thackeray wished away the guilt he felt for both his and his stepfather's speculation in the Anglo-Indian agency houses of Calcutta—and perhaps even more his resentment over the loss of his fortune—by projecting those feelings onto the stereotype of the deceitful Bengali. Clive and Clive's father are forever innocent of sharp business practices; as Barnes Newcome sums it up, "here is a hot-headed old [Anglo-]Indian dragoon . . . who knows no more about business than I do about cavalry tactics or Hindostanee; who gets into a partnership with other dragoons and Indian wiseacres, with some uncommonly wily old native practitioners" (2:279). Thus are readers of *The Newcomes* led to believe that the blameless conquerors of India are being subverted and swindled by the very people they have conquered.

Pen protests his own innocence of the world of commerce: "These subjects are mysterious, terrifying, unknown to me" (2:267). Yet the rise and fall of the bank serves as the "real foundation," to borrow Marx's phrase, for about two-thirds of the novel, through much of which Pen calls Rummun Loll nearly every hard name but the devil. The improba-ble fantasy that is Thackeray's characterization of the Indian tycoon so patently results from a hateful wishful thinking that we naturally ask to what extent Thackeray was aware of what he was doing. If he was at all aware, why did he fail to take seriously the Colonel's own better judg-ment: *I used to think meanly of the honesty of natives?* But Thackeray was always a highly unsystematic, self-indulgent writer, one who rarely brought himself to criticize his most autobiographical characters, always lovingly if somewhat cynically portrayed. His stereotypic rendering of Rummun Loll is merely a corollary to his inability or unwillingness to follow through his moral themes to either personal or political conclusions. As J. Y. T. Greig puts it, "the trouble with [Thackeray] was that he had no relatively firm social theory to control his pen. He had no standards, except the vague ones of a 'gentleman,' by which he could measure social aberrations. Like many another social physician, he could only name the disease, and attack its symptoms. To get down to ultimate causes would have needed more systematic thinking than his untrained and inconstant mind was capable of undertaking."[37] Yet for this very reason, Thackeray's novels offer a clear expression of average, bourgeois, mid-Victorian values and ideas about many social issues. And the portrayal of India in his major novels, albeit with the intrusion of the sinister Rummun Loll and the failure of the Bundelcund Bank, is a perfectly complacent, uncritical image of Anglo-India—he was no more interested in depicting "native" India than he was in depicting factory workers and strikes in Manchester. Anglo-India and the Empire were givens, and these facts of life the mildly cynical portrait painter of Vanity Fair never questioned at any fundamental level.

Lacking a "relatively firm social theory," Thackeray moralizes about individuals, personifying rather than generalizing social and political forces. In contrast to the utilitarian and evangelical reformers, he seems almost obsessively to avoid political statements concerning India.[38] For him the Anglo-Indian experience is a matter of either warfare or business. The two do not connect in his thinking—indeed, they are antithetical, because warfare is honorable and business always a bit despicable. Yet in both spheres Thackeray never questions that the British presence in India is proper, inevitable, perhaps eternal. The proof of these assumptions lies in the character of Rummun Loll himself. By his very success in business and in penetrating Anglo-Indian and London social circles, the heathen humbug shows his innate tendency to fraud. But his success also implies that for Thackeray he has attained the highest, most westernized state to which his race could progress. By thinking in terms of the immutable features of racial stereotypes, Thackeray in effect rules out genuine progress for any non-European peoples. In any event, both London and Calcutta kowtow to Rummun Loll; even the good Colonel, initially hostile, is taken in by the great oriental swindler. Rummun Loll's chief con game is not necessarily connected to the Bundelcund Bank at all, which until the end of the story remains distinct from his native company and mainly under European control. Long before Rummun Loll has filched thousands and the bank has failed, he has learned to ape English manners, to ogle fair-haired English girls, to compete on an equal basis in Englishmen's business, and to aspire to Englishmen's power. The ultimate scam for Thackeray is not the Bundelcund Bank but Rummun Loll himself.

In a brief consideration of racism in Thackeray, John Sutherland points out that, whereas Dickens and George Eliot seem to have approached "a more humane position at the ends of their writing careers," Thackeray moved "in just the opposite direction, his views on race hardening as he grew older and, paradoxically, otherwise more mellow and philanthropic towards his fellow-men."[39] Responses to the Indian Mutiny and the Governor Eyre controversy suggest another conclusion about Dickens, but Sutherland bears out his point about Thackeray by tracing through the novels various mocking allusions to the abolitionist slogan "Am I not a man and a brother?" The last words of *Pendennis* contain such an allusion, as Sutherland notes, though the mockery there is faint. It is strongest in *Philip*, where Captain Woolcomb, "the mulatto dandy who steals Agnes from the blue-eyed hero," runs for Parliament with the ludicrous campaign slogan "Am I not a man and a brudder?" (444). But there are earlier unsettling figures—Miss Swartz, "the Hottentot Venus" in *Vanity Fair*, for example, and Mr. Nebuchadnezzar and various other Hebrew gentlemen throughout Thackeray's cartoons and spoofs—which suggest that Thackeray's views about race did not alter much over the years.[40] Whether or not his views hardened, Thackeray relied on racial stereotypes as a substitute—as in all racist thinking—for political analysis and self-criticism.

The evangelicals and utilitarians insisted that the chief objects of British imperialism were the conversion and civilization of India. Macaulay and James Mill partially recognized the violence, rapacity, even criminality with which Clive and the East India Company had often acted. By the early nineteenth century the deed was done, however, and the object now was to bring progress to Asia. The utilitarian project of social reform often conflicted with the Christian conversion advocated by the evangelicals, but both goals involved a belief that ran counter to the more extreme forms of racism: no matter how benighted or tyrannized by custom and false religion, Indians were capable of education, improvement, progress. Indeed, they were themselves heirs of ancient social traditions and civilizations that, though crippling to modern progress, could at least be respected by more sympathetic British analysts as major historical achievements.

To the writer who substituted individualistic moralizing and racial stereotyping for politics, however, India appeared only as it does in *The*

Newcomes—a field for potential *British* achievement, conquest, and fortune making and a background of changeless oriental deceit, lasciviousness, and obsequious bowing and scraping to the master race. For Thackeray, as for Carlyle and Dickens, it seemed clear that no dark-skinned native could ever be "a man and a brudder" to whites. But then Thackeray's strength as a novelist is his ability to chronicle with sympathetic good humor the struggles of small middle-class folk like himself, for most of whom India seemed at best distant, exotic, and perhaps ominous, posing some sort of mysterious threat to home values. Henry James was correct to suppose that Thackeray's "large and easy" genius owed much to his Anglo-Indian background—but what it owed was not its "large and easy" qualities.

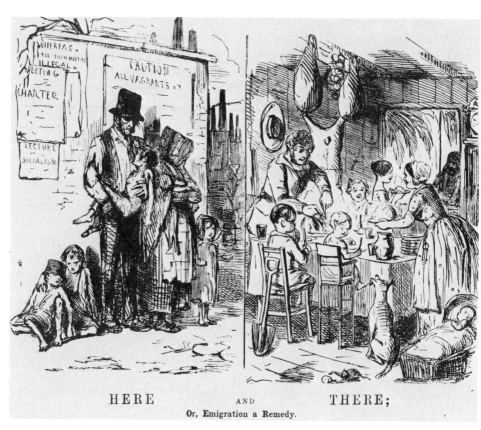

Cartoon from *Punch*, 1848.

4. Black Swans; or, Botany Bay Eclogues

"I'm an Englishman, ain't I? Where are my priwileges?"
—The Artful Dodger

i

Out of his wartime experiences Captain Marryat fashioned his midshipman novels, celebrations of combat and youthful heroism which stand at the head of a long line of imperialist adventure stories. Related to these adventure narratives, often endings or sequels to them, are numerous accounts of settlers and settled life in new colonies—versions of pastoral which lead from the epic themes of discovery and conquest to the pacific themes of domestication and steady colonial progress. In *Masterman Ready* and *The Settlers in Canada*, Marryat combined adventure with colonial pastoral in ways foreshadowed by *The Tempest* and *Robinson Crusoe*. And in *Dawn Island* and countless other conversion fantasies, both evangelical and utilitarian, Harriet Martineau and other proselytizers for progress created versions of pastoral in which the shepherds are white explorers, soldiers, settlers, missionaries, and their flocks the originally wild creatures—savages and cannibals—of the "dark places" of the earth. Unlike earlier pastoral writing, these conversion fantasies do not suggest that exiles from civilization need to relearn innocence from rustic types and an Edenic nature. On the contrary, what is primitive must be converted to civilization, or else contained or eliminated. The colonial setting is not only backdrop for the conquest and conversion of cannibals, however, but also an enabling space where the colonizers can be at least partially redeemed. Conversion thus works in two directions. Just as the rigors of shipboard life shape Marryat's boy-heroes into men, so the rigors of pioneering and Indian fighting shape the

Campbell family into successful immigrants in *The Settlers in Canada*, in part by teaching them the ways of the Indians.

Australia serves as the colonial setting for some of the most complex, contradictory treatments of the conversion motif. The colonizers of the Bush described by numerous authors must themselves be redeemed for civilization; the aborigines hardly count at all. Both because of Australia's early history as a penal colony and because of efforts toward systematic colonization which influenced British debate about overpopulation and emigration from the 1820s onward, Botany Bay acquired a powerful ideological significance. Emigration, it has often been said, provides a convenient device for novelists wanting to provide happy endings for characters; for decades Australia provided an actual device for the disposal of criminals and other outcasts. [1] Banishment, it was hoped, would lead to redemption, but redemption was not always expected. In time a second hope emerged, that Australia itself would be redeemed from savagery and mere desert waste, though this later hope conflicted with the fact that Australia's first colonizers were themselves "white savages." To many observers, transported convicts seemed no more eligible for redemption than the aborigines, who at least were innocent of the crimes of civilized life.

The penal colony at Botany Bay was established in 1788, and as early as 1794 Robert Southey's "Botany Bay Eclogues" helped give it mythic status. In Southey's four poems, several transported felons describe their experiences. Then still a radical sympathizer with the French Revolution, Southey tried to treat his criminal subjects as victims of unjust social circumstances. (The idea that the criminal was society's victim was central to William Godwin's theories, and it was later to become central to several "Newgate novelists.")[2] Southey's first convict is Elinor, who recollects how she betrayed her parson father and abandoned the "lowly lovely dwelling" of her childhood to become "the slave / Of Vice and Infamy."[3] Because of her righteous upbringing, she cannot be seen as a victim of poverty, lack of education, or other social circumstances—she has instead, seemingly of her own free will, become "the hireling prey / Of brutal appetite." Thus, also, it is impossible to imagine that banishment to Australia, by placing Elinor close to nature, will reform her. Yet the main points Southey apparently wishes to make in each of the eclogues are that his criminal characters have been victimized by injustice at home, and that the pastoral, wilderness setting of Australia has redemptive power. Elinor apostrophizes "Nature's domain," where "the comforts and the crimes of polish'd life" are "as yet unknown." But is

Nature supposed to be redemptive in an Arcadian sense merely because innocent of civilized vice? Or is Australian Nature in particular supposed to cause criminals like Elinor to repent because of its harsh rigors and isolation? In contrast to the paradisal imagery of Arcadian nature, the wild landscape of Botany Bay suggests an infernal domain of guilt and torment:

> Once more to daily toil, once more to wear
> The livery of shame, once more to search
> With miserable task this savage shore!

So Elinor begins her dismal monologue. Her memory of childhood in England takes on the trappings of pastoral innocence, whereas Australia offers only barren wilderness and exile—"savage lands," "barbarous climes," and "joyless shores" where "angry England sends her outcast sons." In this mythic confusion of realms only "the saving hand of Grace" can be expected to "fit the faithful penitent for Heaven."

In the other three eclogues the same contradictions recur. Australia offers a setting for pastoral redemption, but the idea blurs because the convict characters remember Britain in pastoral terms. In the second and third eclogues male characters exchange reminiscences about soldiering, sailoring, and the injustices—the press gang, for example—that have led them to commit the crimes for which they have been exiled. Although several of them can "thank God" that they are now "safe quarter'd at Botany Bay," memory also transports them back to a precriminal, pastoral innocence in Britain. The confusion is perhaps most evident in the final eclogue, where Frederic makes his way back to his hut at night through the Australian wilderness, listening to "the midnight howl / Of hungry monsters prowling for their prey." Frederic too remembers Britain both as a realm of innocence and as a realm of injustice that has led to his fall:

> What if I warr'd upon the world? the world
> Had wrong'd me first: I had endured the ills
> Of hard injustice.

Just as Frederic perceives Britain as childhood Eden and as land of injustice, so Australia, both Eden and howling wilderness, echoes his guilt. Given such contrariness, "all this goodly earth" appears to be "one wide waste wilderness" from which only God's grace can redeem the sinner—a conclusion surely at odds with Southey's youthful radicalism.

The penal colony history of Australia elicits similar contradictions from many later writers. Botany Bay eclogues always involve a confusion of mythic realms which corresponds in a quite precise way to the contradictory aims underlying the practice of transportation. Was transportation a punishment or a means of redemption? And was the criminal entirely to blame for his actions, or was he in some measure a victim of the society that banished him? In 1797 London magistrate Patrick Colquhoun wrote that "transportation to an unknown region, inhabited by savages, and placed at such a remote distance from England, would exhibit this species of punishment in a light so terrific, as to prove the means of preventing crimes."[4] In one of his reports on the penal colonies J. T. Bigge later wrote: "Transportation to New South Wales is intended as a severe Punishment . . . and must be rendered an Object of real Terror."[5] Colquhoun added, however, that "a hope was probably entertained that . . . the great expence of a passage home, joined to the fertility of the soil, and the salubrity of the climate, would induce convicts to remain after the expiration of their banishment, so as not to become troublesome again in their native country" (321). Colquhoun nevertheless remarks that neither of these contradictory expectations proved correct. On the one hand, the terror of transportation did not lead to a diminution of crime at home. On the other, "the great distance of New South Wales has not proved a bar to the return of a considerable number of the more atrocious and adroit thieves, several of whom are known to be again upon the town" (321).

From the colony's very beginning, some commentators felt that transportation was letting criminals off lightly. In his *Serious Admonition to the Public on the Intended Thief Colony at Botany Bay* (1786), Alexander Dalrymple declared: "For what is the Punishment intended to be afflicted? *Not* to make the felons undergo *servitude* for the *benefit* of *others* as was the Case in America; but to place them as their own masters in a temperate climate, where they have *every object* of comfort for *Ambition* before them!"[6] As more convicts became "emancipists" and as increasing numbers of free settlers arrived, the terrors of transportation diminished; the utilitarian line between pain and pleasure, punishment and reward, became harder to draw. But clearly the transportation of criminals profoundly influenced British attitudes toward the Antipodes, from 1788 to the last shipments of convicts to Western Australia in the 1860s and beyond. As Eleanor Hodges points out, "For almost the first half-century of its existence, White Australia was primarily an extensive gaol, with 'Old Australians'—convicts, ex-convicts, and native-born people . . .

outnumbering free settlers and officials by seven to one in 1828, and remaining a majority of the population until the discovery of gold in 1851."[7]

The conflicting social values evident in Botany Bay eclogues present in extreme form contradictions that characterize the entire literature of emigration and colonization. Were emigrants themselves outcasts, social misfits, criminals? If so, how could they be viewed as the vanguard of an Empire whose goal was nothing less than semidivine, the redemption of the nonwestern world from darkness and barbarism? The desolate, perhaps vengeful backward gaze of the emigrants in Ford Madox Brown's famous painting *The Last of England* suggests the ambiguity inherent in its subject. In "Lines on the Departure of Emigrants for New South Wales" (1828), Thomas Campbell strikes the same troubled note:

> On England's shore I saw a pensive band,
> With sails unfurled for earth's remotest strand,
> Like children parting from a mother, shed
> Tears for the home that could not give them bread.
> Grief marked each face receding from the view.[8]

Just as England for Campbell is both mother and a country that cannot feed its poor, so New South Wales is both a place inconceivably far away—"the home-sick heart / Quails" when thinking about it—and also a "delightful land," "benign" even "in wildness." Perhaps because he was writing about free emigrants rather than transported felons, however, Campbell is both more optimistic and more patriotic than Southey:

> The glorious past is ours, the future thine.
> As in a cradled Hercules, we trace
> The lines of empire in thine infant face—

so shall a glorious empire arise from the wilderness of New South Wales.

British victory in the Napoleonic Wars formed the context for Marryat's first novels; few works of nineteenth-century fiction are more optimistic than *Peter Simple* and *Mr. Midshipman Easy.* But the end of the long conflict with France bred trouble at home. Thomas Malthus's dismal analysis of the adverse effects of population growth on all forms of social improvement may not have seemed particularly troublesome or persuasive in its first formulation—*The Essay on the Principle of Population* of 1798. By the time Malthus published his *Principles of Political Economy* in 1820, however, he could attach his analysis to symptoms of

economic decline which must have been evident to all thoughtful readers:

> The powerful stimulus . . . given to population by the continued demand
> for labour during the war, occasioned the pouring in of fresh supplies of
> labour, which, aided by the disbanded soldiers and sailors . . . reduced
> generally both wages and profits, and left the country with a generally
> diminished capital and revenue. . . . For the four or five years since the
> war . . . a check has been given to the rate of production, and the
> population, under its former impulse, has increased, not only faster than
> the demand for labour, but faster than the actual produce. . . . Though
> labour is cheap, there is neither the power nor the will to employ it all.[9]

Malthus never considered that emigration offered more than a short-
term palliative to overpopulation and unemployment. In the first edition
of the *Essay* he simply denied that emigration could have much effect on
population; by 1817, however, he had come to believe that for specific
social conditions emigration could provide at least a temporary relief: "If,
for instance, from a combination of external and internal causes, a very
great stimulus should be given to the population of a country for ten or
twelve years together, and it should then comparatively cease, it is clear
that labour will continue flowing into the market with almost un-
diminished rapidity, while the means of employing and paying it have
been essentially contracted. It is precisely under these circumstances that
emigration is most useful as a temporary relief."[10] In just such circumstances, Malthus believed, Britain found itself at the end of the Napoleonic Wars. Although the relief afforded by emigration could be only
temporary, in effect because population abhors a vacuum, "at the present
moment" (1817) Malthus asserted that emigration was "well worthy the
attention of the government, both as a matter of humanity and policy"
(354).

Malthus was, if anything, lukewarm toward emigration in comparison
with the majority of classical economists. After an early, anti-imperialist
phase represented by *Emancipate Your Colonies!* (1792) Jeremy Bentham
adopted the view that colonization could be a valuable means for the
maintenance of prosperity at home through the export of surplus population and surplus capital. By 1808, according to Donald Winch,
Bentham's opinions "verge on jingoism." The future, according to
Bentham, is bright with the prospect of "men spreading in distant climes,
through distant ages, from the best stock, the earth covered with British
population, rich with British wealth, tranquil with British security, the
fruit of British law."[11] According to Colquhoun in 1814, "No nation ever

possessed such resources for the beneficial employment of a redundant population as Great Britain at the present moment." The resources he had in mind were the colonies.[12] Similarly, in an 1817 "Paper on the Means of Reducing the Poor Rates," the economist Robert Torrens declared that "a well-regulated system of colonization acts as a safety-valve to the political machine, and allows the expanding vapour to escape, before it is heated to explosion."[13] Twenty-seven years later, in *The Budget* (1844), Torrens could assert that it was "the mission of the Anglo-Saxon race to multiply and to replenish the earth." Through colonization, "England might become a vast industrial metropolis, and the colonies agricultural provinces of unlimited extent."[14] And, towards the end of the Hungry Forties, John Stuart Mill put the stamp of orthodoxy on emigration as an instrument of economic prosperity when, in his *Principles of Political Economy* (1848), he wrote: "To appreciate the benefits of colonization, it should be considered in relation, not to a single country, but to the collective economical interest of the human race. . . . The exportation of labourers and capital from old to new countries, from a place where their productive power is less, to a place where it is greater, increases by so much the aggregate produce of the labour and capital of the world. . . . There needs to be no hesitation affirming that Colonization, in the present state of the world, is the best affair of business, in which the capital of an old and wealthy country can be engaged."[15]

Mill was writing in the midst of what has been called "the greatest upsurge in emigration which the world had ever seen," much of it from Britain.[16] Between 1847 and 1852 over 1.6 million migrants left Britain for the United States and Canada, Australia, and other parts of the Empire. Many were Irish, and it was largely in response to poverty and overpopulation in Ireland, to divert the "tide" of Irish emigrants from England's shores, that the first systematic colonization schemes were proposed in the 1820s and 1830s. In 1826, commenting on the Report of the Select Committee on Emigration issued in May of that year, the economist J. R. McCulloch advocated a governmental expenditure of nearly £14 million to convey one-seventh of the entire population of Ireland—roughly one million "redundant" people—to the colonies or other parts of the world, preferably far away from Britain. McCulloch believed it imperative to "protect and secure our own population from being overrun and degraded by the influx of Irish poor."[17] Just as Malthus had imagined redundant or surplus population in liquid, hydraulic terms, so McCulloch conceived of emigration in the 20s as sanitary engineering on the grand scale. The "torrent of pauperism" in Ireland was already deluging England and Scotland. Though expensive, transplantation of the redundant Irish population to the colonies was far preferable, McCulloch believed, to the inundation of England and Scotland by the disease of pauperism. Without a program of government-assisted emigration, "the tide of beggary and degradation will flow in this direction, until the plague of poverty has spread its ravages equally over both divisions of the empire" (54). Already, McCulloch reported, "half-famished hordes . . . are daily pouring in from the great *officina pauperum*" of Ireland (56). He stressed his hydraulic-sanitary metaphors by declaring: "Pauperism, like water, will find its level. It cannot be heaped up in Leinster and Ulster without overflowing upon England and Scotland" (54).

McCulloch's imagery—the diarrhea of paupers from Ireland carrying the contagion of poverty to England and Scotland—foreshadows the many mid-Victorian treatments of overpopulation as a problem also of sanitation. In an 1853 essay entitled "Immortal Sewerage," the Rev. Sidney Godolphin Osborne wrote of "the draining of civilization" as an urgent necessity. The "festering mass of depraved physical matter" which needed to be removed from Glasgow and other cities was both actual excrement and the people who produced it.[18] Osborne wrote as a social reformer, sympathetic to the cause of improving the lives of the poor. As Gertrude Himmelfarb points out in *The Idea of Poverty*, often it was those middle-class writers most sympathetic to the poor, such as Dickens and Henry Mayhew, who were most ready to portray them in the terms of an excremental vision that reduced them to "superfluous masses," heaped up in festering slums such as Seven Dials and Jacob's Island.[19] The conversion motif, when focused upon slumdwellers of Britain rather than savages abroad, acquired the status of a problem of public health (not to mention control of the sex lives of the poor). According to Mayhew:

> The consciences of the London costermongers . . . are as little developed as their intellects; indeed, the moral and religious state of these men is a foul disgrace to us, laughing to scorn our zeal for the "propagation of the gospel in *foreign* parts," and making our many societies for the civilization of savages on the other side of the globe appear like a "delusion, a mockery, and a snare," when we have so many people sunk in the lowest depths of barbarism round about our very homes. It is well to have Bishops of New Zealand when we have Christianized all *our own* heathen; but with 30,000 individuals, in merely *one* of our cities, utterly creedless, mindless, and principleless, surely it would look more like earnestness on our parts if we

created Bishops of the New-Cut and sent "right reverend fathers" to watch over the "cure of souls" in the Broadway and the Brill. If our sense of duty will not rouse us to do this, at least our regard for our own interests should teach us, that it is not safe to allow this vast dungheap of ignorance and vice to seethe and fester, breeding a social pestilence in the very heart of our land.[20]

Mayhew makes the typical reformist point that the savagery or barbarism in the heart of civilization is as bad as anything in New Zealand. At the same time, social reclamation takes the form of conversion and of sanitary engineering: the "vast dungheap of ignorance and vice" must somehow be swept away from Britain—perhaps to New Zealand.

Numerous Victorian social reformers viewed a "redundant population"—Malthus's favorite phrase—as nonproductive waste, the unfortunate byproduct of the social organism. If only this waste population could be drained away to the colonies, it might there fertilize "waste lands" and make the deserts bloom. Festering at home, this human excrement bred the diseases of discontent, crime, and revolution. The contagion was spreading from the slums upward, just as the smallpox spreads from Tom-All-Alone's in *Bleak House*. In the same anthology of reformist essays which included "Immortal Sewerage," Alexander Thomson, sounding like Midshipman Jack Easy, declared that society was a pyramid—but unlike Marryat's hero, Thomson believed the pyramid rested precariously upon "an unstable agglomeration of mixed materials, often decaying and rotting away, whose corrupting influences are perpetually spreading upwards, and whose material is perpetually receiving increase by portions of the masses next above being crushed down into its bosom."[21]

Such a vision of the dangerous, contagious effects of overpopulation made colonization appear through much of the nineteenth century an almost self-evident source of relief, a chief hope for the continued health of the body politic. Drainage or good sewerage—metaphorically speaking—was a key to the future prosperity of Britain and of the colonies. In the 1820s Wilmot Horton's emigration committees proposed a national system for alleviating poverty, through which "large numbers of paupers would be converted into landholders in British North America while much smaller numbers would become indentured servants at the Cape . . . New South Wales, and Van Diemen's Land."[22] Modest experiments in government-assisted emigration were conducted in 1823 and 1825. Although Charles Buller accused Horton of merely "shovelling out paupers," Horton's efforts pointed ahead to the systematic colonization schemes of Edward Gibbon Wakefield in the 1830s and 1840s, which led to the establishment of South Australia in the thirties and the first white settlement of New Zealand in 1839. Wakefield's were only the most elaborate of the several forms of assisted emigration which swelled the stream from Britain to Australasia and other parts of the world. "Colonization is a natural means of seeking relief from the worst of our social ills, and of thus avoiding formidable political dangers"—so Wakefield wrote in his *View of the Art of Colonization,* published in 1849.[23] By that time perhaps the majority of middle and upper-class Britons agreed that colonization was an urgent necessity for the health of the body politic.

ii

No matter how vigorously opponents of Malthus mounted their campaigns against him in the early 1800s, most came around to the view that Britain was afflicted with a redundant population that needed somehow to be shoveled out. This redundant population was not just criminal but consisted of all the poor—paupers, vagrants, landless Irish peasants, unemployed handloom weavers, idled factory workers. These were the "dangerous classes," from whose ranks sprang criminals and incendiary types—Luddites, trade unionists, Chartists, socialists.[24]

The main refutation of Malthus offered by many commentators was emigration (not really a refutation at all). Coleridge, Southey, Shelley, Wordsworth, and Carlyle all responded angrily to what Coleridge called "the monstrous practical sophism of Malthus."[25] Byron wrote satirically that "Malthus does the thing 'gainst which he writes," and Wordsworth, in the more philosophical tones of *The Excursion,* called upon Britain to educate the "ignorance . . . which breeds . . . Dark discontent":

> With such foundations laid, avaunt the fear
> Of numbers crowded on their native soil,
> To the prevention of all healthful growth
> Through mutual injury! Rather in the law
> Of increase and the mandate from above
> Rejoice!

An educated populace, Wordsworth apparently believes, cannot be too numerous. But he undercuts the implication by next declaring that Britain has "special cause for joy":

> For, as the element of air affords
> An easy passage to the industrious bees

> Fraught with their burdens; and a way as smooth
> For those ordained to take their sounding flight
> From the thronged hive, and settle where they list
> In fresh abodes—their labor to renew;
> So the wide waters, open to the power,
> The will, the instincts, and appointed needs
> Of Britain, do invite her to cast off
> Her swarms, and in succession send them forth;
> Bound to establish new communities
> On every shore whose aspect favors hope
> Or bold adventure, promising to skill
> And perseverance their deserved reward. [26]

In similar fashion Carlyle, as early as *Sartor Resartus* (1833–34), thought that emigration to the supposedly empty parts of the world offered a means to refute Malthus. Hofrath Heuschrecke in *Sartor* has written a piece of Malthusian propaganda, his *Institute for the Repression of Population*, but Teufelsdröckh calls for new heroes to arise and lead the "superfluous masses" abroad, to conquer and cultivate the untilled portions of the globe. [27] And in *Past and Present*, despite categorizing emigration as a "Morrison's pill" in an early chapter, Carlyle later equates it with education as part of the answer to "the condition-of-England question":

> An effective "Teaching Service" I do consider that there must be. . . .
> Then again, why should there not be an "Emigration Service" . . . with
> funds, forces, idle Navy-ships, and ever-increasing apparatus; in fine an
> *effective system* of Emigration; so that, at length . . . every honest willing
> Workman who found England too strait, and the "Organisation of Labour"
> not yet sufficiently advanced, might find likewise a bridge to carry him
> into new Western Lands, there to "organise" with more elbow-room some
> labour for himself? There to be a real blessing, raising new corn for us,
> purchasing new webs and hatchets from us; leaving us at least in peace;—
> instead of staying here to be a Physical-Force Chartist, unblessed and no
> blessing! [28]

Carlyle moves from this argument, in which he accepts the Malthusian vision of overpopulation he claims to reject, to a rhapsodic vision of the future of the "new colonies" that Britain's "redundant" emigrants will establish:

> A free bridge for Emigrants. . . . Our little Isle is grown too narrow for us;
> but the world is wide enough yet for Six Thousand Years. England's sure

markets will be among new Colonies of Englishmen in all quarters of the Globe. . . . "Hostile Tariffs" will arise, to shut us out; and then again will fall, to let us in: but the Sons of England, speakers of the English language were it nothing more, will in all times have the ineradicable predisposition to trade with England. [Therefore] why should not London long continue the *All-Saxon-home*, rendezvous of all the "Children of the Harz-Rock," arriving . . . from the Antipodes and elsewhere, by steam and otherwise, to the "season" here!—What a Future; wide as the world, if we have the heart and heroism for it. (264)

Carlyle thus anticipates by some forty years his disciple James Anthony Froude's *Oceana*, with its vision of a worldwide federation of Anglo-Saxons in Britain's colonies and former colonies.

The same optimistic note can be heard in much early and mid-Victorian fiction—in *Dawn Island*, for example, and *The Settlers in Canada*. If fiction about emigration to Australia was not always so upbeat, it was in part because of Botany Bay: crime was added to overpopulation and unemployment as among the social problems that emigration was to solve. When Dickens first wrote about Australia, it was in terms of crime and transportation, in the story "The Convict's Return" in *Pickwick Papers*. The guilt-stricken criminal John Edmunds has his death sentence commuted to fourteen years' transportation. Those years pass almost as a blank in the story; Australia is not a place in which Dickens, at least in 1836, takes an interest. Edmunds is "sent a considerable distance up the country on his arrival at the settlement," and he "remains in the same place during the whole fourteen years."[29] Time passes. Edmunds eventually returns to England and "to his native place." He learns that his good mother is long since dead; he encounters his wicked father, who dies from the shock of his son's accusations. "Contrite, penitent, and humbled," Edmunds lives out the remaining three years of his life in quiet service to the old clergyman who tells his story. Only upon his return does Edmunds come to terms with his guilty past and his parents; there is no suggestion that his time in Australia is meaningful, or that the *location* of his punishment has a reformative influence upon him. Dickens's more elaborate version of a convict's return, twenty-five years later in *Great Expectations*, is even more negative about the possibility of repentance and reform. Though in some ways a better man after Australia, Magwitch is also crazed by his expectations about making a gentleman out of Pip. His vicarious success story is also a failure story, leading of course to his apprehension for returning. Both of Dickens's returned convicts suggest a sociological "return of the repressed" quite at odds with the more numerous, optimistic figures of colonial progress, prosperity, and happiness—the Peggottys and the Micawbers—who populate British fiction from the late 1840s through the 1870s.

The New South Wales passages in *David Copperfield*, as well as the upbeat, pro-emigration propaganda of the many articles about Australia Dickens published in *Household Words* in the 1850s, obviously clash with the theme of the convict's return. They present Australia not as a dreary blank or a wilderness where convicts struggle unsuccessfully to come to terms with their guilt but as a land of promise and social rehabilitation for various basically honest characters who deserve better lives than they can make for themselves in Britain. This is the chief message of the *Household Words* articles where, in contrast to the histories of John Edmunds and Abel Magwitch, the Australian experience reclaims even convicts to lives of freedom and usefulness: "Under the wise . . . government of [Lachlan] Macquarie . . . [all] prudent, industrious settlers, whether free or 'emancipists,' as freed convicts are called, had ample means of independence within their reach . . . every prisoner knew that, if well conducted, he would obtain his liberty, a grant of land, and, perhaps, in the end, become a magistrate, and dine with the Governor!" When in 1821 "free settlers of capital began to arrive in considerable numbers," they were "anxious to receive the benefits of the thieves."[30]

The Australia of *David Copperfield* is a place where ne'er-do-wells at home can do well in the Bush. A similar vision characterizes Edward Bulwer-Lytton's novel of failure in Britain and success in the colonies, *The Caxtons*, published slightly before *David Copperfield* and probably a model for its emigration passages. Virtually bankrupted by the speculations of his wayward Uncle Jack (Micawber's twin in waywardness), Pisistratus Caxton decides to emigrate. He chooses Australia with the approval of his old employer and friend, the politician Trevanion, who tells him: "Yes, how many young men must there be like you, in this Old World, able, intelligent, active, and persevering enough, yet not adapted for success in any of our conventional professions—'mute, inglorious Raleighs.'"[31] Trevanion approves "the sending out not only the paupers, the refuse of an over-populated state, but a large proportion of a better class—fellows full of pith and sap, and exuberant vitality, like yourself, blending . . . a certain portion of the aristocratic with the more democratic element; not turning a rabble loose upon a new soil, but planting in the foreign allotments all the rudiments of a harmonious state, analogous to that in the mother country—not only getting rid of hungry craving mouths, but furnishing vent for a waste surplus of intelligence and courage, which at home is really not needed, and more often comes to ill than to good;—here only menaces our artificial embankments, but there, carried off in an aqueduct, might give life to a desert" (380). Trevanion proceeds to envisage the self-conscious importation into Australia or other colonies "of a constitution and a civilisation similar to our own— with self-developed forms of monarchy and aristocracy." Colonies, he believes, should be rendered aristocratic "and not left a strange motley chaos of struggling democracy—an uncouth livid giant, at which the Frankenstein may well tremble" (380).

If Bulwer perceives the home country as deluged, overloaded with redundant population to the extent that members of the middle and upper-classes are themselves becoming superfluous, Australia is virtually empty, a desert vacuum. Yet he also perceives the Bush in explicitly Arcadian terms, as a realm of potential redemption through direct contact with innocent nature: "A bright, clear, transparent atmosphere . . . a broad and fair river, rolling through wide grassy plains; yonder, far in the distance, stretch away vast forests of evergreen, and gentle slopes break the line of the cloudless horizon; see the pastures, Arcadian with sheep in hundreds and thousands—Thyrsis and Menalcas would have had hard labour to count them, and small time, I fear, for singing songs about Daphne" (520). Of course the Bush is a rough-hewn, pioneering, hard-working Arcadia, but its colonizers—including "Sisty" Caxton—are no less than the "lords of the land . . . and of those numberless flocks; and better still, of a health which an antediluvian might have envied, and of nerves so seasoned with horse-breaking, cattle-driving, fighting with wild blacks—chases from them and after them, for life and for death—that if any passion vex the breast of those kings of the Bushland, fear at least is erased from the list" (520). Theirs is an existence at once heroic and pastoral, warlike and Arcadian, and chases after wild blacks seem not to contradict the innocence of the lords of Bushland.

Into this Arcadian New World, Sisty imports—besides himself—other young ne'er-do-wells who cannot succeed at home but who nonetheless make their fortunes in the wilderness. Instead of a fable of the conversion of the savages, the Australian saga in *The Caxtons* becomes the story of the redemption of the colonists, and the eventual return "home" of at least the main sometime ne'er-do-well, now rich, socially and morally reformed. Accompanying Sisty to Australia is Guy Bolding, a "fast man" at Oxford whose "great fault" has been "his absolute incontinence of money" (394). In Bushland, Bolding's spendthrift tendencies cannot hamper him, and—as his name implies—he makes a wonderfully brave, cheerful pioneer. Sisty also takes "the son of our old shepherd" and his wife, the only woman who accompanies them into the wilderness. And he takes Will Peterson, a skillful poacher known as "Will o' the Wisp," who escapes a life of crime and imprisonment at home by emigrating and making a success on the grand scale as a "pastoralist." Miles Square, sickly factory worker with dangerously democratic opinions, also makes the journey and discovers in the colonial setting health and a completely contrary set of political values. Miles, too, succeeds "first as a shepherd, next as a superintendent, and finally, on saving money, as a land-owner" (400). Bulwer's former Chartist eventually writes "a little pamphlet, published at Sydney, on the *Sanctity of the Rights of Property*" (400). And although a pacifist at home, Miles, declares Sisty, "was no sooner in possession of a comfortable log homestead, than he defended it with uncommon gallantry against an attack of the aborigines, whose right to the soil was, to say the least of it, as good as his claim to my uncle's acres" (400).

The hardest case in *The Caxtons* in terms of social rehabilitation is Sisty's cousin Vivian, who has tried to elope with Trevanion's daughter Fanny. He is thus similar to Steerforth in *David Copperfield*; perhaps because of the "gipsy" blood in his veins, Vivian comes as close to being a villain as anyone in the novel. While Sisty and Bolding take care of the sheep-herding side of their joint enterprise in Bushland, Vivian manages the cattle-raising side, which fits his wilder character. Bolding settles down to life as a prosperous pastoralist, while Sisty—once he has made his fortune—returns to resume the life of a gentleman in England. But Vivian is rewarded for his reformed behavior with a different sort of colonial ending: he takes a commission in the army and dies in combat in India, a scapegrace ultimately redeemed by heroism on the battlefield.

And so the poor are redeemed in the colonies by being made rich (through hard work, of course). The morally suspect are redeemed by new opportunities and new responsibilities. The sickly and sedentary are redeemed by wholesome, outdoor living. The wild, improvident, and reckless are redeemed by heroic action and, as in Vivian's case, heroic deaths. All those who are superfluous or redundant at home can discover roles for themselves in the colonies, fighting the wild animals and the wild blacks, taming the wilderness, turning deserts into Arcadias. Numerous characters in Victorian fiction experience secular rebirths in the Bush; even convicts can strike it rich and be redeemed, though they generally must stay in the land of their redemption. Those convicts who return to Britain—John Edmunds, Abel Magwitch, John Armstrong (alias Altamont) in Thackeray's *Pendennis*, among others—remain convicts whether they have completed their sentences or not, shadowed by crimes and guilt they cannot shake off.

After gold was discovered in Australia in 1851, Eldorado merged with Arcadia as part of the mythic version of colonial experience "down under." To a certain extent, "gold fever" reinforced the success-story pattern established in *David Copperfield* and *The Caxtons*, but Dickens and Bulwer had insisted that plain, hard work was fundamental to the pastoral redemption of the Bush. The gold rush engendered a strike-it-rich-quick mentality that undercut the theme of the reformative power of labor. Charles Reade imitated the plot of *The Caxtons* but also mixed Arcadia with Eldorado in his play *Gold!* (1853) and his novel *It Is Never too Late to Mend* (1856). Henry Kingsley emigrated to Australia in 1853 hoping to strike it rich in the gold fields, only to return disappointed to Britain five years later. He nevertheless continued to believe that, though "the new country [was] the most wonderfully scentless cesspool for a vast quantity of nameless rubbish, convicted and unconvicted," it also "gave an opening for really honest, upright fellows."³² And he turned his experience to literary success of sorts by writing a highly conventional colonial success story, *The Recollections of Geoffrey Hamlyn* (1859), part pastoral and part treasure hunt, which contains "every known cliché of Australian life" (Lansbury, 119). Similarly Anthony Trollope, whose youngest son Frederic had emigrated but failed to make good as a sheep farmer, insisted that Australia was a place where failures in Britain could hope to succeed. Alaric, the embezzler in *The Three Clerks* (1858), serves time in jail in Britain but afterward goes to Australia to begin a new life. And the protagonist of *John Caldigate* (1879) strikes it rich in the gold fields, though after his return to Britain he falls into difficulties with the law. In between Trollope wrote an Australian Christmas story for *The Graphic, Harry Heathcote of Gangoil* (1873), in which the young hero makes good as a sheep farmer.

Despite his son Frederic's struggles, Trollope clearly believed—with Dickens, Bulwer, Reade, and many others—that Australia was a land of potential prosperity for all who could not prosper at home. In *Australia and New Zealand* (1873), Trollope declared:

> The life of the artisan there is certainly a better life than he can find at home. He not only lives better, with more comfortable appurtenances around him, but he fills a higher position in reference to those around

him, and has a greater consideration paid to him than would have fallen to his lot at home. He gets a better education for his children than he can in England, and may have a more assured hope of seeing them rise above himself, and has less cause to fear that they shall fall infinitely lower. Therefore I would say to any young man whose courage is high and whose intelligence is not below par, that he should not be satisfied to remain at home; but should come out . . . and try to win a higher lot and a better fortune than the old country can afford to give him.[33]

When Vivian de Caxton wonders if it is "from the outcasts of the work-house, the prison, and the transport-ship, that a second Rome is to arise," Sisty replies: "There is something in this new soil—in the labour it calls forth, in the hope it inspires, in the sense of property, which I take to be the core of social morals—that expedites the work of redemption with marvellous rapidity. Take them altogether, whatever their origin, or whatever brought them hither, they are a fine, manly, frank-hearted race, these colonists now!" (534).

iii

Not all accounts of life in the Bush were as sanguine as those in *David Copperfield*, *The Caxtons*, and *Geoffry Hamlyn*. Dickens himself offered a different vision in his stories of returned convicts; and the occasional, usually fleeting references to aborigines or wild blacks in novels with Australian settings point to an actual racism and violence that were anything but Arcadian. At best, aborigines appear in faithful servant roles, like Jacky in Reade's *It Is Never too Late to Mend*. More often they appear as savages to be chased and gunned down, as they do in the brief allusions in *The Caxtons*. Samuel Sidney, author of *Sidney's Australian Handbook*, which Bulwer quotes, and also of many of the articles on Australia which Dickens published in *Household Words*, believed that, if it proved difficult to gun down aborigines, poison might do the trick (Lansbury, 64). In several of Sidney's pieces for Dickens, white pastoralists are harassed by war parties of aborigines and of course defend themselves manfully (in these stories the aborigines always attack first).

The narrator of "Two Letters from Australia," published in *Household Words* in 1850, explains the only way to deal with "the Blacks": "Although I had heard that kindness was of no avail, I never could be brought to believe it, and determined, therefore, to do all in my power to propitiate them by trifling gifts, kind treatment, and avoiding everything that could hurt their feelings. It was of no use; no kindness—nothing, in fact—will teach them the law of *meum* and *tuum* but the white man's gun and his superior courage."[34] After describing several bloody encounters, in which one Irishman and perhaps forty or fifty blacks are slain, the narrator concludes with a vision of the future civilization of the Bush in which the aborigines clearly have no place.

> To detail all the skirmishes . . . with the Blacks for the eighteen months which ensued, would only weary you. Where, little more than three years ago, ours was the only station in this direction, being five miles beyond any other, there are now stations formed a hundred miles below us, and even ladies grace the river forty miles down, one of them married to an old school-fellow of ours, viz., Brougham, nephew of Lord Brougham. Among other diversions, I have been employing myself in making a flower-garden, for . . . I think their contemplation, and . . . cultivation, has a humanising, or . . . civilising effect on the mind, such as I can assure you we require in the Bush. (480)

Sidney believed, with many others, that the aborigines were a "dying race," doomed to extinction by contact with a "higher race." This extinction might happen rapidly or only gradually, depending on whether the higher race used direct violence or permitted the aborigines to retreat into the desert and die off at their own pace. That Dickens shared Sidney's genocidal attitudes can be seen not merely from the articles he accepted for *Household Words* but in Dickens's own writings—for example, in his "Noble Savage" essay for *The Examiner* and in his reactions to the Indian Mutiny of 1857 and the Jamaica Rebellion of 1865.

"'Aborigines' are a mistake."[35] So declared the first great writer in Australian literary history, Marcus Clarke, in 1868. Of course it is debatable whether Clarke, schoolboy friend of Gerard Manley Hopkins and emigrant to New South Wales in 1863, was more genuinely Australian than, say, Henry Kingsley. But Clarke's bitterly ironic realism offers a vision of Australian history far more clear-sighted—and therefore distinctly less Arcadian—than that of any of the writers I have mentioned so far. When Clarke called the aborigines a mistake, he was being ironic and stating his actual opinion, for he too believed that the primitive peoples of Australasia were doomed to extinction. A religious skeptic, he apparently considered it a waste of time to try to convert the aborigines to Christianity, in part because they were racially so inferior that they could not understand the missionaries' message. When fighting broke out in New Zealand in the 1860s between white settlers and Maoris, moreover, Clarke thought about joining up to do battle against "the savages."

Clarke's attitude toward the blacks is pitiless, racist, but also utterly without illusions about the violence and bloodshed entailed by the civilizing process. In this respect, he seems much closer to Conrad than to Bulwer: "I regard the occupation of New Zealand by the British as a gross swindle from beginning to end. . . . [But] having got the land, established ourselves there, and built churches and public houses, and so on, we would be fools not to use our best endeavours to keep [it]. To do this in peace, the Maoris must be exterminated. . . . To make treaties and talk bunkum is perfectly useless; they must be stamped out and utterly annihilated. If England will send out a sensible man with a genius for slaughter, New Zealand should be grateful. Free fire and sword for six months, and a 'smoking-out' or two would speedily put matters to rights" (446).

If there is no fighting with doomed savages in Clarke's great novel, *For the Term of His Natural Life* (1874), it is simply because most of the action takes place after the early 1830s, by which time the majority of the Tasmans had been exterminated or rounded up and relocated on Flinders Island. In one of his articles on the convict settlement at Port Arthur, Clarke speaks of an 1830 "war of extermination, known as the Black War. The settlers banded themselves together, drew a cordon of armed men across the island, drove the natives to the extremity of a narrow neck of land known as Tasman's Peninsula, and slaughtered them at their leisure. The capabilities of this place [for a convict settlement] struck [Colonel] Arthur at once."[36] But though black savagery is not a problem in Clarke's novel, white savagery is another matter. Just as Clarke will tolerate no bunkum about the extinction of the Tasmans, the Maoris, or the aborigines, so he will tolerate no sentimentality with regard to the convict history of Australia. The administrators of the convict settlements in Clarke's Tasmania include no idealistic rehabilitationists or conversionists. As the brutal Lt. Maurice Frere says, "We must treat brutes like brutes" (101). When the alcoholic, secretly freethinking Rev. James North talks conversion, Frere says it is "no use preaching to stones" (405). In Clarke's world of unredeemable convicts and sadistic guards, the opposite of conversion—"breaking a man's spirit"—works much more effectively. When the Reverend North speaks to the novel's hero, Rufus Dawes, "of hope, of release, of repentance and redemption," Dawes laughs in his face. "'Who's to redeem me?' he said, expressing his thoughts in phraseology that to ordinary folks might seem blasphemous. 'It would take a Christ to die again to save such as I'" (408).

The settlement of Tasmania by convicts and their warders goes on accordingly: "All that the vilest and most bestial of human creatures could invent and practise, was in this unhappy country invented and practised without restraint and without shame" (90). The result is a colony which, even among the military and emancipists, is indeed a sort of moral sewer: "Of the social condition of these people . . . it is impossible to speak without astonishment. According to the recorded testimony of many respectable persons . . . the profligacy of the settlers was notorious. Drunkenness was a prevailing vice. Even children were to be seen in the streets intoxicated. . . . As for the condition of the prisoner population, that, indeed, is indescribable" (90). The condition of the prisoner population in Tasmania in the 1820s may be indescribable, but the power of Clarke's remarkable novel lies partly in its detailed, relentless, documentary description of life in the convict settlements at Macquarie Harbour, Port Arthur, and Norfolk Island. Its power lies also in its dramatic reversals and questionings of the motifs of conversion, rehabilitation, and the civilizing process which characterize the novels of Bulwer, Dickens, Reade, and Kingsley. Sometimes hailed as the first major work of Australian literature, the tormented life of convict Rufus Dawes can be read as a historical novel, but to British versions of that genre, which celebrate the epic glories of discovery, conquest, and colonization—for example, Charles Kingsley's *Westward Ho!*—*His Natural Life* offers nearly the antithesis. Reading the narrative of the mutineers of the prison-brig *Osprey*, Sylvia Vickers, the chief figure of innocence in the novel besides Dawes himself, exclaims: "Oh, how strangely must the world have been civilised, that this most lovely corner of it must needs be set apart as a place of banishment for the monsters that civilisation had brought forth and bred!" (260).

Sylvia thus expresses the paradox that Clarke's novel, in its graphic depictions of brutalization and violence, presents from beginning to end. The cannibals in Clarke's tale are not blackskinned savages, to be slaughtered by white conquistadors or converted to civilization by white missionaries. They are instead escaped convicts, the first white settlers of Tasmania and New South Wales. Whereas Dickens only toys with the idea of cannibalism in Magwitch's threat to Pip that "your heart and your liver shall be tore out, roasted and ate," Clarke offers in graphic detail the story of Gabbett and eight other escapees who murder and eat each other one by one until only Gabbett is left, a crazed, bloodthirsty monster alone with his axe. A boat's crew landing on a wild part of the Tasmanian coast in search of fresh water discovers "a gaunt and blood-stained man, clad in tattered yellow [convict's garb], who carried on his back an axe and a bundle. When the sailors came within sight of him, he made signs to them to approach, and opening his bundle with much ceremony offered them some of its contents. Filled with horror at what the maniac displayed, they seized and bound him. At Hobart Town he was recognized as the only survivor of the nine desperadoes who had escaped from Colonel Arthur's 'Natural Penitentiary'" (360).

Ultimately no one escapes from the penitentiary world of Clarke's Tasmania, where the civilizing process seems to reverse itself. Combining the melodrama of sensation fiction with the unrelenting documentary thoroughness of French naturalism, Clarke produces a story of fate and injustice which has genuine tragic power.[37] The dehumanized colony of convicts and sadistic warders seems an antisociety, the exact shadow-image of the bright, prosperous, liberal England that Rufus Dawes leaves behind. Clarke's description of the "barracoon" or slave-hold on the prison ship bearing Dawes to Tasmania suggests that an entire Dickensian slumload of criminals and social riffraff is being exported to the Antipodes. The barracoon contains a "hideous phantasmagoria of shifting limbs and faces which moved through the evil-smelling twilight of this terrible prison-house."

> Callot might have drawn it, Dante might have suggested it. . . . Old men, young men, and boys, stalwart burglars and highway robbers, slept side by side with wizened pickpockets or cunning-featured area-sneaks. The forger occupied the same berth with the body-snatcher. The man of education learned strange secrets of house-breakers' craft, and the vulgar ruffian of St. Giles took lessons of self-control from the keener intellect of the professional swindler. The fraudulent clerk and the flash "cracksman" interchanged experiences. . . . The fast shopboy, whose love of fine company and high living had brought him to this pass, had shaken off the first shame that was on him, and listened eagerly to the narratives of successful vice that fell so glibly from the lips of his older companions. (36)

In such company, ideas of redemption and conversion seem the merest hypocrisy. The term barracoon suggests that convict transportation is the slave trade in reverse: now British men, women, and children rather than Africans are being shipped off in chains to do the dirty work of stone-breaking and cultivating the wilderness.

To the convicts in the barracoon, "to be transported seemed no such uncommon fate" (36). On the contrary, crime takes on the appearance of shared social rebellion: "Society was the common foe, and magistrates, jailers, and parsons, were the natural prey of all noteworthy mankind.

Only fools were honest, only cowards kissed the rod, and failed to meditate revenge on that world of respectability which had wronged them. Each new comer was one more recruit to the ranks of ruffianism, and not a man penned in that reeking den of infamy but became a sworn hater of law, order, and 'free-men'" (36). The opposite of redemption or conversion—their complete dehumanization—is the fate of most of those thrown into such a living hell. Even the most innocent man or child, "herded with the foulest of mankind, with all imaginable depths of blasphemy and indecency sounded hourly in his sight and hearing . . . lost his self-respect, and became what his jailers took him to be—a wild beast to be locked under bolts and bars, lest he should break out and tear them" (36).

Clarke reverses Dickens's theme in *Oliver Twist*, the incorruptibility of human nature. But Dickens's treatment of that theme is ambiguous and contradictory. Though Oliver and Nancy, at least in the deepest part of her being, remain uncorrupted by the world of slums and thieves which imprisons them, the thieves themselves—Sikes, Fagin, Charlie Bates, the Artful Dodger—are figures of degradation and guilt. After murdering Nancy, Sikes is clearly beyond redemption; for the child criminals there is at least the hope of a better future. Charlie, "appalled by Sikes's crime," decides that "an honest life" is "the best" and takes to the countryside, where, "from being a farmer's drudge, and a carrier's lad, he is now the merriest young grazier in all Northamptonshire" (410). Perhaps such a pastoral redemption awaits the Dodger, too, though he seems unrepentant as he is sentenced to transportation.

A different fate attends Clarke's juvenile convicts, as we learn from the case of Peter Brown at Port Arthur, "a refractory little thief . . . aged twelve years" who jumped off a cliff "and drowned himself in full view of the constables" (308). One of the warders muses about this "unlucky accident": "These 'jumpings off' had become rather frequent lately, and Burgess was enraged at one happening this particular day. If he could by any possibility have brought the corpse of poor little Peter Brown to life again, he would have soundly whipped it for its impertinence" (309). Burgess is incensed mainly because visitors are present, Captain Frere and his wife Sylvia. Frere is about to take over the convict station at Port Arthur; he asks to see Peter Brown's record:

> 20th November, disorderly conduct, 12 lashes. 24th November, insolence to hospital attendant, diet reduced. 4th December, stealing cap from another prisoner, 12 lashes. 15th December, absenting himself at roll call,

two days' cells. 23d December, insolence and insubordination, two days' cells. 8th January, insolence and insubordination, 12 lashes. 20th January, insolence and insubordination, 12 lashes. 22nd February, insolence and insubordination, 12 lashes and one week's solitary. 6th March, insolence and insubordination, 20 lashes. (309)

And then Peter Brown jumps off the cliff. The narrator comments: "Just so! The magnificent system starved and tortured a child of twelve until he killed himself. That was the way of it."

Nor is that the end of it. The narrator continues, in a vein of bitter condemnation of institutionalized cruelty and injustice that sounds like Dickens but goes much farther because it suggests that, from such torment, unfairness, and hypocrisy there can be no redemption: "'Suffer little children to come unto Me, and forbid them not, for of such is the Kingdom of Heaven,' said, or is reported to have said, the Founder of our Established Religion. Of such it seemed that a large number of Honourable Gentlemen, together with Her Majesty's faithful Commons in Parliament assembled, had done their best to create a Kingdom of Hell" (309–10).

As in works of naturalistic fiction, so in Clarke's novel the "free" characters are themselves bound, imprisoned by their own weaknesses and by the narrow brutality of early Tasmanian society. In a paradoxical way the freest character of all—besides the innocent Sylvia—is the convict-hero Rufus Dawes, though from start to finish he is the victim or prisoner of circumstance. The paradox arises in part from his innocence, in part from his resistance to all attempts *either* to break his spirit *or* to convert and redeem him. Wrongly accused of the murder and robbery of his father, Dawes serves out his life sentence as the archetypal victim of injustice. Until the very end of the story, after years of the living hell of Tasmanian imprisonment, he experiences only the redemption that comes to him through stern survival and the consciousness of innocence. Even the end of the story, moreover, which holds out to Rufus the hope of escape and a new life in another country with Sylvia, avoids the easy way out. Rufus and Sylvia recognize their love for each other in melodramatic fashion, at the very last moment, and they perish in the cyclone that sinks their ship a few miles off shore. The storm that overwhelms them with darkness and death, Clarke suggests, is analogous to the circumstances that overwhelmed them in life.

> At day-dawn on the morning after the storm, the rays of the rising sun fell upon an object which floated on the surface of the water not far from where the schooner had foundered.

This object was a portion of the mainmast head of the *Lady Franklin*, and entangled in the rigging were two corpses—a man and a woman. The arms of the man were clasped round the body of the woman, and her head lay on her breast.

The Prison Island appeared but as a long, low line on the distant horizon. The tempest was over. As the sun rose higher the air grew balmy, the ocean placid; and, golden in the rays of the new risen morning, the wreck and its burden drifted out to sea. (466)

From the beginning, the myths of Australia were double, contradictory: Arcadian redemption versus social damnation. These polar extremes seem almost to parody the general contradictions of imperialist ideology, as also of penal servitude: salvation through conquest, reformation through bondage. Given the rigors of Australian climate and geography that free settlers as well as convicts had to struggle against, and given also the bloody facts of racial extermination, the Arcadian myth was impossible to sustain. But the other myth, over which, as Robert Hughes points out, Thomas Hobbes and the Marquis de Sade presided, was impossible to accept. For generations, "convict history was ignored in schools and little taught in universities. . . . An unstated bias rooted deep in Australian life seemed to wish that 'real' Australian history had begun with Australian respectability—with the flood of money from gold and wool, the opening of the continent, the creation of an Australian middle class. [But] behind the bright diorama of Australia Felix lurked the convicts, some 160,000 of them, clanking their fetters in the penumbral darkness. . . . They were statistics, absences and finally embarrassments" (Hughes, xi).

In metaphor, at least, the pollution of an entire continent, the "down under" of the world, began with the debarkation of 736 white convicts and 294 white sailors and soldiers on the Australian coast toward the end of January 1788. Out of sight, out of mind: that was one of the results wished for by the advocates of transportation. But the convicts were also colonists and empire-builders, although the first governor of Botany Bay, Captain Arthur Phillip, declared: "I would not wish convicts to lay the foundation of an empire" (quoted by Hughes, 68). Jeremy Bentham, for one, thought that convicts should be incarcerated in Britain rather than transported, locked up in prisons based on his panopticon design where they could be kept under proper surveillance, punished, and reformed. He did not believe that the "excrementitious mass" of criminals should be "projected . . . as far out of sight as possible."[38] Not that he had any concern for what they might do to the native Australians who, as he declared in *Panopticon versus New South Wales* (1802), were only "a set of brutes in human shape—the very dregs even of savage life" (182). But removed from panoptical inspection, Bentham argued, transported convicts would only go from bad to worse: "Colonizing-transportation-system: characteristic feature of it, radical incapacity of being combined with any efficient system of inspection. Penitentiary system: characteristic feature of it, in its original state, frequent and regular inspection; in its extraordinary and improved [panoptical] state, that principle of management carried to such a degree of perfection as till then had never been reached . . ." (Bentham, 175).

For Bentham, the chief difference between the panoptical penitentiary and the prison colonies in Australia was the amount of disciplinary surveillance or power each generated. Whereas Botany Bay seemed immensely distant from any proper exercise of power (but not distant enough to prevent the return of the transported), the panopticon would be, in essence, an ideal colony, completely mapped and visible, with the warden as ruler and the prisoners his totally dominated subjects. The panopticon offers the clearest expression of that utopian—or dystopian—daydream shared by all of the social reformers whom Bentham influenced, of a world entirely penetrated, illuminated, and governed by the gaze of rational justice and science, a prison from which there could be no escape. In contrast, in New South Wales, Bentham believed, the reformation of criminals was at best erratic because not subject to the absolute inspection and control he deemed necessary. Indeed, Bentham contended, the evidence from Australia showed that "the number of the unreformed is to that of . . . reformed characters, as a hundred or so to one. A bettermost sort of rogue—a man in whom on any occasion the smallest degree of confidence can be reposed, appears in that country to be . . . a scarcer animal than a *black swan*" (Bentham, 178).

Those who were to be [transported] belonged neither to the list of souls to be saved, nor to the list of moral beings. On these principles, how the people thus sent thither behaved while there, was a point which, so long as they did but stay *there*, or, at any rate, did not come back *here*, was not worth thinking about. Such was the religion, such the morality, which presided over the design and execution of the picture of industry and reformation in New South Wales. (Bentham, 183)

"The Hhareem" (ca. 1850). Painting by John Frederick Lewis, R.A. Courtesy the Victoria & Albert Museum.

5. The New Crusades

Wake! For the Sun, who scatter'd into flight
The Stars before him from the Field of Night,
    Drives Night along with them from Heav'n, and strikes
The Sultan's Turret with a Shaft of Light.
                    —*The Rubaiyat of Omar Khayyam*

As an adult Thackeray thought about visiting the land of his birth but never did so. In the summer of 1844, however, he went on a tour of the Near East arranged by the Peninsular and Oriental Company and wrote about it in *Notes of a Journey from Cornhill to Grand Cairo*. In the guise of Michael Angelo Titmarsh, Thackeray as tourist pares the "mysterious Orient" down to size. "The life of the East is a life of brutes," says the unromantic Titmarsh, sounding like Podsnap; "the much-maligned Orient, I am confident, has not been maligned near enough; for the good reason that none of us can tell the amount of horrible sensuality practised there."[1]

Nevertheless, like many British travelers before and since, Titmarsh-Thackeray indulges happily in many of the sensual pleasures of the East: he is both mildly scared and thrilled by his first Turkish bath; he enjoys smoking hookahs and narghiles; he is smitten by the numerous picturesque views of minarets, bazaars, and dancing dervishes; he dines well, both on shipboard and in port; and though he is unawed by the Pyramids in Egypt, he waxes suitably sanctimonious amid the shrines of Jerusalem: "With shame and humility one looks towards the spot . . . where the great yearning heart of the Saviour interceded for all our race; and whence the bigots and traitors of His day led Him away to kill Him!" (200).

The 1840s saw the advent of the modern tourist industry and Thackeray was one of many Britons who in that decade flocked to the Holy Land and the Pyramids. (Though it was not until the 1860s that

Cook's Tours began plying the waters of the Nile, Thomas Cook first ventured into the tourist business in 1841.) On board his P&O steamer Thackeray found that all the British excursionists were reading Alexander Kinglake's *Eothen*, just published—a book addressed to another eastern traveler, Eliot Warburton, whose *The Crescent and the Cross* was also published in 1844. The redoubtable Harriet Martineau took ship with friends in 1846 to the East, publishing *Eastern Life, Present and Past* in 1848—a volume R. K. Webb describes as containing "travels and a torrent of philosophizing," both utilitarian and Unitarian.[2] If contemporary travelogues were not enough, romantically inclined readers could fall back on Byron's *Childe Harold's Pilgrimage*, and the religious had numerous works such as the Rev. Thomas Hartwell Horne's *The Biblical Keepsake; or, Landscape Illustrations of the Most Remarkable Places Mentioned in the Holy Scriptures* (1835).[3]

The East, and particularly the Near East, was for British writers preeminently a land of romance, evoking responses often based as much on *The Arabian Nights* as on contemporary information. As Thackeray understood, Titmarsh's chief modern rival for shaping public attitudes toward the Orient was not Kinglake but Byron. Though Byronism was ostensibly antagonistic toward imperialism, several later writers—Benjamin Disraeli and Richard Burton, for example—combined Byronic with imperialist attitudes in writing about the Near East. As home to three of the world's major religions, moreover, the Near East was obviously a focus for much religious rivalry with nationalistic overtones. As the site of the earliest known civilizations, it was the focus for intense archaeological rivalry, often with nationalistic implications also. And, fixated on the harems and veiled women of various Muslim societies, the Victorians found the Orient's alleged sensuality both abhorrent and endlessly fascinating.[4]

It was, however, as much the shaky political circumstances of the Near East as any of these factors which contributed to its romantic aura. From Napoleon's invasion of Egypt in 1798, through the Crimean War of 1853–56, down to World War I, Gallipoli, and the exploits of Lawrence of Arabia, the Near East was a hotbed of intricate diplomatic maneuvering, espionage, and frequent war. Decrepit though it may have been, the Ottoman Empire was the chief buffer between Russia and India; through its domains lay the vital overland routes to Britain's own oriental empire. The lands between Russia and India thus became, inevitably, pawns in the Great Game in Asia. Successive British governments, overcoming religious considerations, strove to prop up and "reform" the tottering sultanate at Constantinople. These diplomatic maneuverings were part of the context for Disraeli's purchase of Suez Canal shares in 1875, the furor over "Bulgarian atrocities" the year after, Gladstone's reluctant take-over of Egypt in 1882, and the eventual imperialization of other parts of North Africa and the Near East. The realities of political struggle often evoked clandestine, temporizing, or Machiavellian actions rather than those suggested by the first crusades. Nevertheless, a crusading spirit—usually Tory or conservative, occasionally evangelical, sometimes even utilitarian and radical, but always at least implicitly imperialist—informs most nineteenth-century British writing that took the Near East for its subject. [5]

i

Titmarsh-Thackeray, though not inclined to philosophize or to evangelize, still does plenty of moralizing in his Biedermeier way. He is especially hard on Jews, whom he sees as the modern representatives of the "bigots and traitors" who crucified Jesus. Otherwise, however, he treats with some latitude and amused sympathy the "orientals" he encounters—Greeks, Turks, Syrians, Palestinians. They are inferior races, no doubt, but less inferior than the Jews. At one point Titmarsh-Thackeray even goes so far as to assert that "in the Crusades my wicked sympathies have always been with the Turks" (166). Sir Walter Scott, he says, "has led all the world astray" concerning the difference between Saladin and Richard Coeur de Lion: "As far as I can get at the authentic story, Saladin is a pearl of refinement compared to the brutal beef-eating Richard," and the Turks "seem to me the best Christians of the two; more humane, less brutally presumptuous about their own merits, and more generous in esteeming their neighbours" (166). This is Thackeray in a Dickensian mode, subverting the medievalism of reactionary celebrators of "the good old days"—Scott, Carlyle, Disraeli and his Young England comrades who were making their mark in the 1840s. Thackeray's travelogue itself, like many another, can be read as an ironic inversion of the crusading legend made famous by Scott in *Ivanhoe* and *The Talisman*. Instead of a red cross knight in shining armor riding forth to do battle against the infidel Saracen, the modern English gentleman orders his valet to pack his trunk and, armed only with an umbrella, boards the P&O steamer bound for the not-so-mysterious East.

The unromantic Titmarsh has no particular reason to mount a crusade, for the P&O Company will take care of the crusading business as it takes care of the tourist business. Perhaps there is something regrettable about the antiheroic ease of modern transportation, but the machinery that brings Titmarsh to the Pyramids is the same machinery that brings civilization, automatically and apolitically, to the barbarians. "Wherever the steamboat touches the shore adventure retreats into the interior, and what is called romance vanishes," says Titmarsh; but this is a small price to pay for the spread of civilization. He is pleased to observe that in Muslim countries "cursing and insulting of Giaours" or unbelievers is almost obsolete (136). Though a few mosques are difficult to get into, "strangers may enter scores . . . without molestation." The "infidel Turk" has learned the commercial value of tourism, and both the sultan at Constantinople and his supposed subordinate, the pasha at Cairo, know the political value of British protection. The influence of modern Europe sweeps like a fresh breeze through the domains of the Sublime Porte. "The paddle-wheel is the great conqueror. Wherever the captain cries, 'Stop her,' Civilization stops, and lands in the ship's boat, and makes a permanent acquaintance with the savages on shore." This inevitable modernization leads Titmarsh to allude again to the crusades: "Whole hosts of crusaders have passed and died, and butchered here in vain. But to manufacture European iron into pikes and helmets was a waste of metal: in the shape of piston-rods and furnace-pokers it is irresistible; and I think an allegory might be made showing how much stronger commerce is than chivalry, and finishing with a grand image of Mahomet's crescent being extinguished in Fulton's boiler" (137).

Progress through commerce is the axiom of Thackeray's free trade imperialism: steam conquers all. In Constantinople, Titmarsh repeats the lesson when he sees a "Turkish lady drive up to Sultan Achmet's mosque *in a brougham*." Startled by this sharp juxtaposition of ancient and modern, oriental and western, he concludes "that the knell of the Turkish dominion is rung; that the European spirit and institutions once admitted can never be rooted out again; and that the scepticism prevalent amongst the higher orders must descend ere very long to the lower; and the cry of the muezzin from the mosque become a mere ceremony" (160). Thackeray here mixes a perception widespread in the nineteenth century of the political decrepitude of the Ottoman Empire with another, much less credible forecast of the demise of Islam. The Ottoman Empire finally crumbled during World War I (its official death-knell was the

Treaty of Sèvres in 1920). Far from disappearing, however, Islam has experienced numerous revivals, especially in Near Eastern countries suffering from the pangs of modernization or westernization—names for the same revolutionary process.

Paeans to steam and modern commerce occur throughout early Victorian literature, but in these passages Thackeray is specifically echoing one of the primary themes of *Eothen*. In his opening chapter Kinglake presents a comic illustration of the difficulties of cross-cultural understanding between a British traveler and "the Pasha of So-and-So" who is "particularly interested in the vast progress which has been made in the application of steam."[6] The Pasha "remarked upon the gigantic results of our manufacturing industry; showed that he possessed considerable knowledge . . . of the constitution of the [East India] Company; and expressed a lively admiration of the many sterling qualities for which the people of England are distinguished" (15). The actual conversation between hypothetical traveler and Pasha, through the mediation of the inevitable dragoman or translator, meanders in strange directions. When the Pasha makes various whizzing and whirring noises, the dragoman says that he means that "the English talk by wheels and by steam." The traveler responds that this is an "exaggeration" but asks the dragoman to "say that the English really have carried machinery to great perfection" and that "whenever we have any disturbances to put down, even at two or three hundred miles from London, we can send troops by the thousand to the scene of action in a few hours" (17). The dragoman then translates: "Whenever the Irish, or the French, or the Indians rebel against the English, whole armies . . . are dropped into a mighty chasm called Euston Square, and in the biting of a cartridge they rise up again in . . . Dublin, or Paris, or Delhi, and utterly exterminate the enemies of England from the face of the earth." To which embellished translation the Pasha responds: "I know it—I know all . . . my mind comprehends locomotives. The armies of the English ride upon vapours of boiling cauldrons, and their horses are flaming coals! Whir! whir! all by wheels!—whiz! whiz! all by steam!" Then, as if steam were not miracle enough, the Pasha adds the related miracle of British imperialism in the East: "The ships of the English swarm like flies; their printed calicoes cover the whole earth, and by the side of their swords the blades of Damascus are blades of grass. All India is but an item in the Ledger-books of the Merchants, whose lumber-rooms are filled with ancient thrones! Whir! whir! all by wheels!—whiz! whiz! all by steam!" (18). The Pasha, of course, is not far from the truth, but the traveler fears that his host may be getting a wrong impression: "These foreigners are always fancying that we have nothing but ships, and railways, and East India Companies." He therefore asks the dragoman to "tell the Pasha that our rural districts deserve his attention, and that even within the last two hundred years there has been an evident improvement in the culture of the turnip" (19). But the lesson is clear—steam rather than turnips is the key to British power and glory. Both Kinglake and Thackeray traversed the Near East fully confident that the machinery then beginning to transport flocks of tourists was also the machinery of British imperial expansion and the ultimate conversion to civilization of the subjects of pasha and sultan.

Barbarism yields to steam power, Thackeray believes, but as it does so one source of romanticism disappears. "Now that dark Hassan sits in his divan and drinks champagne, and Selim has a French watch, and Zuleika perhaps takes Morrison's pills, Byronism becomes absurd instead of sublime, and is only a foolish expression of cockney wonder" (136). Titmarsh seems just as happy to dispense with Byronism as with barbarism, although for many Victorian readers no oriental traveler was more influential than Byron. Thackeray's Biedermeier imperialism is clearly at odds with Byron's celebrations of the wild, fiercely independent Albanians and Greeks. *Childe Harold* and the Turkish tales almost seem to celebrate a barbarism identified not with oriental despotism but with the desire for personal liberty and national independence from empire. Byron's legendary death at Missolonghi in 1824, hoping to liberate Greece from Ottoman rule, made him a martyr for romantic nationalism—and so for anti-imperialism. Childe Harold and Don Juan both traversed the Near East as enemies to imperialism, whether Turkish, Napoleonic, Austrian, or British.

> Imperial anarchs, doubling human woes!
> GOD! was thy globe ordain'd for such to win and lose?[7]

In Greece, Childe Harold pleads for the liberation of its "hereditary bondsmen" from the Turks; at Constantinople he envisages the downfall of the Ottoman Empire:

> The city won for Allah from the Giaour,
> The Giaour from Othman's race again may wrest;
> And the Serai's impenetrable tower
> Receive the fiery Frank. (2:77)

The fiery Frank, one infers, will come as a liberator rather than as a new imperializer of the sultan's domains.[8]

Although the poet's image as a nationalist freedom-fighter became widely popular, for many of Byron's early readers his anti-imperialist message probably did not extend to British territory. Much romantic writing about the Near East, moreover, particularly historical writing dealing with chivalry and the crusades, offers a very different pattern, based on a righteous invasion of the Holy Land by western knights in shining armor, seeking to recapture Jerusalem for Christendom. Nineteenth-century medievalism could obviously serve as a vehicle for a wide range of political values, from Carlyle's Hero-Worship to William Morris's anarchistic Marxism. Nevertheless, writing focused on chivalry and the crusades often carries an imperialist message directed toward the Near East and the Holy Land. In that inspiration to gentlemanly valor and Tory medievalism, for instance, *The Broad Stone of Honour* (1828–29), Sir Kenelm Digby asks: "Who can read the account . . . of the entrance of the Crusaders into Jerusalem without emotion?" He declares that "we have our honourable East India Company; and the Dutch have their honourable companies to monopolize the riches and luxury of the East," but this is mere vainglory without the sacred ideals of "piety and honour" which carried "the hoary Palmer and the Red-cross knight" to Jerusalem.[9]

One might dismiss Digby as a mere romantic enthusiast for the Middle Ages, were it not that similar attitudes toward chivalry and the crusades are evident in Scott's medieval novels. Of the treatment of chivalry in *Ivanhoe*, Dwight Culler says that "contrary to popular impression, it is a very mixed report."[10] The reason is, however, that Scott has it both ways, presenting chivalry as the highest type of personal and national idealism while also suggesting that Europe has progressed well beyond the barbarous times when knights mowed each other down in the lists. *Ivanhoe* is one of many nineteenth-century texts to juxtapose the chivalrous values of honor and war against the prudent virtues of peace and domestic harmony. Readers with the correct gentlemanly spirit will recognize that Rebecca's objections to knightly combat are of a piece with her defense of her unwarlike Jewish "race," and that Ivanhoe's praise of chivalry goes to the heart of a "useless" but nonetheless world-conquering heroism:

> Thou wouldst quench the pure light of chivalry [says Ivanhoe to Rebecca] which alone distinguishes the noble from the base, the gentle knight from the churl and the savage. . . . Thou art no Christian, Rebecca; and to thee

are unknown those high feelings which swell the bosom of a noble maiden when her lover hath done some deed of emprize which sanctions his flame. Chivalry! Why, maiden, she is the nurse of pure and high affection, the stay of the oppressed, the redresser of grievances, the curb of the power of the tyrant. Nobility were but an empty name without her, and liberty finds the best protection in her lance and sword. [11]

In such romantic celebrations of chivalry and the crusades lie the roots of the late Victorian and Edwardian insistence on the relation between the Empire and gentlemanly valor, the public school ethos of "useless" games, pluck, and war. [12]

The connection between Scott's medievalism and imperialist ideology is perhaps clearer in *The Talisman* than in *Ivanhoe*. In both stories, political themes relevant to modern times emerge from Scott's shaping of Richard Coeur de Lion, despite his Norman origin, into a champion of specifically *British* chivalry and liberty. In *Ivanhoe* the thesis of the medieval origin of British liberty—Burke's "liberal descent"—is worked out in terms of the struggle of the Saxon "race" against the "Norman yoke." [13] In *The Talisman* it is worked out in terms of Christian versus Saracen and, implicitly at least, civilization versus barbarism. Scott says that the contrast between the Christian Richard and the Muslim Saladin does not favor the former: "The Christian and English monarch showed all the cruelty and violence of an Eastern sultan; and Saladin, on the other hand, displayed the deep policy and prudence of a European sovereign." [14] Richard improves in the story, however, and Scott leaves no doubt that true chivalry and its central ideals of honor and courtly love are of Christian origin, even though Saladin himself behaves in highly chivalrous ways. Richard's European allies show weakness through their treachery and in-fighting, but they are superior to their Saracen enemies in religion, physical prowess, and liberty. Chivalry for Scott is paradoxically egalitarian and hence a source of specifically British liberty; as Sir Kenneth explains to the strange Emir (who turns out to be Saladin) with whom he first does combat: "Know, Saracen . . . that the name of a knight, and the blood of a gentleman, entitle him to place himself on the same rank with sovereigns" (34).

The Talisman might be described as an early nineteenth-century Western (perhaps we should call it an Eastern). Christian knights on horseback wage war against infidel Saracens on horseback for dominion of the Holy Land; oddly, perhaps perversely, medieval chivalry shadows forth progress and civilization as well as the true religion. Yet to the paradoxically progressive sort of Eastern represented by Scott's tales of chivalry, we should add another, a type that underscores the perpetual circularity, despotism, and barbarism of the Orient. This is the general pattern of the story of Scheherezade and her Bluebeard husband in *The Arabian Nights*, for example—medieval Islam tended to represent modern Islam for many western readers—as well as of Edward FitzGerald's rendering of *The Rubaiyat of Omar Khayyam*. Such texts needed no overt moralizing to stress the contrast between enlightened, progressive west and benighted, nonprogressive east. This self-evident stereotyping also characterizes Tennyson's early poems with oriental themes. The flow of time reverses itself on several levels in Tennyson's "Recollections of the Arabian Nights":

> When the breeze of a joyful dawn blew free
> In the silken sail of infancy,
> The tide of time flowed back with me,
>   The forward-flowing tide of time;
> And many a sheeny summer-morn,
> Adown the Tigris I was borne,
> By Bagdat's shrines of fretted gold,
> High-walled gardens green and old;
> True Mussulman was I and sworn,
>   For it was in the golden prime
>   Of good Haroun Alraschid.

The flowing back of time here seems charming, beautiful; but Tennyson could also condemn the Orient for its backwardness, as he does in "Locksley Hall": "Better fifty years of Europe than a cycle of Cathay."

In the introduction to *The Talisman*, together with Byron's poetry, Southey's *Thalaba*, and Moore's *Lalla Rookh*, Scott mentions Thomas Hope's *Anastasius* (1819) and James Morier's *Hajji Baba* (1824), both nonprogressive Easterns, and to these we might add some other early nineteenth-century novels. One would be R. R. Madden's *The Musulman* (1830), which Norman Daniel describes as "a sensationalized exploitation of cruelty and sensuality."[15] Daniel also criticizes *Anastasius* (1819) as "already anachronistic with its harem sexuality and picaresque manner," but these were standard features of Easterns throughout the century (59). Morier's fictions do not escape the stereotypic emphasis on "cruelty and sensuality," but they are informed by a wry, sympathetic amusement at the foibles of both eastern and western characters which renders them superior to the works of Hope and Madden. Like Meadows Taylor's *Confessions of a Thug*, the enduringly popular *Adventures of Hajji Baba of Ispahan* offers the supposed autobiography of an oriental— an attractive Persian rogue who begins life as a barber's son, advances through many picaresque vicissitudes to become assistant executioner for the Shah, and then, after being "bastinadoed" and nearly beheaded himself, goes through a haphazard round of careers and identities. By the end of his account, Hajji Baba has risen once more into the Shah's favor and is persuaded—that is, bribed—by the Grand Vizier to travel to England as secretary to the Persian ambassador.

Despite his apparent personal success at the novel's conclusion, Hajji Baba encounters the principle of progress only through the connection with Britain. Hajji Baba's amusing ups and downs illustrate oriental despotism through the Shah's entourage, which is made up largely of cruel, corrupt executioners, but otherwise there seems to be no particular point to his career—which is just the point. Unlike the adventures of Marryat's midshipmen, which lead to victory in battle, promotion through the ranks, and the aggrandizement of British power and glory, Hajji Baba's adventures take him meandering through Persia and Turkey, escaping from one tight spot after another but never progressing by European standards. And the story itself meanders. "The art of a story- teller," says Hajji Baba, "is to make his tale interminable, and still to interest his audience."[16] Easterns like his are aimless, merely episodic tales, though they are inevitably framed by the western reader's sense of what it would take to give them a crusading goal or to shape them in terms of a linear, progressive plot or career.

"Peregrine Persic," Morier's editorial persona, states the obvious moral in his introduction to *Hajji Baba*:

A distinct line must ever be drawn between "the nations who wear the hat and those who wear the beard." . . . What is moral and virtuous with the one, is wickedness with the other—that which the Christian reviles as abominable, is by the Mohamedan held sacred. Although the contrast between their respective manners may be very amusing, still it is most certain that the former will ever feel devoutly grateful that he is neither subject to Mohamedan rule, nor educated in Mohamedan principles; whilst the latter, in his turn, looking upon the rest of mankind as unclean infidels, will continue to hold fast to his bigoted persuasion, until some powerful interposition of Providence shall dispel the moral and intellectual darkness which, at present, overhangs so large a portion of the Asiatic world. (13)

The "interposition of Providence" in Morier's novel takes the shape of the British ambassador and the British doctor (who insists on vaccinating Persian mothers and children for smallpox, much against the wishes of Persian officials, including Hajji Baba). Their efforts to do good seem irrational to the Persian characters. The Grand Vizier tells Hajji Baba that "the Franks talk of feelings in public life of which we are ignorant." The idea of service to one's country is, he contends, meaningless in the East: anything the Shah or his ministers do today, the next shah will undo tomorrow. Evil repeats itself; history is circular. Nothing is ever done for the public good in Persia, but for enhancing the "privileges and enjoyments" that are "the lawful inheritance of the shahs . . . let them possess them in the name of Allah!" The Grand Vizier sees no reason why the Shah's—or his own—privileges should be abridged, "certainly not for the good of the country, because not one individual throughout the whole empire even understands what that good means, much less would he work for it" (447–48). Hajji Baba agrees that "one of the most remarkable features in the character" of the British is "their extreme desire to do us good against our inclination." The British even, he says, "do not refrain from expense to secure their ends"—an obvious contrast to the observation that *riswah* or bribery, a word that also means manure, is what greases the creaking wheels of Persian society. The British, says Hajji Baba, "felt a great deal more for us than we did for ourselves; and what they could discover in us worthy of their love, we, who did not cease to revile them as unclean infidels, and as creatures doomed to eternal fires, were quite at a loss to discover" (448–49).

Just as Morier's novel reduces the Shah's government to an arbitrary, cruel despotism, uninformed by any sense of public service or progress, so it reduces "Mahomedan principles" to the single standard of impudence. This is the chief moral that Hajji Baba learns from the dervish Sefer, as it is also the chief quality that propels him from episode to episode, often rescuing him from catastrophe. When Sefer proposes to Hajji Baba that he become a dervish, the latter pleads that he lacks the necessary religious training. Sefer replies: "Ah, my friend . . . little do you know of dervishes, and still less of human-kind. It is not great learning that is required to make a dervish: assurance is the first ingredient. . . . By impudence I have been a prophet, by impudence I have wrought miracles, by impudence I have restored the dying to health—by impudence, in short, I lead a life of great ease and am feared and respected by those who, like you, do not know what dervishes are" (59). By impudence, Sefer goes on to say, Mahomed himself founded Islam, practicing magic tricks upon his ignorant followers. And by impudence, the inference follows, the Shah holds sway at Teheran and the Sultan at Constantinople. Only with the Shah's signing of the treaty with the British, Morier indicates, does a new day begin to dawn for Persia. This event opens the way also, at the very end of the novel, for Hajji Baba's impending journey to the West and the continuation of his adventures in *Hajji Baba in England* (1828). That the light at the end of the Near Eastern tunnel is specifically British, of course, is the central political lesson of Morier's comic portrayal of "eastern manners."

ii

The contrast between the progressive West and the nonprogressive East occurs also in the final novel of Benjamin Disraeli's Young England trilogy, *Tancred; or, The New Crusade* (1847). Instead of impudence, however, "intrigue" is the more positive name that Disraeli attaches to the complexities of oriental politics; and he invests the Near East with a spirituality absent from Morier's account. Named for a medieval crusader, Tancredus de Montecaute (the title also of the second volume of *The Broad Stone of Honour*), Disraeli's Young England hero starts his political career by refusing to run for Parliament and by going instead on an oriental "pilgrimage" resembling Byron's or Disraeli's own tour in 1830–31. Of the many British travelers to the Near East during the first half of the nineteenth century, none had more influence on the later history of the British Empire than the future Conservative Prime Minister. According to Disraeli's biographers, after his eastern tour the "Oriental tendency in his nature . . . was henceforth to dominate his imagination and show itself in nearly all his achievements." This tendency is apparent, they claim, "in the bold stroke of policy which laid the foundations of English ascendancy in Egypt, in the Act which gave explicit form to the conception of an Indian Empire with the Sovereign of Great Britain at its head, and in the settlement imposed on Europe at the Berlin Congress."[17] This is to attribute mighty political results to the oriental side of Disraeli's personality or to his oriental tour, or both. Disraeli himself liked to play up his oriental roots, both in his fiction and in his political career—a theatrical assertiveness that began about the time of his journey and was one way to counteract antisemitism.

Disraeli went on his eastern journey for relief from the mental doldrums, for a respite from his creditors, and, of course, for that experience of the world which most travelers seek. At the same time he was perhaps already sensing that affinity with the mysterious Orient which would help him solve the puzzle of his own social and political identity. On 27 December 1830 Disraeli wrote to Bulwer from Constantinople: "I confess to you that my Turkish prejudices are very much confirmed by my residence in Turkey. The life of this people greatly accords with my taste, which is naturally somewhat indolent and melancholy. . . . To repose on voluptuous ottomans and smoke superb pipes, daily to indulge in the luxuries of a bath which requires half a dozen attendants for its perfection; to court the air in a carved caïque, by shores which are a perpetual scene; and to find no exertion greater than a canter on a barb; this is, I think, a far more sensible life than all the bustle of clubs, all the boring of drawing-rooms, and all the coarse vulgarity of our political controversies" (1:174). As Robert Blake points out, Disraeli's Turkish prejudices place him directly contrary to Byron, despite the fact that Byron was one of his early heroes and the subject of his sixth novel, *Venetia* (1837).[18] Disraeli the young oriental traveler was quite conscious of following Childe Harold, visiting sites made famous by Byron and trying to locate Byron's old servants and guides. Nevertheless, Disraeli both approved of Turks and Turkish life and wrote that "I detest the Greeks" (quoted in Blake, 47). Whereas Byron died in the cause of Greek independence, Disraeli off the coast of Albania considered joining "the Turkish Army as volunteer in the Albanian war" (1:162). Though the war was over by the time Disraeli came ashore, he sent his autobiographical hero, Contarini Fleming, into battle on the side of the Turks rather than the Greeks. The young Disraeli may have considered himself a political radical, but his home politics evidently did not apply to foreign turf—or else, as seems more likely, his radicalism was never as thoroughgoing as other values and attitudes, values that made him sympathetic to imperialism abroad and led him by the end of the 1830s to adopt a Tory-Radical position.

The immediate effects of Disraeli's oriental journey were registered in his fiction rather than his politics, in two novels partially written while he traveled. *Alroy* is an odd, stylistically prolix attempt at a prose epic, based on the medieval Jewish figure David Alroy, whom Disraeli makes out to be a would-be liberator of Israel, a Zionist before his time. The romantic nationalism of the story seems to align Disraeli with Byron, but Alroy's ambition is presented as much in terms of "universal empire" as of the creation of an independent Jewish state in Palestine.[19] In composing *Alroy*, however, Disraeli seems to have been concerned less about politics or historical accuracy than about "the celebration of a gorgeous incident in the annals of that sacred and romantic people from whom I derive my blood and name" (1:198). Certainly *Alroy* is the "gorgeous" daydream of imperial power of an extremely ambitious young man, as well as a highly idiosyncratic contribution to romantic medievalism.

A better gauge of Disraeli's early political attitudes is *Contarini Fleming*, his most directly autobiographical novel. In the last quarter of the story the hero goes on an eastern tour that corresponds almost exactly to Disraeli's journey. Many of the sites and experiences are given in the novel in verbatim transcriptions of letters Disraeli sent home—or perhaps he transcribed the letters from the manuscript of the novel (Blake, 109). Following Byron's trail into Albania, the protagonist draws a conclusion very different from Byron's about the destruction and signs of warfare everywhere visible—the Albanian rebels, he says, have "revenged themselves on tyranny by destroying civilisation."[20] Fighting with the Turks against the Albanians, Contarini participates in the Battle of Bitoglia, which led to the "complete pacification of Albania, and the temporary suppression of the conspiracies in the adjoining provinces." Disraeli's hero continues: "Had it been in the power of the Porte to reinforce at this moment its able and faithful servant [Reschid Pasha, the Ottoman vizier,] it is probable that the authority of the Sultan would have been permanently consolidated in these countries. As it is, the finest regions in Europe are still the prey of civil war, in too many instances excited by foreign powers for their miserable purposes" (316–17). Disraeli offers no hint that he understands how un-Byronic is Contarini's allegiance to the Ottoman Empire. On the contrary, he treats the Ottoman Empire as an obsolete but nonetheless splendid political structure, and the struggles of Greeks and Albanians against that empire as a provincial, rather miserable throwback to barbarism. The Sublime Porte represents tyranny but also civilisation—perhaps what tips the balance in its favor is the reality of present power, which Disraeli always respected.

It may be unwise to treat anything in the early novels as an exact foreshadowing of Disraeli's later political attitudes. But the oriental passages of *Contarini Fleming* anticipate *Tancred*, which as the third of the Young England trilogy expresses opinions Disraeli adhered to throughout his career. Often perceived as confused, disconnected from, and less realistic than its predecessors, *Tancred* was Disraeli's favorite of all his novels. From the description of its relation to *Coningsby* and *Sybil* which Disraeli offers in his "general preface" of 1870, moreover, it appears to be a logical culmination of the trilogy. The theme of *Coningsby*, Disraeli declares, is "the derivation and character of political parties"; that of *Sybil* "the condition of the people which had been the consequence of" those parties; that of *Tancred* "the duties of the Church as a main remedial agency in our present state." This is, of course, much too neat an account of what actually happens in the three novels; the stated theme of *Tancred* is especially wide of the mark. In the rest of Disraeli's explanation of *Tancred* the subject of "the duties of the Church" gives way to another—race—which fits the events of the story much more accurately than anything ecclesiastical:

> In recognizing the Church as a powerful agent in the previous development of England . . . it seemed to me that the time had arrived when it became my duty to . . . consider the position of the descendants of that race who had been the founders of Christianity. Familiar as we all are now with such themes, the House of Israel being now freed from the barbarism of mediaeval misconception, and judged like other races by their contributions to the existing sum of human welfare, and the general influence of race on human action being universally recognized as the key of history, the difficulty and hazard of touching for the first time on such topics cannot now be easily appreciated. But public opinion recognised both the truth and sincerity of these views, and, with its sanction, in TANCRED OR THE NEW CRUSADE, the third portion of the Trilogy, I completed their development.[21]

In fact *Tancred* says precious little about the role of the church in the political life of Britain and a great deal about the role of race as "the key of history." Perhaps Disraeli adopted a positive version of racist theory to counteract the negative versions he experienced because of his Jewish heritage. It is possible to read the novel as being mainly about religion; but if the author himself has any fixed religious views, these involve a mysticism of race. And the subject of race leads inevitably to that of empire. The sequence of the trilogy, then, moves from a consideration of political parties in *Coningsby*, through domestic reform in *Sybil*, to foreign affairs and the Empire in *Tancred*.[22]

This is not to say Disraeli is uninterested in religion as a subject. But the genius for religion has been, he believes, the gift of certain inspired races—none more inspired than the Jews, although other "orientals" have also been touched by the visionary flame. Tancred goes on his new crusade not to reconquer the Holy Land but to explore the sources of faith and to renew his own faith. As he explains to his fabulously wise and wealthy Jewish mentor Sidonia, Jerusalem "is the land of inspiration," and "inspiration is not only a divine but a local quality."[23] Britain is corrupt; the Anglican church is riddled with contradictions and doubt. Like Disraeli's other Young England heroes, Tancred could take up his political career by entering Parliament, but he refuses to do so until he has gone on his oriental journey because he recognizes that both he and his country lack ideals. The East—the Holy Land—is the locus of religious vision and hence of political idealism. With Disraeli's and Sidonia's blessing, though not that of his parents, Tancred sets out on his new crusade to visit the Holy Sepulchre and, he hopes, be touched by a spark from heaven where such sparks have fallen in the past.

There is, of course, an air of quixotic improbability about Tancred's quest which Disraeli emphasizes for ironic effect. His hero is already so idealistic that he is misunderstood by most of those around him.

> Why should Tancred go to Jerusalem? [asks the narrator.] What does it signify to him whether there be religious truth or political justice? He has youth, beauty, rank, wealth, power, and all in excess. He has a mind that can comprehend their importance and appreciate their advantages. What more does he require? Unreasonable boy! And if he reach Jerusalem, why should he find religious truth and political justice there? He can read of it in the traveling books, written by young gentlemen, with the best letters of introduction to all the consuls. They tell us what it is, a third-rate city in a stony wilderness. (105)

Half-inspired already by his family's crusading tradition, Tancred asks Sidonia: "Is it so wild as some would think it . . . that I should wish to do that which, six centuries ago, was done by my ancestor whose name I bear, and that I should cross the seas, and—?" Sidonia fills in the blank: "And visit the Holy Sepulchre" (122–23). Sidonia does not think Tancred unreasonable, though there is an obvious ironic distance between his worldly wisdom and the younger man's idealism. Sidonia knows the value of idealism, as of everything else, though he also points out that, whereas "it is no longer difficult to reach Jerusalem . . . the real difficulty is the one experienced by the crusaders, to know what to do when you have arrived there" (121).

Sidonia adds that "the crusades were of vast advantage to Europe . . . and renovated the spiritual hold which Asia has always had upon the North" (123). His point, that religious inspiration comes from the East, obviously differs from Scott's, whose crusaders, though as barbaric as the Saracens, represent progress. It is also an idea based on the assumption that race is the key to history. At the dinner at Sidonia's which Tancred attends before his departure, a discussion takes place concerning the nature of civilization and progress. When Mr. Vavasour defines civilization as "the progressive development of the faculties of man," Sidonia asks where such development is occurring? He lists countries—Italy, China, France, Germany—which, he claims, are either stationary or regressive. They are thus all foils to progressive Britain, which alone "flourishes" in the historical present. Sidonia then asks:

> Is it what you call civilisation that makes England flourish? Is it the universal development of the faculties of man that has rendered an island, almost unknown to the ancients, the arbiter of the world? Clearly not. It is her inhabitants that have done this; it is an affair of race. A Saxon race, protected by an insular position, has stamped its diligent and methodic character on the century. And when a superior race, with a superior idea to Work and Order, advances, its state will be progressive, and we shall, perhaps, follow the example of the [now] desolate countries. All is race; there is no other truth. (148–9)

Sidonia adds that "the decay of a race is an inevitable necessity, unless it lives in deserts and never mixes its blood" (150). The gist of this remark is partly explained by Sidonia's earlier account of his family history. He tells Tancred there has been no intermarriage by his relations with other races—"We are pure Sephardim" (125). (The fact that Sidonia no longer "lives in deserts" may suggest an inconsistency, but racist thinking even of a positive sort has never been noted for its logicality.) In Sidonia's doctrine of race Disraeli anticipates the pseudo-scientific racists of the 1850s such as Robert Knox, who in *The Races of Men* (1850) proclaims that "race is everything: literature, science, art, in a word, civilization, depend on it."[24]

Armed with his crusading idealism and Sidonia's grand idea of race, Tancred sets out on his journey "to penetrate the great Asian mystery" (124). His voyage is not described; the novel skips over the various scenes along the route to Jerusalem which young Disraeli found so fascinating and which compose the bulk of Contarini Fleming's narrative. Disraeli was impressed by the historical significance of Jerusalem, and, if *Contarini Fleming* accurately renders his own experience, he engaged in interesting though not especially impassioned theological conversations with fellow-tourists. Unlike Tancred, however, Contarini—and presumably Disraeli—visited the Holy Land without any thought of experiencing visionary illumination or receiving some new dispensation from on high.[25]

Tancred realizes his wish, and on Mount Sinai, in a moment of high vision (or perhaps high self-delusion), he is visited by "the angel of Arabia." This interesting creature, perhaps only the mirage of Tancred's dream or trance, identifies himself as "the guardian spirit of that land which governs the world; for power is neither the sword nor the shield, for these pass away, but ideas, which are divine. The thoughts of all lands come from a higher source than man, but the intellect of Arabia comes from the Most High. Therefore it is that from this spot issue the principles which regulate the human destiny" (290). The Angel stresses "*Arabian* principles" as much as divine revelation—again emphasizing the importance of race. Jesus he calls a "Galilean Arab," who "advanced and traced on the front of the rude conquerors of the Caesars the subduing symbol of the last development of Arabian principles." From there he jumps forward to the French Revolution. Since the beginning of the nineteenth century, he says, "the intellectual colony of Arabia, once called Christendom, has been in a state of partial and blind revolt." The "God of Sinai and of Calvary" has been abandoned in favor of liberty, equality, and fraternity. But "the equality of man can only be accomplished by the sovereignty of God." The Angel of Arabia proceeds therefore to command Tancred to "announce the sublime and solacing doctrine of theocratic equality" and to "obey the impulse of thine own spirit." Tancred is then roused from his trance by "a sound, as of thunder"; the moment of divine revelation has ended.

What has Tancred learned that he did not already believe? He was already convinced of the basic truth of the biblical revelation, or he would not have set out on his new crusade. He himself tells Sidonia that religious vision is a local phenomenon (and therefore a racial phenomenon) centered at Jerusalem, and this idea his dream vision appears to confirm. He is obviously a conservative young aristocrat, not at all enamored of liberty, equality, and fraternity. By "theocratic equality" it seems unlikely that the Arabian angel means anything other than the standard notion that, as equality is impossible in reality, so the illusion of equality supplied by religion is vital for the maintenance of political stability. Though Tancred's vision teaches the hero no new lesson, however, it does underscore the two main themes of the story: first, the visionary power of Tancred's moral idealism (Disraeli always liked to assert the primacy of imagination in politics); and second, the significance of race (especially the historical and religious significance of the "Arabian race," which for Disraeli includes the "Hebrew race").

Framing the apparition of the Angel of Arabia on Mount Sinai is a highly romantic plot in which Tancred meets Eva, "the Rose of Sharon," and is kidnaped by her half-brother Fakredeen, who hopes with the ransom money to buy arms that will allow him to liberate—that is, conquer—Syria and Lebanon. Tancred falls in love with Eva, and he and Fakredeen become close friends. These kindred spirits represent two contrary sides of Disraeli's own complicated personality, the idealistic and the Machiavellian, though a romantic valorization of youthful ambition blurs the edges of the contrast.

Being held hostage in the desert is to Tancred more pleasurable than otherwise; he modestly likens his captivity to Coeur de Lion's, except that it comes at the start instead of the end of his new crusade (254). Besides, as a hostage Tancred gets to know several oriental characters, especially Fakredeen, on an intimate basis, which is just as important for his future political career as what the Angel has told him. If Tancred represents the religious and medievalizing idealism of Young England, Fakredeen represents the romantic orientalism and also Machiavellian scheming of "Young Syria"—and of Disraeli's own mercurial political personality: "Fakredeen possessed all the qualities of the genuine Syrian character in excess; vain, susceptible, endowed with a brilliant though frothy imagination, and a love of action so unrestrained that restlessness deprived it of energy, with so fine a taste that he was always capricious, and so ingenious that he seemed ever inconsistent" (213). Fakredeen is an ironic self-portrait of Disraeli, but not the idealistic though rather colorless, humorless Tancred. Disraeli enjoys portraying slightly dull western aristocrats learning from sharp-witted eastern friends.

Like Disraeli, Fakredeen sees the political realm in terms less of high ideals than of high intrigue. "Stratagems came to him as naturally as fruit comes to a tree. He lived in a labyrinth of plans" (214). Disraeli himself believed that "dissimulation" was the key to success, at least in oriental politics. In Albania, hearing "of the massacre of the principal rebel Beys at Monastir, at a banquet given by the Grand Vizir," Contarini Fleming is at first indignant at "this savage treachery" (300). But his host, "a Frank experienced in the Turkish character," mollifies him:

> Live a little longer in these countries before you hazard an opinion as to their conduct. Do you indeed think that the rebel Beys . . . were so simple as to place the slightest trust in the Vizir's pledge? The practice of politics in the East may be defined by one word, dissimulation. The most wary dissembler is the consummate statesman. The Albanian chiefs went up to the divan in full array, and accompanied by a select body of their best troops. They resolved to overawe the Vizir; perhaps they even meditated, with regard to him, the very stroke which he put in execution against themselves. He was the most skilful dissembler, that is all. (300–301)

Disraeli here offers an argument that he would use to rationalize his continued support of the Ottoman Empire after the Bulgarian crisis of 1876. According to Robert Blake: "No one who reads Disraeli's own account of his visit to the Near East in 1830–31 could be surprised that he tended to dismiss the Bulgarian atrocities . . . as grossly exaggerated and to react with particular distaste against the committees and meetings which took the opposite line in London and all over the country" (*Disraeli's Grand Tour*, 58).

In *Tancred*, Fakredeen views politics from much the same Machiavellian perspective as Contarini's host, offering his sister Eva an elaborate defense of intrigue: "It is life! It is the only thing! How do you think Guizot and Aberdeen got to be ministers without intrigue? Or Riza Pacha himself? How do you think Mehemet Ali got on? Do you believe Sir [Stratford] Canning [British ambassador to Constantinople] never intrigues? He would be recalled in a week if he did not. Why, I have got one of his spies in my castle at this moment, and I make him write home for the English all that I wish them not to believe. Intrigue! Why, England won India by intrigue. Do you think they are not intriguing in the Punjaub at this very moment? Intrigue has gained half the thrones of Europe" (204). Disraeli clearly agrees with Fakredeen, but he also knows that intrigue must be inspired by high principles; otherwise it can express only cynicism in the service of expediency and material interests.[26] What saves Fakredeen from cynicism is his romantic ambition to unite and rule over the Near East. As the leader of Young Syria, he seems to represent precisely that romantic nationalism which Disraeli rejected in the case of Greece; but Fakredeen's desire is less to liberate his countrymen from the

Turks than to found an empire of his own. Without the higher principle that Tancred injects into the novel's treatment of politics, however, Fakredeen's aim would be merely egotistical, a barren self-aggrandizement. "The world was never conquered by intrigue," Tancred tells Fakredeen; "it was conquered by faith. Now, I do not see that you have faith in anything." To this criticism Fakredeen replies: "Faith! that is a grand idea. If one could only have faith in something and conquer the world!" (259).

This, then, is the true subject of *Tancred:* not religion, much less the role of the church in the political life of Britain, but the proper formula for "conquering the world"—for founding and governing empires.[27] In large part this formula is racial. Disraeli adheres in *Tancred* not to his "Turkish prejudices" but to Sidonia's insistence on the virtues of pure desert races whose blood is unmixed. To the Arabian races Sidonia and Tancred both attribute religious or visionary qualities, for these races have founded three of the world's great religions. But it is Tancred who has the visionary experience, Fakredeen who is the political schemer and would-be imperialist. Through this ironic reversal Disraeli gives the young Syrian emir the usual stereotypic qualities of the oriental despot while insisting that Syrians and Arabs are "of the holy race." The young English aristocrat, meanwhile—who by virtue of his being English is much more obviously an actual imperialist or world-ruler than Fakredeen—goes to the Holy Land seeking faith, though he is the most religious character from the very outset of the novel.

Join the qualities of Young Syrian and Young Englander, Disraeli suggests, and you have the combination of intrigue and faith necessary to found empires—the ideal character for the aspiring statesman and for Disraeli as he saw himself in 1847. Fakredeen is certainly ready; in reference to his pure desert race, he declares: "The game is in our hands, if we have energy." Moreover, "it is finished with England." He proposes that Tancred should, on his return home, convince Queen Victoria to abandon England for her Indian empire: "You must . . . quit a petty and exhausted position for a vast and prolific empire. Let the Queen of the English collect a great fleet, let her stow away all her treasure, bullion, gold plate, and precious arms; be accompanied by all her court and chief people, and transfer the seat of her empire from London to Delhi. There she will find an immense empire ready made" (263). Fakredeen, in the meantime, will split the Ottoman Empire with Mehemet Ali of Egypt; they will then acknowledge Victoria "as our suzerain, and secure for her the Levantine coast" (263).

It is Fakredeen's misconception of the weakness of Queen Victoria's position in England that alone renders the entire wild scheme ludicrous. Tancred himself enters his Asiatic friend's schemes, at least insofar as they entail breaking up the Ottoman Empire and founding some new imperial structure on the ruins. "Why, the most favoured part of the globe at this moment is entirely defenceless," Tancred observes; "there is not a soldier worth firing at in Asia except the Sepoys. The Persian, Assyrian, and Babylonian monarchies might be gained in a morning with faith and the flourish of a sabre" (303). Of course the only new imperialist dispensation in the Near East must be British or British-dominated, though Tancred does not say so to Fakredeen. When his dragoman Baroni objects that "you would have the Great Powers interfering" if he tried to conquer the Near East, Tancred responds: "What should I care for the Great Powers, if the Lord of Hosts were on my side!" (303). If Tancred earlier seemed half-crazed by religious romanticism, he now joins Fakredeen in seeming half-crazed by a political romanticism that thinks in terms not of liberty, equality, and fraternity but of Napoleonic world conquest.

Tancred advises Fakredeen that "the whole country to the Euphrates might be conquered in a campaign" (369), a project he is obviously eager to support. And when they visit the Queen of the Ansaray in the Syrian mountains to enlist her aid, it is Tancred, not Fakredeen, who tells her: "We wish to conquer [the] world, with angels at our head, in order that we may establish the happiness of man by a divine dominion, and, crushing the political atheism that is now desolating existence, utterly extinguish the groveling tyranny of self-government" (422). By self-government Tancred appears to mean both national independence and democracy. He wants, specifically and clearly, the overthrow of the Ottoman Empire by a new imperial power, one originating in the deserts and presumably led by Fakredeen and the Young Syrians. In fact, Mehemet Ali's recent conquest of Palestine and Syria from his base in Egypt, not to mention Napoleon's earlier conquest, made such a scheme less fantastic than it might sound today. Because the empire building of both Napoleon and Mehemet Ali had been effectively squelched by the Royal Navy, moreover, Disraeli's first readers might easily have inferred that Tancred's enthusiasm for Fakredeen's cause involved another, hardly hidden agenda for the development of British hegemony in the Near East.

His conviction regarding the religious genius of both Jews and Arabs makes Tancred on occasion sound more like an oriental prophet preaching a new jihad than like a young, romantic aristocrat from England. What were the conquests of the Greeks and Romans, he asks, "to those of Jesus Christ?" The Greek and Roman empires have long since vanished; "the house of David is worshipped at Rome itself, at every seat of great and growing empire in the world, at London, at St. Petersburg, at New York." He offers a vision of a revolutionary imperialism sweeping out of Arabia and demolishing that "Tataric system," the Ottoman Empire:

> Asia alone is faithless to the Asian [Jesus, or at least "the house of David"]; but Asia has been overrun by Turks and Tatars. For nearly five hundred years the true Oriental mind has been enthralled. Arabia alone has remained free and faithful to the divine tradition. From its bosom we shall go forth and sweep away the mouldering remnants of the Tataric system; and then, when the East has resumed its indigenous intelligence, when angels and prophets again mingle with humanity, the sacred quarter of the globe will recover its primeval and divine supremacy; it will act upon the modern empires, and the faint-hearted faith of Europe, which is but the shadow of a shade, will become as vigorous as befits men who are in sustained communication with the Creator. (428)

How much of this farrago of politics and religion Disraeli actually believed it is impossible to tell. Though Disraeli was not a young man in 1847, *Tancred* is a novel about young men, and the author clearly enjoys putting extravagant ambitions and naïveté under the microscope. If one judges by his political practice, however, the racist and imperialist ingredients of *Tancred* meant far more to Disraeli than its hero's rather nutty religious idealism. *Tancred's* vision on Mount Sinai is a stunning piece of theatrical double-take, in part because the revelation proffered him by the Angel of Arabia is in the final analysis not religious at all. It is instead a worldly vision of imperial power and glory, and afterward Tancred behaves less like a saint or mystic than like a political intriguer on the grand scale, sharing Fakredeen's ambitions of conquest. But what can the ambitions of Young Syria amount to in the shadow of the truly world-conquering energies of the British? The romantic, crusading zeal of Young England would inspire the British Empire with new, paradoxical, Tory-Radical ideals and lead it to new conquests in the decades to come.

iii

"But the question is, what is the Eastern question?" asks one of the characters in *Tancred* (395). By the 1850s the Eastern Question meant the entire panoply of diplomatic controversies associated with the Near East which precipitated the Crimean War. These ranged from the squabble over rights to the Holy Places in Palestine to diplomatic jockeying in anticipation of the dissolution of the Ottoman Empire, from the rivalry of French, British, and German archaeologists in Egypt and Persia to the defense of the Afghan frontier in India.[28] The Crimean conflict signaled the breakdown of a diplomacy that, through the Concert of Europe, had maintained peace among the great powers since 1815. After the 1850s the great powers would behave with increasing suspicion toward each other as they accelerated their competition for the spoils of empire. Among those spoils none would prove more spectacular than Egypt and the Sudan, the locations of several new crusades by British gentlemen and knights-at-arms—the search for the Nile's sources starting in the 1850s, the bombardment of Alexandria and the take-over of Egypt in 1882, the death of General Gordon at Khartoum three years later, and the revenge for Gordon at the Battle of Omdurman in 1898.

A key figure in the search for the Nile's sources, a scholar who "could hold his own with any academic Orientalist in Europe" according to Edward Said, and an important harbinger of the late Victorian imperialization of Egypt, the Sudan, and the Near East was Captain Richard F. Burton.[29] Unlike Disraeli, Burton never engaged in imperial decision making from the centers of power; on the contrary, he was often treated as something of an embarrassment by his various employers—the Indian army, the Foreign Office, and even the Royal Geographical Society, which sponsored several of his expeditions. Often as obstinate in his opinions as he was painstaking in his researches, Burton deserves to be remembered for no one grand discovery, expedition, or publication. His greatest feat of exploration, the trek to the central African lakes with John Hanning Speke, is flawed by its aftermath—his public quarrel with Speke, who was more nearly correct than he about the Nile's sources, and Speke's subsequent death by hunting accident or by suicide (it is impossible to know which). Burton's greatest scholarly endeavor, his translation and annotation of *The Arabian Nights*, is also flawed by the charge that he plagiarized, or at least relied too heavily upon, John Payne's translation.[30] Nevertheless, Burton offers a paradigm of nineteenth-century careers in the service of the Empire. Coningsby says in *Tancred* that "the East is a career" (141), and to no Victorian was this aphorism more applicable than Burton. Soldier, explorer, linguist, author of some two dozen travelogues ranging from Arabia to Iceland and from India to

Paraguay, Burton also merits consideration as one of the founders of the new science of anthropology. (That he shows up in none of the standard histories of that discipline perhaps stems from the understandable desire of modern anthropologists to play down an influential but embarrassing heritage of racism and imperialism.)

Burton's numerous activities were all informed by a code of military and gentlemanly chivalry—he was an authority on fencing and falconry as well as on India and Islam—and by "scientific" racism that led him to defend various past and present forms of slavery.[31] All of his expeditions can be understood as modern crusades motivated by sometimes conflicting desires for personal adventure and romantic image making, for contributing to scientific knowledge, and ultimately for increasing his country's world domination. He believed the "dark races" much inferior to his own—unprogressive, prone to deceit, laziness, and cruelty, and lacking intelligence. But at least with certain Muslim peoples, especially the nomadic "desert races," Burton felt a sympathetic identification similar to Disraeli's feeling of kinship with the "Arabian" or "Hebrew race" (synonymous terms in *Tancred*).

In *Personal Narrative of a Pilgrimage to Al-Madinah and Meccah* (1855), Burton declares that the Arabs, like Afghans and "American aborigines," are one of the "chivalrous races."[32] Burton on several occasions expresses his keen delight in "the chivalry of the Desert" (2:19), comparing the barbarous customs of the "Badawis" (Bedouin) to the unchivalric, semicivilized customs of the town-dwellers of Medina and Mecca: "The almost absolute independence of the [desert] Arabs, and of that noble race the North American Indians of a former generation, has produced a similarity between them worthy of note, because it may warn the anthropologist not always to detect in coincidence of custom identity of origin. Both have the same wild chivalry, the same fiery sense of honour, and the same boundless hospitality. . . . Both, recognising no other occupation but war and the chase, despise artificers and the effeminate people of cities, as the game cock spurns the vulgar roosters of the poultry-yard" (2:118). Burton identified with the game cock rather than with the vulgar roosters—the personal side of his career entailed the careful construction and projection of a dangerous, warlike, aristocratic persona who is as much the subject of his travelogues as the various countries he explored. Burton's image making owes a good deal to Byron's example, moreover; in her admiring biography his wife says that he "had a curious characteristic which he shared with Lord Byron—that of loving to paint himself much blacker than he really was, and to affect vices, much as most men affect virtues, and with the same insincerity."[33]

In the comparison between Arabs and native Americans, Burton thinks the Arabs do better: "Of these two chivalrous races of barbarians, the Badawi claims our preference on account of his treatment of women, his superior development of intellect, and the glorious page of history which he has filled" (2:119). Burton finds in the desert Arabs several virtues he associates with chivalry: nomadic freedom, fierce pride, bravery in combat, a strict code of honor, and the treatment of women which involves both romanticizing and dominating them. The individual Arabs he encounters on his hajj all fall short of the full chivalric ideal; it seems apparent that Burton's ideal Arab is an idealized self-portrait. Above all, the desert for Burton means liberation from the "artificial restraints" of civilisation, though such liberation demands courage, for it entails the constant proximity of death:

> Above, through a sky terrible in its stainless beauty . . . the Samun caresses you like a lion with flaming breath. Around lie drifted sand-heaps . . . the very skeletons of mountains, and hard unbroken plains, over which he who rides is spurred by the idea that the bursting of a water-skin, or the pricking of a camel's hoof, would be a certain death of torture,—a haggard land infested with wild beasts, and wilder men,—a region whose very fountains murmur the warning words "Drink and away!" What can be more exciting? what more sublime? Man's heart bounds in his breast at the thought of measuring his puny force with Nature's might, and of emerging triumphant from the trial. This explains the Arab's proverb, "Voyaging is victory." In the Desert, even more than upon the ocean, there is present death. (1:149)

In such passages Burton expresses his highest social values, those of a Victorian officer and gentleman for whom the arts of war and self-defense are paramount. The true knight or gentlemanly adventurer disdains the "degradation, moral and physical," of town life and sedentary labor for "the freedom of the Desert"; "the loom and the file do not conserve courtesy and chivalry like the sword and spear" (2:10). But Burton does not travel to Mecca overtly as a crusader, out to battle the Saracens for possession of the Holy Land, much less as a modern tourist armed with umbrella and *Eothen*. On the contrary, he travels disguised as a Muslim pilgrim from Afghanistan—a false identity he dramatizes throughout the *Pilgrimage*—and he travels to Mecca rather than to Jerusalem. The modern crusader ironically adopts the identity of a Saracen—"going

native," if only temporarily—and plays the dangerous role of anthropological spy.

Burton was not the first European to don Arab costume and enter
Mecca as a Muslim pilgrim. He stresses the danger of his disguise but also
points out that he could not have entered Mecca undisguised: Europeans
in the Arabian peninsula ran great risks. By refusing to travel as anything
other than an orthodox Christian and rather stiff-necked Englishman,
the author of *Arabia Deserta*, Charles M. Doughty, often met with rough
treatment.[34] Burton was risking his life both by desert travel and by the
chance of being unmasked: exposed as an infidel at Mecca, he would
probably have been executed. He wishes the reader to understand both
the peril of his journey and the meticulous skill with which he adopts his
fraudulent persona.

Because of the author's Afghan disguise, Burton's *Pilgrimage* acquires
the suspenseful ambiguity of a spy novel. His narrative looks forward to
Kipling's *Kim*, a tale of espionage full of disguises and characters like Kim
himself whose identities are ambiguous or multiple, playing the Great
Game in Asia. In later specimens—the novels of John le Carré, for
instance—identities and allegiances are often so tenuous and compro-
mised as to become mysterious even to the protagonists themselves.
Burton seems untroubled about his own selfhood, and yet from the outset
he dramatizes both the danger and the mysterious ambiguity of his
oriental disguise. In the first four chapters he offers a detailed account of
his metamorphosis, bit by bit shedding his western habits and adopting
eastern ones. At Alexandria, "the better to blind the inquisitive eyes of
servants and visitors, my friend, Larking, lodged me in an outhouse,
where I could revel in the utmost freedom of life and manners. And
although some Armenian Dragoman, a restless spy like all his race,
occasionally remarked *voilà un Persan diablement dégagé*, none, except
those who were entrusted with the secret, had any idea of the part I was
playing" (1:11). Shortly after this, "Abdullah" Burton studies "to assume
the character of a wandering Darwaysh" or dervish, also changing his
title from Mirza to Shaykh Abdullah. "No character in the Moslem
world," he says, "is so proper for disguise as that of the Darwaysh," a
Protean figure in Islamic societies (1:14). Finally, at Cairo, living in the
"khan" or "wakalah," Shaykh Abdullah adds the finishing touches to his
identity: "After long deliberation about the choice of nations, I became a
'Pathan.' Born in India of Afghan parents, who had settled in the country,
educated at Rangoon, and sent out to wander, as men of that race

frequently are, from early youth, I was well guarded against the danger of detection" (1:44–45).

As his outward self undergoes transformation, Burton plays up his own ambivalent attitudes toward Christianity, civilization, and western values, declaring, for example, that "there are honest men who hold that Al-Islam, in its capital tenets, approaches much nearer to the faith of Jesus than do the Pauline and Athanasian modifications . . . a visit after Arab Meccah to Angle-Indian Aden, with its 'priests after the order of Melchisedeck,' suggested to me that the Moslem may be more tolerant, more enlightened, more charitable, than many societies of self-styled Christians" (1:xxii–xxiii). Dubbed the "White Nigger" by his colleagues in Sindh, Burton now grumbles half-humorously about the "jocose editors" of certain Indian papers who "during my journey, and since my return" have "made merry upon an Englishman 'turning Turk'" (1:23). He was always, he implies, a Turk with a difference, never forgetting his imperial and racial allegiance (his religion is another matter); and yet he revels in the Protean ambiguity of his various roles.

If Burton is either a crusader or a pilgrim, then obviously from a religious perspective he is a fraudulent one, whether Muslim or Christian. When the climactic moment arrives and he views the Kaabah at Mecca, the thrill Burton experiences has nothing to do with religion. Instead it derives from the fulfillment of scientific curiosity and from an evidently sacrilegious pride:

> There at last it lay, the bourn of my long and weary Pilgrimage, realising the plans and hopes of many and many a year. The mirage medium of Fancy invested the huge catafalque and its gloomy pall with peculiar charms . . . and how few have looked upon the celebrated shrine! I may truly say that, of all the worshippers who clung weeping to the curtain, or who pressed their beating hearts to the stone, none felt for the moment a deeper emotion than did the Haji from the far-north. It was as if the poetical legends of the Arab spoke truth, and that the waving wings of angels, not the sweet breeze of morning, were agitating and swelling the black covering of the shrine. But, to confess humbling truth, theirs was the high feeling of religious enthusiasm, mine was the ecstasy of gratified pride. (2:160–61)

"How few have looked upon the celebrated shrine"—at least, how few *westerners*. The phrase inadvertently expresses the contradiction in Burton's situation. In a sea of Muslim pilgrims, all crowding around and into the shrine, Burton remains isolated by his consciousness of difference, by his sense of personal and racial superiority. Yet the superior man has stooped to deception to reach his goal, and this awareness increases his sense of isolated difference. Burton proceeds to relate how, on shouldering through the crowd to kiss the stone and rub his hands and forehead upon it, "I narrowly observed it, and came away persuaded that it is an aerolite" (2:169). Burton casts upon the black stone not the gaze of another worshipful pilgrim but the panoptical gaze of western science, which penetrates all corners of the globe, prying into the deepest, most sacred mysteries of every culture.

Anthropological fieldwork is inevitably a form of spying—a fact some modern anthropologists acknowledge—particularly so when, as in Burton's case, the information gathered is to be used for defending and enlarging empire.[35] Kipling was not being capricious when he had Colonel Creighton and the other pro-British agents in *Kim* disguise their espionage work in the Great Game as an ethnological survey. Burton began as an intelligence officer for the army in India, though his military career was nearly cut short because he was, in a sense, too good at his work. His phenomenal linguistic skill and his facility for disguise led to the adoption of his first false identity in the early 1840s, that of a half-Arab, half-Persian merchant selling his wares throughout the newly conquered territory of Sindh. The disguise, Burton declares, was essential for getting beneath the surface of native life: "The European official in India seldom, if ever, sees anything in its real light, so dense is the veil which the fearfulness, the duplicity, the prejudice and the superstitions of the natives hang before his eyes."[36]

Burton repeats this point in the *Pilgrimage*: the average Indian, he asserts, views his British rulers with a contempt and fear the British fail to recognize. "Like the fox in the fable, fulsomely flattering at first," the Indian will befriend an Englishman, but in the latter's absence he will descant complacently upon the probability of a general Bartholomew's Day in the East, and look forward to the hour when enlightened Young India will arise and drive the 'foul invader' from the land." In a footnote Burton adds: "When, in the history of the world, do we read that such foreign dominion ever made itself loved?" (1:37–38) Such passages show how clearly Burton understood the violent divisiveness of imperialism. Never ceasing to be a racist and imperialist himself, he often expresses contempt for his compatriots' insensitivity to the psychological costs of racism and imperialism. Disguise was a means of crossing the gulf between superior and inferior races, civilization and barbarism—a means that led to ethnological knowledge as well as to adventure. Disguise also allowed Burton to criticize western society while permitting him eventually to return to it.

Disguise thus entails a double arrogance characteristic of Burton's entire career: contempt for the peoples among whom he travels and upon whom he spies or anthropologizes (in his case these activities are inseparable), and contempt for the ignorance and superficiality of his compatriots. This double arrogance has its roots partly in Burton's gentlemanly pretensions, as does his valorization of chivalry. Burton presents himself as one of a superior breed, in knowledge as well as in martial bravery and honor, not only in relation to Indians, Arabs, and Africans but also to most other Britons. Identifying himself with both the world of the civilized imperialist *and* the world of the sometimes imperialized, sometimes still free barbarian, he simultaneously finds both worlds deficient. Both lack the virility, strength of will, and intelligence to be a match for him.

In Sindh, as Mirza Abdullah of Bushire, Burton adopted a false identity socially superior to that of the Indian peasants and villagers among whom he moved. The same is true of his later disguise for the hajj to Mecca: Shaykh Abdullah is a learned dervish and also *hakim* or doctor from Afghanistan, and as a doctor Burton was able to pry into the private lives and sexual behaviors of the Arabs who became his patients. Of his first oriental persona, Burton writes:

> When the Mirza arrived at a strange town, his first step was to secure a house in or near the bazaar, for the purpose of evening *conversazioni*. Now and then he rented a shop and furnished it with clammy dates, viscid molasses, tobacco, ginger, rancid oil and strong-smelling sweetmeats; and wonderful tales Fame told about these establishments. Yet somehow or other, though they were more crowded than a first-rate milliner's rooms in Town, they throve not in a pecuniary point of view; the cause of which was, I believe, that the polite Mirza was in the habit of giving the heaviest possible weight for their money to all the ladies,—particularly the pretty ones. (*Sindh*, xvi)

How much we should believe what Burton says about Mirza Abdullah— or about the other personas and adventures his writings describe—is not always easy to determine. But H. T. Lambrick declares that *Sindh and the Races That Inhabit the Valley of the Indus* (1851) is a stunning achievement; on every aspect of Sindhian culture "Burton's knowledge will be found to throw into the shade the sum of all that had been recorded by his predecessors" (Editor's Introduction, *Sindh*, viii). Lambrick also suggests that no better work has been written on the subject since Burton's time.

Burton's spying on certain aspects of Sindhian culture went too far, however, for some of his superiors. Sir Charles Napier had learned that in Karachi, then a town of only 2,000 people a mile from a key military base, there were "no less than three lupanars or bordels, in which not women but boys and eunuchs, the former demanding nearly a double price, lay for hire."[37] Burton says that, because he was "the only British officer who could speak Sindi," he was "asked indirectly" to investigate these lupanars and report on them. He claims he was told that his report would not be passed on to the British authorities at Bombay, but somehow it found its way there and "produced the expected result." Burton was threatened with expulsion from the service, but—presumably because his talents were too valuable to dismiss—this did not happen. In any event, it was the first instance in which Burton challenged not only a native culture but his own home culture by penetrating both too deeply: he knew how to unmask both pederasty and hypocrisy, as well as most other forms of sexual practice, prudery, and deviation, anywhere in the world, and he prided himself on penetrating especially these tabooed subjects.

Burton the anthropological espionage agent merits inclusion in histories of anthropology not because of any theories he developed but rather because of the thoroughness and seeming objectivity (or scientific ruthlessness) with which he went about his explorations of other cultures. His most original and also half-baked theory about the nonwestern cultures he explored concerns the existence of a Sotadic Zone, running through the tropics and semitropics and representing that half of the world where, he claims, pederasty is as common as heterosexuality.[38] If this were Burton's chief contribution to anthropology, he would deserve to be forgotten. But his courageous, though often cranky, investigations of sexuality foreshadow the work of Bronislaw Malinowski and Margaret Mead, and his books on Sindh, Arabia, and parts of both east and west Africa are clearly much more than mere explorers' narratives. Burton does include detailed geographical information in each of his accounts, but he is always just as interested in describing the physical and racial qualities, the languages, the economies, the religious beliefs, the marital and sexual practices of the peoples among whom he travels.

Burton makes a troublesome figure for the modern anthropologist not because of anything he failed to do but because he did too much. All of the information he gathered, from India to Fernando Po, he viewed as a form of power over nonwestern peoples. If Burton is one of the greatest British anthropologists before 1900 in terms of fieldwork among living societies, then clearly anthropology is the social science discipline of imperial domination, just as classical political economy is the discipline of early industrial capitalism at home. Throughout his writing Burton recognizes the direct link between ethnological knowledge and power. For Disraeli the equation between imagination and power leads to a similar conclusion: world dominion is open to the strong-willed, the bold, the clever, whether the individuals concerned are idealists or intriguers. That both Disraeli and Burton could expect to influence the course of history as *individuals*, whether through imagination or through knowledge, is obviously more than the result of mere personal arrogance and brilliance—it is also the result of their positions as citizens and officials of the most powerful imperialist nation in the world.

Burton thought of himself as establishing a new social science called anthropology: he served as both vice-president and president of the Anthropological Society of London, which he helped found in 1863, and he refers throughout his writings to his researches as anthropological or ethnographical—his extensive commentaries on *The Arabian Nights*, for instance, he calls "anthropological notes."[39] For the modern anthropologist who might otherwise acknowledge Burton as a pioneer of the discipline, perhaps the chief obstacle is that, in common with most members of the Anthropological Society, Burton saw the new science as concerned with the apparently great differences among the races of mankind. When it broke away from the Ethnological Society in 1863, the Anthropological Society aimed to be a freer, more general forum for the investigation of every aspect of human behavior.[40] Its founders specifically aimed to be (as they saw it) more honest than the older organization about the issues of slavery, the place of "the negro" in nature, and the relative superiority or inferiority of different races. The first president, Dr. James Hunt, was of two minds about whether the negro was just a different, lower race of mankind, or a separate species, but he inclined toward the latter view. Hunt, Burton, and other members believed in a relatively rigid hierarchy of races, with the English and other Germanic peoples at the top and the Australian aborigines at the base, an enormous distance away. They placed a priority on investigating the causes for the worldwide extinction of the "inferior" or "primitive" or "dark races."

Theirs was not a sentimental hope to preserve inferior races from extinction, however. Rather, they tended to think of racial extinction as the other side of the coin of the progress of civilization, and they wished to understand the laws governing both phenomena.[41]

As a corollary to their racist tendencies, the members of the Anthropological Society made large claims about the potential contributions of anthropology to the aggrandizement of the British Empire. In a presidential address for 1864 Hunt declared:

> It is frequently the habit of scientific men to exaggerate the importance of their own special study to the detriment of other branches of knowledge; but do I exaggerate when I say that the fate of nations depends on a true appreciation of the science of anthropology? Are the causes which have overthrown the greatest of nations not to be resolved by the laws regulating the intermixture of the races of man? Does not the success of our colonisation depend on the deductions of our science? Is not the composition of harmonic nations entirely a question of race? Is not the wicked war now going on in America caused by an ignorance of our science?[42]

In an address marking the organization's fifth anniversary (1868), its treasurer, the Rev. Dunbar J. Heath, declared that "anthropological science . . . concerns each man and woman within these realms . . . it is, in fact, the anthropologist . . . who must be consulted for the future help and guidance in the government of alien races."[43] Heath went on to say that "the best legislator or politician is he who best understands the elements he governs; or, in other words, the best practical anthropologist" (lxxxvii). Burton himself hoped that the society would support the work of exploration and empire building throughout the world while also publishing the tabooed information he could not publish elsewhere.

Burton thought of all of his military, geographical, anthropological, and linguistic work as contributing to imperial power and glory. In a concluding note to *The Arabian Nights* he justifies even his study of proscribed sexual practices as having political value: "I . . . maintain that the free treatment of topics usually taboo'd and held to be 'alekta'— unknown and unfitted for publicity—will be a national benefit to an 'Empire of Opinion,' whose very basis and buttresses are a thorough knowledge by the rulers of the ruled."[44] Burton also states his imperialist creed explicitly in the preface to *First Footsteps in East Africa* (1856), where he recommends a much more forceful stance regarding both the Sublime Porte and the Arabians, even if such a policy leads to war.

"Peace," observes a modern sage, "is the dream of the wise, war is the history of man." To indulge in such dreams is but questionable wisdom. It was not a "peace-policy" which gave the Portuguese a seaboard extending from Cape Non to Macao. By no peace policy the Osmanlis of a past age pushed their victorious arms from the deserts of Tartary to Aden, to Delhi, to Algiers, and to the gates of Vienna. It was no peace policy which made the Russians set themselves upon the shores of the Black, the Baltic, and the Caspian seas: gaining in the space of 150 years . . . a territory greater than England and France united. No peace policy enabled the French to absorb region after region in Northern Africa, till the Mediterranean appears doomed to sink into a Gallic lake. The English of a former generation were celebrated for gaining ground in both hemispheres: their broad lands were not won by a peace policy, which, however, in this our day, has . . . well nigh lost for them the "gem of the British Empire"— India. The philanthropist and the political economist may fondly hope, by outcry against "territorial aggrandizement," by advocating a compact frontier, by abandoning colonies, and by cultivating "equilibrium," to retain our rank amongst the great nations of the world. Never! The facts of history prove nothing more conclusively than this: a race either progresses or retrogrades, either increases or diminishes: the children of Time, like their sire, cannot stand still.[45]

As for Disraeli, race for Burton is "the key to history," and a "truly fighting people" like the British must prove its worth by making constant progress in the military acquisition and government of new lands. Steam and free trade will not suffice; sword and spear remain the necessary tools for the advance of civilization—that is, especially for the advance of the British race—against the forces of barbarism and darkness. Burton proceeds to advocate the British "occupation of the port of Berberah" in Somalia, "the true key to the Red Sea" and "the centre of East African traffic."

Much the same imperialist message is evident in the *Pilgrimage*. His first Arabian journey was sponsored by the Royal Geographical Society, "for the purpose of removing that opprobrium to modern adventure, the huge white blot which in our maps still notes the Eastern and the Central regions of Arabia" (1:2). No doubt adventure and scientific curiosity were Burton's principle motives, but "the secondary objects were numerous" and of some strategic importance for the defense of India, as was Burton's own continued training as an intelligence agent capable of penetrating oriental and African societies. Along the way, he frequently makes observations about the fighting capacity of the peoples he sees and about the fortifications of the towns (1:255, 268). Describing his stay in Egypt, he contends that Egyptians are eager for an imperial yoke: "Egyptian human nature is, like human nature everywhere, contradictory. Hating and despising Europeans, they still long for European rule. This people admire an iron-handed and lion-hearted despotism; they hate a timid and a grinding tyranny," that is, that of the Turkish mamelukes (1:111–12). Burton is afraid Egypt will fall again into the hands of France, for "whatever European nation secures Egypt will win a treasure" (1:112). Apart from its economic value, Egypt has obvious strategic value: "This country in western hands will command India, and by a ship-canal between Pelusium and Suez would open the whole of Eastern Africa" (1:113). Of Arabia, Burton says that "it requires not the ken of a prophet to foresee the day when political necessity . . . will compel us to occupy in force the fountain-head of Al-Islam" (2:231n), a point he returns to when urging the appointment of a British consul "in Al-Hijaz . . . till the day shall come when the tide of events forces us to occupy the mother-city of Al-Islam" (2:268n).

The British never occupied Mecca, but they did occupy much of the Near East and Africa which Burton explored in oriental disguise. In his narratives Burton always presents himself as eager to abandon the West, to plunge into the wilderness, to experience again "the freedom of the Desert." But also he always holds his Byronic rebelliousness in check, precariously balanced by the authoritarian political attitudes involved in his military and social status and which inform his racist anthropology. These attitudes led him to look forward to a renewal of the barbarism of war (supposedly tempered by chivalry). In his posthumous "country house dialogue" on the chivalrous art of fencing, *The Sentiment of the Sword*, he declares that "now, when 'la force prime le droit,' when Europe stands up like Minerva in her panoply ready for the trial by what sciolists call 'brute strength,' I would see the old nation, England," prepared for victorious struggle.[46] "We are fast returning to those fine old days, still preserved in Asia and Africa, where every free-born man was a born man-at-arms, when every citizen was a soldier, and our falling back on the 'wisdom of antiquity' in this, as in other matters, is not one of the least curious features of the age" (6). Burton on war suggests how an era of progress could also be one of retrogression, sliding backward through imperial rivalry toward the medieval barbarism of the crusades.

iv

Burton's clearest exposition of his political ideas comes in an essay that he wrote in 1876 and Isabel appended to *The Life*; the essay was an installment of a projected work to be entitled *Labours and Wisdom of Richard Burton*. In the essay Burton denigrates Disraeli's "Suez Canal measure" as "a patch of tinsel gold plastered upon the rags of foreign and continental policy" (2:497). Burton declares himself to be a Conservative but says that his own party has failed to support true conservatism. He advocates the total rejection of democratic institutions and a return to a strong aristocracy and monarchy. He clearly wishes that Disraeli—or some more conservative, preferably non-Jewish leader—would invade Egypt and the rest of the Near East, and be done with "half measures":

> I would have bought the Canal wholly out and out, and put a fortress at each end, and taken a mild nominal toll to show my right. I would annex Egypt and protect Syria, occupy the Dardenelles, and after that let the whole world wrangle as much as it pleased. What is the use of having a Navy superior to all the united navies of the rest of the world, if we can't do this? The world will never be still till Constantinople returns to the old Byzantine kingdom; and we might put a Royalty there, say the Duke of Edinburgh, who, being married to the Czar's daughter, would unite the interests of Russia and England. Let the Turk live, but retire into private life; he is a good fellow there, and we can respect El Islam so long as he has nothing to butcher. (2:497)

Six years after Burton wrote his political essay, one year after Disraeli's death, a reluctant Liberal administration under Gladstone ordered the bombardment of Alexandria and the occupation of Egypt to defeat the nationalist rebellion of Arabi-Pasha. Three years later General Gordon's death at Khartoum precipitated the crisis that would lead to the occupation of the Sudan. The Scramble for Africa, and also for much of the Near and Far East, had begun in earnest. The press and public opinion portrayed Gordon as a glorious martyr for the British Empire and civilization. Despite his middle-class evangelicalism, he was often depicted as a modern St. George, slaying the dragons of slavery, barbarism, and oriental despotism.[47] Burton, a friend of Gordon's, was almost sent to the Sudan in Gordon's place or as Gordon's partner. Apart from religion, their values were similar, and the political results might have been the same had Burton gone to Khartoum instead of Gordon. The news of Gordon's death came as a great shock to Burton; according to Isabel, her husband initiated the speculation that Gordon was not dead but had fled down the Nile into darkest Africa. Burton believed that Gordon, "disgusted at the cruel treatment of being abandoned to his fate" by Gladstone's government, "had escaped and would come out Congowards, but that he would never let himself be rediscovered, nor reappear in England" (2:280). Gordon did not escape from Khartoum, but the myth of his martyrdom—less at the hands of the Mahdists than at those of the Liberals who supposedly failed to rescue him—inspired the British to undertake new crusades throughout the world.

"Dr. Livingstone, I presume?" From Henry Morton Stanley, *How I Found Livingstone* (1872).

6. The Genealogy of the Myth of the "Dark Continent"

We are thrown back in imagination to the infancy of the world.

—DAVID LIVINGSTONE

In *Heart of Darkness*, Marlow says that Africa is no longer the "blank space" on the map he had once daydreamed over. "It had got filled since my boyhood with rivers and lakes and names. . . . It had become a place of darkness."[1] Marlow is right: Africa grew dark as Victorian explorers, missionaries, and scientists flooded it with light, because the light was refracted through an imperialist ideology that urged the abolition of "savage customs" in the name of civilization. As a product of that ideology, the myth of the Dark Continent developed during the transition from the British campaign against the slave trade, which culminated in the outlawing of slavery in all British territory in 1833, to the imperialist partitioning of Africa, which dominated the final quarter of the nineteenth century.

The transition from the altruism of antislavery to the cynicism of empire building involved a transvaluation of values which we can aptly describe in Michel Foucault's genealogical language. For middle- and upper-class Victorians, dominant over a vast working-class majority at home and increasing millions of "uncivilized" peoples of "inferior races" abroad, power was self-validating. The world might contain many stages of social evolution and many seemingly bizarre customs and "superstitions," but there was only one civilization, one path of progress, one true religion. At home, culture might often seem threatened by anarchy: through Chartism, trade unionism, and socialism the alternative voices of the working class could at least be heard by anyone who cared to listen. Abroad, the culture of the "conquering race" seemed, at least to the insular and insulated sources of British public opinion, unchallenged: in imperialist discourse the voices of the dominated are represented almost entirely by their silence or their alleged acquiescence. According to Edward Said, "the critic is responsible to a degree for articulating those voices dominated, displaced, or silenced" by the authority of a dominant culture. This is one function of Foucault's genealogy, which seeks to analyze "the various systems of subjection: not the anticipatory power of meaning, but the hazardous play of dominations."[2]

Paradoxically, abolitionism contained the seeds of empire. If the general outline of Eric Williams's thesis in *Capitalism and Slavery* is valid, abolition was not purely altruistic but as economically conditioned as Britain's later empire building in Africa. The contradiction between the ideologies of antislavery and imperialism may be more apparent than real. Although the idealism that motivated the great abolitionists is unquestionable, Williams argues that Britain could *afford* to legislate against the slave trade only after that trade had helped provide the surplus capital necessary for industrial takeoff. Britain had lost much of its slave-owning territory as a result of the American Revolution; as the leading industrial power in the world Britain found in abolition a way to work against the interests of rivals who were still heavily involved in colonial slavery and a plantation economy.[3] There was nothing Machiavellian or even conscious about this aspect of abolition; what was conscious was the desire to right injustices and behave with a social benevolence unparalleled in history.

Nevertheless, the British abolitionist program entailed deeper and deeper involvement in Africa—the creation of Sierra Leone as a haven for freed slaves was just a start—although abolitionists before the 1840s were neither jingoists nor deliberate expansionists. Applied to Africa, however, humanitarianism did point insistently toward imperialism.[4] By the 1860s the success of the antislavery movement, the impact of the great Victorian explorers, and the merger in the social sciences of racist and evolutionary doctrines had combined, and the public widely shared a view of Africa which demanded imperialization on moral, religious, and scientific grounds. It is this view I call the myth of the Dark Continent; by mythology I mean ideology, or modern, secularized, "depoliticized speech" (to adopt Roland Barthes's phrase)—discourse that treats its subject as universally understood, scientifically established, and therefore no longer open to criticism by a political or theoretical opposition. According to Nancy Stepan, "a fundamental question about the history of racism in the first half of the nineteenth century is why it was that, just as the battle against slavery was being won by abolitionists, the war against racism was being lost. The Negro was legally freed by the Emancipation Act of 1833, but in the British mind he was still mentally, morally and physically a slave."[5] It is this fundamental question which a genealogy of the myth of the Dark Continent can help answer.

i

From the 1790s to the 1840s, the most influential kind of writing about Africa was abolitionist propaganda. Most of the great Romantics wrote poems against what Wordsworth in *The Prelude* called "the traffickers in Negro blood." Blake's "Little Black Boy" is perhaps the most familiar of these:

> My mother bore me in the southern wild,
> And I am black, but O! my soul is white;
> White as an angel is the English child;
> But I am black as if bereav'd of light.[6]

To Blake's poem can be added Coleridge's "Greek Prize Ode on the Slave Trade," Wordsworth's "Sonnet to Thomas Clarkson," and stanzas and poems by Byron and Shelley. Several of Southey's poems deal with the slave trade, including the final stanza of "To Horror":

> Horror! I call thee yet once more!
> Bear me to that accursed shore,
> Where on the stake the Negro writhes.[7]

We can hear the echo of Southey's "Dark Horror" in Conrad's "The horror! The horror!" a century later.

Two main points about antislavery literature stand out.[8] First, abolitionist writing involves the revelation of atrocities. Simon Legree's beating Uncle Tom to death is only the most familiar example. Abolitionist propaganda depicted in excruciating detail the barbaric practices of slave traders and owners in Africa, during the infamous Middle Passage, and in the southern states and West Indies. The constant association of Africa with the inhuman violence of the slave trade did much to darken its landscape even before the Romantic period. The exposé style of abolitionist propaganda, moreover, influenced much British writing about

Africa well after slavery had ceased to be an urgent issue. Though *Heart of Darkness* is not directly about slavery, an exposé style is evident there, as it is also, for example, in Olive Schreiner's fictional diatribe against Cecil Rhodes, *Trooper Peter Halket of Mashonaland* (1897). The frontispiece to Schreiner's tale is a photograph showing white Rhodesians with three lynched Mashona rebels—an accurate summary of much of the history of Europe's relations with Africa.

The second main point about antislavery literature is that pre-Victorian writers were often able to envisage Africans living freely and happily without European interference. Strike off the fetters European slavers had placed on them, and the result was noble savages living in pastoral freedom and innocence. In sonnet 5 of Southey's "Poems Concerning the Slave Trade," a slave's rebelliousness is inspired by

> the intolerable thought
> Of every past delight; his native grove,
> Friendship's best joys, and liberty and love
> For ever lost.[9]

Similarly, in "Africa Delivered; or, The Slave Trade Abolished" (1809), James Grahame writes:

> In that fair land of hill, and dale, and stream,
> The simple tribes from age to age had heard
> No hostile voice

—until the arrival of European slave traders who introduced to an Edenic Africa the characteristic products of civilization: avarice, treachery, rapine, murder, warfare, and slavery.[10]

Abolitionist portrayals of Africans as perhaps noble but also innocent or simple savages were patronizing and unintentionally derogatory. Nevertheless, such portrayals were both more positive and often more open-minded than those from about 1840 to World War I.[11] Ironically, the expansion of the slave trade had required Europeans to develop more accurate knowledge of Africans—both those Africans with whom they did business and those who became their commodities. Many factors contributed to a period of relative sympathy in writing about Africa between 1790 and 1830, among them the satiric tradition of the noble savage, turned to effective popular use in 1688 in Aphra Behn's *Oroonoko; or, The Royal Slave* (and later by many abolitionists); the Enlightenment belief that all people should be treated equally under the law; the growth of the abolitionist movement; and the exploration of the Niger River by Mungo Park and others, starting in the late 1700s. This relative sympathy is evident in the abolitionist poetry of Southey and Grahame and also in such works of social observation as Thomas Bowdich's *Mission from Cape Coast Castle to Ashantee* (1819). Bowdich condemned the Ashanti practice of ritual human sacrifice but did not treat that aspect of their culture as representative of the whole, nor allow it to interfere with his appreciation of other Ashanti customs, arts, and institutions.[12]

The abolition of slavery in all British territories did not eliminate concern about slavery elsewhere, but the British began to see themselves less as perpetrators of the slave trade and more as potential saviors of the African. The blame for slavery could now be displaced onto others, Americans, for example, and increasingly onto Africans themselves for maintaining the slave trade as a main form of economic exchange. This shifting of the burden of guilt is already evident in the Niger Expedition of 1841, which one historian calls "the first step toward a general 'forward policy' in West Africa."[13] Thomas Fowell Buxton, leader of the British antislavery movement after William Wilberforce, recognized that the emancipation legislation of 1833 would not eliminate slavery from non-British parts of the world. He therefore proposed to attack slavery at its source, planning the Niger Expedition to initiate the introduction of Christianity and "legitimate commerce" to West Africa. In *The African Slave Trade and Its Remedy* (1840), Buxton portrays Africa as a land "teeming with inhabitants who admire, and are desirous of possessing our manufactures."[14] In the past Africans learned to trade in human lives; in the future they must learn to produce something other than slaves. Buxton's message is close to Martineau's in *Dawn Island*: the British will teach Africans to be both religious and industrious, and to engage in free trade.

Although Buxton repudiated empire building, the Niger Expedition aimed to establish bases from which European values could spread throughout Africa. Buxton's portrayal of Africa is almost wholly negative: "Bound in the chains of the grossest ignorance, [Africa] is a prey to the most savage superstition. Christianity has made but feeble inroads on this kingdom of darkness" (10–11). In a chapter titled "Superstitions and Cruelties of the Africans," Buxton extracts the most grisly descriptions of such customs as human sacrifice from the writings of Bowdich and others and offers these as the essence of African culture. Buxton's "dark catalogue of crime" combines slavery and savagery; both disrupt Africa's chances for civilization and salvation (270). "Such atrocious deeds, as have been detailed in the foregoing pages, keep the African population in a state of callous barbarity, which can only be effectually counteracted by Christian civilisation" (244).

The Niger Expedition ended in disaster: most of its European participants were laid low by malaria, forty-one of them perishing. For at least a decade the failure supported arguments that Europeans should stay out of central Africa—the harsh facts of disease and death themselves darkened the continent. In his 1848 essay on the Niger Expedition, Dickens attacked the aims of philanthropists and decried Africa as a continent not fit for civilization, best left in the dark: "The history of this Expedition is the history of the Past [rather than the future] in reference to the heated visions of philanthropists for the railroad Christianisation of Africa, and the abolition of the Slave Trade. . . . Between the civilized European and the barbarous African there is a great gulf set. . . . To change the customs even of civilised . . . men . . . is . . . a most difficult and slow proceeding; but to do this by ignorant and savage races, is a work which, like the progressive changes of the globe itself, requires a stretch of years that dazzles in the looking at."[15] A Buxton or a Martineau might look upon conversion of the savages as a mere matter of showing them the light, whether of religion or of the gospel of free trade, but Dickens thought savages so far beneath Europeans on the great chain of being that only fools expected to "railroad" them into civilization. In *Bleak House* he places Mrs. Jellyby's Borrioboola-Gha mission on the banks of the Niger to suggest its utter and absurd futility, like that of the Niger Expedition. In his occasional rantings against "natives," "Sambos," and "ignoble savages," Dickens also vents his hostility toward evangelical philanthropy. He regarded missionaries as "perfect nuisances who leave every place worse than they find it." "Believe it, African Civilisation, Church of England Missionary, and all other Missionary Societies!" he writes. "The work at home must be completed thoroughly, or there is no hope abroad."[16] This was also Carlyle's attitude in "The Nigger Question" (1849) and again in his response to the Jamaica Rebellion of 1865. Both Carlyle and Dickens held that abolitionist and missionary activities were distractions from more appropriate concerns about poverty and misgovernment at home.

As the Governor Eyre controversy showed, many Victorians sympathized with the poor at home but not with the exploited abroad, and a sizable portion of the British public sided with the South during the American Civil War. Slavery, however, remained an important issue from the 1840s to the end of the century. Slavery is central, for example, to an 1847 novel by Sarah Lee Wallis (whose first husband was Thomas Bowdich), *The African Wanderers*, in which "from one end of Africa to the other we find traces of that horrible traffic." Some of Wallis's "natives" are restless and hostile because they are cannibals "who file their teeth" and lust after human flesh, but more are restless and hostile because their normally pacific lives have been disrupted by the slave trade. When *Uncle Tom's Cabin* appeared in 1852, moreover, it sold more copies in Britain than America.[17] One of Harriet Beecher Stowe's most ardent British admirers, Elizabeth Barrett Browning, contributed to the abolitionist cause with her poems "The Runaway Slave at Pilgrim's Point" and "A Curse for a Nation," and Harriet Martineau was also an ardent abolitionist. After 1865 slavery seemed to be largely confined to Africa; along with such staples of sensational journalism as human sacrifice and cannibalism, slavery looked more and more like a direct extension of African savagery.

After abolishing slavery on their own ground, the British turned to the seemingly humane work of abolishing slavery—and all "savage customs"—on African ground. By the time of the Berlin Conference of 1884–85, which is often identified as the start of the Scramble for Africa, the British tended to see Africa as a center of evil, a part of the world possessed by a demonic darkness or barbarism, represented above all by slavery, human sacrifice, and cannibalism, which it was their duty to exorcise. The writers most responsible for promoting this view—and for maintaining the crusade against slavery and the slave trade even after Britain and the United States had ceased to engage in them—were the explorers and missionaries, with Buxton's disciple David Livingstone in the lead.

ii

The so-called opening up of Africa by the great Victorian explorers commenced in the late 1850s, facilitated by quinine as a prophylactic against malaria. Earlier explorers had excited public interest, but the search for the sources of the White Nile, initiated by Burton and Speke in 1856 and followed by the expeditions of Speke and Grant, Samuel White Baker, Livingstone, and Stanley, raised public interest to fever pitch.[18] When Alec MacKenzie, hero of Somerset Maugham's *The Explorer* (1907), first reads "the marvellous records of African exploration," his "blood tingled at the magic of those pages." Inspired by those narratives,

Alec becomes an explorer who struggles mightily against savagery and the internal slave trade, not to mention European villainy, and thus contributes mightily to imperial expansion. Maugham offers a fictional hagiography of all the great explorers of Africa, "men who've built up the empire piece by piece" and whose chief aim has been to add "another fair jewel to her crown." If the connection between exploration and empire building was not always evident to MacKenzie's originals, it is paramount for Maugham: "Success rewarded [MacKenzie's] long efforts. . . . The slavers were driven out of a territory larger than the United Kingdom, treaties were signed with chiefs who had hitherto been independent . . . and only one step remained, that the government should . . . annex the conquered district to the empire."[19]

The books the explorers wrote took the Victorian reading public by storm. In the first few months after its publication in 1857 Livingstone's *Missionary Travels* sold 70,000 copies and made its author wealthy and so famous that he was mobbed by admirers. A national hero in the late 1850s, by the end of his last African journey in 1872 he was a national saint. The obverse of the myth of the Dark Continent was that of the Promethean and, at least in Livingstone's case, saintly bestower of light. Even Dickens, with his dislike of evangelical types, made an exception of Livingstone, calling him one of "those who carry into desert places the water of life."[20] Livingstone's apotheosis was complete in 1872 when Stanley, with his great journalistic scoop, published his first bestseller, *How I Found Livingstone.* Stanley's other books were also bestsellers: *In Darkest Africa,* for example, sold 150,000 copies in English, was frequently translated, and according to one reviewer "has been read more universally and with deeper interest than any other publication of" 1890.[21] Still another bestseller was Samuel White Baker's *The Albert N'Yanza* of 1866, and many others were widely read, including Burton's *Lake Regions of Central Africa* (1860), John Speke's *Discovery of the Sources of the Nile* (1864), and Joseph Thomson's *To the Central African Lakes and Back* (1881). Although such accounts of African exploration do not figure in standard histories of Victorian literature, they exerted an incalculable influence on British culture and the course of modern history. It would be difficult to find a clearer example of the Foucauldian concept of discourse as power, as "a violence that we do to things."[22]

The great explorers' writings are nonfictional quest romances in which the hero-authors struggle through enchanted, bedeviled lands toward an ostensible goal: the discovery of the Nile's sources, the conversion of the cannibals. But that goal is also sheer survival and return home to the regions of light. The humble but heroic authors move from adventure to adventure against a dark, infernal backdrop where there are no other characters of equal stature, only bewitched or demonic savages. Although they sometimes individualize the Africans they encounter, explorers usually portray amusing or dangerous obstacles or objects of curiosity, whereas missionaries see weak, pitiable, inferior mortals who need to be shown the light. Center stage is occupied not by Africa or Africans but by a Livingstone or a Stanley, a Baker or a Burton, Victorian St. Georges battling the armies of the night. Kurtz's career in deviltry suggests that at least sometimes it was a losing battle.

Livingstone offers a striking example of how humanitarian aims could contribute to imperialist encroachment. Deeply influenced by Buxton, Livingstone also advocated the opening up of Africa by commerce and Christianity. He had more respect for Africans than most explorers and missionaries, though he still viewed them as "children" and "savages." Occasionally he even expressed doubt that a European presence in Africa would be beneficial, but he also believed the African was "benighted" and the European bore the light of civilization and true religion. Just as Martineau in *Dawn Island* identified salvation from savagery with the gospel of free trade, so Livingstone held that Africa could not hope to "raise itself" without "contact with superior races by commerce." Africans were "inured to bloodshed and murder, and care[d] for no god except being bewitched"; without commerce and Christianity, "the prospects for these dark regions are not bright." Of this most humanitarian of explorers Tim Jeal writes that "with his missionary aims and his almost messianic passion for exporting British values [Livingstone] seemed to his successors to have provided the moral basis for massive imperial expansion."[23]

Economic and political motives are, of course, easier to detect in Livingstone's doppelgänger, Henry Morton Stanley. The purpose behind Stanley's work in the Congo for King Leopold II of Belgium was not far removed from the aims of the Eldorado Exploring Expedition in *Heart of Darkness*: "To tear treasure out of the bowels of the land was their desire, with no more moral purpose at the back of it than there is in burglars breaking into a safe." But blatant economic motive was not what impelled Livingstone and the horde of missionaries who imitated him. The melodrama of Africa called for intervention by a higher moral power, and the Victorians increasingly saw themselves—again with Livingstone in the lead—as the highest moral power among nations. The success of the British antislavery movement, after all, seemed to prove that Britain was more virtuous than its rivals for empire. For Livingstone, as for other missionaries and abolitionists, the African was a creature to be pitied, to be saved from slavery and also from his own darkness, his savagery. At least Livingstone believed that the African could be rescued from darkness—that he could be Christianized and perhaps civilized. Such an attitude was, of course, necessary for any missionary. At the same time missionaries were strongly tempted to exaggerate savagery and darkness to rationalize their presence in Africa, to explain the frustrations they experienced in making converts, and to win support from mission societies at home.[24]

The titles of missionary accounts express typical attitudes: *Daybreak in the Dark Continent* by Wilson S. Naylor, for example, and *Dawn in the Dark Continent; or, Africa and Its Missions* by James Stewart. Typical, too, are these assertions from *By the Equator's Snowy Peak*, May Crawford's 1913 autobiography about missionary life in British East Africa: "With the coming of the British," she says, "dawned a somewhat brighter" day for Africa—only somewhat brighter because of the great backwardness of the natives, not because of any British failing. "Loving darkness rather than light," she continues, the "natives . . . resent all that makes for progress."[25] Perhaps what the Africans resented was British intrusion into their land, but this Crawford could not see. I have read of no instances where cannibals put missionaries into pots and cooked them, but Africans did sometimes kill, capture, or drive missionaries away, thus fueling arguments for armed intervention and imperialist annexation.[26] In Anthony Hope's 1895 novel *The God in the Car*, Lord Semingham is asked how his great scheme for investing in central Africa is faring. "Everything's going on very well," he replies. "They've killed a missionary." This may be "regrettable in itself," Semingham smiles, "but [it's] the first step towards empire."[27]

The missionary idea that Africa could be redeemed for civilization was more than some explorers were willing to grant. Burton believed that the African was "unimprovable." "He is inferior to the active-minded and objective . . . Europeans, and to the . . . subjective and reflective Asiatic. He partakes largely of the worst characteristics of the lower Oriental types—stagnation of mind, indolence of body, moral deficiency, superstition, and childish passion."[28] Burton goes to some lengths to undermine the missionary position. He declares that "these wild African fetissists [sic] are [not] easily converted to a 'purer creed' . . . their faith is a web woven with threads of iron." Yet he agrees with the missionaries in depicting fetishism as witchcraft and devil worship, Kurtz's unspeakable rites. "A prey to base passions and melancholy godless fears, the Fetissist . . . peoples with malevolent beings the invisible world, and animates material nature with evil influences. The rites of his dark and deadly superstition are" entirely nefarious, as almost all Victorian writers claimed.[29] In their books and essays the Victorians demote all central Africa's kings to "chiefs" and all African priests, with the exception of Muslims, to "witchdoctors."

Even if Africans are doomed by their "negro instincts" (Burton's phrase) always to remain savage, Burton still has in mind for them a role in the work of civilization. Like Carlyle, he argues both that abolitionist philanthropy is mistaken and that primitive peoples need civilized masters. His argument is explicitly imperialist: "I unhesitatingly assert—and all unprejudiced travellers will agree with me—that the world still wants the black hand. Enormous tropical regions yet await the clearing and draining operations by the lower races, which will fit them to become the dwelling-places of civilized men."[30] Other explorers agreed with Burton. Though a hero in the late stages of the antislavery crusade, Baker believed that "the African . . . will assuredly relapse into an idle and savage state, unless specially governed and forced by industry."[31]

Burton was a marginal aristocrat; Baker came from a well-to-do family of shipowners and West Indian planters. Their racist view of Africans as a natural laboring class, suited only for the dirty work of civilization, expresses a nostalgia for lost authority and for a pliable, completely subordinate proletariat that is one of the central fantasies of imperialism. For opposite reasons, that fantasy also appealed to explorers from working-class backgrounds, such as Livingstone and Stanley, whose subordinate status at home was reversed in Africa. Livingstone the factory boy could be Livingstone the great white leader and teacher in Africa; Stanley the pauper orphan became the great pioneer and field marshal, blazing the trail for civilization.

That Africans were suited only for manual labor is an idea fiction often repeats. In Henry S. Merriman's *With Edged Tools* (1894), for example, African porters "hired themselves out like animals, and as the beasts of the field they did their work—patiently, without intelligence. . . . Such is the African." The comparison with British labor is made explicit when the narrator adds: "If any hold that men are not created so dense and unambitious as has just been represented, let him look nearer home in our own merchant service. The able-bodied seaman goes to sea all his life, but he never gets any nearer navigating the ship—and he a white man." The English protagonists are shocked to discover that the Africans whom their villainous half-breed partner has hired are his "slaves," to whom he pays no wages—slavery by the 1890s was patently a violation of "one of Heaven's laws."[32] But when offered the choice between freedom and continuing in slavery, most of the Africans choose slavery. Africans are not suited for freedom, Merriman implies, though whether they can ever be elevated to freedom or are racially doomed to a life no higher than that of beasts of burden is an issue he leaves clouded.

Racism functions as a displaced or surrogate class system, growing more extreme as the domestic class alignments it reflects are threatened or erode. As a rationalization for the domination of "inferior" peoples, imperialist discourse is inevitably racist; it treats class and race terminology as covertly interchangeable or at least analogous. There exist both a hierarchy of classes and a hierarchy of races; both are the results of evolution or of the laws of nature; both classes and races are simpler than but similar to species; and both are developing but are also, at any given moment, fixed, inevitable, not subject to political manipulation. But class is more or less subject to political reform, and in that way the class hierarchy never seemed as absolute as the hierarchy of races. Compared to the social Darwinian rhetoric of imperialism, the socialist, liberal, and even conservative discourses of domestic reform at least acknowledged the existence of political alternatives to the status quo.

As in South Africa now, so in the Empire the conquered races were treated as a new proletariat, their status much less distinct from slavery than that of the working class at home. The desire for—indeed, the creation of—a new, subordinate underclass contradicted the abolitionist stance taken by Victorian explorers and missionaries, but it influenced all relations between Victorians and Africans. Aside from South Africa, perhaps its most virulent form was the forced labor system of King Leopold's Congo which Stanley helped establish, though it appears in so small an item as the design by Sir Harry Johnston for the first postage stamp of British Central Africa. The Africans who flank the shield and the motto "Light in Darkness" hold a spade and a pickax—the implements, no doubt, to build the future *white* civilization of Africa.[33]

iii

The racist views held by Burton and Baker were at least as close to the science of their day as the somewhat less negative views of the missionaries. Burton, as a member of the Anthropological Society, agreed with its founder James Hunt that the Negro race probably formed a distinct species.[34] In contrast, most Darwinians held that the races of mankind had a common origin and therefore believed the unity of human nature. But Darwinism was only relatively more advanced than Hunt's racism. The development of physical anthropology and ethnology as disciplines concerned with differences among races strengthened the stereotypes expressed by explorers and missionaries. Evolutionary anthropology often suggested that Africans, if not nonhuman or a different species, were such an inferior "breed" that they might be impervious to "higher influences."

Concerted investigations of race and evolution were beginning at the same time as investigations of prehistory and the anthropoid apes. Some of the results can be seen in Thomas Henry Huxley's *Man's Place in Nature* (1863) and Darwin's *Descent of Man* (1872). Huxley's essay involves a refutation of the idea that Africans, Australians, and other primitive peoples are the "missing link" or evolutionary stage between the anthropoid apes and civilized (white) mankind. But Huxley repeatedly cites evidence that suggests a proximity between African, chimpanzee, and gorilla, including the story of an African tribe who believe that the great apes were once their next of kin. Into the middle of his otherwise logical argument, moreover, he inserts a wholly gratuitous account of "African cannibalism in the sixteenth century," drawn from a Portuguese source and illustrated with a grisly woodcut depicting a "human butcher shop."[35]

When an astute, scientific observer indulges in fantasies about cannibalism, something more than mere caprice is at work. As Dorothy Hammond and Alta Jablow note, cannibalism was not an important theme in British writing about Africa before mid-century. But "in the imperial period writers were far more addicted to tales of cannibalism than . . . Africans ever were to cannibalism."[36] Typical of the more sensational treatments of anthropophagy is Winwood Reade, who in *Savage Africa* (1863) writes that "the mob of Dahomey are *man-eaters*; they have cannibal minds; they have been accustomed to feed on murder." Reade nonetheless describes his flirtations with cannibal maidens, and in a capricious chapter on "the philosophy of cannibalism" he distinguishes between ritual cannibalism, practiced by some West African societies, and another (mythical) sort that is "simply an act of *gourmandise*." "A cannibal is not necessarily ferocious. He eats his fellow-creatures, not because he hates them, but because he likes them."[37] The more Europeans dominated Africans, the more savage Africans came to seem; cannibalism represented the nadir of savagery, more extreme even than slavery (which, of course, a number of "civilized" nations practiced through much of the nineteenth century).

Evolutionary thought seems almost calculated to legitimize imperialism. The theory that man evolved through distinct social stages—from savagery to barbarism to civilization—led to a self-congratulatory anthropology that actively promoted belief in the inferiority, indeed the bestiality, of the African. In *The Origin of Civilization* (1870), Sir John Lubbock argues not just that contemporary savages represent the starting point of social evolution but that they are below that starting point. The original primitives from whom we evolved contained the seeds of progress; modern savages have not progressed, according to Lubbock, and hence must be lower on the evolutionary scale than our ancestors. All the more reason, of course, to place them under imperial guardianship and to treat them as nothing more than potential labor.[38] Similar is the evolutionary hierarchy of both race and social class in George Romanes's 1889 essay *Mental Evolution in Man*: "When we come to consider the case of the savages, and through them the case of prehistoric man, we shall find that, in the great interval which lies between such grades of mental evolution and our own, we are brought far on the way toward bridging the psychological distance which separates the gorilla from the gentleman."[39] Presumably, everyone is a link somewhere in this late Victorian version of the great chain of being: if gentlemen are at the farthest remove from our anthropoid ancestors, the working class is not so far removed, and savages are even closer.

In her examination of the "scientific" codification of racist dogmas, Nancy Stepan writes: "By the 1850s, the shift from the earlier ethnographic, monogenist, historical and philosophical tradition to a more conservative, anthropological, and polygenist approach . . . had advanced quite far in Britain. . . . Races were now seen as forming a natural but static chain of excellence" (45–46). By the end of the century eugenicists and social Darwinists were offering "scientific" justifications for genocide as well as for imperialism (the two were inseparable, but while imperialism could be advocated in public, the liquidation of "inferior" races obviously could not). In *Social Evolution* (1894), Benjamin Kidd argued that, try as they might to be humane, the British would inevitably kill off the weaker races in "the struggle for existence":

> The Anglo-Saxon has exterminated the less developed peoples with which he has come into competition . . . through the operation of laws not less

deadly [than war] and even more certain in their result. The weaker races disappear before the stronger through the effects of mere contact. . . . The Anglo-Saxon, driven by forces inherent in his own civilisation, comes to develop the natural resources of the land, and the consequences appear to be inevitable. The same history is repeating itself in South Africa. In the words [of] a leading colonist of that country, "the natives must go; or they must work as laboriously to develop the land as we are prepared to do."⁴⁰

In *National Life from the Standpoint of Science* (1901), the eugenicist Karl Pearson goes beyond the vision of the black African with spade and pickax performing the groundwork for white civilization in the tropics: "No strong and permanent civilization can be built upon slave labour, [and] an inferior race doing menial labour for a superior race can give no stable community." The solution? Whereas the abolitionists sought to liberate the slaves, Pearson's science seeks to eliminate them, or at least to push them out of the path of civilization. "We shall never have a healthy social state in South Africa until the white man replaces the dark in the fields and the mines, and the Kaffir is pushed back towards the equator. The nation organized for the struggle [of existence] must be a *homogeneous* whole, not a mixture of superior and inferior races."⁴¹

Darwin himself speculated about the apparently inevitable extinction of primitive races in the encounter with higher ones. Genocide decimated the American Indians, Tasmanians, Maoris, and aboriginal Australians, but Darwin believed these races would have withered on the vine anyway—the less fit vanishing as the fitter advanced. Africans did not dwindle away as Europeans encroached on their territory, despite the slave trade, which to some observers seemed proof of their hardiness, their fitness. Others, however, saw this apparent fitness as only showing inferiority in a different light—Africans were made of coarser stuff than the sensitive and poetic Maoris. Darwin is comparatively cautious in his speculations about race, but throughout *The Descent of Man* he emphasizes the distance between savage and civilized peoples, contrasting savages who practice infanticide to such examples of moral and intellectual excellence as John Howard and Shakespeare. In the last paragraph of the book he declares he would rather be related to a baboon than to "a savage who delights to torture his enemies, offers up bloody sacrifices without remorse, treats his wives like slaves, knows no decency, and is haunted by the grossest superstitions."⁴² In general, Darwinism lent scientific status to the view that there were higher and lower races, progressive and nonprogressive ones, and that the lower races ought to be governed by—even completely supplanted by—civilized, progressive races like the British.

There is much irony in the merger of racist and evolutionary theories in Victorian anthropology. For the Victorians the distance between primitive and civilized peoples seemed immense and perhaps unbridgeable. In the modern era, through another sharp transvaluation, anthropology has shifted from evolutionism to cultural relativism. First in the work of Franz Boas and then more generally after World War I, the morally judgmental and racist anthropology of the Victorians gave way to a new version of "objectivity," what might even be called scientific primitivism.[43] What Claude Lévi-Strauss says in *Tristes tropiques* about the religious attitudes of primitives is exemplary of the transvaluation that anthropology has undergone since its nineteenth-century inception as the study of racial differences and a scientific rationalization for empire. Primitive beliefs are not "superstitions," Lévi-Strauss declares, but rather "preferences . . . denoting a kind of wisdom [acceptance of individual and ecological limits, reverence for nature] which savage races practised spontaneously and the rejection of which, by the modern world, is the real madness."[44]

iv

Although the antislavery crusade inspired much poetry before 1833, Victorian poets wrote little about Africa (except for patriotic verses on such topics as General Gordon's last stand at Khartoum). Tennyson's "Timbuctoo" is an apparent exception, but it was written in 1829 for a Cambridge poetry contest and offers a Romantic account of how the visionary city of Fable has been "darkened" by "keen discovery" (a paradoxical application of "darken" similar to Marlow's). More typical of Victorian attitudes is Thackeray's "Timbuctoo," written for the same contest that Tennyson's poem won. Thackeray parodied abolitionist propaganda:

> Desolate Afric! thou art lovely yet!
> One heart yet beats which ne'er shall thee forget.
> What though thy maidens are a blackish brown,
> Does virtue dwell in whiter breasts alone?
> Oh no, oh no, oh no, oh no, oh no!
> It shall not, must not, cannot, e'er be so.
> The day shall come when Albion's self shall feel
> Stern Afric's wrath, and writhe neath Afric's steel.[45]

Other far-flung parts of the world inspired the Victorian muse—Edward FitzGerald's *Rubaiyat* and Edwin Arnold's *The Light of Asia* come to mind—but Victorian imaginative discourse about Africa tended toward discredited forms, Gothic romance and boys' adventure story. For the most part, fiction writers imitated the explorers, producing quest romances with Gothic overtones in which the heroic white penetration of the Dark Continent is the central theme. H. Rider Haggard's stories fit this pattern, and so—with ironic differences—does Joseph Conrad's *Heart of Darkness*.

Explorers themselves sometimes wrote adventure novels: Baker's *Cast Up by the Sea* (1866) and Stanley's *My Kalulu: Prince, King, and Slave* (1889) are both tales addressed to boys, and both carry abolitionist themes into Africa well after the emancipation of slaves in most other parts of the world. "I had in view," writes Stanley, "that I might be able to describe more vividly in such a book as this than in any other way the evils of the slave trade in Africa."[46] His story traces an Arab slaving caravan to Lake Tanganyika; when the Arabs are attacked by the blacks they have come to enslave, the only survivors—a few Arab boys—are enslaved instead. Later they are rescued from slavery by Prince Kalulu, who himself escaped from slavery in an earlier episode. But Kalulu and the Arab boys are once more captured, by slave-trading blacks, "the Wazavila assassins and midnight robbers," whose attacks on innocent villages provide what Stanley calls "a true picture" of the horrors of the slave trade. Even the Arab slavers are morally superior to the "fiendish" Wazavila. After many scrapes, Kalulu and the Arab boys, well-experienced in the horrors of slavery and the Dark Continent, reach Zanzibar and freedom. Stanley's moral is plain: the internal slave trade will cease only when European forces quash the Wazavila and other slave-trading tribes and harness the African to the wheel of what Buxton called legitimate commerce.

In 1888 the great Scottish explorer of Kenya, Joseph Thomson, published an ostensibly adult novel. The protagonist of *Ulu: An African Romance* is a disgruntled Scotsman named Gilmour (partly modeled on Thomson himself) who escapes from corrupt civilization to the Kenyan highlands. Gilmour accepts as his fiancée a fourteen-year-old African girl, Ulu, whom he proceeds (inconsistently, given his rejection of civilization) to try to civilize before marrying. This African Pygmalion story seems daring for the first fifty pages—a direct assault on Victorian stereotypes of race and empire. But the hero never marries or even civilizes Ulu; instead, he realizes the terrible mistake he has made when he meets the blonde, blue-eyed daughter of the local missionary. Ulu then becomes for the white lovers an object of patronizing, cloying concern. Gilmour acknowledges "the impossibility of making Ulu other than she is, an out-and-out little savage, childlike and simple, and lovable in many ways, perhaps, but utterly incapable of assimilating any of the higher thoughts and aspirations of the civilized life." While Gilmour's Pygmalion scheme is collapsing, the story falls into a stereotypic adventure pattern. The ferocious Masai attack and capture Ulu and the missionary's daughter. "What had [Kate] to expect from these licentious, bloodthirsty savages, the indulgence of whose brutal passions was their sole rule in life?"[47] Fortunately the Masai have never seen anything as beautiful as Kate, and they proceed to worship her. Gilmour rescues Kate, and Ulu conveniently sacrifices herself so the intrepid white couple, who were of course meant for each other all along, can live happily ever after. (It is tempting to correlate this wishful fantasy of love and extermination with scientific rationalizations of genocide: progress and fulfillment are the domain of Europeans, even on an individual level. Nevertheless, among the great explorers Thomson was one of the more liberal defenders of Africans and African rights.) Thomson's story is ludicrously inconsistent, but it is also remarkable for suggesting that the European invasion of Africa might corrupt innocent savages without civilizing them and for even broaching the possibility of intermarriage. White/black unions were not uncommon in reality, as the history of the Griqua and other racially mixed peoples in southern Africa attests, but in fiction intermarriage was unheard of.

Except for its stress on love and marriage, Thomson's adult novel contains little to distinguish it from the whole subgenre of boys' adventure tales to which Stanley's and Baker's stories belong. An adolescent quality pervades imperialist literature, as it would fascist culture in the 1920s and 1930s. Africa was a setting where British boys could become men, and British men, like Haggard's heroes, could behave like boys with impunity. Africa was a great testing (or teething) ground for moral growth and moral regression (the two processes were often indistinguishable). And because imperialism always entailed violence and exploitation and therefore could never bear much scrutiny, propagandists found it easier to leave it to boys to "play up, play up, and play the game" than to supposedly more mature audiences. Much imperialist discourse was thus directed at a specifically adolescent audience, the future rulers of the world. In the works of Marryat, Mayne Reid, G. A. Henty, W. H. G. Kingston, Dr. Gordon Stables, Stevenson, Haggard, and Kipling, Britain turned youthful as it turned outward, following a regressive path parallel to "going native."

In *Black Ivory: A Tale of Adventure among the Slaves of East Africa*

(1873), another boys' novelist, R. M. Ballantyne, emulated Livingstone in seeking to expose "the horrible traffic in human beings." "Exaggeration has easily been avoided," Ballantyne assures us, "because—as Dr. Livingstone says in regard to the slave trade—'exaggeration is impossible.'" Ballantyne wishes to expose both the atrocities of the slave trade and anti-Negro stereotypes. His character Chief Kambira, Ballantyne writes, has "nothing of our nursery savage . . . [he] does not roar, or glare, or chatter, or devour his food in its blood."[48] This is all to the good, but Ballantyne is inconsistent. His Africans are sympathetic mainly as melodrama victims, and otherwise he portrays their customs as laughably childish. He has only praise for British antislavery squadrons patrolling the coasts and for the British intruding inland in East Africa to stop the slave trade.[49]

More ingenious than *Black Ivory* is Sir Harry Johnston's *The History of a Slave* (1889), which takes the form of an autobiographical slave narrative. Himself an explorer and an artist, illustrator of his own story, Johnston attacks slavery as an extension of savagery. The atrocities that his slave narrator depicts are more grisly than anything in Ballantyne; most grisly of all are the slow tortures practiced by the Executioner of Zinder under the Tree of Death. But if the slave's life under various Muslim masters is violent and cruel, his life before slavery is just as bloody and even more irrational. Thus the narrator recounts his earliest memory: "When . . . the men of our town killed someone and roasted his flesh for a feast . . . the bones . . . were laid round about the base of [a] tree. The first thing I remember clearly was playing with [a] skull."[50] Johnston's exposé of the atrocities of the slave trade is preceded by an exposé of the alleged atrocities of tribal savagery—no pastoral innocence here. The solution to the slave trade entails more than persuading Muslim sheikhs to set black Africans free; it also entails the abolition of tribal savagery, which requires imperialist annexation, the fulfillment of Britain's civilizing mission.

Other fictions about Africa, even when written long after the American Civil War, also attack the slave trade as part of a larger pattern of violence and savagery. In *The Congo Rovers: A Story of the Slave Squadron* (1885), by the American William Lancaster, the hero is captured by slave-trading natives and narrowly escapes sacrificial murder in a chapter entitled "A Fiendish Ceremonial." The work exhibits all of the stereotypes about the Dark Continent exploited by another popular American writer, Edgar Rice Burroughs, in the Tarzan books. Novels not about slavery also stress the violence and irrationality of tribal customs. The publication dates of Haggard's *King Solomon's Mines* (1885) and John Buchan's *Prester John* (1910) span the period of the Scramble for Africa, and in both novels civilization is juxtaposed with savagery in ways that call for the elimination of the latter. For Haggard and Buchan too, the Dark Continent must be made light.

Haggard and Buchan also give new life to the Romantic figure of the noble savage, however—Haggard through his magnificent Zulu warriors Umbopa and Umslopogaas, Buchan through his black antihero John Laputa, also from Zulu country. Haggard sees clearly the destruction of Zulu society by the encroachment of whites (*King Solomon's Mines* appeared six years after the Zulu War of 1879), and he contrasts primitive customs favorably with civilized ones. He nevertheless maintains a sharp division between savage and civilized; his white heroes penetrate the darkness as representatives of vastly higher levels of social evolution. Like aristocrats in Renaissance pastoral they cleave to their own kind and return to the light. Their friendship with Umbopa cannot hold them in Kukuanaland, and only one other relationship threatens to do so, the romance between Captain John Good and the beautiful Foulata, nipped in the bud when like Ulu she is killed near the end of the story. The narrator Allan Quatermain concludes: "I consider her removal was a fortunate occurrence, since, otherwise, complications would have been sure to ensue. The poor creature was no ordinary native girl, but a person of great . . . beauty, and of considerable refinement of mind. But no amount of beauty or refinement could have made an entanglement between Good and herself a desirable occurrence; for, as she herself put it, 'Can the sun mate with the darkness, or the white with the black?' "[51]

Buchan depicts a revolutionary conspiracy led by John Laputa, the self-proclaimed heir of Prester John. To the narrator, Davie Crawfurd, Laputa is a noble but also satanic savage; Davie finds him intensely attractive, but the attraction is charged with a deeply racist and erotic dread. Buchan portrays the conspiracy in Gothic romance terms, as a nightmare from which Davie struggles to awake. "You know the [kind of] nightmare when you are pursued by some awful terror," Davie says; and again: "Last night I . . . looked into the heart of darkness and the sight . . . terrified me."[52] But this heart of darkness is not within Davie's psyche, it is Africa and the murderous savagery of Laputa. Haggard can entertain the thought of a free society of noble savages as long as it is distant and mythical, and so can Buchan in *A Lodge in the Wilderness*. In *Prester John*, however, the idea of independence for Africans is a source only of terror. Laputa must be destroyed, the nightmare dispelled.

Even at its most positive the romance genre renders the hero's quest as a journey to an underworld, a harrowing of hell, and into this pattern the myth of the Dark Continent fits perfectly. Conrad dealt with these associations more consciously than other writers, producing a quest romance that foreshadows the atrocity literature of the Congo Reform Association—works such as Arthur Conan Doyle's *Crime of the Congo* and Mark Twain's *King Leopold's Soliloquy,* to name two examples by prominent novelists.[53] By combining romance and exposé, Conrad creates a brilliantly ironic structure in which the diabolical Kurtz demonstrates how the Dark Continent grew dark. For Conrad the ultimate atrocity is not some form of tribal savagery but Kurtz's regression. Kurtz has been "tropenkollered" or "maddened by the tropics"; he has gone native.[54] In one sense, going native was universal, because in Africa or in any foreign setting every traveler must to some extent adopt the customs of the country, eat its food, learn its language, and so on. Kurtz does something worse, of course—he betrays the ideals of the civilization he is supposedly importing from Europe. Conrad does not debunk the myth of the Dark Continent: Africa is the location of his hell on earth. But at the center of that hell is Kurtz, the would-be civilizer, the embodiment of Europe's highest and noblest values, radiating darkness.

Ian Watt identifies nine possible models for Kurtz, and the very number suggests how common it was to go native. Stanley is among these models, and so is Charles Stokes, "the renegade missionary," who abandoned the Church Missionary Society, took a native wife, and led a wild career as a slave trader and gunrunner.[55] Stokes was not particular about his stock in trade or his customers: he sold guns to Germans working against the British in East Africa, and also to French Catholic converts in Buganda waging a miniature religious war against the Protestant converts of his former colleagues. He was finally arrested and executed without trial in the Congo for selling guns to Arab slavers, his demise adding to the scandal back in Britain about King Leopold's empire. Stokes's backsliding was extreme but not unusual. "I have been increasingly struck," wrote Johnston in 1897, "with the rapidity with which such members of the white race as are not of the best class, can throw over the restraints of civilization and develop into savages of unbridled lust and abominable cruelty."[56] Here is another way in which savages and the working class could seem alike. But Kurtz is of "the best class," not a "lower" one: going native could happen to anyone, even to entire societies. The Boers in Charles Reade's novel A *Simpleton* (1873), for example, have "degenerated into white savages"; the British hero finds that Kaffir savages are "socially superior" to them, a typical assertion well before the Boer War of 1899–1902.[57]

Perhaps missionaries were especially susceptible to going native; at least they frequently expressed fears about regressing, about being converted to heathenism instead of converting the heathen. According to J. S. Moffat, a missionary had to be "deeply imbued with God's spirit in order to have strength to stand against the deadening and corrupting influence around him. . . . I am like a man looking forward to getting back to the sweet air and bright sunshine after being in a coal-mine." Another missionary, S. T. Pruen, believed that merely witnessing heathen customs could be dangerous: "Can a man touch pitch, and not be himself defiled?"[58] That Africa held strong temptations for the Victorian is evident in the frequent references to allegedly promiscuous sexual customs of Africans—in Burton's prurient anthropology, for example, or again in the sensuality that Haggard attributes to Foulata and Joseph Thomson to Ulu. Europeans found their savage impulses were never far from their civilized surfaces; the potential for being "defiled," for going native, led them again and again to displace these impulses onto Africans, as well as onto other nonwhite peoples. Just as the social class fantasies of the Victorians (*Oliver Twist*, for example) often express the fear of falling into the abyss of poverty, so the myth of the Dark Continent contains the submerged fear of falling out of the light into the abyss of social and moral regression. In both cases the fear of backsliding has a powerful sexual dimension. If, as Freud argued, civilization is based on the repression of instincts, then when the demands of repression become excessive, civilization itself is liable to break down.

In *Prospero and Caliban*, Dominique Mannoni asks to what extent Europeans "project upon . . . colonial peoples the obscurities of their own unconscious—obscurities they would rather not penetrate." In European writings about Africa, Mannoni says, "the savage . . . is identified with the unconscious, with a certain image of the instincts. . . . And civilized man is painfully divided between the desire to 'correct' the 'errors' of the savages and the desire to identify himself with them in his search for some lost paradise (a desire which at once casts doubt upon the merit of the very civilization he is trying to transmit to them)."[59] Kurtz is a product of this painful division. Yet not even Marlow sees Kurtz's going native as a step toward the recovery of a lost paradise; it is instead a fall into hell, into the darkness of self-disintegration. For modern Europeans—Lévi-Strauss again comes to mind—as for the Romantics, the association of primitive life with paradise has once more become possible.[60] For the Victorians, however, that association was taboo, so repressed that the African landscapes they explored and exploited were painted again and again with the same tarbrush image of pandemonium. Yet when they penetrated the heart of darkness, only to discover lust and depravity, cannibalism and devil worship, they always also discovered, as the central figure in the shadows, a Stanley, a Charles Stokes, a Kurtz— an astonished white face staring back.

Nothing points more uncannily to the projection and displacement of guilt for the slave trade, guilt for empire, guilt for one's own savage and shadowy impulses, than those moments when white man confronts white man in the depths of the jungle. The archetypal event is Stanley's discovery of Livingstone; the famous "Dr. Livingstone, I presume?" scene suggests a narcissistic doubling, a repetition or mirroring, and consequently a solipsistic repression of whatever is nonself or alien that characterizes all forms of cultural and political domination. In analogous fashion, in *King Solomon's Mines*, Haggard's Britons discover the ruins of a great white civilization, with a black race, unconscious of their significance, living among them. When Karl Mauch discovered the ruins of Zimbabwe in 1871, no European believed they had been constructed by Africans; so arose the theory that they were the ruins of King Solomon's Golden Ophir, the work of a higher, fairer race—a myth that archaeologists began to controvert only in 1906.[61] Haggard repeats this myth in other stories. In *She*, Ayesha is a beautiful white demigoddess ruling over a brown-skinned race; and in *Allan Quatermain*, the white explorers discover a mysterious white race in the heart of darkness. So Dark Continent turned into mirror, reflecting on one level the heroic and saintly self-images the Victorians wanted to see, but on another casting the ghostly shadows of guilt and regression.

v

The myth of the Dark Continent was largely a Victorian invention. As part of the larger discourse about empire, it was shaped by political and economic pressures, and also by a psychology of blaming the victim through which Europeans projected onto Africans their own darkest impulses. The product of the transition or transvaluation from abolition to Scramble, the myth of the Dark Continent defined slavery as the offspring of tribal savagery and portrayed white explorers and missionaries as the leaders of a Christian crusade that would vanquish the forces of darkness. Blame for the slave trade, which the first abolitionists had placed mainly on Europeans, had by midcentury been displaced onto Africans. This displacement fused with sensational reports about cannibalism, witchcraft, and apparently shameless sexual customs to drape Victorian Africa in that pall of darkness which the Victorians themselves accepted as reality.

The invasion of preindustrial, largely preliterate societies by men with industrialized communications, weapons, and transportation meant a deluge of ruling discourse on one side and, on the other, what appeared to be total acquiescence and silence. As Frantz Fanon declares, "a man who has a language . . . possesses the world expressed and implied by that language. . . . Mastery of language affords remarkable power."[62] Victorian imperialism both created and was in part created by a growing monopoly on discourse. Unless they became virtually "mimic men," in V. S. Naipaul's phrase, Africans were stripped of articulation: the Bible might be translated into numerous African languages, but the colonizers, even the few who learned Wolof or Zulu, rarely translated in the other direction. African customs and beliefs were condemned as superstitions, their social organizations despised and demolished, their land, belongings, and labor appropriated often as ruthlessly as they had been through the slave trade.

But the ethnocentric discourse of domination was not met with silence. Though the reaction has not been easy to recover, modern historians have begun piecing together how Africans responded to their Victorian savior-invaders.[63] The wars of resistance fought by Zulu, Ashanti, Matabele, Ethiopian, Bugandan, and Sudanese peoples offer perhaps the best evidence. The writings of literate nineteenth-century Africans such as the Liberian Edward Blyden, pioneer of the negritude movement, have also been important. Still other responses can be found in modern independence movements and the writings of nationalists— Frantz Fanon, Kwame Nkrumah, Jomo Kenyatta. But the myth of the Dark Continent and imperialism more generally left a legacy both massive and impossible to evade, as stereotypic treatments of Africa by today's mass media continue to demonstrate. The work of liberation from racism and the politics of domination is far from over. Discourse, that most subtle yet also inescapable form of power, in its imperial guise persists, for example, in the most recent assumptions about the antithesis between "primitive" or "backward" and "civilized" or "advanced" societies, about the cultural and historical differences between Afro-Americans and white Americans, and about the legitimacy of the white apartheid regime in South Africa. In this regard what Nkrumah said in

1965 about the impact especially of the American mass media on the African situation is still relevant:

> The cinema stories of fabulous Hollywood are loaded. One has only to listen to the cheers of an African audience as Hollywood's heroes slaughter red Indians or Asiatics to understand the effectiveness of this weapon. For, in the developing continents, where the colonialist heritage has left a vast majority still illiterate, even the smallest child gets the message. . . . And along with murder and the Wild West goes an incessant barrage of anti-socialist propaganda, in which the trade union man, the revolutionary, or the man of dark skin is generally cast as the villain, while the policeman, the gum-shoe, the Federal agent—in a word, the CIA-type spy—is ever the hero. Here, truly, is the ideological under-belly of those political murders which so often use local people as their instruments.[64]

The spirit of Tarzan lives on in Western culture, as in the sophisticated buffoonery of Saul Bellow's *Henderson the Rain King*. Criticizing recent American and European failures to imagine Africa without prejudice, Chinua Achebe notes the continuing "desire—one might indeed say the need—in Western psychology to set Africa up as a foil to Europe, a place of negations at once remote and vaguely familiar in comparison with which Europe's own state of spiritual grace will be manifest." As Achebe points out, whether they come from Victorian or modern England, the America of Grover Cleveland or that of Ronald Reagan, "travellers with closed minds can tell us little except about themselves."[65]

Miss Wheeler defending herself against the Mutineers. From Charles Ball, *History of the Indian Mutiny* (1858).

7. The Well at Cawnpore: Literary Representations of the Indian Mutiny of 1857

> Even the Bay of Bengal might, in ages, be filled up; but the yawning well of Cawnpore—never!
>
> —Vinayak Savarkar

No episode in British imperial history raised public excitement to a higher pitch than the Indian Mutiny of 1857. In 1897, Hilda Gregg remarked that "of all the great events of this century, as they are reflected in fiction, the Indian Mutiny has taken the firmest hold on the popular imagination." By comparison, "the impression made on imaginative literature by the Crimean War is a very faint one."[1] Gregg examined nine novels about the Mutiny, but at least fifty were written before 1900, and at least thirty more before World War II.[2] There was also a deluge of eyewitness accounts, journal articles, histories, poems and plays dealing with the 1857–58 rebellion. But the sheer quantity of Victorian writing about the Mutiny seems inversely proportional to its quality. Gregg was unable to identify any story as "*the* novel of the Indian Mutiny," and she lamented that Rudyard Kipling had not yet written about it. Perhaps Kipling intuitively avoided a subject that so tempted other writers to bar the doors against imaginative sympathy: great literature does not mix well with calls for repression and revenge.

Victorian writing about the Mutiny expresses in concentrated form the racist ideology that Edward Said calls Orientalism, the hegemonic discourse of imperialist domination which applies specifically to the Near and Far East. Said poses "the main intellectual issue raised by Orien-

199

talism" as whether one can "divide human reality . . . into clearly
different cultures, histories, traditions, societies, even races, and survive
the consequences humanly." In relation to representations of the Indian
Mutiny, the answer is clearly negative. With few exceptions, the texts
concerned are instances of "the nineteenth-century academic and imaginative demonology of 'the mysterious Orient,'" which dehumanizes
both the dominated and the imperialist dominators.[3]

Victorian accounts of the Mutiny display extreme forms of extropunitive projection, the racist pattern of blaming the victim expressed
in terms of an absolute polarization of good and evil, innocence and
guilt, justice and injustice, moral restraint and sexual depravity, civilization and barbarism.[4] These categories are perceived as racially determined attributes in an imperialist allegory that calls for the total
subjugation of India and at times for the wholesale extermination of
Indians. British writing about India before 1857 was also racist, but it
frequently admitted the possibility that Indians might be helped to progress in the scale of civilization. Evangelical or utilitarian reforms would
convert Indians, more or less rapidly, from barbarism to western and
specifically British ways. After the Mutiny these hopeful though obviously ethnocentric possibilities are often denied. India is portrayed as
mired in changeless patterns of superstition and violence which can be
dominated but not necessarily altered for the better. If a humanist text
can be imagined which will break down national, social class, religious,
racist, and sexist barriers to understanding, then nearly all nineteenth-
and many twentieth-century accounts of the Mutiny are versions of its
antithesis.

i

The immediate cause of the rebellion was ammunition for the new
Enfield rifles; the sepoys of the Bengal Army suspected that the cartridges
had been greased with cow and pig fat. The paper ends had to be bitten
off before use, and because cow fat was taboo for Hindus and pork fat for
Muslims, the British seemed to be forcing both groups of sepoys to
commit sacrilege. Of course there were more important causes—Disraeli
said in Parliament that "the rise and fall of empires are not affairs of
greased cartridges"—but most British analysts found discontent only
within the native regiments, which saved them from acknowledging
widespread unrest. Among both British and Indian historians, debate still
focuses on whether the uprising was only an army "mutiny," or a "civil

rebellion" as well, or, as Indian nationalists have held it to be, "the first Indian war of independence."[5]

Trouble started early in 1857 at Dum-Dum, Barrackpore, and Ambala. On 10 May the sepoys mutinied at Meerut, burning the cantonments and killing their British officers and other Europeans. They then marched to Delhi, where they massacred many European residents and installed Bahadur Shah II, hypothetical ruler of the Moghul Empire, as their reluctant leader. In June the Mutiny spread to Cawnpore, where Nana Sahib offered terms and then either ordered the massacre of the British, including women and children, or looked the other way during the slaughter. On 27 June, under assurances of safe passage to Allahabad, the British were led down to the river; as they boarded the boats, their escorts turned guns and sabers on them. The surviving women and children were led back to a prison house, where on 17 July they were hacked to death and their bodies thrown into a well. (It was these atrocities more than any other events which enraged the British public and provoked demands for revenge; Nana Sahib, "the Demon of Cawnpore," figures again and again in Victorian writing about India as a treacherous monster who deserves no quarter.) The Mutiny flared up in many other locations, including Lucknow, where the British were besieged from 30 June until mid-November, and guerrilla resistance continued well into 1858.

The British retaliated with atrocities of their own, hanging and shooting without trial, blowing prisoners from the mouths of cannons, looting, and massacring the Indian residents of recaptured towns. There was little protest against these actions in the British press, which for the most part either ignored them or celebrated them as excesses of heroism, performed in the heat of battle. If the "red year" of 1857 called forth a "red revenge," as the titles of Mutiny novels by Tracy Louis and Charles E. Pearce attest, that was all to the good. Nevertheless, it is likely that British atrocities at Benares and Allahabad early in June 1857 were known to Nana Sahib and the rebels at Cawnpore so that the betrayal and massacre of the British prisoners there were retaliatory.[6] Even recent histories often fail to treat General Neill's Bloody Assizes as reprehensible, and some mention them only after describing Nana Sahib's "treachery" in grisly detail. But several thousand Indians may have been slaughtered at Allahabad alone before the slaughter of the few hundred British at Cawnpore. Such facts have remained suppressed, and Nana Sahib's villainy is still the most vivid feature in many British accounts.[7]

Although racist and imperialist attitudes toward India grew more dogmatic after 1857, the Mutiny also evoked sharp criticisms of British policies. In seeking causes more important than greased cartridges, Disraeli, for example, attacked the administration of India for disrupting Indian customs in the name of utilitarian and evangelical progress. As a Conservative, Disraeli understood Hindu and Muslim attempts to protect beliefs and customs, and he disapproved of the reformism that had influenced British policy since the late 1820s: "I would range under three heads the various causes which have led . . . to a general discontent among all classes . . . first, our forcible destruction of native authority; next, our disturbance of the settlement of property; and thirdly, our tampering with the religion of the people."[8]

From a contrary perspective Karl Marx, in several *New York Daily Tribune* articles, paid little heed to greased cartridges. He stressed British incomes in India, rapacious land tenure policies, and evidence that tax collectors resorted to torture. He thus emphasized economic exploitation and interpreted the Mutiny as at least foreshadowing a full-scale nationalist revolution. But he also rightly predicted that the British would crush the rebellion and assume a more repressive dominion afterward.[9] Together, Disraeli and Marx suggest the range of thoughtful interpretation available to the contemporary British public. An enormous public outcry swamped analysis, however, and influenced most writing about the Mutiny well beyond the turn of the century.

Innumerable essays, sermons, novels, poems, and plays expressed a general racist and political hysteria about the Mutiny. Sensational eyewitness accounts, such as Mrs. J. A. Harris's *Lady's Diary of the Siege of Lucknow* (1858), Robert Gibney's *My Escape from the Mutineers in Oudh* (1858), and Mowbray Thompson's *Story of Cawnpore* (1859), were immediately popular and influential. After these came histories, everything from the popular fare of Charles Ball's *History of the Indian Mutiny* (1858) to more sophisticated accounts, Sir John William Kaye's *Sepoy War in India* (1864–80) and T. Rice Holmes's *History of the Indian Mutiny* (1898). The Mutiny called for an epic, according to S. N. Sen, and "the epic was written in prose by Sir George Trevelyan." This was *Cawnpore* (1865), probably the most popular and influential of the Victorian histories. The epic distorts, as Sen shows: by accepting unreliable evidence, Trevelyan "spun out of very flimsy material a horror story which surpasses anything in cold cruelty."[10]

What is of greater interest than Trevelyan's reliance on dubious sources is his concentration of the massacres at Cawnpore, which from 1857 forward were the primary focus of all popular accounts. Nana Sahib's treachery serves as a reductive synecdoche for the entire rebellion—one that is its own instant explanation, transforming politics into crime and widespread social forces into questions of race and personality. The problem of general causes is reduced to that of the motives of the mutineers, which are in turn reduced to Nana Sahib's allegedly deceitful, lustful, bloodthirsty impulses: "The great crime of Cawnpore blackens the page of history with a far deeper stain than Sicilian Vespers, or September massacres; for this atrocious act was prompted, not by diseased and mistaken patriotism, nor by the madness of superstition. . . . The motives of the deed were as mean as the execution was cowardly and treacherous. Among the subordinate villains there might be some who were possessed by bigotry and class-hatred, but the chief of the gang was actuated by no higher impulse than ruffled pride and disappointed greed."[11] Explanation takes the form of naming Nana Sahib's degraded motives for villainy while asserting that the sepoys were deluded and misled. Trevelyan might have granted more importance to "the madness of superstition" had he viewed either Hinduism or Islam with any respect, but the best he can offer is that "the mind of the sepoy reeked with religious prejudice" (30). The Mutiny was "a cause . . . detestable to God and man" for which even the purest motives could offer no justification.

Trevelyan works constantly to narrow the focus and restrict the range of explanation. Nana Sahib emerges as the personification of much larger forces, the spider in the web's eye of the "gigantic conspiracy." Although there is some evidence that the Mutiny was partially planned, Trevelyan and many other Victorian writers emphasize conspiracy while often insisting that the rebels were racially incapable of following a coordinated plan; they thereby reduce conspiracy to Nana Sahib's treachery, suggesting the paranoid basis of their response.[12] Everything in Trevelyan's reductive epic verges toward one spot, the well at Cawnpore. Looking into the depths of the well, the reader is meant to understand the absolute villainy of the Mutineers and the heroic purity of their victims.

> It is interesting to observe the neat garden that strives to beguile away the associations which haunt the well of evil fame, and to peruse the inscription indicted by a vice-regal hand. It may gratify some minds, beneath the roof of a memorial church that is now building, to listen while Christian worship is performed above a spot which once resounded with ineffectual prayers and vain ejaculations addressed to quite other ears. But it is beside that little shrine on the brink of the yellow flood that none save they who live in the present alone can speak with unaltered voice, and gaze with undimmed eye. For that is the very place itself where the act was accomplished. (228–29).

On the one hand are the motiveless, bloodthirsty mutineers and "the madness of superstition"; on the other, the spotless innocence of English women and children and of "Christian worship." At Cawnpore the world splits apart: the well becomes a widening chasm dividing the forces of absolute righteousness from the demonic armies of the night.

Trevelyan might be excused for treating the Mutiny reductively on the ground that he aimed not at a complete history, only what passed at Cawnpore. But other Victorian accounts also make Cawnpore the main setting of a melodrama, its chief villain Nana Sahib and its chief victims the women and children whose mutilated bodies were cast into "the well of evil fame." According to the first historian of the Mutiny, Charles Ball, "the crowning atrocity . . . demands that the crimes of the Bithoor rajah [Nana Sahib] should be recorded as a warning and a terror to mankind."[13] For Ball the warning seems to be never to trust an Indian, or perhaps any native anywhere; the terror is clear enough.

William Fitchett's *Tale of the Great Mutiny* (1901) is another account that purports to tell the entire story but, by treating Cawnpore as the essence, instead reveals the persistence of the public mythology about the Mutiny. For Fitchett the chief cause of the uprising was the mutinous state of mind of the Mutineers: "The men had the petulance and the ignorance of children."[14] He considers the possibility that British behavior may have provoked the Mutiny, but that behavior is only good: "The very virtues of the British rule, thus proved its peril. Its cool justice, its steadfast enforcement of order, its tireless warfare against crime, made it hated of all the lawless and predatory classes. Every native who lived by vice, chafed under a justice which might be slow and passionless, but which could not be bribed, and in the long-run could not be escaped" (17). Thus the Mutiny appears to be the work of criminal elements in Indian society; thus too Fitchett implies that criminality comes easily to Indians, a point dramatized by his portrayal of Nana Sahib, whose "name has become an execration, his memory a horror" (147). Fitchett draws the chief moral of the Mutiny at the start of his narrative: in contrast to Indian criminality, "what a demonstration the whole story is, of the Imperial genius of the British race!" (21).

The obsessive emphasis on Cawnpore and Nana Sahib is even more evident in fictional and poetic representations than in histories. By the turn of the century Nana Sahib, Satanic locus of all oriental treachery, lust, and murder, was one of the most familiar villains in novels and melodramas, and by far the most familiar Indian character. His evil visage peers out of countless texts, the miragelike product of the projective mechanisms by which Victorians displaced their repressed sexual desire and guilt for imperial domination onto the dark places of the earth. Like the historians, writers of imaginative literature lead their readers to the well of evil fame and bid them peer into it, after which, they imply, no further explanation should be necessary. *Punch* established the pattern in its most basic form in 1857; its masterpiece in the Mutiny line is surely one of the least humorous poems ever to appear in a comic journal. The first stanza of "Liberavimus Animam" (12 September 1857) reads:

> Who pules about mercy? The agonised wail
>   Of babies hewn piecemeal yet sickens the air,
> And echoes still shudder that caught on the gale
>   The mother's—the maiden's wild scream of despair.

Mercy is out of the question; "the Avengers are marching—fierce eyes in a glow," and "terrified India shall tell to all time / How Englishmen paid her for murder and lust."

> . . . woe to the hell-hounds! Their enemies know
> Who hath said to the soldier that fights in His name—
> "THY FOOT SHALL BE DIPPED IN THE BLOOD OF THY FOE,
> AND THE TONGUE OF THY DOGS SHALL BE RED THROUGH THE SAME."

Only slightly more temperate are the sentiments expressed by other poets. Tennyson had celebrated British valor in "The Charge of the Light Brigade," but the deaths of many of the "noble six hundred" occurred because "someone had blundered." In the gallant leaders who defeated the Mutiny, however, Tennyson saw only heroism, no blundering: "every man in Britain / Says 'I am of Havelock's blood!'" So Tennyson wrote late in 1857, in response to the news of Havelock's death by dysentery after the relief of Lucknow. Twenty-three years later, in "The Defense of Lucknow," Tennyson commemorated "our Lawrence the best of the brave" and the other besieged Britons ("women and children among us, God help them, our children and wives"), the intrepid "handful" whom the Mutineers "could not subdue."[15] Whatever his interpretation of the Crimean campaign, Tennyson expressed no doubt about the rightness of British actions in India.

The Mutiny inspired numerous dramatic representations featuring Nana Sahib as the chief villain, as in *Keereda and Nena Sahib (sic)*, first presented at the Victoria Theatre in November 1857, and *Nana Sahib; or, A Story of Aymere*, presented at the Victoria some six years later. Other early productions include *India in 1857*, a spectacle staged at the Surrey late in 1857; *The Fall of Delhi*, a "military drama" also presented late in 1857 at the Marylebone; *The Storming and Capture of Delhi*, an "equestrian spectacle" offered by the Astley Theatre at the same time; and Edmund Glover's *The Indian Revolt; or, The Relief of Lucknow*, first staged in Glasgow in 1860. The most successful of the early Mutiny plays, at least from the box office standpoint, seems to have been *Jessie Brown; or, The Relief of Lucknow*, which Dion Boucicault first presented at Wallack's Theatre in New York on 22 February 1858 and later transported to Britain.[16]

Melodrama reduces social and moral complexities to simplistic oppositions between good and evil, victims and villains; these polarities readily lend themselves to the white/black patterns of racist fantasy. In *Jessie Brown*, Boucicault does not try to avoid stereotypes or even to be historically accurate. Although the setting of his play is Lucknow, Boucicault transplants Nana Sahib from Cawnpore onto center stage. He also converts Nana from Hinduism to Islam, making him swear by Allah in every other line. Nana's main motive—and hence the only motive suggested for the Mutiny as a whole—is to kidnap one Mrs. Campbell for his harem. Thus does Boucicault express both public outrage over the massacre of women and children and the stereotypic lasciviousness of Indians. The chief lesson of *Jessie Brown*, British racial superiority and Indian inferiority, is summed up by Nana Sahib's evil henchman, Achmet, who at least feigns agreement with the hero that the Mutineers are "black rascals" and "scum" like himself: "Allah Akbar! it is so—we are scum. . . . In Hindoostan there are one hundred millions such as I am, and there are one hundred thousand such as you; yet for a century you have had your foot on our necks; we are to you a thousand to one—a thousand black necks to one white foot. Allah is great, and Mohammed is his prophet. We are SCUM!" The audiences who pelted actors playing Nana Sahib with rotten fruit and broken umbrellas, forcing Boucicault himself to play the villain, must have relished Achmet's groveling admission.

The earliest work of fiction to deal with the Mutiny is just as melodramatic as *Jessie Brown* and in some respects even more wildly inaccurate. This is "The Perils of Certain English Prisoners," co-authored by Charles Dickens and Wilkie Collins for the 1857 Christmas number of *Household Words*. Dicken's journal for 1857–58 was full of essays about the Indian crisis; Dickens was deeply disturbed by the news from India, and on 4 October he wrote to Angela Burdett Coutts: "I wish I were Commander in Chief in India. The first thing I would do to strike that Oriental race with amazement . . . should be to proclaim to them . . . that I should do my utmost to exterminate the Race upon whom the stain of the late cruelties rested; and that I was . . . now proceeding, with . . . merciful swiftness of execution, to blot it out of mankind and raze it off the face of the Earth."[17] Dickens's sympathy for the downtrodden poor at home is reversed abroad, translated into approval of imperial domination and even, if necessary, of the liquidation by genocide of "niggers" and "natives." His "Noble Savage" essay (1853) echoes Carlyle's "On the Nigger Question" (1849), and his response to the Jamaica Rebellion of 1865 also agrees with Carlyle's vigorous defense of Governor Eyre and demand for the repression of uppity former slaves. Dickens thinks no savage can be noble; he wishes to see them all civilized off the face of the earth.

Dickens records his shock and dismay over events in India in his strangest—certainly his least compassionate—Christmas story, in which, as he told Miss Coutts, he hoped to commemorate "without any vulgar catchpenny connexion or application, some of the best qualities of the English character that have been shown in India." The setting of "Perils" is "Silver Store," on the "Mosquito coast" of Central America, rather than India, but the similarities are obvious. The narrator, Gill Davis, a private in the Royal Marines, is sent to "West India" to help protect an English mining colony against "pirates." The central villain, patterned after Nana Sahib at least in his treachery, is a "native Sambo"—half American Indian and half Negro—named Christian George King. Davis hates this interracial monster, a ludicrous compound of savagery and "darky" minstrelsy, from the moment he sets eyes on him: "If I had been Captain . . . I should have kicked Christian George King—who was no more a Christian than he was a King or a George—over the [ship's] side, without exactly knowing why, except that it was the right thing to do."[18] Davis's impulse proves correct: highly trusted by the residents of Silver Store, just as Nana Sahib had been trusted by the British at Cawnpore, the "Sambo pilot" betrays them to the pirates.

Dickens's placement of his tale in West rather than East India does not provide the distance needed for considering the Mutiny dispassionately. Rather, it extends his view of the Mutiny to other parts of the Empire. The equation between Christian George King and Nana Sahib suggests that Indians are no better than "Sambos" or "niggers" and also that Africans, American Indians, and all other natives are likely to be just as untrustworthy as Dickens held East Indians to be. Gill Davis says: "I have stated myself to be a man of no learning, and, if I entertain prejudices, I hope allowance will be made . . . but, I never did like Natives, except in the form of oysters" (217). About the only aspect of "Perils" which befits a Christmas story is its happy ending: the English escape from the pirates by rafting down a river much as the Cawnpore victims almost escaped down the Ganges, and Captain Carton shoots Sambo King. After all, King was "a double-dyed traitor, and a most infernal villain," which is about what Dickens thinks natives are anywhere. Dickens's way to deal with pirates, mutineers, and perhaps also "Sambos" in general is described by Captain Carton: "Believing that I hold my commission by the allowance of God . . . I shall certainly use it, with all . . . merciful swiftness of execution, to exterminate these people from the face of the earth" (229). Carton's echo of what Dickens had said he would do if he were commander in chief again suggests genocide as a solution to the Mutiny.

In analyzing Dickens's response to the events of 1857–58, William Odie argues that A Tale of Two Cities (1859) is in some sense a Mutiny novel. Dickens decided to write about the French Revolution while the Mutiny was running its course. His Carlylean view of the Revolution as irrational, frenzied, and bloodthirsty is close to his view of the Mutiny. The coincidence of names between Captain Carton and Sidney Carton and some of the metaphors in the novel also suggest India: Dickens frequently likens his French characters to tigers, as when he says of Madame Defarge that "opportunity had developed her into a tigress."[19] But no obvious parallels are drawn in the novel between the events of the French Revolution and those of the Mutiny, and for Dickens there was at least one essential difference: he did not view the Mutiny as the result of oppressive government. The French had been goaded to rebellion by aristocratic misgovernment, but the same was not true, Dickens thought, of mutinous Indians or, for that matter, of any other "Sambos" under British dominion.

ii

Hilda Gregg identifies George Lawrence's Maurice Dering (1864) as the first novel in which the Mutiny is featured. There were earlier stories she did not know or consider, including "Perils," but Lawrence's novel is interesting even though the Mutiny comes only at the end. Lawrence produces a sensation novel involving near-adultery, robbery, blackmail, a duel, and the death of the beautiful near-adulteress by heart attack. After these melodramatic events, in a penultimate chapter titled "Darkest of All," the hero returns to India to wreak vengeance upon the Mutineers for the "foul murder" of his fiancée: "Has any one of forgotten the evil Spring, when there swept over this country of ours a blast from the East—fatal to many households as the wind from the wilderness that smote the banqueting-hall in Uz—chilling to many hearts as the deadly Sarsar? Have we forgotten how, with each successive mail, the wrath and the horror grew wilder; till the sluggish Anglo-Saxon nature became, as it were, possessed by a devil, and through the length and breadth of the land . . . there went up one awful cry for vengeance?"[20] With Lawrence's tacit approval, Maurice Dering acts out the revenge demanded by much of the British public. A parson tries to convince him to be merciful, but Dering responds that he can show no mercy because none was shown when " 'my innocent darling was given up to those unchained devils.' He gnashed his teeth as he spoke, and his moustache grew white and wet with foam" (485). Religion may be on the parson's side, but heroism, passion, romance, justice, and the implied reader are on Dering's, and in the great "Pandy-killing" that follows the Mutiny no one surpasses him.

Equally vindictive is James Grant's *First Love and Last Love: A Tale of the Indian Mutiny* (1868). Grant retails the sexual atrocity stories spawned by the hysteria of 1857, even though the investigations that followed the Mutiny had discredited them. As his Mutineers go to work, "women were outraged again and again, ere they were slaughtered, riddled with musket balls, or gashed by bayonets; and every indignity that the singularly fiendish invention of the Oriental mind could suggest, was offered to the dying and the dead."[21] To "religious fanaticism and Oriental cruelty" (2:141) as causes of the Mutiny, Grant adds an oriental sex drive close to pornographic. "Had not the Nana Sahib at Cawnpore . . . slain the Christian women by the hundreds and flung them into a well, because not one of them would enter his zenana?" (3:232-33). The behavior of the Mutineers at Delhi, as Grant describes it, is even worse: "The women were always stripped of their clothing, treated with every indignity, and then slowly tortured to death, or hacked at once to pieces, according to the fancy of their captors" (2:58). That fancy is sadistic in the extreme: "The king, the princes, and leaders [of Delhi] seized . . . 'forty-eight females [who] were kept for the base purposes of the leaders of the insurrection for a whole week.' At the end of that time, their clothes were rent from them, and they were surrendered to the lowest ruffians in Delhi, to abuse in the streets in the open light of day. Fingers, breasts, and noses were cut off; 'one lady was three days dying; they flayed the face of another, and made her walk through the streets, perfectly nude,' according to a native eye witness" (2:75).

The heroine of Grant's tale is held captive by one of the princes of Delhi, but he behaves better than the average oriental sadist, wooing her rather than raping and hacking her to pieces—although for Grant there seems to be little difference. *First Love* might be dismissed as prurient sensation mongering were it not for the window it opens onto the relation between racism and sexual repression. The atrocity rumors in general involved the projection of "devilish" sexual impulses onto Indians, a blaming the victim that pervades Orientalism and other expressions of racism. The rape and castration fantasies offered by Grant and other Mutiny writers, in common with those spawned in the American South and South Africa, express the incestuous wishes that lie at the root of what Dominique Mannoni calls "the Prospero complex."[22]

Henry Kingsley is less willing to describe sadistic fantasies than Grant but indulges in them anyway. In *Stretton* (1869), Kingsley takes three young Englishmen out of a peaceful country house setting and sends them to India for the last third of the story. "Roland, Eddy, and Jim . . . like Shadrach, Meshach, and Abednego, [enter] the fiery furnace of the Indian Mutiny, and . . . come out unscathed."[23] At the center of the furnace are the Cawnpore massacres; Kingsley writes that "things were done with women and children that night at Belpore, of which there is no need to speak. If there were, one would speak" (3:265). Instigator of the atrocities is the treacherous "Rajah of Beethoor" or Nana Sahib, who "for lust or ferocity . . . would have matched the worst man in any of our great towns. He had the lust of blood on him. . . . Matters which shall be nameless had gone on" (3:265). The many nameless hiatuses in Kingsley's text function like miniature Cawnpore wells, as holes to be filled with the imagination of atrocities. Kingsley's reluctance to name the nameless is matched by his opinion of the Mutiny as "causeless." He means partly that the event is beyond human reckoning, partly that the Mutineers had no rational motives. The Mutiny is "the most reckless, causeless, stupidest revolution ever planned." Confronted with such inexplicable behavior, Kingsley offers the most rudimentary explanation of what happened: "Like all ill-considered and causeless revolutions, it failed. It was evil against good, and good won" (3:183–84).

The incarnation of evil in *Stretton*, the lustful Rajah, stands for both the individual Nana Sahib and the native princes in general as presented in "the contemporary evidence about the state of Indian courts" (3:33). The Rajah's palace is "more unutterably given to the devil than possibly that of Heliogabalus" (3:33). The princely state of Oudh and other semi-independent domains, Kingsley suggests, should be annexed for the good of Indians, a message often expressed in post-Mutiny fiction. In Sarah Jeannette Duncan's *The Story of Sonny Sahib* (1895), for example, an English child is rescued from the Cawnpore bloodbath by two kindly Muslim servants and brought up at the court of an Indian prince until reunited with his soldier father. An imperial Oliver Twist, Sonny shows the superiority of British nature to Indian nurture: at every turn his ingenuity, industry, and valor clash with the ignorance, lethargy, and cowardice of his Indian hosts. Like Fagin's roost, the Indian court is an odd mixture of comic and diabolical, the Maharajah himself combining debauchery and murderous deceit with bungling ineptitude. Again, Kipling's "The Man Who Would Be King," which can almost be read as a critique of imperial expansion, describes native courts as "the dark places of the earth, full of unimaginable cruelty."[24]

Like George Lawrence, Sir George Chesney uses the Mutiny, in *The Dilemma* (1876), to accentuate the melodramatic aspects of an already sensational story.[25] The dilemma of Chesney's title has nothing directly to do with the Mutiny but rather with a tangled love story in which the heroine's husband, Colonel Falkland, appears to be killed during the siege of Mustaphabad (based on Lucknow). After Mustaphabad is relieved by Kirke's Horse (based on Hodson's Horse), Kirke and the hero Arthur Yorke come across a palanquin. Kirke orders his men to kill the rich Indian occupant and loot the palanquin, keeping some of the jewels for himself rather than turning them over to the army's prize fund (an episode recalling Hodson's murder of the princes of Delhi). Yorke is not much disturbed by the murder, though he does object to Kirke's dishonorable appropriation of the jewels. After the Mutiny, Yorke loses to Kirke in the contest for the heroine's hand, and for the newlyweds then comes a downhill slide into bankruptcy and disgrace. The couple absconds, Kirke entering the army of the pasha of Egypt and sending Olivia and the children to America. Yorke later discovers Olivia, as does Falkland, who escaped death at Mustaphabad but was grotesquely maimed. The dilemma at last emerges: Olivia's house catches fire; Falkland rescues her and the children; she recognizes him; he dies; she realizes she has been living in bigamy. Accusing herself of being no better than a "streetwalker" and her children "bastards," she jumps into an icy river. Yorke pulls her out, but she expires from shock.

Bigamy is the dilemma, not the Mutiny. Events at Mustaphabad, however, occupy nearly two-thirds of Chesney's story. Does he import the

Mutiny into his tale merely to serve as a backdrop, or does the unraveling of the love story provide a distraction from Chesney's inability to deal with the Mutiny on any but a melodramatic level? The failure of the two parts of the novel—Mutiny and love story or, better, repression-of-love story—to intersect mirrors precisely the failure of many Victorians after 1857 to imagine any common ground between themselves and Indians. On the one hand, the violence and lust of the Mutineers are repositories for feelings and impulses that Chesney cannot attribute to his English characters; on the other, the hollowed-out love story ostensibly deals with the consequences of marital infidelity but unconsciously shadows forth the destructive side of sexual repression. Olivia's suicide is the antithesis to the oriental lasciviousness portrayed in most Mutiny novels: self-destruction is the cost of even an unintended breach of sexual restraint. Far from being a streetwalker, Olivia is cheated of love and life for failing to remain a faithful widow; Mutineers are gunned down partly because they embody sexual urges that neither Yorke nor Olivia is allowed to indulge. Yorke's tacit approval of the murder of the rich Indian, more-over, like James Grant's approving the murder of the princes of Delhi, suggests how far some Victorians were prepared to go for revenge.

iii

For the first two decades after the event, most novels about the Mutiny are flawed by structural contradictions like those in *Stretton* and *The Dilemma*. One exception is Meadows Taylor's *Seeta* (1872), in many ways the most remarkable of Mutiny novels just as his *Confessions of a Thug* is the fullest, most powerful fictional expression of the utilitarian reformism of the 1830s as applied to India. *Seeta* is the third book in a trilogy dealing with critical periods of Indian history. *Tara* (1863) illustrates "the rise of the Marathas, and their first blow against the Mussulman power in 1657." *Ralph Darnell* (1865) describes "the rise of the English political power in the victory of Plassey in June 1757." And *Seeta* deals with "the attempts of all classes alike to rid themselves of the English by the Mutiny of 1857."[26] Taylor's brief description suggests a remarkable feature of his novel: the Mutiny he sees not as restricted to sepoys and a few native princes but as affecting "all classes alike." *Seeta* offers the most fully imagined account in any Victorian novel both of the scope and of the motives for the Mutiny.

Taylor's version of the Mutiny seems at first to be an extension of Thuggee, because the chief conspirator, Azrael Pande, is a former Thug who, disguised as a Muslim priest, goes about the countryside preaching rebellion. Such a device seems as reductive as Kingsley's diabolical Rajah, but just as Taylor's captured Thug makes a wonderfully convincing case for himself in *Confessions*, so Azrael Pande displays enough rhetorical fireworks to be an Indian Patrick Henry. Pande preaches that the East India Company "is not as it used to be; it is no longer an incarnation of our gods. It has changed into a mean, cheating robber, who farms this great Hind of ours from the Government of England and robs it of all it can carry away. Where do those great ships yonder take the cotton, and the indigo, and the silk which the poor ryots [peasants] have produced, but to England? Do they bring us anything in return? No! nothing but what we have to buy, and very dearly; and even the old Moghuls did not tax our salt and our opium."[27] As Marx understood, it is difficult to answer charges of economic exploitation; Taylor makes no effort to do so.

Taylor's Mutineers are good men goaded to rebellion by the dread of losing caste. The author recognizes that the greased cartridges and other caste-violating regulations involved serious threats to Hindu and Muslim orthodoxy. What other writers dismiss as superstition, Taylor depicts as a religious striving for purity: "The Sepoys had completed their contract of a hundred years of faithful service, and yet their masters were now seeking . . . to defile them and pollute their social caste, which was more precious than life, for without it life and honour would be dead. What cause had they given for this outrage on their faith . . .? Had they not marched devotedly through the bitter snows and frosts of Afghanistan and the burning plains of India, everywhere shedding their best blood, while their achievements were splendid victories? Yet now, all seemed forgotten and flung aside" (216). Faith of any sort can be admirable; it can also be dangerous. Taylor illustrates both possibilities, in the religiously motivated actions of Indian and British characters. Religious misunderstanding is one of the causes of the Mutiny; it also causes most of the difficulties encountered by the Indian heroine Seeta in her love affair with the British hero Cyril Brandon. *Seeta* is the only Victorian novel about India I know that presents an interracial love affair in a sympathetic light. Even Kipling deals with relations between British men and Indian women with a heavy hand: in "Without Benefit of Clergy," John Holden leads a less than happy double life with his Indian mistress Ameera, his work flagging, until she and their son are "taken away as many things are taken away in India—suddenly and without warning." Their deaths will depress Holden for a while, Kipling seems to feel, but perhaps Holden's work will pick up. In the melodramatic moment when Seeta steps in front of Brandon to ward off Azrael Pande's spear, one also feels that a terrible difficulty has been removed from the hero's path: he is free to marry the English girl for whom he has been hankering even as he loves Seeta.

Taylor's story cannot easily be dismissed, however, for by the time Seeta sacrifices herself for her lover, a great deal has passed between them. From the beginning, Taylor dramatizes the scruples and prejudices that both characters have to overcome in their union. He also portrays the reactions of Indian and British family and friends. The typical response is the intolerance of Mrs. Smith who, referring to Seeta and Brandon, declares: "If men will have black 'companions,' you know, they ought to keep them to themselves, and not stuff them under our noses. I hate the thought of it" (182). Brandon is fired from his post for entering into a "native connection" and receives a letter from his brother in England, Lord Hylton, about Seeta: "She could *never* take her place as your wife here" (238–39). On the other hand, several British women come to a sympathetic (though still patronizing) attitude toward Seeta, and Brandon's friend Philip Mostyn says: "I often think that if there were not our horrible social prejudices against it, many of us would be happier with such a wife than with some of our own people." But the idea is next to impossible, "because of our social prejudices, which you and I can't overcome. Because of old Mrs. Grundy, who is as powerful here as elsewhere in the world" (87).

As Brandon is ostracized by the British, so Seeta runs afoul of the Indian community—between British racism and Hindu fanaticism about purity of caste and belief, Taylor suggests, there is little to choose. The easy way out would be for Brandon to take Seeta as his mistress, as in Kipling's story, but both characters insist on marriage, for moral and religious reasons as well as for love. "I can give scores of instances of native connections in far higher places than mine," Brandon thinks, but "few have dared, as I have, to avow marriage" (240). Marriage, ironically, is more scandalous than his taking a mistress would have been. Marriage, however, is difficult also, because she is a devout Hindu and he a devout Christian. Brandon marries her by Hindu ceremony, expecting gradually to convert her and marry her a second time by Christian rite. Taylor does not clearly approve of this rigmarole, though neither does he approve of treating Indian women only as mistresses or prostitutes.

Brandon looks forward to the "dawning of true light" in Seeta's mind (273), and apparently so does Taylor. The novel reaches a sentimental climax with the heroine's conversion or near-conversion to Christianity just before her death. Her final expressions of faith are (compared to the claims of absolute conviction in evangelical stories) ambivalent, however, blending "strange snatches of . . . Sanscrit prayers . . . with lines of simple Christian hymns" (382–83).

> Suddenly, and as though the vivid light had roused her, she raised herself a little, and stretched out her hands, and said the Vedantic invocation to the sun, which is called Gayatri. It seemed as if she would have repeated the hymn also, but she had no strength, and as she fell back she cried faintly, "Cyril! . . . kiss me. Mother! He calls me again!—Listen! And there are the bright flowers of heaven!—Lord!—I come!" As they put their arms under her to support her she smiled, and sighed once, and as the glory of the sun rested on her face, her humble, loving spirit had passed away forever. (382–83)

Mawkish though it may be, this deathbed scene does not express a straightforward rejection of Hinduism and conversion to Christianity. Nor is Taylor throughout the novel nearly so interested in preaching a positive gospel for Indians as he is in criticizing the religious and racial intolerance of his compatriots. *Seeta* is a study of how religion even of the highest sort—whether Christian, Hindu, or Islamic—can create obstacles to love and sympathy. It is even more obviously a study of how religion in degenerate forms—superstition, prejudice, Mrs. Grundyism on both sides—helped spawn the violence and race hatred that flared up in 1857.

Like Kipling, Taylor expresses a moral idealism that calls upon British imperialism to practice what it preaches. He recognizes that the civilizing mission is contradicted by the prejudices of its agents. Taylor believes that the main cause of the Mutiny is the failure of Anglo-Indians to shoulder the "white man's burden"; foreshadowing Kipling's hard-working civil servants and soldiers, Brandon is less a character than a receptacle for all the virtues the ideal servant of the Empire should possess. "Firm, just, confident, yet deliberate in his acts and judgements, he was at once loved and respected by the loyal, while his name was a terror to evil-doers. The secret of his success . . . lay in his true sympathy with all classes, and his ready attention to all demands on his time and patience" (417). Brandon's restoration of order in his own district after the Mutiny is obviously wishful thinking on Taylor's part, a daydream of justice, service, and loyalty which looks backward to the ideals of the utilitarian reformers, among whom Taylor began his own career: "Brandon pressed on through the country, not only delivering the people from petty local oppressors, but reestablishing the authority of Government soundly and satisfactorily; and it was a great assurance to him to find how deeply the people rejoiced in the return to old laws and customs. They might be hard; they might be unsympathetic; but they were just. They furnished personal and general security, and the tyranny of the strong over the weak was at an end. Cyril's progress was indeed almost a triumphal procession" (399). Taylor understood that the Mutiny was partly a reaction against British attempts to reform or eradicate Indian customs and to convert Indians to Christianity, but he also believed that the work of men like Brandon was invaluable, and that many Indians appreciated that work. Even during the Mutiny, he thought, "at the very worst, there was a strong, deep-lying attachment to English rule, to English faith and honour, and to that ample protection of property to the meanest as well as to the richest, which a powerful English Government had afforded, that pervaded all the most valuable portions of the population, and bore good fruit in time" (315–16). His view that the Mutiny would not have occurred had every Briton lived up to his or her responsibilities is of course simplistic. Nevertheless, *Seeta* portrays the only complexly imagined intersection between British and Indian characters in Mutiny novels before 1914, unless one counts groveling Anglophiles or Indians in completely subordinate roles. The love affair between Brandon and Seeta is Victorian fiction's only approach to an adequate symbolic antithesis to the Mutiny. And *Seeta* is the only pre-1890s novel about that event which does not focus reductively on Nana Sahib and the massacres at Cawnpore.

iv

Most of the Mutiny novels written after the 1870s express no better understanding of India and Indians than those by Kingsley and Chesney. G. A. Henty wrote two Mutiny novels, one for boys and one for adults, that preach an imperialist faith obviously closer to public opinion than Taylor's critical attitudes. For the adolescent readers of *In Times of Peril* (1881) Henty names what Kingsley refuses to name for his supposedly adult readers: "The floor was deep in blood, the walls were sprinkled thickly with it. Fragments of clothes, tresses of long hair, children's shoes with the feet still in them—a thousand terrible and touching mementos of the butchery . . . there met the eye. Horror-struck and sickened, the officers returned to the courtyard, to find that another discovery had been made; namely, that the great well near the house was choked to the brim with the bodies of women and children."[28] Ironically, in his later adult novel, *Rujub the Juggler* (1893), Henty is less explicit about Cawnpore, even though Nana Sahib imprisons the heroine along with the massacre victims.

Rujub is in several ways a less realistic fantasy than *In Times of Peril*. Through Rujub's "juggling" or magic Henty attempts to portray Indian customs in a sympathetic light while also providing a ready-made excuse for rejecting them as irrational. The hero, Bathurst, even more a do-gooder than Cyril Brandon, rescues Rujub's daughter from a tiger; the magician repays the Englishman and his friends by using his clairvoyant powers to rescue them from Nana Sahib and the Mutineers. Rujub would perhaps have helped the British anyway, because he is, like Kingsley's Nawab, an Anglophile: "I saw that, though the white men were masterful and often hard . . . and viewed our beliefs as superstitions . . . yet they were a great people. Other conquerors, many of them, India has had, but none who have made it their first object to care for the welfare of the people at large . . . as soon as the white man was gone the old quarrels would break out and the country would be red with blood."[29]

If the hero is typical of British rule, then Rujub is right to be an Anglophile, because Bathurst is in every way admirable. Indeed, whereas Taylor presents Brandon as an ideal type whom all too few Anglo-Indians approximate, Henty treats his hero almost as an imperial commonplace. Bathurst has some small difficulty about being gun-shy, which leads his rival to accuse him of cowardice, but he is in truth the bravest of the brave. He is one of Henty's boy heroes grown up, but grown up into a fantasy world less truthful about India and life than the worlds Henty creates for adolescent readers. Captured by Nana Sahib, who of course lusts after her in his slimy way, the heroine Isobel Hannay douses her face with the nitric acid Bathurst has given her. By marring her beauty she hopes to repel Nana; like the Miss Wheeler of popular legend, who was alleged to have taken her life after being raped during the Mutiny, Isobel would even commit suicide to escape a fate worse than death.[30] But she neither dies nor falls prey to Nana's lurid desires; with Rujub's help, Bathurst rescues her from the Cawnpore prison-house. On their way out Isobel sensibly asks: "But the others, Mr. Bathurst, can't you save them too?" This fictive snag would too clearly violate history by caving in to wishful fantasies; Bathurst replies that it is "impossible. . . . Even if they got out they would be overtaken and killed at once" (3:173)—perhaps the one realistic remark in the story. By the time Bathurst and Isobel learn of the massacre of the other Cawnpore prisoners, the scars are already vanishing from the heroine's lovely visage. Bathurst would have married her anyhow, being as much above the lures of sex as he is above fear and dishonesty, but by the wedding day her beauty has magically mended.

In *Rujub*, Henty does not lead his readers to the well's edge as he does in his boys' novel; where Ned and Dick are concerned, there must be no flinching from hard facts. In writing for boys Henty is also less evasive about his racist beliefs than in the supposedly grown-up novel. Ned and Dick are superior to every Indian they meet because of their English "blood," that of the "conquering race." As the beautiful Ranee tells them: "How brave you English boys are. No wonder your men have conquered India" (141). Empire is the result of natural selection; Ned and Dick survive every scrape because they belong to the fittest race. When Dick worries about killing an Indian sentry, Ned tells him: "These scoundrels are all mutineers and murderers. [Furthermore,] this is no ordinary war, Dick; it is a struggle for existence" (55). Remembering that the world is Darwinian, Dick goes straight to work on the sentry's throat. The boys escape from Cawnpore, are besieged at Lucknow, and take a hand in the reconquest and looting of Delhi. *In Times of Peril* describes most of the major events of the Mutiny in some detail, freely borrowing passages from histories and eyewitness accounts. Of course it contains miraculous escapes and coincidences galore, but at least there is no nonsense about magic or nitric acid—Henty saves such romantic twaddle for adults. It is thus more honest and a better historical novel than *Rujub*, and superior for similar reasons to Grant's *First Love and Last Love*, Kingsley's *Stretton*, and Chesney's *The Dilemma*.

The lesson most Victorians drew from Cawnpore was not that the Mutiny was a response to the greater violence of imperial domination. Occasional criticism of British rule creeps into these novels (noticeably in *Seeta*, which is critical of many aspects of British behavior). But such perception never interferes with the main purpose, damning the Mutineers and praising British martyrs and heroes. Toward the end of the century a deeper critical perspective does almost emerge in several Mutiny novels—Henry Merriman's *Flotsam* (1892), Hume Nisbet's *The Queen's Desire* (1893), and Flora Annie Steel's *On the Face of the Waters* (1897). But Merriman, like Chesney, fails to unite the parts of his story; Nisbet offers a wild romance in which questions of social justice boil down to a universal law of the jungle; and Steel's irony undercuts potentially critical ideas. One indication of the critical distance of these authors from earlier Mutiny fiction, however, is that they do not focus reductively on Nana Sahib and the horrors of Cawnpore.

Merriman has only praise for the Empire yet creates a hero who is less than admirable. Harry Wylam is brave but impulsive, good material for a subaltern, but, as a friend says, "India is a very easy country to go to the devil in."[31] Before the Mutiny, Harry loses most of his fortune gambling and jilts the fiancée he left in England. His new flame is the daughter of traitorous Philip Lamond, who though English spies for the Mutineers and cajoles Harry into looting a temple. Harry fights heroically, but afterwards everything goes downhill. He marries Lamond's daughter, who bilks him out of the rest of his fortune. Lamond is exposed as a spy, and Harry is cashiered for looting. Harry now regrets what he has lost; he extracts his daughter from his wife's clutches and takes her to England, where he deposits her with his incredibly joyful ex-fiancée. Then he goes to South Africa to bury his ruinous past, there "drift[ing] northwards with the scum that ever floats on the wave of civilization" (342). The meaning of the title becomes clear: Harry is "flotsam" on "the tide of rascaldom" that is "ever flowing" (344), phrases that recall the excremental metaphors in writing about Botany Bay. *Flotsam* is thus a spy novel in which the British are their own worst enemies.

In *The Dilemma*, Chesney hinted at rascaldom through his character Lieutenant Kirke, though without suggesting it was typical of either human nature or Empire. But rascaldom is at the center of *Flotsam*, although it is hard to square with Merriman's interpretation of the Mutiny as "a corner-stone of our race." "A race . . . is a chain hung down into the centuries," the narrator asserts. "Our English chain has hung through fair and foul, and at times a great strain has been put upon it, testing it. . . . Forty years ago such a strain tugged at us, and we held good" (144–45). Perhaps Merriman means that even a weak link like Harry holds good in a crisis, but Lamond and his rascally daughter are at the center rather than the margin of the story. Like Chesney, Merriman writes two stories that do not connect. The British presence in India is both heroic and rascally, a contradiction Merriman cannot resolve, especially because he does not think of rascaldom as a cause of the Mutiny. What the British do and what Indians do seem completely disjoined; they are two distinct "races" acting on separate sides of a widening chasm of incomprehensibility.

In *The Queen's Desire*, Hume Nisbet acknowledges the violence of British domination as one cause of the Mutiny. The opening depicts "Tommy Atkins" and a gang of British soldiers insulting Indian women in the streets of Delhi; Tommy gets his head cut off for his trouble by a brave princess. She is then rescued from Tommy's friends by the hero, George

Jackson; she turns out to be the Rani of Jhansi, famous for her guerrilla resistance in the late stages of the Mutiny. George and the Rani become lovers, but in the finale George engages in hand-to-hand combat with a masked, richly garbed rebel. He mows the rebel down and discovers he has killed the Rani. He expresses little remorse, however; after all, he is engaged to a proper English girl. Woven through this preposterous tale is a subplot featuring Nana Sahib and the "damnable deed of treachery and cold-blooded cruelty" at Cawnpore.[32]

Unlike the oriental monster of earlier Mutiny fiction, however, Nisbet's Nana has good reasons for his treachery. "His just and moral claims had been scornfully denied by the Government, as were those of his friend the Ranee of Jhansi, and scores of other less important personages . . . who had given their friendship to the overbearing conquerors" (15–16). Nisbet's Scottish roots perhaps sensitized him to issues of conquest and empire. He repeatedly likens episodes in the Mutiny to events in European history, often alluding to violent past relations between Scotland and England. At one point, for instance, the Mutineers flee "with that relentless white-haired Nemesis [Havelock] and his cavalry after them, slaughtering, as the horse of Cromwell slaughtered the Presbyterians after the battle of Dunbar" (284). Again, Nana Sahib's treachery can only "be compared with the relentless . . . double-dealing of Queen Elizabeth and her advisers about her trusting guest, Mary of Scotland, which ended in the latter's bloody taking-off" (185–86). Elizabeth's treachery is only one of many instances of bloody "diplomacy," Nisbet says, "which have stained the pages of our own and other civilized races' histories; humanity is much the same in all countries and periods, but never so cruel, so remorseless, and so treacherous, as when fighting for a holy cause." He draws the obvious moral: "Nana Sahib was fighting for his country, his religion, and his own lost estates—three good motives which are enough to change the most Christian of monarchs into devils incarnate." But Nisbet's historical analogies generalize bloody diplomacy and might-makes-right; if the Mutineers' violence is no different in kind from the violence of civilized races, blood-letting is rationalized as a fact of history. Nisbet treats the victory of the British over the Mutineers as a final justice, at least in Darwinian terms: the triumph of the fitter over the weaker race in a world where power usually overrules morality.

Flora Annie Steel's *On the Face of the Waters* offers a portrayal of the Mutiny richer, more complex than any nineteenth-century novel except *Seeta*. Steel enters into the thoughts and feelings of a variety of characters, both British and Indian, often without maintaining a distinct narrative voice. It is therefore not always possible to separate her judgments from those of her characters. The hero Jim Douglas has had a baby by his Indian mistress Zora, for example, but the baby has died: "He never told [Zora] of the relief it was to him, of the vague repulsion which the thought of a child had always brought with it."[33] Whether Steel shares or is criticizing Douglas's feeling of relief is unclear. Similarly, as Hodson's Horse march on Delhi, their attitudes are described in a manner that could be taken to mean either that they are heroes, or that they are vindictive fanatics, or both: "For, to the three thousand marching upon Delhi that cool dewy night, sent—so they told themselves—for special solace and succor of the Right, there were but two things to be reckoned with in the wide world: Themselves—Men. Those others—Murderers" (307). Only later, with Hodson's three thousand holding out against fifty thousand, does Steel's opinion of their heroism become explicit, as does her belief that Hodson is fighting for India and Indians ("the millions of peasants plowing their land peaceably in firm faith of a just master") and also "for law and order" (338).

Steel often renders judgment against both Indians and British, thus maintaining the appearance of impartiality. She cites pro-Mutiny views in native newspapers (277), and she portrays the motives and attitudes of the Mutineers in detail. A judgment emerges from even the seemingly most impartial passages, however, as in the description of the arrival of the Mutineers at the Moghul's palace in Delhi, calling on their "brothers" to "close the gates": "It was a cry to heal all strife within those rose-red walls, for the dearest wish of every faction was to close [the gates] against civilization; against those prying Western noses, detecting drains and sinks of iniquity" (213–14). Toward the end of the novel Captain Morecombe says that "there have been terrible things on both sides. There always are. You can't help it when you sack cities" (450). This apparently balanced view leaves untouched the pervasive impression of the Mutineers' barbarism, cruelty, and irrationality. Whenever the narrator appears to criticize the British, the text always contains an at least implicit exoneration, as in this description of the forging of fetters for a group of captive Mutineers: "The clang of cold iron upon hot, rising from the regimental smithy [was a] cruel sound at best, proclaiming the indubitable advantage of coolness and hardness over glow and plasticity. Cruel indeed when the hardness and insistency goes to the forging of fetters for emotion and ignorance" (165). Again a balanced judgment seems to emerge: the British have been too hard, perhaps too arrogant; the Indians have reacted from emotion and ignorance. But the balance is only superficial, because the analogy also suggests that something is occurring on a vaster scale than fetters for Mutineers. Wielding the hammer are the British; the metal being shaped is Indian character, the Indian nation—British industry against oriental inertia. It is a work that will ultimately transform emotion and ignorance into civilization. For Steel, as for almost all Victorian writers, the Mutiny is evidence of Indian racial and cultural inferiority, as she makes plain in her portrayals of the feuding and chaos at the court of Delhi. Steel declares in her autobiography that the subject of *On the Face of the Waters* "was one to touch all hearts, to rouse every Britisher's pride and enthusiasm. The Indian Mutiny was the Epic of the Race. It held all possible emotion, all possible triumph."[34]

Unlike most Mutiny novelists, Steel at least understands how the violence of 1857–58 has helped make violence inevitable in later relations between Britain and India. When her heroine Kate Erlton watches Captain Mainwaring go off to battle, "her own gentler nature was conscious of a pride, almost a pleasure in the thought of the revenge which would surely be taken sooner or later, by such as he, for every woman, every child killed, wounded—even touched. She was conscious of it, even though she stood aghast before a vision of the years stretching away into an eternity of division and mutual hate" (251–52).

Most British writing about the Mutiny before 1914 is part of an imperialist heritage of division and mutual hate. In all of the novels surveyed here except *Seeta*, the bridges between British and Indian characters have broken down, if indeed they ever existed. Only incredible, Anglophile Indians remain to soothe the shaken egos of their masters. For the rest, all that can be shared is the experience of the Mutiny, staring down the barrels of each other's guns. In the basic fantasy, repeated endlessly in novels, plays, poems, and histories, the imperialist dominators become victims and the dominated, villains. Imagining the Mutiny in this way totally displaced guilt and projected repressed, sadistic impulses onto demonicized Indian characters. Most Victorian accounts insistently mystify the causes of the Mutiny, treating the motives of the rebels as wholly irrational, at once childish and diabolic. Politics turns into crime (mutiny, massacre) and is further trivialized by personification: Nana Sahib as the incarnation of the essential viciousness of all Indians. These reductive, racist fantasy patterns shape a literature antithetical to sympathy; its features betray the violence that crushed the rebellion and restored British authority.[35]

Awareness of the ultimate result of the Mutiny—perhaps "an eternity of division and mutual hate" or perhaps, as Marx thought, the bonding together of forces that would eventually overthrow British rule—lies at the center of E. M. Forster's *A Passage to India* (1924). Following Miss Quested's charge of sexual harassment against Dr. Aziz, the Mutiny becomes the touchstone by which several of Forster's English characters try to comprehend what they see as a new revelation of Indian criminality. When Mr. McBryde, the superintendent of police, tells Fielding that the psychology of Indian crime is different from that of English crime, he adds, "read any of the Mutiny records; which, rather than the Bhagavad Gita, should be your Bible in this country."[36] At the club before the trial there is much agitation, "and several parents had brought their children into the rooms reserved for adults, which gave the air of the Residency at Lucknow. One young mother [whose] husband was away in the district . . . dared not return to her bungalow in case the 'niggers attacked'" (178). The Mutiny atmosphere makes all of the British characters, with the exception of Fielding, behave hysterically. Major Callendar declares "it's not the time for sitting down. It's the time for action. Call in the troops and clear the bazaars" (183). Nobody takes the Major quite seriously, "but he made everyone uneasy on this occasion. The crime was even worse than they had supposed—the unspeakable limit of cynicism, untouched since 1857." Of course "the crime" is the product of another hysterical English imagination—Miss Quested's—who at least has the decency to admit her mistake during the trial. While the other Britons magnify the crime in their imaginations, Fielding contemplates their paranoia: "The evil was propagating in every direction, it seemed to have an existence of its own, apart from anything that was done or said by individuals" (184).

Poor Dr. Aziz is no Indian Bluebeard, no Nana Sahib; he has wanted only to make friends with one or two English people. He succeeded in doing so, at least with Fielding. By the end of the story, however, with Aziz insisting on nationhood for India and Fielding mocking him, the entire history of British imperialism in India stands in the way of their mutual desire to remain friends. "'Why can't we be friends now? . . . It's what I want. It's what you want.' But the horses didn't want it—they swerved apart; the earth didn't want it, sending up rocks through which riders must pass single file; the temples, the tank, the jail, the palace, the birds, the carrion, the Guest House . . . they didn't want it, they said in their hundred voices, 'No, not yet,' and the sky said, 'No, not there'" (317). As Forster knew, it was not just the Mutiny that fixed the great gulf between Aziz and Fielding. The Mutiny itself, like Miss Quested's hysteria in the Marabar Cave, was only a revelation that the gulf existed. Forster was sadly conscious that imperialism, economic exploitation, racism, and religious prejudice made friendship between nations as between individuals impossible. In *Nightrunners of Bengal* (1961), John Masters says much the same thing: "The Great Bengal Mutiny lives as history's cruelest example of the inherent melancholy of power."[37]

Part III   DUSK

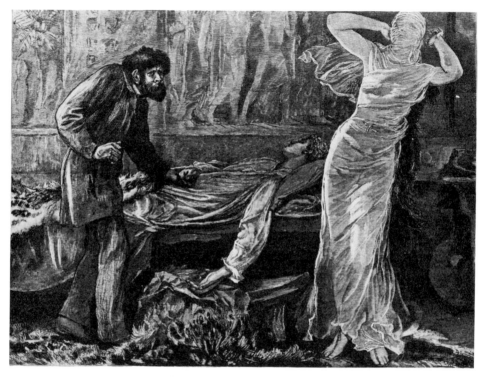

From the first, serial edition of H. Rider Haggard's *She* (1886).

8. Imperial Gothic: Atavism and the Occult in the British Adventure Novel, 1880–1914

> How thinkest thou that I rule this people? . . . It is by terror. My empire is of the imagination.
>
> —Ayesha in *She*

i

In "The Little Brass God," a 1905 story by Bithia Croker, a statue of "Kali, Goddess of Destruction," brings misfortune to its unwitting Anglo-Indian possessors. First their pets kill each other or are killed in accidents; next the servants get sick or fall downstairs; then the family's lives are jeopardized. Finally the statue is stolen and dropped down a well, thus ending the curse.[1] This featherweight tale typifies many written between 1880 and 1914. Its central feature, the magic statue, suggests that Western rationality may be subverted by the very superstitions it rejects. The destructive magic of the Orient takes its revenge; Croker unwittingly expresses a social version of the return of the repressed characteristic of late Victorian and Edwardian fiction, including that blend of adventure story with Gothic elements—imperial Gothic, as I will call it—which flourished from H. Rider Haggard's *King Solomon's Mines* in 1885 down at least to John Buchan's *Greenmantle* in 1916. Imperial Gothic combines the seemingly scientific, progressive, often Darwinian ideology of imperialism with an antithetical interest in the occult. Although the connections between imperialism and other aspects of late Victorian and Edwardian culture are innumerable, the link with occultism is especially symptomatic of the anxieties that attended the climax of the British

Empire. No form of cultural expression reveals more clearly the contradictions within that climax than imperial Gothic.

Impelled by scientific materialism, the search for new sources of faith led many late Victorians to telepathy, séances, and psychic research. It also led to the far reaches of the Empire, where strange gods and "unspeakable rites" still had their millions of devotees. Publication of Madame Blavatsky's *Isis Unveiled* in 1877 marks the beginning of this trend, and the stunning success of Edwin Arnold's *The Light of Asia* (1879) suggests the strength of the desire for alternatives to both religious orthodoxy and scientific skepticism.[2] For the same reason, A. P. Sinnett's *Esoteric Buddhism* (1883) was widely popular, as was his earlier *The Occult World* (1881).[3] The standard explanation for the flourishing of occultism in the second half of the nineteenth century is that "triumphant positivism sparked an international reaction against its restrictive world view." In illustrating this thesis, Janet Oppenheim lists some manifestations of that reaction: "In England, it was an age of . . . the Rosicrucian revival, of cabalists, Hermeticists, and reincarnationists. In the late 1880s, the Hermetic Order of the Golden Dawn first saw the light of day in London, and during its stormy history, the Order lured into its arcane activities not only W. B. Yeats, but also the self-proclaimed magus Aleister Crowley. . . . Palmists and astrologers abounded, while books on magic and the occult sold briskly."[4] Oppenheim's thesis that "much of the attraction of these and related subjects depended on the dominant role that science had assumed in modern culture" (160) is borne out by the testimony of those drawn to occultism, among them Arthur Conan Doyle, Annie Besant, Arthur J. Balfour, and Oliver Lodge. At the same time an emphasis on the occult aspects of experience was often reconciled with "science" and even with Darwinism; such a reconcilation characterizes Andrew Lang's interests in both anthropology and psychic research, as well as the various neo-Hegelian justifications of Empire. Thus in *Origins and Destiny of Imperial Britain* (1900), J. A. Cramb argues that "empires are successive incarnations of the Divine ideas," but also that empires result from the struggle for survival of the fittest among nations and races. The British nation and Anglo-Saxon race, he contends, are the fittest to survive.[5]

Imperialism itself, as an ideology or political faith, functioned as a partial substitute for declining or fallen Christianity and for declining faith in Britain's future. The poet John Davidson, for instance, having rejected other creeds and causes, "committed himself to a cluster of ideas centering on heroes, hero worship, and heroic vitalism," according to his biographer, which led him to pen ardent celebrations of the Empire.[6] In "St. George's Day," Davidson writes:

> The Sphinx that watches by the Nile
> Has seen great empires pass away:
> The mightiest lasted but a while;
> Yet ours shall not decay—

a claim that by the 1890s obviously required extraordinary faith.[7] The religious quality of late Victorian imperialism is also evident in much of Rudyard Kipling's poetry, as in "Recessional":

> God of our fathers, known of old,
>   Lord of our far-flung battle-line,
> Beneath whose awful Hand we hold
>   Dominion over palm and pine—
> Lord God of Hosts, be with us yet,
> Lest we forget—lest we forget![8]

In his study of William Ernest Henley, who did much to encourage the expression of imperialism in fin-de-siècle literature, Jerome Buckley remarks that "by the last decade of the century, the concept of a national or racial absolute inspired a fervor comparable to that engendered by the older evangelical religion."[9]

Imperialism and occultism both functioned as ersatz religions, but their fusion in imperial Gothic represents something different from a search for new faiths. The patterns of atavism and going native described by imperialist romancers do not offer salvationist answers for seekers after religious truth; they offer instead insistent images of decline and fall or of civilization turning into its opposite just as the Englishman who desecrates a Hindu temple in Kipling's "Mark of the Beast" turns into a werewolf. Imperial Gothic expresses anxieties about the waning of religious orthodoxy, but even more clearly it expresses anxieties about the ease with which civilization can revert to barbarism or savagery and thus about the weakening of Britain's imperial hegemony. The atavistic descents into the primitive experienced by fictional characters seem often to be allegories of the larger regressive movement of civilization, British progress transformed into British backsliding. So the first section of Richard Jefferies's apocalyptic fantasy *After London* (1885) is entitled "The Relapse into Barbarism." Similarly, the narrator of Erskine Childers's spy novel *Riddle of the Sands* (1903) starts his tale in this way: "I have read of men who, when forced by their calling to live for long periods in utter solitude—save for a few black faces—have made it a rule to dress regularly for dinner in order to . . . prevent a relapse into barbarism."[10] Much imperialist writing after about 1880 treats the Empire as a barricade against a new barbarian invasion; just as often it treats the Empire as a "dressing for dinner," a temporary means of preventing Britain itself from relapsing into barbarism.

After the mid-Victorian years the British found it increasingly difficult to think of themselves as inevitably progressive; they began worrying instead about the degeneration of their institutions, their culture, their racial "stock." In *Mark Rutherford's Deliverance* (1885), William Hale White writes that "our civilization is nothing but a thin film or crust lying over a volcanic pit," and in *Fabian Essays* (1889), George Bernard Shaw contends that Britain is "in an advanced state of rottenness."[11] Much of the literary culture of the period expresses similar views. The aesthetic and decadent movements offer sinister analogies to Roman imperial decline and fall, while realistic novelists—George Gissing and Thomas Hardy, for instance—paint gloomy pictures of contemporary society and "the ache of modernism" (some of Gissing's pictures are explicitly anti-imperialist). Apocalyptic themes and images are characteristic of imperial Gothic, in which, despite the consciously pro-Empire values of many authors, the feeling emerges that "we are those upon whom the ends of the world are come."[12]

The three principal themes of imperial Gothic are individual regression or going native; an invasion of civilization by the forces of barbarism or demonism; and the diminution of opportunities for adventure and heroism in the modern world. In the romances of Stevenson, Haggard, Kipling, Doyle, Bram Stoker, and John Buchan the supernatural or paranormal, usually symptomatic of individual regression, often manifests itself in imperial settings. Noting that Anglo-Indian fiction frequently deals with "inexplicable curses, demonic possession, and ghostly visitations," Lewis Wurgaft cites Kipling's "Phantom Rickshaw" as typical, and countless such tales were set in Burma, Egypt, Nigeria, and other parts of the Empire as well.[13] In Edgar Wallace's *Sanders of the River* (1909), for example, the commissioner of a West African territory out-savages the savages, partly through police brutality but partly also through his knowledge of witchcraft. Says the narrator: "You can no more explain many happenings which are the merest commonplace in [Africa] than you can explain the miracle of faith or the wonder of telepathy."[14]

In numerous late Victorian and Edwardian stories, moreover, occult phenomena follow characters from imperial settings home to Britain. In Doyle's "The Brown Hand" (1899), an Anglo-Indian doctor is haunted after his return to England by the ghost of an Afghan whose hand he had amputated. In "The Ring of Thoth" (1890) and "Lot No. 249" (1892), Egyptian mummies come to life in the Louvre and in the rooms of an Oxford student.[15] In all three stories, western science discovers or triggers supernatural effects associated with the "mysterious Orient." My favorite story of this type is H. G. Wells's "The Truth about Pyecraft," in which an obese Londoner takes an Indian recipe for "loss of weight" but instead of slimming down, begins levitating. The problem caused by oriental magic is then solved by western technology: lead underwear, which allows the balloonlike Mr. Pyecraft to live almost normally, feet on the ground.

The causes of the upsurge in romance writing toward the end of the century are numerous, complex, and often the same as those of the upsurge of occultism. Thus the new romanticism in fiction is frequently explained by its advocates—Stevenson, Haggard, Lang, and others—as a reaction against scientific materialism as embodied in "realistic" or "naturalistic" narratives. The most enthusiastic defender of the new fashion for romances was Andrew Lang, who thought the realism of George Eliot and Henry James intellectually superior but also that the romances of Stevenson and Haggard tapped universal, deep-rooted, "primitive" aspects of human nature which the realists could not approach. "Fiction is a shield with two sides, the silver and the golden: the study of manners and of character, on one hand; on the other, the description of adventure, the delight of romantic narrative."[16] Although he sees a place for both kinds of fiction, Lang has little patience with, for example, Dostoevsky's gloomy honesty: "I, for one, admire M. Dostoieffsky so much . . . that I pay him the supreme tribute of never reading him at all" (685). Lang prefers literature of a middle-brow sort, on a level with his own critical journalism, or, farther down the scale of cultural value, he prefers adventure stories written for boys: " 'Treasure Island' and 'Kidnapped' are boys' books written by an author of whose genius, for narrative, for delineation of character, for style, I hardly care to speak, lest enthusiasm should seem to border on fanaticism" (690). Lang feels that Haggard is by no means so sophisticated a writer as Stevenson, but this is almost an advantage: the less sophisticated or the more boyish, the better.

All the same, Lang believes, realism in fiction should coexist with romanticism just as the rational, conscious side of human nature coexists with the unconscious. Lang can appreciate realistic novels intellectually, but "the natural man within me, the survival of some blue-painted

Briton or of some gipsy," is "equally pleased with a *true* Zulu love story" (689). He therefore declares that "the advantage of our mixed condition, civilized at top with the old barbarian under our clothes, is just this, that we can enjoy all sorts of things" (690). Romances may be unsophisticated affairs, but because they appeal to the barbarian buried self of the reader, they are more fundamental, more honest, more natural than realism. In Lang's criticism, romances are "'savage survivals,' but so is the whole of the poetic way of regarding Nature" (690).

An anthropologist of sorts, Lang acquired his theory of savage survivals from his mentor Edward Burnett Tylor, who contends that occultism and spiritualism—indeed, all forms of superstition (and therefore, implicitly, of religion)—belong to "the philosophy of savages." Modern occultism, according to Tylor, is "a direct revival from the regions of savage philosophy and peasant folk-lore," a reversion to "primitive culture."[17] At the same time Tylor associates poetry with the mythology of primitive peoples: "The mental condition of the lower races is the key to poetry, nor is it a small portion of the poetic realm which these definitions cover" (2:533). Literary activity in general thus appears to be a throwback to prerational states of mind and society. Similarly, Arthur Machen, author of numerous Gothic horror stories from the 1890s onward, defines literature as "the endeavour of every age to return to the first age, to an age, if you like, of savages."[18]

Robert Louis Stevenson, who echoes Lang's defenses of romances as against novels, discovered sources of "primitive" poetic energy in his own psyche, most notably through the nightmare that yielded *Dr. Jekyll and Mr. Hyde*. Stevenson entertained ambivalent feelings toward the popularity of that "Gothic gnome" or "crawler," in part because *any* popular appeal seemed irrational or vaguely barbaric to him. Although not overtly about imperial matters, *Jekyll and Hyde*, perhaps even more than *Treasure Island* and *Kidnapped*, served as a model for later writers of imperial Gothic fantasies. Because "within the Gothic we can find a very intense, if displaced, engagement with political and social problems," it is possible, as David Punter argues, to read *Jekyll and Hyde* as itself an example of imperial Gothic: "It is strongly suggested [by Stevenson] that Hyde's behaviour is an urban version of 'going native.' The particular difficulties encountered by English imperialism in its decline were conditioned by the nature of the supremacy which had been asserted: not a simple racial supremacy, but one constantly seen as founded on moral superiority. If an empire based on a morality declines, what are the implications . . .? It is precisely Jekyll's 'high views' which produce morbidity in his *alter ego.*"[19] Jekyll's alchemy releases the apelike barbarian—the savage or natural man—who lives beneath the civilized skin. Not only is this the general fantasy of going native in imperial Gothic, but Hyde—murderous, primitive, apelike—fits the Victorian stereotype of the Irish hooligan, and his dastardly murder of Sir Danvers Carew resembles some of the "Fenian outrages" of the early 1880s.[20]

Imperial Gothic is related to several other forms of romance writing which flourished between 1880 and 1914. Judith Wilt has argued for the existence of subterranean links between late Victorian imperialism, the resurrection of Gothic romance formulas, and the conversion of Gothic into science fiction. "In or around December, 1897," she writes, "Victorian gothic changed—into Victorian science fiction. The occasion was . . . Wells's *War of the Worlds*, which followed by only a few months Bram Stoker's . . . *Dracula.*"[21] A similar connection is evident between imperial Gothic and the romance fictions of the decadent movement, as in Oscar Wilde's *Picture of Dorian Gray*, which traces an atavistic descent into criminal self-indulgence as mirrored by a changing portrait. Both Stoker's and Wells's romances can be read, moreover, as fanciful versions of yet another popular literary form, invasion-scare stories, in which the outward movement of imperialist adventure is reversed, a pattern foreshadowed by the returned convict theme in Botany Bay eclogues. *Dracula* itself is an individual invasion or demonic possession fantasy with political implications. Not only is Stoker's bloodthirsty Count the "final aristocrat," he is also the last of a "conquering race," as Dracula explains to Jonathan Harker:

> We Szekelys have a right to be proud, for in our veins flows the blood of many brave races who fought as the lion fights, for lordship. Here, in the whirlpool of European races, the Ugric tribe bore down from Iceland the fighting spirit which Thor and Wodin gave them, which their Berserkers displayed to such fell intent on the seaboards of Europe, aye, and of Asia and Africa, too, till the peoples thought that the were-wolves themselves had come. Here, too, when they came, they found the Huns, whose warlike fury had swept the earth like a living flame, till the dying peoples held that in their veins ran the blood of those old witches, who, expelled from Scythia, had mated with the devils in the desert. Fool, fools! What devil or what witch was ever so great as Attila, whose blood is in these veins? . . . Is it a wonder that we were a conquering race?[22]

The whirlpool of the Count's own ideas, confounding racism with the mixing of races, pride in pure blood with blood-sucking cannibalism, and aristocratic descent with witchcraft and barbarism, reads like a grim parody of the "conquering race" rhetoric in much imperialist writing, a premonition of fascism. In common with several other Gothic invaders in late Victorian fiction, moreover, Dracula threatens to create a demonic empire of the dead from the living British Empire. "This was the being I was helping to transfer to London," says Jonathan Harker, "where, perhaps for centuries to come, he might, amongst its teeming millions, satiate his lust for blood, and create a new and ever widening circle of semi-demons to batten on the helpless" (67).

A similar demonic invasion is threatened in Haggard's *She*: Ayesha plans to usurp the British throne from Queen Victoria, though fortunately her second dousing in the flames of immortality kills her before she can leave the Caves of Kôr for London.[23] Horace Holly, the principal narrator of Haggard's romance, explains the situation: "Evidently the terrible *She* had determined to go to England, and it made me shudder to think what would be the result of her arrival. . . . In the end, I had little doubt, she would assume absolute rule over the British dominions, and probably over the whole earth, and, though I was sure that she would speedily make ours the most glorious and prosperous empire that the world has ever seen, it must be at the cost of a terrible sacrifice of life."[24] Though Haggard resurrects Ayesha in later romances, his archetype of feminine domination grows tamer and never travels to Britain. Several critics have seen in both *She* and *Dracula* the threat of the New Woman to Victorian patriarchy, and Queen Tera, the mummy who comes to life in Stoker's *Jewel of the Seven Stars* (1903), represents the same threat. Norman Etherington calls Ayesha "a Diana in jack-boots who preaches materialism in philosophy and fascism in politics" (47), while Nina Auerbach notes that Ayesha's dream of eternal love and immortality is fused with the nightmare of universal empire. In Ayesha's case, "love does not tranquilize womanhood into domestic confinement, but fuels her latent powers into political life."[25] Although the New Woman is one of the threats underlying the demonism of Ayesha and also of Dracula and his female victims, however, Haggard's and Stoker's apocalyptic fears are comprehensive: the demons who threaten to subvert the Empire and invade Britain are of both sexes and come in many guises.

Often Wells's translations of Gothic conventions into quasi-scientific ones also suggest demonic subversions of the Empire or—what amounts to the same thing in late Victorian and Edwardian writing—of civilization. "It occurred to me that instead of the usual interview with the devil or a magician, an ingenious use of scientific patter might with advantage be substituted," Wells writes of his "scientific romances." "I simply brought the fetish stuff up to date, and made it as near actual theory as possible."[26] *The War of the Worlds* is the classic science fiction, invasion-from-outer-space fantasy, though Wells wrote many related stories—"The Empire of the Ants," for example, in which superintelligent, poisonous ants from the Amazon Basin threaten to overwhelm first British Guiana and then the entire world, founding their insect empire upon the ruins of human ones.

Numerous invasion fantasies were written between 1880 and 1914 without Gothic overtones. The ur-text is Sir George Chesney's *The Battle of Dorking*, which first appeared in *Blackwood's Magazine* in 1871. In the bibliography to *Voices Prophesying War*, I. F. Clarke lists dozens of "imaginary war" novels published between 1871 and 1914, many of them following an invasion-of-Britain pattern. Among them are T. A. Guthrie's *The Seizure of the Channel Tunnel* (1882), H. F. Lester's *The Taking of Dover* (1888), and the anonymous *The Sack of London in the Great French War of 1901* (1901). Several novels also appeared, both in Britain and elsewhere, with titles along the lines of *Decline and Fall of the British Empire*, as well as invasion-of-India stories.[27] Clearly this was not the fiction of a generation of writers confident about the future of Britain or its Empire. The essence of the genre is captured in P. G. Wodehouse's 1909 parody *The Swoop . . . A Tale of the Great Invasion*, in which Britain is overwhelmed by simultaneous onslaughts of Germans, Russians, Chinese, Young Turks, the Swiss Navy, Moroccan brigands, cannibals in war canoes, the Prince of Monaco, and the Mad Mullah, until it is saved by a patriotic Boy Scout named Clarence Chugwater. The only question left to the reader's imagination is why these various forces of barbarism should want to invade so decrepit a country.[28]

Invasion-scare stories often intersect with spy stories. David Stafford gives 1893 as the date of "the birth of the British spy novel," with publication of William Le Queux's *The Great War in England in 1897*, and the subgenre includes many stories, among them Childers's *Riddle of the Sands*, that contain elements of imperial Gothic.[29] Spy stories can be as upbeat as Kipling's *Kim*, full of an evident delight in playing the Great Game in Asia, with little to fear from the bungling French and Russian agents whom Kim helps to foil, or as fear-ridden as Buchan's *Thirty-Nine Steps*, characterized by a breathless paranoia as the hero flees his would-be assassins through a British countryside where no one is to be trusted. Even *Kim*, however, fits Stafford's general description of spy fiction: "The world presented by these novels is a . . . treacherous one in which Britain is the target of the envy, hostility, and malevolence of the other European powers" (497–98).

All of these popular romance formulas—imperial Gothic, Wellsian science fiction, invasion fantasies, spy stories—betray anxieties characteristic of late Victorian and Edwardian imperialism both as an ideology and as a phase of political development. To Wilt's and Stafford's mainly literary perspectives can be added a socioeconomic one, related to those theories of J. A. Hobson and Joseph Schumpeter which treat imperialism itself as an atavistic stage of economic and political development. Although Schumpeter argues against the economic imperialism espoused by Hobson and later, in modified forms, by Lenin and other Marxists, his contention that "imperialism is . . . atavistic in character" fits both imperial Gothic and the flourishing of occultism. [30] Schumpeter identifies capitalism with progress through rational self-interest and therefore fails to see it as a source of social irrationality and regression. Hobson, on the other hand, sees imperialism as a direct result of underconsumption at home and capitalism's consequent search for ever-expanding markets abroad. But in terms of ideological and cultural effects, both Schumpeter and Hobson view imperialism as a retrograde social development, a backsliding toward barbarism.

Hobson locates the causes of "national hate" and international aggression as much in cultural as in economic factors, though for him culture and economics are finally inseparable. [31] Hobson was as much influenced by John Ruskin as by Richard Cobden (the best book on Ruskin published during the nineteenth century is Hobson's); his condemnation of industrialism is less sweeping than Ruskin's, but his "economic humanism" nevertheless echoes *Unto This Last* and *Fors Clavigera*. [32] Ruskin, however, like his own mentor Carlyle, celebrated war as a supreme social value and offered little criticism of British overseas aggression, whereas Hobson contends that uncontrolled industrial capitalism generates wars and leads to the imperialization of preindustrial peoples. Ruskin saw that so-called industrial progress adversely affected nature, town life, workers, owners, the arts; Hobson sees that it also entails an expansive militarization that rides roughshod over older patterns of democracy and liberal nationalism toward an era of ruinous wars.

Both Ruskin and Hobson interpret in terms of regression much that their contemporaries understand as progress. According to Hobson, "the rapid and numerous changes in the external structure of modern civilization have been accompanied by grave unsettlement of the inner life; a

breaking up of time-honoured dogmas, a collapse of principles in politics, religion, and morality have sensibly reduced the power of resistance
to strong passionate suggestions in the individuals of all classes. Hence
the common paradox that an age of universal scepticism may also be an
age of multifarious superstitions, lightly acquired and briefly held, but
dangerous for character and conduct while they hold their sway."[33] By
superstitions Hobson appears to mean a variety of ideological phenomena, including both imperialism and occultism. In any event, he is
especially distressed that universal education and the new mass literacy
have failed to increase democratic rationality but instead seem to have
undermined the intelligence of public opinion. "The popularization of
the power to read has made the press the chief instrument of brutality. . . . A biassed, enslaved, and poisoned press has been the chief
engine for manufacturing Jingoism" (29, 125). The very machinery that
makes mass literacy possible Hobson sees as having deleterious side-
effects. The "terse, dogmatic, unqualified, and unverifiable cablegram,"
for example, seems to represent technological progress but is instead,
Hobson believes, a source of "emotional explosive" and mob sentiment
(11). On the one hand, industrialization has created "mechanical facilities for cheap, quick carriage of persons, goods, and news"; on the other,
a newly literate but poorly educated urban population is easy prey for
sensational journalists and warmongering financiers. These new shapers
of public opinion diffuse a potent ideological mix consisting of adulter-
ated versions of social Darwinism, the chauvinistic ethos of the public
schools and universities, the "khaki Christianity" of the churches, and
above all the racism and narrow-mindedness of the music halls: "The
glorification of brute force and an ignorant contempt for foreigners are
ever-present factors which . . . make the music-hall a very serviceable
engine for generating military passion" (2).

For Hobson, therefore, the path of social regression is marked by the
signs of a corrupting, degenerate mass culture. He believes that "the
physical and mental conditions of . . . town-life" breed "the very atmosphere of Jingoism. A coarse patriotism, fed by the wildest rumours
and the most violent appeals to hate and the animal lust of blood, passes
by quick contagion through the crowded life of cities, and recommends
itself everywhere by the satisfaction it affords to sensational cravings" (8–
9). Hobson is thinking partly of the riotous celebrations in London and
other British cities which followed the lifting of the sieges of Ladysmith
and Mafeking during the Boer War. Something was at work in those mob
scenes far more destructive than the breaking of the Hyde Park railings

which had distressed Matthew Arnold in 1866, even though the later rioters were presumably patriots celebrating British victories. Jingoism fused with the social imperialism of Joseph Chamberlain in the 1890s to emerge as the chief rival to liberalism and socialism for the allegiance of the new working- and lower middle-class voters, foreshadowing fascism. In *The Psychology of Jingoism*, Hobson interprets the ideological success of imperialism as threatening the entire project of civilizing humanity, including British humanity at home. During mob expressions of jingoism, Hobson declares, "the superstructure which centuries of civilization have imposed upon . . . the individual, gives way before some sudden wave of ancient savage nature roused from its subconscious depths" (19). If such a regression is possible for the individual who joins the mob, then it is also possible for an entire society—even the seemingly most civilized, most progressive society—and for Hobson one name for such a reversion to barbarism is imperialism, "a depraved choice of national life" transforming democratic civilization into a savage anarchy clamoring for war. "For the purposes of the present study . . . the hypothesis of reversion to a savage type of nature is distinctly profitable. The [modern] war-spirit . . . is composed of just those qualities which differentiate savage from civilized man" (19).

ii

Numerous travel writers from about 1870 onward lament the decline of exploration into mere tourism. In "Regrets of a Veteran Traveller" (1897), Frederic Harrison declares: "Railways, telegraphs, and circular tours in twenty days have opened to the million the wonders of foreign parts." These signs of technological progress, however, conceal losses: "Have they not sown broadcast disfigurement, vulgarity, stupidity, demoralisation? Europe is changed indeed since the unprogressive forties! Is it all for the better?"[34] The old ideal of opening up the dark places of the world to civilization, commerce, and Christianity fades into the tourist trade: "Morally, we Britons plant the British flag on every peak and pass; and wherever the Union Jack floats there we place the cardinal British institutions—tea, tubs, sanitary appliances, lawn tennis, and churches; all of them excellent things in season. But the missionary zeal of our people is not always according to knowledge and discretion" (241). Before the ugly American came the ugly Briton, clutching a Baedeker or a Cook's travel guide. Harrison thinks it has all become too easy, too common, too standardized to be heroic or adventuresome—"We go abroad, but we travel no longer."

Imperial Gothic frequently expresses anxiety about the waning of opportunities for heroic adventure. With regression and invasion, this is the third of its major themes (ironic today, given Hollywood's frequent regressions to Haggard and Kipling for its adventure tales, as in *Raiders of the Lost Ark*). Early Victorian adventure writers—Marryat, Chamier, Mayne Reid, R. M. Ballantyne—took as self-evident the notion that England was the vanguard nation, leading the world toward the future. As one of the marooned boys in Ballantyne's *Coral Island* (1856) says, "We'll take possession of [this island] in the name of the King; we'll . . . enter the service of its black inhabitants. Of course we'll rise, naturally, to the top of affairs. White men always do in savage countries."[35] Upbeat racism and chauvinism continued to characterize boys' adventure fiction well into the twentieth century, but in imperial Gothic white men do not always rise to the top—just as often they sink into savagedom, cowardice, or exotic torpor, as in Tennyson's "Lotos Eaters." Conrad's fictions frequently read like botched romances in which adventure turns sour or squalid, undermined by moral frailty, and the same is true also of Stevenson's most realistic stories—*The Beach of Falesá*, *The Wreckers*, *Ebb-Tide*. Lord Jim's failure to live up to his heroic self-image has analogues in many imperial Gothic stories that are not ostensibly critical of imperialism.

The fear that adventure may be a thing of the past in the real world led many writers to seek it in the unreal world of romance, dreams, imagination. "Soon the ancient mystery of Africa will have vanished," Haggard laments in an 1894 essay appropriately titled "'Elephant Smashing' and 'Lion Shooting.'" Where, he dolefully asks, "will the romance writers of future generations find a safe and secret place, unknown to the pestilent accuracy of the geographer, in which to lay their plots?"[36] In similar fashion, in both *Heart of Darkness* and his autobiographical essays, Conrad registers his youthful excitement over the blank places on the map of Africa and the disillusionment he felt when he arrived at Stanley Falls in 1890: "A great melancholy descended on me . . . there was . . . no great haunting memory . . . only the unholy recollection of a prosaic newspaper 'stunt' and the distasteful knowledge of the vilest scramble for loot that ever disfigured the history of human conscience and geographical exploration. What an end to the idealized realities of a boy's daydreams! I wondered what I was doing there."[37] The stunt was Stanley's

1871 trek into Central Africa in search of Livingstone for the *New York Herald*, the scramble for loot that Conrad saw at first hand King Leopold's rapacious private empire in the Congo.

Arguments defending theosophy and spiritualism often sound like Haggard's and Conrad's laments for the waning of geographical adventure: the disappearance of earthly frontiers will be compensated for by the opening of new frontiers in the beyond. Not only were occultists seeking proofs of immortality and of a spiritual realm above or beneath the material one, they were also seeking adventure. The fantasy element in such adventure seeking is its most obvious feature, as it is also in the literary turn away from realism to romanticism. According to Lang: "As the visible world is measured, mapped, tested, weighed, we seem to hope more and more that a world of invisible romance may not be far from us. . . . The ordinary shilling tales of 'hypnotism' and mesmerism are vulgar trash enough, and yet I can believe that an impossible romance, if the right man wrote it in the right mood, might still win us from the newspapers, and the stories of shabby love, and cheap remorses, and commonplace failures."[38] But even a well-written impossible romance, as Lang well knows, carries with it more than a hint of childish daydreaming.

If imperialist ideology is atavistic, occultism is obviously so, a rejection of individual and social rationality and a movement backward to primitive or infantile modes of perception and belief. "Ages, empires, civilisations pass, and leave some members even of educated mankind still, in certain points, on the level of the savage who propitiates with gifts, or addresses with prayers, the spirits of the dead"—so Lang writes in *Cock Lane and Common Sense* (1894), intended in part to expose the spurious aspects of spiritualism.[39] Lang believes that much of what goes by that name is fraudulent: "As to the idea of purposely evoking the dead, it is at least as impious, as absurd, as odious to taste and sentiment, as it is insane in the eyes of reason. This protest the writer feels obliged to make, for while he regards the traditional, historical, and anthropological curiosities here collected as matters of some interest . . . he has nothing but abhorrence and contempt for modern efforts to converse with the manes, and for all the profane impostures of 'spiritualism'" (*Cock Lane*, 22).

Like many other well-known Victorians, Lang participated in the Society for Psychical Research, founded in 1882, and even served as its president. But his opinions about psychic phenomena always retain a healthy skepticism. Stopping short of supernatural explanations, Lang favors instead explanations in terms of extraordinary, hitherto unidentified mental powers, including the power of "unconscious cerebration" to create illusions of ghosts or spirits and to perform telepathic feats. If we assume psychic phenomena do occur, then the theory that they emanate from the subconscious is the chief alternative to what Lang calls "the old savage theory" of "the agency of the spirits of the dead."[40]

Just how the subconscious works—how to explain its mechanisms of projection, hallucination, dreams, and forgetting—was a major issue in late nineteenth-century psychology. British psychologists followed paths similar to those that led to psychoanalysis, and their explanations of psychic phenomena, in common with Freud's, tend toward ideas of regression and unconscious cerebration.[41] In *The Future of an Illusion*, Freud writes that the beliefs of the "spiritualists" are infantile: "They are convinced of the survival of the individual soul. . . . Unfortunately they cannot succeed in refuting the fact that . . . their spirits are merely the products of their own mental activity. They have called up the spirits of the greatest men . . . but all the pronouncements and information which they have received . . . have been so foolish . . . that one can find nothing credible in them but the capacity of the spirits to adapt themselves to the circle of people who have conjured them up."[42] Freud interprets spiritualist beliefs, as he does all of the "fairy tales of religion," as backsliding from adult, conscious rationality into the irrational depths of the subconscious.

Such an explanation of superstitions might do for the psychologists and also for Lang, who as an anthropologist was more interested in the products of myth making and religion than in experiencing the miraculous himself. For many of Lang's colleagues in psychic research, however, the realm of spirit was not reducible to that of the unconscious, even though the latter might contain unknown, potentially miraculous powers. In his *Encyclopedia Britannica* article on psychical research, Lang notes F.W.H. Myers's various studies; regrettably, Myers "tended more and more to the belief in the 'invasion' and 'possession' of living human organisms by spirits of the dead." He points to the same tendency in the work of the physicist and psychic researcher Oliver Lodge, and adds: "Other students can find, in the evidence cited [by Lodge and Myers], no warrant for this return to the 'palaeolithic psychology' of 'invasion' and 'possession'" (547).

Other late Victorians and Edwardians moved in the direction Lang held to be retrograde—away from an early skepticism toward increasing and occasionally absolute faith in occult phenomena, including demonic invasions and possessions of reality. Obviously the will-to-believe in such cases was powerful. A. J. Balfour, for example, Conservative prime minister from 1902 to 1905, produced several "metaphysical" essays—*A Defence of Philosophic Doubt* (1879), *The Foundations of Belief* (1895), and others—that make the case for faith by sharply dividing science and religion. Balfour argues that the two are separate, equally valid realms; the methods and discoveries of science cannot invalidate those of religion. That his sympathies lie with religion is obvious. In his presidential address to the Society for Psychical Research in 1894, Balfour expresses his joy that the society's work demonstrates "there are things in heaven and earth not hitherto dreamed of in our scientific philosophy."[43] Small wonder that in 1916, when the former prime minister (aided by several automatic writers, including Kipling's sister Alice Fleming) began to receive spirit communications from the love of his youth, Mary Lyttelton, he came to believe that the messages were genuine. Small wonder, too, given his political career, that among the themes in the three thousand messages directed to him from the beyond is the establishment of a harmonious world order (Oppenheim 133).

Several early modern writers followed roughly similar paths from doubt to faith. In Kipling's case, the faith was perhaps never firm. While lightly tossing off such ghost stories as "The Phantom Rickshaw" (1888) and "The Return of Imray" (1891), the young Kipling showed what he actually thought of occultism in "The Sending of Dana Da" (1888)—and what he thought was skeptical to the point of sarcasm: "Once upon a time, some people in India made a new Heaven and a new Earth out of broken teacups, a missing brooch or two, and a hair-brush. These were hidden under bushes, or stuffed into holes in the hillside, and an entire Civil Service of subordinate Gods used to find or mend them again; and every one said: 'There are more things in Heaven and Earth than are dreamt of in our philosophy.'"[44] Kipling's satire, perhaps inspired by recent exposures of Mme. Blavatsky's fraudulence, takes aim at all branches of occultism including theosophy. The new "Religion," he says, "was too elastic for ordinary use. It stretched itself and embraced pieces of everything that the medicine-men of all ages have manufactured," including "White, Gray, and Black Magic . . . spiritualism, palmistry, fortune-telling by cards, hot chesnuts, double-kernelled nuts, and tallow droppings." It would even "have adopted Voodoo and Oboe had it known anything about them" (308).

In the story that follows this introduction, Dana Da, a magus from Afghanistan or parts unknown, is hired by an unnamed Englishman to produce a psychic sending or visitation to annoy the Englishman's enemy,

Lone Sahib. Because Lone Sahib hates cats, the sending takes the form of an invasion of his bungalow by a plague of supposedly spirit kittens. Lone Sahib and his "co-religionists" see the kittens as materializations from the beyond, write up a report on them "as every Psychical Observer is bound to do," and grow ever more convinced that "spirits . . . squatter up and down their staircases all night" (313). At the story's end the Englishman who has paid for the sending asks Dana Da how he produced it; the alleged magus replies that he gave Lone Sahib's servant "two-eight a month for cats—little, little cats. I wrote, and he put them about—very clever man" (320).

Just when Kipling put aside skepticism and began to be something of an occultist himself is not clear, though some accounts attribute the change to the death of his daughter Josephine in 1899. Certainly her death inspired Kipling to write the psychic story "They" (1904), in which the protagonist communicates with ghostly children in a ghostly country-house setting. But by that time Kipling had also written stories dealing with reincarnation—"The Finest Story in the World" (1891) and "Wireless" (1902)—a subject of increasing interest also to his friend Haggard, whose views about spiritual matters are easier to trace because he was always less defensively ironic than Kipling. Some critics dismiss the problem, suggesting that Kipling occasionally includes supernatural elements in his stories merely for artistic purposes, but this approach seems no more explanatory than arguing that Dante writes about heaven and hell for artistic purposes. Nor did Kipling drop the supernatural after the early 1900s: several stories in *Debits and Credits* (1926) deal with the supernatural—"The Gardener," "The Madonna of the Trenches," and "The Wish House"—and so do other works among his late fiction.[45]

Haggard was interested in occultism from the time when, as a young man in London, he attended séances at the house of Lady Paulet, who gave him his "entree to the spiritualistic society of the day."[46] The apparitions that he saw were not exactly spirits, he thought, but rather the products of "some existent but unknown force" (1:41). Occultism shows up in his first novel, *Dawn* (1884), which combines realism with, as George Saintsbury put it, the "elements of occult arts and astral spirits."[47] Haggard's second novel, *The Witch's Head* (1884), also supposedly realistic, touches upon the theme of reincarnation. After about 1900, according to Norman Etherington, Haggard dwelt with "increased fervor on the truth of reincarnation. The idea he had first tentatively expressed in *Witch's Head*, that lovers worked out their relationships in successive lives and literally eternal triangles, became a dominant theme in his later

novels. He believed he had caught glimpses of his own previous exis-
tences in dreams and visions" (17). In *The Days of My Life*, Haggard
describes a series of these visions of former lives, which might almost,
Etherington says, "be tableaux from the ethnographic section of a museum," similar to "displays on 'the ascent of man' from the Stone Age to
the Iron Age" (17). In the first reincarnation Haggard is a primitive man,
perhaps of the Stone Age; in the second he is black, again primitive,
defending his rude home against attackers who kill him; in the third he is
an ancient Egyptian, in love with a "beautiful young woman with violet
eyes"; and in the fourth he is probably an early medieval barbarian, living
in "a timber-built hall" in a land of "boundless snows and great cold,"
though again in love with a violet-eyed woman, the same "as she of the
Egyptian picture." Haggard believes that these "dream-pictures" can be
explained in one of three ways: "(1) Memories of some central incident
that occurred in a previous incarnation. (2) *Racial* memories of events
that had happened to forefathers. (3) Subconscious imagination and
invention" (2:168). The third explanation is the easiest to accept, he says,
but he clearly favors the first or the second.

Kipling and Haggard often discussed telepathy, ghosts, and reincarnation. Although it is likely that Kipling believed—perhaps always with a
certain ambivalence or ironic distance—in some version of occultism at
least from 1904 onward, Haggard later opined that he converted Kipling
to faith in reincarnation in the 1920s. "He is now convinced," Haggard
wrote in his diary in 1923, "that the individual human being is not a
mere flash in the pan, seen for a moment and lost forever, but an
enduring entity that has lived elsewhere and will continue to live, though
for a while memory of the past is blotted out" (quoted in Cohen, 122).
This may have been only wishful thinking on Haggard's part. In any
event, it seems likely that the very ambivalence with which Kipling
approached any belief in the supernatural made him all the more ardent
an imperialist. On political issues Haggard often seems more supple and
thoughtful than Kipling, though always also ardently imperialistic.[48]
Thus Haggard was not prepared to blame "all our Russian troubles" on
"the machinations of the Jews." Puzzled by Kipling's often belligerent
antisemitism, Haggard wrote in 1919: "I do not know, I am sure, but
personally I am inclined to think that one can insist too much on the Jew
motive, the truth being that there are Jews and Jews. . . . For my own
part I should be inclined to read Trade Unions instead of Jews" (quoted in
Cohen, 110–11). In contrast, Kipling, ambivalent about so many matters, is often dogmatic about politics: "Any nation save ourselves, with

such a fleet as we have at present, would go out swiftly to trample the guts out of the world," Kipling declaimed to Haggard in 1897; "and the fact that we do not seems to show that even if we aren't very civilized, we're about the one power with a glimmering of civilization in us" (quoted in Cohen, 33). The only ambivalence here has to do with the meaning of civilization: perhaps it is a weakness, a disease; perhaps the brave if not civilized thing to do would be to "trample the guts out of the world."

Haggard's comparative uncertainty about politics is dimly reflected in the romance conventions he employs in most of his fictions. In common with other advocates of the romance as against the novel, Haggard hesitates at defending his tales as truer than realistic fictions or even as somehow true. He agrees with Lang that he is expressing universal, mythic concerns—writing about what Jung would later call archetypes. But he also knows that his landscapes shade into the fantastic and are therefore highly subjective landscapes of the mind. Just as Lang is inclined to attribute psychic phenomena to the unconscious, so Haggard often suggests that his stories refer more to his own—or perhaps to universal—dream states than to outward reality. Haggard shares this emphasis on fantasy with all Gothic romancers, whose stories always veer toward dreams and the subliminal reaches of the mind.

The subjectivism of Gothic romance as a genre thus intersects with the atavistic character of both imperialist ideology and occultist belief. According to Theodor Adorno, "occultism is a reflex-action to the subjectification of all meaning, the complement of reification." Adorno contends that "occultism is a symptom of regression in consciousness," diagnosing it specifically as a "regression to magic under late capitalism" whereby "thought is assimilated to late capitalist forms" (239).

> The power of occultism, as of Fascism, to which it is connected by thought-patterns of the ilk of anti-semitism, is not only pathic. Rather it lies in the fact that in the lesser panaceas, as in superimposed pictures, consciousness famished for truth imagines it is grasping a dimly present knowledge diligently denied to it by official progress in all its forms. It is the knowledge that society, by virtually excluding the possibility of spontaneous change, is gravitating towards total catastrophe. The real absurdity is reproduced in the astrological hocus-pocus, which adduces the impenetrable connections of alienated elements—nothing more alien than the stars—as knowledge about the subject.[49]

Adorno's analysis of the interior parallelism between occultism and fascism suggests also the interior significance (the political unconscious) of imperial Gothic fantasy. The subjective nature of the genre is more or less apparent to all of its best practitioners. The motif of the exploration of the Dark Continent or of other blank spaces of external reality whose meaning seems inward—the fabled journey into the unconscious or the heart of darkness of the explorer—is omnipresent in late Victorian and Edwardian literature. Graham Greene is writing at the end of a long tradition when, in *Journey without Maps* (1936), he likens African travel to a landscape of the mind, a dream geography, to be understood as much in psychoanalytic as in geographical terms. [50] Africa, India, and the other dark places of the earth become a terrain upon which the political unconscious of imperialism maps its own desires, its own fantastic longitudes and latitudes.

All of Haggard's romances, from *King Solomon's Mines* onward, can be interpreted as journeys into the dreams of the protagonists and ultimately of Haggard himself. "I closed my eyes," says Horace Holly in *She*, "and imagination, taking up the thread of thought, shot its swift shuttle back across the ages, weaving a picture on their blackness so real and vivid in its detail that I could almost for a moment think that I had triumphed over Time, and that my vision had pierced the mystery of the Past" (141). After describing his fantasy of Ayesha in her youthful power and glory, Holly adds: "Let him who reads forgive the intrusion of a dream into a history of fact" (141). Or, as Captain John Good says after the battle with the Masai in *Allan Quatermain*, "the whole thing seemed more as though one had enjoyed a nightmare just before being called, than as a deed done" (485). Over and over Haggard's adventurers liken their experiences to dreams as they leave the actual geography of Africa or Asia for landscapes that obviously have more affinity to the world of fantasy than to the real one. For Haggard, it requires merely a flip-flopping of the equation to claim the reality of reincarnation and the spirit world that dreams appear to shadow forth.

Haggard's fantasy landscapes often refer less to mental processes than to downright visceral ones, as his characters are swallowed up or temporarily entombed in chasms, tunnels, crypts, and caves: the Place of Death in *King Solomon's Mines*, the underground river down which the explorers plummet to the land of the Zu-Vendis in *Allan Quatermain*, the Caves of Kôr in *She*. As Holly and Leo Vincy escape the midnight storm that shipwrecks them on the coast of Africa, "we shot out between the teeth-like lines of gnashing waves into the comparatively smooth water of the mouth of the sea" (*She*, 43). As Conrad recognized, the basic regression fantasy of imperial Gothic involves a reverse cannibalism: the nightmare of being swallowed by the world's dark places has as its obverse side the solipsistic fantasy of swallowing the world. In *Heart of Darkness*, Marlow describes Kurtz as an eloquent voice, though uttering emptiness, "the horror, the horror." The restraint of the African "cannibals" who serve as Marlow's crew stands in obvious contrast to the fact that "Mr. Kurtz lacked restraint in the gratification of his various lusts."[51] At one point Marlow describes Kurtz opening "his mouth wide—it gave him a weirdly voracious aspect, as though he had wanted to swallow all the air, all the earth, all the men before him" (61). George Gissing, too, sensed in late Victorian imperialism a cannibalism in reverse. In *The Whirlpool* (1897), after his friend Carnaby has ironically mentioned "nigger-hunting" as an excellent modern sport, Harvey Rolfe responds: "There's more than that to do in South Africa. . . . Who believes for a moment that England will remain satisfied with bits here and there? We have to swallow the whole, of course. We shall go on fighting and annexing until—until the decline and fall of the British Empire. That hasn't begun yet. Some of us are so over-civilized that it makes a reaction of wholesome barbarism in the rest. We shall fight like blazes in the twentieth century."[52]

Gissing here captures the tone of much late Victorian imperialist propaganda. Rolfe's statement, though ironically made, seems almost to echo Cecil Rhodes's grandiose claims about painting the map of Africa red, or his famous assertion that he "would annex the planets if I could."[53] The latter assertion, often quoted out of context, seems much less self-assured when read in relation to what proceeds it—a near-lament about the closing off of global frontiers, a lament suspiciously close to spiritualist concerns with astral bodies and astrology: "The world . . . is nearly all parcelled out, and what there is left of it is being divided up, conquered, and colonised. To think of these stars . . . that you see overhead at night, these vast worlds which we can never reach. I would annex the planets if I could; I often think of that. It makes me sad to see them so clear and yet so far" (190). Rhodes made this statement to the journalist W. T. Stead, who quotes it in his hagiographic *Last Will and Testament of Cecil John Rhodes* (1902). About the only criticism Stead has is that Rhodes was a social Darwinist who never crossed the invisible line between secular ideology and spiritualism. Nevertheless, Stead does his best to bring Rhodes into the occultist fold, attributing an imaginary chain of reasoning to Rhodes which couples survival of the fittest with God's will. Assuming that God *does* exist, Stead makes Rhodes speculate, then in a social Darwinian world He would no doubt make it His will that

Britain and the British, the fittest nation and race that history has ever known, should annex as much of the globe as possible, if not the stars. "If there be a God, I think that what He would like me to do is to paint as much of the map of Africa British red as possible, and to do what I can elsewhere to promote the unity and extend the influence of the English-speaking race" (98).

Of all late Victorian and Edwardian occultists, none was more sanguine than Stead about the truth of his convictions. He believed that God had given him a personal mission as a journalist, to defend the Empire and to trumpet the truths of spiritualism through the world. In reporting the news, he made innovative use of interviews with the great and powerful, and when the great were not available—when they happened to be dead, for example—he questioned them anyway through what he called "automatic interviews." Thus he was able to publish the opinions of Catherine the Great on the Russian Question and those of Gladstone's ghost on the budget of 1909. The headline on the front page of the *Daily Chronicle* for 1 November 1909 read: "Amazing Spirit Interview: The Late Mr. Gladstone on the Budget." In her study of spiritualism Ruth Brandon notes that "Mr. Gladstone, as it happened, had not much of interest to say; but the news (to paraphrase Dr. Johnson) lay in his saying it at all" (201).

Through the urgings of his dead friend Julia Ames, Stead made plans to open better communications with the spirit world. In his occultist journal *Borderland* and elsewhere, Stead projected a highly original sort of news agency—one that would transmit news of the beyond through spirit mediumship and that would be named Julia's Bureau. "What is wanted is a bureau of communication between the two sides," Julia's ghost told Stead. "Could you not establish some sort of office with one or more trustworthy mediums? If only it were to enable the sorrowing on the earth to know, if only for once, that their so-called dead live nearer them than ever before, it would help to dry many a tear and soothe many a sorrow. I think you could count upon the eager co-operation of all on this side."54

Over the years Julia sent Stead many spirit letters containing news from the borderland, and she often exhorted him to open a bureau of communication. He saw these exhortations as a great opportunity but also, considering the numbers of both dead and living who might want to avail themselves of the bureau's services, as an enormous undertaking. On this score Julia was reassuring. In a communiqué dated 6 October 1908, four years before Stead went down in the *Titanic*, Julia acknowl-

edged that the population of the spirit world was vast—of course far larger
than the one and a half billion in the world of the living. But the desire of
the dead to communicate with the living tended to wane quickly; therefore "I should say that the number of the 'dead' who wish to communicate with the living are comparatively few." Julia's ghost then offers what
to any imperialist must have seemed an obvious analogy:

> It is with us as with immigrants to my former country [Australia]. When
> they arrive their hearts are in the old world. The new world is new and
> strange. They long to hear from the old home; and the post brings them
> more joy than the sunrise. But after a very little time the pain is dulled,
> new interests arise, and in a few years . . . they write no more. . . . The
> receipt of letters and telegrams has taken away the death-like edge of
> emigration. "We shall hear from them again." "Write soon." These are the
> consolations of humanity even on the physical plane. What the Bureau
> will do is to enable those who have newly lost their dead to write soon, to
> hear messages. (175–76)

The emigration analogy suggests once again the complex, unconscious
interconnections between imperialist ideology and occultism. To the
ardent imperialist, "away" can never be "away"; nothing is foreign, not
even death; the borderland itself becomes a new frontier to cross, a new
realm to conquer. And with the help of friendly spirits like the Australian
Julia, how easy the conquest seems! Just at the moment actual frontiers
were vanishing, late Victorian and Edwardian occultist literature is filled
with metaphors of exploration, emigration, conquest, colonization. Nor
is the news agency metaphor of Julia's Bureau unique. An imagery of
telegraphy and cablegrams, telephone and radio, permeates the millen-
nial expectations of the spiritualists, as Kipling shows in "Wireless."
According to the persistent modernist Stead: "The recent applications of
electricity in wireless telegraphy and wireless telephony, while proving
nothing in themselves as to the nature or permanence of personality, are
valuable as enabling us to illustrate the difficulties as well as the possibilities of proving the existence of life after death" (xii). But though hard
to prove, the discoveries of the spiritualists are at least as immense as
those of Christopher Columbus: "In order to form a definite idea of the
problem which we are about to attack, let us imagine the grave as if it
were the Atlantic Ocean" (xii). Using similar language in *Phantom Walls*,
Lodge writes of his hope "to be able to survey the ocean of eternity from
Darien-like peaks," while Arthur Conan Doyle often seems willing to
don armor and go crusading in order to conquer death or convince

doubters of the truths of spiritualism: "The greater the difficulty in breaking down the wall of apathy, ignorance, and materialism, the more is it a challenge to our manhood to attack and ever attack in the same bulldog spirit with which Foch faced the German lines."[55]

Both Doyle's and Stead's "sublime self-certainty" in their spiritualist writings, Brandon speculates, is a reflection of imperial domination (193). But they frequently express fears about foreign rivals and British slippage in the real world, so the self-certainty of their spiritualism must be largely compensatory. In any event, Brandon reports that three weeks after Stead drowned in the *Titanic*, "he appeared in his inner sanctuary in Mowbray House, where his daughter, his secretary and other devoted ladies were waiting. His face (so they said) shone out; and as it faded his voice rang through the room saying: 'All I told you is true'" (205). Stead's ghost showed up a few years later, at one of the Doyle family séances, announcing that he had "looked into the eyes of Christ with Cecil Rhodes by my side and he said tell Arthur that his work on Earth is holy and divine—that his Message is Mine" (quoted by Brandon, 220). This message came after the death of Doyle's son Kingsley, who had been wounded in combat during the world war and, while recovering, contracted the pneumonia that killed him.

Doyle's path to spiritualism was much like the one traversed by many late Victorians and Edwardians. In his *Memories and Adventures* (1924), he writes that his youthful education had trained him in "the school of medical materialism," formed by "the negative views of all my great teachers" (77). At first he was generally skeptical about occultism:

> I had at that time the usual contempt which the young educated man feels towards the whole subject which has been covered by the clumsy name of Spiritualism. I had read of mediums being convicted of fraud, I had heard of phenomena which were opposed to every known scientific law, and I had deplored the simplicity and credulity which could deceive good, earnest people into believing that such bogus happenings were signs of intelligence outside our own existence. . . . I was wrong and my great teachers were wrong, but still I hold that they wrought well and that their Victorian agnosticism was in the interests of the human race, for it shook the old iron-clad unreasoning Evangelical position which was so universal before their days. For all rebuilding a site must be cleared. (77)

From the 1890s onward, Doyle became increasingly interested in the spiritualist rebuilding of nothing less than world civilization. He engaged in psychic research, experimenting with telepathy and searching for poltergeists in haunted houses, at first with a skeptical air but later with growing belief in an invisible realm of spirits just beyond the boundaries of material reality. If it seemed evident that adventure was vanishing from the modern world, Doyle for one rebelled against the evidence. True, his reinventions of adventure in fiction have about them the same compensatory quality that characterizes most late Victorian romance writing, which senses its inferiority to realistic narration. Romance writers indicate in a variety of ways that their adventure stories are for adolescents; and occultist pursuits are also somehow, even to occultists themselves, childish and subrational. As a young man, at least, Doyle perceived these difficulties but plunged ahead anyway, toward the blinding light (he thought) at the end of the long tunnel of world history.

In Doyle's 1911 novel *The Lost World*, the journalist hero Malone is told by his girlfriend that he must go adventuring and become a hero before she will marry him. The demand seems to him next to impossible because, as his editor exclaims, "the big blank spaces in the map are all being filled in, and there's no room for romance anywhere."[56] But there is room—or Doyle at least will make room—for romance in a fantasy version of the Amazon basin, where the British adventurers regress through a Darwinian nightmare to the days of the dinosaurs. The characters in the story, including the atavistically apelike Professor Challenger, reappear next in *The Poison Belt* of 1913, where adventure shrinks: they watch the end of the world from the windows of an airtight room in Challenger's house. But the world does not end, the poisonous cloud lifts, people revive, and Doyle's band of fantasy adventurers live on to appear in a third novel, *The Land of Mist*, published in 1925, the same year as Yeats's *A Vision*. Challenger and the rest are now participants in what Doyle believes to be the greatest adventure of all, beyond the borders of the material world. Exploration and invasion metaphors abound. Lord John Roxton's newspaper ad sets the tone: Roxton is "seeking fresh worlds to conquer. Having exhausted the sporting adventures of this terrestrial globe, he is now turning to those of the dim, dark and dubious regions of psychic research. He is in the market . . . for any genuine specimen of a haunted house."[57] While the crumbling of the Empire quickened after World War I, Doyle himself turned obsessively to haunted houses, séances, lands of mysticism and mist. The skeptical Challenger exclaims that the "soul-talk" of the spiritualists is "the Animism of savages," but Doyle himself was no longer skeptical (19). He believed in magic, he believed in fairies, he believed in ectoplasmic projections. He believed Spiritualism with a capital S was the successor to

Christianity, the new advent of the City of God after the fall of the City of Man. The creator of that great incarnation of scientific rationalism Sherlock Holmes devoted himself to the spiritualist movement, becoming one of its leaders, and it became for him a substitute for all other causes—for imperialism itself. Just as his friend Stead felt that he had received a call from God, so Doyle after the world war felt that the meaningful part of his life had begun. He had received the call; it was his duty to save the world. "In the days of universal sorrow and loss [after World War I], when the voice of Rachel was heard throughout the land, it was borne in upon me that the knowledge which had come to me thus was not for my own consolation alone, but that God had placed me in a very special position for conveying it to that world which needed it so badly" (*Memories*, 387).

Doyle's version of "Heaven was rather like Sussex, slightly watered down," says Brandon (222), but his plans for the future of the world were somewhat larger than Sussex. He believed the spirit world was arranged in a marvelous, infinite bureaucratic hierarchy very much like the British Raj in India.[58] In 1923 an "Arabian spirit" named Pheneas began to communicate with him through his wife's automatic writing, telling him that the old world would end soon and a glorious new one dawn. Doyle was no doubt reassured to learn that "England is to be the centre to which all humanity will turn. She is to be the beacon light in this dark, dark world. The light is Christ, and all humans will strive to get to that light in the great darkness" (*Pheneas Speaks*, 79). Sherlock Holmes cannot tolerate a mystery without solving it, nor can Doyle: the darkness of this world will soon disperse, and light, radiating especially from England and Sussex, will be universal. Doyle experienced a glimmer of embarrassment toward the end of the decade, shortly before his death, when Pheneas's predictions did not seem to be coming true on schedule, but it was only a minor setback. Material adventure in the material Empire might be on the wane, but over the ruins was dawning the light of the great spiritualist adventure.

As far as geopolitical arrangements were concerned, Doyle believed, the programs of all governments would have to be revised. In spiritualist armor, slaying the dragons of Bolshevism and materialism, Doyle sometimes felt that the future was his. Like the souls of the dead, the glories of the imperialist past would be reborn, purified or rarefied, for they were eternal. In his *History of Spiritualism*, Doyle writes: "I do not say to [the] great and world-commanding . . . powers . . . open your eyes and see that your efforts are fruitless, and acknowledge your defeat, for probably they never will open their eyes . . . but I say to the Spiritualists . . . dark as the day may seem to you, never was it more cheering . . . never . . . more anticipatory of ultimate victory. It has upon it the stamp of all the conquering influences of the age."[59] But the ultimate victory of spiritualism was prefigured for Doyle in the demise of the empires of this world, the precondition for the invasion and reconquest of reality by the realm of spirit, or perhaps of our transubstantiation—a kind of psychic emigration and colonization—into the world beyond reality, an invisible, even more glorious empire rising ghostlike out of the corpse of the old.

As cultural formations, both imperialism and spiritualism have roots in "the dark powers of the subconscious, [and call] into play instincts that carry over from the life habits of the dim past. Driven out everywhere else, the irrational" seeks refuge in imperialism, Schumpeter contends (14), and, I would add, in late Victorian and early modern occultism. Imperial Gothic expresses the atavistic character of both movements, shadowing forth the larger, gradual disintegration of British hegemony. Doyle's phantom empire—and the imperial Gothic themes of regression, invasion, and the waning of adventure—express the narrowing vistas of the British Empire at the time of its greatest extent, in the moment before its fall.

Stanley resisting temptation. From J. W. Buel, *Heroes of the Dark Continent* (1898).

9. Epilogue: Kurtz's "Darkness" and Conrad's *Heart of Darkness*

> Conrad died fifty years ago. In those fifty years his work
> has penetrated to many corners of the world which he saw
> as dark. It is a subject for Conradian meditation.
>
> —V. S. Naipaul, "Conrad's Darkness" (1974)

In a 1975 lecture the Nigerian novelist Chinua Achebe attacked *Heart of Darkness* as "racist." Joseph Conrad, Achebe says, "projects the image of Africa as 'the other world,' the antithesis of Europe and therefore of civilization, a place where man's vaunted intelligence and refinement are finally mocked by triumphant bestiality."[1] Supposedly the great demystifier, Conrad is instead a "purveyor of comforting myths" and even "a bloody racist." Achebe adds: "That this simple truth is glossed over in criticisms of his work is due to the fact that white racism against Africa is such a normal way of thinking that its manifestations go completely undetected." Achebe would therefore strike Conrad's novella from the curriculum, where it has been one of the most frequently taught works of modern fiction in English classes from Chicago to Bombay to Johannesburg.

Achebe's diatribe has provoked vigorous defenses of *Heart of Darkness* which predictably stress Conrad's critical stance toward imperialism and also the wide acceptance of racist language and categories in the late Victorian period. Cedric Watts, for example, asserts that "really Conrad and Achebe are on the same side"; Achebe simply gets carried away by his understandable aversion to racial stereotyping.[2] "Far from being a 'purveyor of comforting myths,'" Watts declares, "Conrad most deliberately and incisively debunks such myths." Acknowledging that Conrad employed the stereotypic language common in his day, Watts contends that he nevertheless rose above racism:

> Achebe notes with indignation that Conrad (in the "Author's Note" to *Victory*) speaks of an encounter with a "buck nigger" in Haiti which gave him an impression of mindless violence. Achebe might as well have noted the reference in *The Nigger of the "Narcissus"* . . . to a "tormented and flattened face . . . pathetic and brutal: the tragic, the mysterious, the repulsive mask of a nigger's soul." He might have noted, also, that Conrad's letters are sprinkled with casual anti-Semitic references. It is the same in the letters of his friend [R. B. Cunninghame] Graham. Both Conrad and Graham were influenced by the climate of prejudice of their times. . . . What is interesting is that the best work of both men seems to transcend such prejudice. (208)

Their work transcends prejudice in part, Watts believes, because both attack imperialism. Watts is one of the many critics who interpret *Heart of Darkness* as an exposé of imperialist rapacity and violence. Kurtz's career in deviltry obviously undermines imperialist ideology, and the greed of the "faithless pilgrims"—the white sub-Kurtzes, so to speak—is perhaps worse. "The conquest of the earth," Marlow declares, "which mostly means the taking it away from those who have a different complexion or slightly flatter noses than ourselves, is not a pretty thing when you look into it too much."[3] There is nothing equivocal about that remark; Conrad entertained no illusions about imperialist violence. But Marlow distinguishes between British imperialism and that of the other European powers: the red parts of the map are good to see, he says, "because one knows that some real work is done in there" (10). *Heart of Darkness* is specifically about what Conrad saw in King Leopold's African empire in 1890; it is unclear how far his critique can be generalized to imperialism beyond the Congo.

The politics of Conrad's story is complicated by the story's ambiguous style. I use "impressionism" as a highly inadequate term to characterize the novella's language and narrative structure, in part because Fredric Jameson uses that term in his diagnosis of the "schizophrenic" nature of *Lord Jim*.[4] Conrad's impressionism is for some critics his most praiseworthy quality; to others it appears instead a means of obfuscation, allowing him to mask his nihilism or to maintain contradictory values, or both. Interpretations of *Heart of Darkness* which read it as only racist (and therefore imperialist), or as only anti-imperialist (and therefore antiracist), inevitably founder on its impressionism. To point to only the most obvious difficulty, the narrative frame filters everything that is said not just through Marlow but also through the anonymous primary narrator. At what point is it safe to assume that Conrad/Marlow expresses a single point of view? And even supposing Marlow to speak directly for Conrad, does Conrad/Marlow agree with the values expressed by the primary narrator? Whatever our answers, *Heart of Darkness* offers a powerful critique of at least some manifestations of imperialism and racism as it simultaneously presents that critique in ways that can be characterized only as imperialist and racist. Impressionism is the fragile skein of discourse which expresses—or disguises—this schizophrenic contradiction as an apparently harmonious whole. Analysis of that contradiction helps to reveal the ideological constraints upon a critical understanding of imperialism in literature before World War I. It also suggests how imperialism influenced the often reactionary politics of literary modernism.

i

In *Conrad and Imperialism*, Benita Parry argues that "by revealing the disjunctions between high-sounding rhetoric and sordid ambitions and indicting the purposes and goals of a civilisation dedicated to global . . . hegemony, Conrad's writings [are] more destructive of imperialism's ideological premises than [are] the polemics of his contemporary opponents of empire."[5] Perhaps. At least it is certain that Conrad was appalled by the "high-sounding rhetoric" used to mask the "sordid ambitions" of King Leopold II of Belgium, Conrad's ultimate employer during his six months in the Congo in 1890. *Heart of Darkness* expresses not only what Conrad saw and partially recorded in his "Congo Diary" but also the revelations of atrocities which began appearing in the British press as early as 1888 and reached a climax twenty years later, in 1908, when the mounting scandal forced the Belgian government to take control of Leopold's private domain. During that period the population of the Congo was decimated, perhaps halved; as many as six million persons may have been uprooted, tortured, and murdered through the forced labor system used to extract ivory and what reformers called "red rubber" from "the heart of darkness."[6] Conrad was sympathetic toward the Congo Reform Association, established in 1903 partly by Roger Casement, whom he had met in Africa, and Casement got him to write a propaganda letter in which Conrad says: "It is an extraordinary thing that the conscience of Europe which seventy years ago . . . put down the slave trade on humanitarian grounds tolerates the Congo state today."[7] There follows some patronizing language contrasting the brutalities visited upon the Congolese with the legal protections given to horses in Europe, but Conrad's intention is clear enough.

There is little to add to Hunt Hawkins's account of Conrad's relations with the Congo Reform Association. The association's leader, Edmund Morel, who quoted Conrad's letter to Casement in *King Leopold's Rule in Africa* (1904), called *Heart of Darkness* the "most powerful thing ever written on the subject."[8] But as Hawkins notes, apart from his letter to Casement, Conrad backed away from involvement with the association. Other prominent novelists who had never been to the Congo contributed as much or more to its work. Mark Twain volunteered "King Leopold's Soliloquy," and Arthur Conan Doyle wrote a book for the association called *The Crime of the Congo*. Conrad, as Hawkins notes, "had little faith in agitation for political reform because words were meaningless, human nature unimprovable, and the universe dying"—hardly views to encourage engagement in the cause of the association.[9]

All the same, in at least one other work of fiction Conrad registered his abhorrence of King Leopold's rape of the Congo. This is the minor but highly revealing fantasy that Conrad co-authored with Ford Madox Hueffer, *The Inheritors: An Extravagant Story* (1901). Conrad's role in writing it may have been slight, but he obviously shared the views it expresses. The protagonist meets a beautiful young woman who claims to come from the fourth dimension and to be one of those who "shall inherit the earth." "The Dimensionists were to come in swarms, to materialise, to devour like locusts. . . . They were to come like snow in the night: in the morning one would look out and find the world white. . . . As to methods, we should be treated as we ourselves treat the inferior races."[10] Far from being meek, the inheritors are modern-day imperialists, satirically depicted as invaders from a spiritualist alternative world. Apart from the young woman and one other character, however, no invaders appear in the novel, although the satire upon imperialism is maintained through the portrayal of the Duc de Mersch and his "System for the Regeneration of the Arctic Regions" (46). Like King Leopold, "the foreign financier—they called him the Duc de Mersch—was by way of being a philanthropist on megalomaniac lines." He proves to be no philanthropist at all, but just the "gigantic and atrocious fraud" that Conrad believed Leopold to be. Greenland is the codeword in *The Inheritors* for the Congo. The journalist hero helps to expose "the real horrors of the Système Groënlandais—flogged, butchered, miserable natives, the famines, the vices, diseases, and the crimes" (280). The authors are not even particular about the color of the Eskimo victims: one character says that the Duc "has the blacks murdered" (246–47).

Hueffer and Conrad write some scorching passages in *The Inheritors* about "cruelty to the miserable, helpless, and defenceless" (282). But the facts of exploitation in the Congo perhaps distress them less than the lying idealism that disguises it: "More revolting to see without a mask was that falsehood which had been hiding under the words which for ages had spurred men to noble deeds, to self-sacrifice, to heroism. What was appalling was . . . that all the traditional ideals of honour, glory, conscience, had been committed to the upholding of a gigantic and atrocious fraud. The falsehood had spread stealthily, had eaten into the very heart of creeds and convictions that we learn upon our passage between the past and the future. The old order of things had to live or perish with a lie" (282). For Conrad, the worst feature of imperialism may have been not violence but the lying propaganda used to cover its bloody tracks.

Conrad did not base his critique of imperialist exploitation in *Heart of Darkness* solely on what he had seen in the Congo. What he witnessed was miserable enough, and personally he was also made miserable and resentful by disease and the conviction that his Belgian employers were exploiting him. As he assured Casement, however, while in the Congo he had not even heard of "the alleged custom of cutting off hands among the natives."[11] The conclusion that Casement drew was that most of the cruelties practiced in the Congo were not traditional but the recent effects of exploitation. The cutting off of hands was a punishment for non-cooperation in Leopold's forced labor system and probably became frequent only after 1890. Moreover, just as Conrad had seen little or no evidence of torture, so he probably saw little or no evidence of cannibalism, despite the stress upon it in his story.[12]

It thus seems likely that much of the horror either depicted or suggested in *Heart of Darkness* represents not what Conrad saw but rather his reading of the literature that exposed Leopold's bloody system between Conrad's return to England and his composition of the novella in 1898–99, along with many of the earlier works that shaped the myth of the Dark Continent. Although Conrad's "Congo Diary" and every facet of his journey to Stanley Falls and back have been scrutinized by Norman Sherry and others, what Conrad learned about the Congo after his sojourn there has received little attention.[13] The exposé literature undoubtedly confirmed suspicions that Conrad formed in 1890, but the bloodiest period in the history of Leopold's regime began about a year later. According to Edmund Morel: "From 1890 onwards the records of the Congo State have been literally blood-soaked. Even at that early date, the real complexion of Congo State philanthropy was beginning to appear, but public opinion in Europe was then in its hoodwinked stage."[14]

The two events that did most to bring Leopold's Congo under public scrutiny were the 1891–94 war between Leopold's forces and the Arab slave-traders and the execution of Charles Stokes, British citizen and renegade missionary, by Belgian officers in 1895. The conflict with the Arabs—a "war of extermination," according to Morel—was incredibly cruel and bloody. "The first serious collision with the Arabs occurred in October 27, 1891; the second on May 6, 1892. Battle then succeeded battle; Nyangwe, the Arab stronghold, was captured in January, 1893, and with the surrender of Rumaliza in January, 1894, the campaign came to an end."[15] Conrad undoubtedly read about these events in the press and perhaps also in later accounts, notably Captain Sidney Hinde's *The Fall of the Congo Arabs* (1897). Arthur Hodister, whom Sherry claims as the original of Kurtz, was an early victim of the fighting, having led an expedition to Katanga which was crushed by the Arabs. According to Ian Watt, "*The Times* reported of Hodister and his comrades that 'their heads were stuck on poles and their bodies eaten.'"[16] This and many similar episodes during the war are probable sources for Conrad's emphasis upon cannibalism in *Heart of Darkness*.

Cannibalism was practiced by both sides, not just the Arabs and their Congolese soldiers. According to Hinde, who must also be counted among possible models for Kurtz, "the fact that both sides were cannibals, or rather that both sides had cannibals in their train, proved a great element in our success."[17] Muslims, Hinde points out, believe they will go to heaven only if their bodies are intact. So cannibalism was a weapon of fear and reprisal on both sides, as well as a traditional accompaniment of war among some Congolese societies. Hinde speaks of combatants on both sides as "human wolves" and describes numerous "disgusting banquets" (69). A typical passage reads: "What struck me most in these expeditions was the number of partially cut-up bodies I found in every direction for miles around. Some were minus the hands and feet, and some with steaks cut from the thighs or elsewhere; others had the entrails or the head removed, according to the taste of the individual savage" (131). Hinde's descriptions of such atrocities seem to be those of an impartial, external observer, but in fact he was one of six white officers in charge of some four hundred "regulars" and about twenty-five thousand "cannibal" troops. His expressions of horror are what one expects of an Englishman; they are also those of a participant, however, and contradict his evident fascination with every bloodthirsty detail.

It seems likely that Conrad read Hinde's lurid account. He must have known about the war also from earlier accounts, such as those in the *Times*, and from E. J. Glave's documenting of "cruelty in the Congo Free State" for the *Century Magazine* in 1896–97. According to Glave, "the state has not suppressed slavery, but established a monopoly by driving out the Arab and Wangwana competitors." Instead of a noble war to end the slave trade, which is how Leopold and his agents justified their actions against the Arabs, a new system of slavery was installed in place of the old. Glave continues: "Sometimes the natives are so persecuted that they [take revenge] by killing and eating their tormentors. Recently the state post on the Lomami lost two men killed and eaten by the natives. Arabs were sent to punish the natives; many women and children were taken, and twenty-one heads were brought to [Stanley Falls], and have been used by Captain Rom as a decoration round a flower-bed in front of his house."[18] Captain Rom, no doubt, must also be counted among Kurtz's forebears. In any event, the practice of seizing Congolese for laborers and chopping off the hands and heads of resisters continued, probably increasing after the defeat of the Arabs, as numerous eyewitnesses testify in the grisly quotations that form the bulk of Morel's exposés. According to a typical account by a Swiss observer: "If the chief does not bring the stipulated number of baskets [of raw rubber], soldiers are sent out, and the people are killed without mercy. As proof, parts of the body are brought to the factory. How often have I watched heads and hands being carried into the factory."[19]

ii

When Marlow declares that "the conquest of the earth . . . is not a pretty thing," he goes on to suggest that imperialism may be "redeemed" by the "idea" that lies behind it. In the real world, however, idealism is fragile, and in *Heart of Darkness*, except for the illusions maintained by a few womenfolk back in Brussels, it has almost died out. In going native, Kurtz betrays the civilizing ideals with which supposedly he set out from Europe. Among the "faithless pilgrims" there are only false ideals and the false religion of self-seeking. "To tear treasure out of the bowels of the land was their desire," says Marlow, "with no more moral purpose at the back of it than there is in burglars breaking into a safe" (31). The true nature of European philanthropy in the Congo is revealed to Marlow by the chain gang and the "black shadows of disease and starvation," left to die in the "greenish gloom," whom he sees at the Outer Station (16–17). Probably these miserable phantoms accurately depict what Conrad saw in 1890; they may also represent what he later learned about Leopold's forced labor system. In any case, from the moment he sets foot in the Congo, Marlow is clear about the meaning of "the merry dance of death and trade" (14). It thus makes perfect sense to interpret *Heart of Darkness* as an attack on imperialism, at least as it operated in the Congo.

In the course of this attack, however, *all* ideals transform into idols— something, in Marlow's words, which "you can set up, and bow down before, and offer a sacrifice to" (7). Conrad universalizes "darkness" in part by universalizing fetishism. Marxist critics of empire describe the era of the Scramble for Africa—roughly 1880 to 1914—as one when the "commodity fetishism" of "late capitalism" was most intense, a thesis that complements Conrad's conservative belief in the decay of heroic adventure, eroded by technology and a dishonorable commercialism.[20] The natives in their darkness set Kurtz up as an idol; the Europeans worship ivory, money, power, reputation. Kurtz joins the natives in their "unspeakable rites," worshiping his own unrestrained power and lust. Marlow himself assumes the pose of an idol, sitting on shipdeck with folded legs and palms outward like a Buddha. And Kurtz's Intended is perhaps the greatest fetishist of all, idolizing her image of her fiancé. Marlow's lie leaves Kurtz's Intended shrouded in the protective darkness of her illusions, her idol worship.

One difficulty with this ingenious inversion, through which ideals become idols, is that Conrad portrays the moral bankruptcy of imperialism by showing European motives and actions as no better than African fetishism and savagery. He paints Kurtz and Africa with the same tarbrush. His version of evil—the form taken by Kurtz's Satanic behavior— is going native. Evil, in short, *is* African in Conrad's story; if it is also European, that is because some white men in the heart of darkness behave like Africans. Conrad's stress on cannibalism, his identification of African customs with violence, lust, and madness, his metaphors of bestiality, death, and darkness, his suggestion that traveling in Africa is like traveling backward in time to primeval, infantile, but also hellish stages of existence—these features of the story are drawn from the repertoire of Victorian imperialism and racism that painted an entire continent dark.

Achebe is therefore right to call Conrad's portrayal of Africans racist.

One can argue, as does Benita Parry, that Conrad works with the white-and-black, light-and-darkness dichotomies of racist fantasy to subvert them, but she acknowledges that the subversion is incomplete: "Although the resonances of white are rendered discordant . . . black and dark do serve in the text as equivalences for the savage and unredeemed, the corrupt and degraded . . . the cruel and atrocious. Imperialism itself is perceived as the dark within Europe. . . . Yet despite . . . momentous departures from traditional European usage . . . the fiction gravitates back to established practice, registering the view of two incompatible orders within a manichean universe."[21] The imperialist imagination itself, Parry suggests, works with the manichean, irreconcilable polarities common to all racist ideology. Achebe states the issue more succinctly: "Conrad had a problem with niggers."[22]

Identifying specific sources for Conrad's knowledge of the horrors of Leopold's regime is less important than recognizing that sources were numerous, swelling in number through the 1890s. Conrad reshaped his firsthand experience of the Congo in light of these sources. The emphasis on cannibalism in *Heart of Darkness* probably derives from Conrad's reading about the war between Leopold's agents and the Arabs. Yet he does not mention the war—indeed, Arab rivals of the Belgians are conspicuous in the story only by their absence. The omission has the effect of sharpening the light-and-dark dichotomies, the staple of racism; evil and darkness are parceled out between only two, antithetical sides, European and African, white and black. Furthermore, because of the omission of the Arabs Conrad treats cannibalism not as a result of war but as an everyday custom of the Congolese.

In simplifying his memories and sources, Conrad arrived at the manichean pattern of the imperialist adventure romance, a pattern radically at odds with any realist, exposé intention. *Heart of Darkness* appears to express two irreconcilable intentions. As Parry says, "to proffer an interpretation of *Heart of Darkness* as a militant denunciation and a reluctant affirmation of imperialist civilisation, as a fiction that [both] exposes and colludes in imperialism's mystifications, is to recognise its immanent contradictions" (39). However, the notion that Conrad was consciously anti-imperialist but unconsciously or carelessly employed the racist terminology current in his day will not stand up. Conrad was acutely aware of what he was doing. Every white-black and light-dark contrast in the story, whether corroborating or subverting racist assumptions, is precisely calculated for its effects both as a unit in a scheme of imagery and as a focal point in a complex web of contradictory political and moral values.

Conrad knows that his story is ambiguous: he stresses that ambiguity at every opportunity, so that labeling the novella anti-imperialist is as unsatisfactory as condemning it for being racist. The fault-line for all of the contradictions in the text lies between Marlow and Kurtz and, of course, it also lies between Conrad and both of his ambiguous characters (not to mention the anonymous primary narrator). Is Marlow Kurtz's antagonist, critic, and potential redeemer? Or is he Kurtz's pale shadow and admirer, his double, finally one more idolator in a story full of fetishists and devil worship? Conrad poses these questions with great care, but he just as carefully refrains from answering them. That evasion, and the ambiguities it generates, reflect the patterns of reification underlying both commodity fetishism and literary modernism—the deliberate ambiguity and refusal of moral and political judgment at the heart of an impressionism and a will-to-style that seem to be ends in themselves, producing finely crafted artifacts and stories with contours smoothed, polished, like carefully sculpted bits of ivory—art itself as the ultimate commodity, object of a rarefied aesthetic worship and consumption.

iii

In the world of *Heart of Darkness*, there are no clear answers. Ambiguity, perhaps the main form of darkness in the story, prevails. Conrad overlays the political and moral content of his novella with symbolic and mythic patterns that divert attention from Kurtz and the Congo to misty halos and moonshine. The anonymous primary narrator uses these metaphors to describe the difference between Marlow's stories and those of ordinary sailors: "The yarns of seamen have a direct simplicity, the whole meaning of which lies within the shell of a cracked nut. But Marlow was not typical . . . and to him the meaning of an episode was not inside like a kernel but outside, enveloping the tale which brought it out only as a glow brings out a haze, in the likeness of one of these misty halos that sometimes are made visible by the spectral illumination of moonshine" (5). This passage announces that locating the "meaning" of the story will not be easy, may in fact be impossible. It seems almost a confession of defeat or at least of contradiction. Conrad here establishes as one of his themes the problem of rendering any judgment whatsoever—moral, political, metaphysical—about Marlow's narrative. It is precisely this complexity—a theme that might be labeled the dislocation of meaning or the disorientation of values in the story—which many critics have treated as the novella's finest feature.

In *The Political Unconscious*, Jameson argues that Conrad's stories

(*Lord Jim* is his main example) betray a symptomatic split between a modernist will-to-style, leading to an elaborate but essentially hollow impressionism, and the reified, mass-culture tendencies of romance conventions. In a fairly obvious way, *Heart of Darkness* betrays the same split, moving in one direction toward the misty halos of a style that seeks to be its own meaning, apart from any kernel or embarrassingly clear content, but also that grounds itself in the conventions of Gothic romance with their devalued, mass-culture status—conventions that were readily adapted to the heroic adventure themes of imperialist propaganda. This split almost corresponds to the contradiction of an anti-imperialist novel that is also racist. In the direction of high style the story acquires several serious purposes, apparently including its critique of empire. In the direction of reified mass culture it falls into the stereotypic patterns of race thinking common to the entire tradition of the imperialist adventure story or quest romance. This double, contradictory purpose, perhaps characteristic of all of Conrad's fiction, Jameson calls schizophrenic.[23]

By "the manichaeanism of the imperialist imagination" Parry means dividing the world between "warring moral forces"—good versus evil, civilization versus savagery, West versus East, light versus darkness, white versus black. Such polarizations are the common property of the racism and authoritarianism that inform imperialist ideology, as they are also of the Gothic romance conventions that numerous writers of imperialist adventure tales appropriated. As Martin Green points out, "Conrad of course offers us an ironic view of that genre. But he affirms its value."[24] Conrad is a critic of the imperialist adventure and its romantic fictions and simultaneously one of the greatest writers of such fictions, his greatness deriving partly from his critical irony and partly from the complexity of his style—his impressionism. But the chief difficulty with Jameson's argument is that the will-to-style in Conrad's text is also a will to appropriate and remake Gothic romance conventions into high art. On some level the impressionism of Conrad's novels and their romance features are identical—Conrad constructs a sophisticated version of the imperialist romance—and in any case both threaten to submerge or "de-realize" the critique of empire within their own more strictly aesthetic project. As part of that project, providing much of the substance of impressionism, the romance conventions that Conrad reshapes carry with them the polarizations of racist thought.

In analyzing Conrad's schizophrenic writing, Jameson notes the proliferation of often contradictory critical opinions which marks the history of his reception: "The discontinuities objectively present in Conrad's

narratives have, as with few other modern writers, projected a bewilder-
ing variety of competing and incommensurable interpretive options."
Jameson lists nine critical approaches, from "the 'romance' or mass-
cultural reading of Conrad as a writer of adventure tales [and] the stylistic
analysis of Conrad as a practitioner of . . . [an] 'impressionistic' will to
style," to the "myth-critical," the Freudian, the ethical, the "ego-psycho-
logical," the existential, the Nietzschean, and the structuralist readings.
Jameson omits from the list his own, Marxist reading; what he wishes to
suggest is how often criticism ignores or downplays the contradictory
politics of Conrad's fiction. Raymond Williams voices a similar com-
plaint:

> It is . . . astonishing that a whole school of criticism has succeeded in
> emptying *Heart of Darkness* of its social and historical content. . . . The
> Congo of Leopold follows the sea that Dombey and Son traded across,
> follows it into an endless substitution in which no object is itself, no social
> experience direct, but everything is translated into what can be called a
> metaphysical language—the river is Evil; the sea is Love or Death. Yet
> only called metaphysical, because there is not even that much guts in it.
> No profound and ordinary belief, only a perpetual and sophisticated
> evasion.[25]

There are wonderfully elaborate readings of Marlow's journey as a descent into hell, playing upon Conrad's allusions to Homer, Virgil, Dante,
Milton, Goethe, and devil worship. There are just as many elaborate
readings of the story as an inward voyage of self-discovery which treat its
geopolitical language as symbolizing psychological states and parts of the
mind. Conrad, Albert Guerard reminds us, was Freud's contemporary,
and in *Heart of Darkness* he produced the quintessential "night journey
into the unconscious."[26] Guerard adds that "it little matters what, in
terms of psychological symbolism, we . . . say [Kurtz] represents:
whether the Freudian id or the Jungian shadow or more vaguely the
outlaw." Perhaps it matters just as little whether we say the story takes
place in Leopold's Congo or in some purely imaginary landscape.

My point, however, is not to take issue with Guerard and other critics
who concentrate on the impressionism of Conrad's story but rather to
restore what their readings neglect. In a great deal of contemporary
criticism, words themselves have almost ceased to have external referents.
Williams does not follow Jameson in accusing Conrad's will-to-style of
emptying *Heart of Darkness* of its social and historical content; rather, he
accuses criticism of so emptying it. The will-to-style—or the will to a

rarefied critical intelligence—devours literary critics, too, leaving structuralists and deconstructionists, Althusserians and Foucauldians. And yet Conrad has anticipated his critics by writing a story in which the meaning does not lie at the center, not even at the heart of darkness, but elsewhere, in misty halos—forever beyond some vertiginous horizon that recedes as the would-be critic-adventurer sails toward it.

iv

> The crowds [in one village] were fired into promiscuously, and fifteen were killed, including four women and a babe on its mother's breast. The heads were cut off and brought to the officer in charge, who then sent men to cut off the hands also, and these were pierced, strung, and dried over the camp fire. The heads, with many others, I saw myself. The town, prosperous once, was burnt, and what they could not carry off was destroyed. Crowds of people were caught, mostly . . . women, and three fresh rope gangs were added. These poor "prisoner" gangs were mere skeletons of skin and bone. . . . Chiyombo's very large town was next attacked. A lot of people were killed, and heads and hands cut off and taken back to the officers. . . . Shortly after the State caravans, with flags flying and bugles blowing, entered the mission station at Luanza . . . and I shall not soon forget the sickening sight of deep baskets of human heads.[27]

Although the primary narrator and many critics seem to believe that the meaning of *Heart of Darkness* lies in "the spectral illumination of moonshine," Marlow knows better. Illumination proves as false as most white men, as false as white civilization; the truth, or at least the meaning of Conrad's story, lies in darkness. That is why, once Marlow learns about the shadowy Kurtz, he is so impatient to get to the Central Station. And yet Kurtz seems inadequate as a central character or as the goal of Marlow's quest—vacuous, a mere shade, a "hollow man." That, however, is part of the point. Ian Watt lists Henry Morton Stanley, Arthur Hodister, and Charles Stokes as possible models for Kurtz. Stokes, the former missionary, was executed in the Congo in 1895 for selling guns to the Arabs, an event following close on the heels of the cannibal war described by Captain Hinde that provided an additional focus for British public indignation. To Watt's list can be added Hinde and also Captain Rom, who decorated the borders of his flower garden with skulls. The Belgian officer responsible for Stokes's illegal execution, Captain Lothaire, must also be counted.[28]

Just as Conrad drew upon many sources in depicting the horrors of the

Congo, so he probably had many models for Kurtz in mind. *All* of the white officers in charge of Leopold's empire were in essence Kurtzes, as eyewitness testimony published by the Congo Reform Association demonstrates. And what about the eyewitnesses? Were they always so objective or so morally appalled as they claimed to be? Hinde's descriptions of atrocities in *Fall of the Congo Arabs* are obviously tinged by a sadistic enthusiasm. What about Conrad himself? Although his role in the building of Leopold's Congo Free State was minor, and preceded the worst horrors, Conrad must have recognized his own complicity and seen himself as at least potentially a Kurtz-like figure. In the novella the African wilderness serves as a mirror, in whose darkness Conrad/Marlow sees a death-pale self-image named Kurtz.

The massive evidence of wholesale torture and slaughter under the direction of Leopold's white agents suggests not only that there were numerous Kurtzes in the heart of darkness but also that, as Hannah Arendt contends in *The Origins of Totalitarianism*, nineteenth-century imperialism prepared the ground in which fascism and Nazism took root after World War I. Arendt has Kurtz and other Conrad characters in mind when she describes the appeal of "the phantom world of colonial adventure" to certain types of Europeans:

> Outside all social restraint and hypocrisy, against the backdrop of native life, the gentleman and the criminal felt not only the closeness of men who share the same color of skin, but the impact of a world of infinite possibilities for crimes committed in the spirit of play, for the combination of horror and laughter, that is for the full realization of their own phantom-like existence. Native life lent these ghostlike events a seeming guarantee against all consequences. . . . The world of . . . savages was a perfect setting for men who had escaped the reality of civilization. [29]

A great many Kurtz-like Europeans went native in Africa and elsewhere and often practiced genocide as a hobby; some were rumored to practice cannibalism. To quote Sir Harry Johnston's observation again, "I have been increasingly struck with the rapidity with which such members of the white race as are not of the best class, can throw over the restraints of civilization and develop into savages of unbridled lust and abominable cruelty." [30] Kurtz is not a member of the *worst* class of the white race, however; Conrad is talking about a quite common pattern of behavior.

One of the most remarkable perversions of the criticism of *Heart of Darkness* has been to see Kurtz not as an abomination, a hollow man with a lust for blood and domination, but as a "hero of the spirit." That phrase is Lionel Trilling's. In describing the establishment of the first course in modern literature at Columbia University, Trilling explains why he put Conrad's novella on the reading list: "Whether or not . . . Conrad read either Blake or Nietzsche I do not know, but his *Heart of Darkness* follows in their line. This very great work has never lacked for the admiration it deserves, and it has been given a . . . canonical place in the legend of modern literature by [T. S.] Eliot's having it so clearly in mind when he wrote *The Waste Land* and his having taken from it the epigraph to 'The Hollow Men.'"[31] Despite the association between Eliot's poem and Conrad's novella, Trilling claims that "no one, to my knowledge, has ever confronted in an explicit way [the latter's] strange and terrible message of ambivalence toward the life of civilization" (17). In *Sincerity and Authenticity*, Trilling adds that Conrad's story is "the paradigmatic literary expression of the modern concern with authenticity," and continues: "This troubling work has no manifest polemical content but it contains in sum the whole of the radical critique of European civilization that has been made by [modern] literature."[32] Trilling appears to interpret literary modernism in its entirety both as apolitical (lacking manifest polemical content) and as offering a "radical critique" of civilization; *Heart of Darkness* he treats as the quintessence of this apolitical critique. He fails to acknowledge that the form of radical critique practiced by high literary modernists (Yeats, Eliot, Pound, and Lawrence, as well as Conrad) readily aligned itself with imperialism and fascism.

Trilling names the political context of *Heart of Darkness*, but the Congo is less important to him than the larger question of the nature of European civilization. Marlow's quest for Kurtz becomes a quest for the truth about that civilization. Trilling arrives at his view of Kurtz partly the way Marlow does, because Kurtz at the end of his Satanic career seems to confront "the horror." "For Marlow," says Trilling, "Kurtz is a hero of the spirit whom he cherishes as Theseus at Colonus cherished Oedipus: he sinned for all mankind. By his regression to savagery Kurtz has reached as far down beneath the constructs of civilization as it was possible to go, to the irreducible truth of man, the innermost core of his nature, his heart of darkness. From that Stygian authenticity comes illumination."[33]

Marlow does paradoxically come to admire Kurtz because he has "summed up" or "judged" in his final moments: "He was a remarkable man" (72). Marlow's admiration for Kurtz, however, carries a terrific burden of irony which Trilling does not recognize. Kurtz has not merely lost faith in civilization and therefore experimented with Stygian authenticity—he is also a murderer, perhaps a cannibal. He has allowed his idolators to make human sacrifices in his honor and, like Captain Rom, has decorated his corner of hell with the skulls of his victims. Perhaps Trilling values Kurtz as a hero of the spirit in part because he himself does not clearly see the horror: the deaths of several million Congolese are a high price to pay for the illumination of Stygian authenticity. Trilling's interpretation of Kurtz's dying words—"The horror! The horror!"—simply does not take account of what transpired in Leopold's Congo. His focus is European civilization, not Africa, and so he reaches this bizarre conclusion: "For me it is still ambiguous whether Kurtz's famous death-bed cry refers to the approach of death or to his experience of savage life."

Either Kurtz thinks death "the horror," according to Trilling's view, or Kurtz thinks African savage life "the horror." There is another possibility, of course, which is that Kurtz's dying words are an outcry against himself—against his betrayal of civilization and his Intended, against the smash-up of his early hopes, and against his bloody domination. No one would ever mistake Conrad's other traitors to civilization (Willems who goes wrong and then goes native in An Outcast of the Islands, Jones and Ricardo in Victory) as heroes of the spirit. Even Lord Jim is no spiritual hero but a moral cripple who regains a semblance of self-respect only after fleeing to Patusan. But how was it possible for Trilling to look past Kurtz's criminal record and identify the horror either with the fear of death or with African savagery? Achebe gives part of the answer: "White racism against Africa is such a normal way of thinking that its manifestations go completely undetected"—so normal that acts which are condemned as the vilest of crimes when committed in the supposedly civilized West can be linked to a heroism of the spirit and to Stygian authenticity when committed in Africa against Africans.

The other part of the answer, however, is that Trilling is right. Conrad himself identifies with and ironically admires Kurtz. He, too, sees him as a hero of the spirit, although the spirit for Conrad is perhaps not what Trilling thinks it is. For Conrad, Kurtz's heroism consists in staring into an abyss of nihilism so total that the issues of imperialism and racism pale into insignificance. It hardly matters if the abyss is of Kurtz's making. No more than Trilling or perhaps most Western literary critics did Conrad concern himself about unspeakable rites and skulls on posts. These appear in Marlow's account like so many melodrama props—the evidence of Kurtz's decline and fall, certainly, but it is still Kurtz who has center stage, with whom Marlow speaks, who is the goal and farthest point of the journey. Kurtz's black victims and idolators skulking in the bushes are only so many props themselves.

Kurtz is not only the hero of the melodrama but an artist, a "universal genius," and a powerful, eloquent voice as well. The African characters, as Achebe points out, are, in contrast, rendered almost without intelligible language. The headman of Marlow's cannibal crew gets in a few phrases of pidgin-minstrelese, something about eating some fellow-Africans. These are the black Kurtz worshipers, shrieking and groaning incoherently in the foggy shrubbery along the river. Kurtz's "superb and savage" mistress, though described in glowing detail, is given no voice, but I imagine that she, at least, unlike the prim, palefaced knitters of black wool back in Brussels, entertained no illusions about Kurtz or imperialism. "It's queer how out of touch with truth women are," says Marlow, but of course he means *white* women (12). Kurtz's black mistress knows all; it's unfortunate that Marlow did not think to interview her.

The voices that come from the heart of darkness are almost exclusively white and male, as usual in imperialist texts. As a nearly disembodied, pure voice emanating from the very center of the story, Kurtz is a figure for the novelist, as is his double Marlow. True, the voice that speaks out of the heart of darkness is a hollow one, the voice of the abyss; but Marlow still talks of Kurtz's "unextinguishable gift of noble and lofty expression." The voice of Kurtz has "electrified large meetings," and through it Kurtz "could get himself to believe anything—anything" (74). Thus Conrad questions or mocks his own voice, his own talent for fiction making, for lying. He knows that the will-to-style, his own impressionism, points toward the production of novels that are hollow at the core—that can justify any injustice—and contain, perhaps, only an abyss, a Kurtz, the horror. Kurtz's devious, shadowy voice echoes Conrad's. It is just this hollow voice, eloquently egotistical, capable both of high idealism and of lying propaganda, which speaks from the center of the heart of darkness to sum up and to judge.

Besides being a painter, musician, orator, and universal genius, Kurtz is also, like Conrad, a writer.[34] What he writes is both an analogue for the story and its dead center, the kernel of meaning or nonmeaning within its cracked shell. True, Kurtz has not written much, only seventeen pages, but "it was a beautiful piece of writing." His pamphlet for the International Society for the Suppression of Savage Customs is a summa of imperialist rhetoric, which Marlow describes as "eloquent, vibrating with eloquence, but too high-strung, I think":

He began with the argument that we whites, from the point of development we had arrived at, "must necessarily appear to [savages] in the nature
of supernatural beings—we approach them with the might as of a deity,"
and so on, and so on. "By the simple exercise of our will we can exert a
power for good practically unbounded," etc., etc. From that point he
soared and took me with him. The peroration was magnificent, though
difficult to remember, you know. It gave me the notion of an exotic
Immensity ruled by an august Benevolence. It made me tingle with
enthusiasm. This was the unbounded power of eloquence [i.e., the unbounded will-to-style]. There were no practical hints to interrupt the
magic current of phrases, unless a kind of note at the foot of the last page,
scrawled evidently much later, in an unsteady hand, may be regarded as
the exposition of a method. It was very simple, and at the end of that
moving appeal to every altruistic sentiment it blazed at you, luminous and
terrifying, like a flash of lightning in a serene sky: "Exterminate all the
brutes!" (50–51)

Viewed one way, Conrad's anti-imperialist story clearly condemns Kurtz's
murderous, imperialist categorical imperative. Viewed another way,
Conrad's racist story voices that very imperative, and Conrad knows it. At
the hollow center of *Heart of Darkness*, far from the misty halos and
moonshine where the meaning supposedly resides, Conrad inscribes a
text that, like the novel itself, cancels out its own best intentions.

Kurtz's pamphlet is not the only text-within-the-text of *Heart of
Darkness*. Fifty miles up river, Marlow comes upon an abandoned hut in
which he finds an apparent antithesis to Kurtz's report: "Its title was, *An
Inquiry into Some Points of Seamanship*, by a man Towser, Towson—
some such name—Master in His Majesty's Navy" (38). Towson's book is
obviously also, like Kurtz's pamphlet, a product of European, imperialist
civilization, but not a lying or hypocritical one. Although "not a very
enthralling book," it has "a singleness of intention, an honest concern for
the right way of going to work, which made those humble pages . . .
luminous with another than a professional light." Marlow's discovery
gives him the "delicious sensation of having come upon something
unmistakably real." Conrad makes Towson sound like a second Captain
Marryat, as the reference to "*His* Majesty's Navy" suggests; both represent
the honorable, unreflecting values of discipline, service, courage, and
stalwart innocence which Conrad finds in Marryat's novels. But Towson's
text has also been scrawled over in strange characters that Marlow takes
for a mysterious "cipher" until he encounters the Russian "harlequin"
who had taken some presumably half-crazed notes on Towson's pages.
When Marlow returns Towson to the Russian, "he made as though he

would kiss me. . . . 'The only book I had left, and I thought I had lost it,' he said, looking at it ecstatically" (55). Between Marlow's discovery of Towson and his returning it to the Russian comes the description of Kurtz's mad, genocidal pamphlet. Just as he idolizes Kurtz, the Russian appears also to idolize Towson, so ultimately there may be little or no difference between the two texts. But this, too, is ambiguous, deliberately left in suspense by Conrad, who likes to judge without judging.

Kurtz's pamphlet, as well as what Marlow reveals about his unspeakable rites, allow us to understand his dying words as something more than an outcry of guilt and certainly more than a mere expression of the fear of death or of loathing for African savagery. Those words can be seen as referring to a lying idealism that can rationalize any behavior, to a complete separation between words and meaning, theory and practice. On this level, *Heart of Darkness* offers a devastating critique of imperialist ideology. On another, more general level, however, it offers a self-critique and an attack upon the impressionistic deviousness of art and language. At this more general level, Conrad stops worrying about the atrocities committed in the Congo and identifies with Kurtz as a fellow-artist, a hero of the spirit of that nihilism which Conrad himself found so attractive, perhaps secretly consoling.

On several occasions Conrad compares the artist with the empire builder in a way obviously counter to his critique of imperialism in *Heart of Darkness*. In A *Personal Record*, Conrad writes of "that interior world where [the novelist's] thought and . . . emotions go seeking for . . . imagined adventures," where "there are no policemen, no law, no pressure of circumstance or dread opinion to keep him within bounds." And in the first manuscript of "The Rescuer," which contains Conrad's most sympathetic treatment of imperialism, empire builders are "one of those unknown guides of civilization, who on the advancing edge of progress are administrators, warriors, creators. . . . They are like great artists a mystery to the masses, appreciated only by the uninfluential few."[35] Kurtz is empire builder, artist, universal genius, and voice crying out from the wilderness, all in one. But he has lost the faith—whether vision or illusion—which can alone sustain an empire and produce great art. Nihilism is no basis upon which to found or administer a colony, or to write a novel, and Conrad knows it. In suggesting his affinity to Kurtz, he suggests the moral bankruptcy of his own literary project, but he also insists that once there were empire builders and great artists who kept the faith. Conrad frequently expresses his admiration for the great explorers and adventurers, from Sir Walter Raleigh and Sir Francis Drake through

James Brooke, the white rajah of Sarawak, and David Livingstone, the greatest of the many great explorers of the Dark Continent.

Conrad's critique of empire is never strictly anti-imperialist. Instead, in terms that can be construed as both conservative and nihilistic, he mourns the loss of the true faith in modern times, the closing down of frontiers, the narrowing of the possibilities for adventure, the commercialization of the world and of art, the death of chivalry and honor. Here the meaning of his emphasis on the lying propaganda of modern imperialism becomes evident. What was once a true, grand, noble, albeit violent enterprise is now "a gigantic and atrocious fraud"—except maybe, Marlow thinks, in the red parts of the map, where "some real work is done." Staring into the abyss of his life, or at least of Kurtz's life, Conrad sees mirrored in his own disillusionment, his own nihilistic darkness, the type of the whole—the path of disintegration which is modern history. It is not just Africa or even just Kurtz that possesses a heart of darkness; Conrad's story bears that title as well.

But I am not going to end by announcing in "a tone of scathing contempt" the death of Conrad's story as a classic, like the insolent manager's boy announcing "Mistah Kurtz—he dead." I agree with Trilling that authenticity, truth telling, far from being a negligible literary effect is the essence of great literature. That almost no other work of British fiction written before World War I is critical of imperialism (Taylor's *Seeta* is indeed exceptional in this regard) is a measure of Conrad's achievement. Yet the real strength of *Heart of Darkness* does not lie in what it says about atrocities in King Leopold's Congo, though its documentary impulse is an important counter to its will-to-style. As social criticism, its anti-imperialist message is undercut by its racism, by its reactionary political attitudes, by its impressionism. There are few novels, however, which so insistently invoke a moral idealism they do not seem to contain and in which the modernist will-to-style is subjected to such powerful self-scrutiny—in which the voice at the heart of the novel, the voice of modern literature, the voice of imperialist civilization itself may in its purest, freest form yield only "The horror! The horror!"

Notes

Introduction

1. George Woodcock, review of *The Spirit of Reform: British Literature and Politics, 1832–1867,* in *Modern Language Quarterly,* 38 (December 1977), 403.

2. C. A. Bodelsen, *Studies in Mid-Victorian Imperialism* (New York: Knopf, 1925), 41.

3. Karl de Schweinitz, Jr., *The Rise and Fall of British India: Imperialism as Inequality* (London: Methuen, 1983), 34n.

4. John Davidson, "Anthony Trollope and the Colonies," *Victorian Studies* 12 (March 1969), 327–28, 329. See also Asa Briggs, "Trollope the Traveller," in *Trollope Centenary Essays,* ed. John Halperin (New York: St. Martin's, 1982), 24–52. On Trollope's ideas about race see Iva G. Johnson, "Trollope, Carlyle, and Mill on the Negro: An Episode in the History of Ideas," *Journal of Negro History* 52 (July 1967), 185–99.

5. Anthony Trollope, *North America,* ed. Donald Smalley and Bradford A. Booth (New York: Knopf, 1951), 86. In *The New Zealander,* written in 1855, Trollope invokes Macaulay's figure of the future visitor from New Zealand contemplating the ruins of London. Trollope's first response is wholly optimistic: Britain and its Empire will never fall to ruin; any future visitor "will come, not to sketch ruins, but to visit the centre of civilization." Trollope then qualifies this glowing view by agreeing that all states and empires must eventually decay, but he argues that the British can postpone the sorry day far into the future if they will only be industrious and honest. Either way, Trollope was optimistic about the future of the Empire; it followed the granting independence to mature colonies was a sign rather of imperial health than of decline and fall. See *The New Zealander,* ed. N. John Hall (Oxford: Clarendon Press, 1972), 4–5.

6. Anthony Trollope, *The Tireless Traveler: Twenty-Five Letters to the Liverpool Mercury, 1875,* ed. Bradford A. Booth (Berkeley: University of California Press, 1978), 181. Because of such sentiments, Booth finds Trollope "vigorously anti-imperialistic" (13).

7. Sir John R. Seeley, *The Expansion of England,* ed. John Gross (Chicago: University of Chicago Press, 1971), 12.

8. W. D. Paden, *Tennyson in Egypt: A Study of the Imagery in His Earlier Work* (Lawrence: University of Kansas Publications, 1942).

9. Alfred, Lord Tennyson, "Hail Briton!" in *The Poems of Tennyson,* ed. Christopher Ricks (London: Longman, 1969), 481.

10. Tennyson, "Akbar's Dream," *Poems of Tennyson,* 1448–49.

11. The best treatment of Tennyson and imperialism is Victor Kiernan, "Tennyson, King Arthur, and Imperialism," in *Culture, Ideology and Politics: Essays for Eric Hobsbawm,* ed. Raphael Samuel and Gareth Stedman Jones (London: Routledge & Kegan Paul, 1982), 126–48.

12. Fredric Jameson, *The Political Unconscious: Narrative as a Socially Symbolic Act* (Ithaca: Cornell University Press, 1981), 17.

13. Edward W. Said, *Orientalism* (New York: Vintage, 1979), 95.

14. Christopher L. Miller, *Blank Darkness: Africanist Discourse in French* (Chicago: University of Chicago Press, 1985).

15. Anthony Brewer, *Marxist Theories of Imperialism: A Critical Survey* (London: Routledge & Kegan Paul, 1980), says little about racism. But see Frantz Fanon, *Black Skin, White Masks* (1952; New York: Grove, 1967), and *The Wretched of the Earth* (1961; New York: Grove, 1968); Paul Gilroy et al., *The Empire Strikes Back: Race and Racism in 70s Britain* (London: Hutchinson, 1982); *Racism and Colonialism: Essays on Ideology and Social Structure*, ed. Robert Ross (The Hague: Martinus Nijhoff, 1982); Sander L. Gilman, *Difference and Pathology: Stereotypes of Sexuality, Race, and Madness* (Ithaca: Cornell University Press, 1985); Henry Louis Gates, Jr., ed., *"Race," Writing, and Difference* (Chicago: University of Chicago Press, 1986); and Gayatri Chakravorty Spivak, *In Other Worlds: Essays in Cultural Politics* (New York: Methuen, 1987). See also the two-volume special issue of *Cultural Critique* on "The Nature and Context of Minority Discourse." The first volume appeared in issue 6, Spring 1987; the second is forthcoming.

16. Martin Green, *Dreams of Adventure, Deeds of Empire* (New York: Basic Books, 1979), 5.

17. Elizabeth Gaskell, *Cranford* (London: Oxford University Press, 1972), 153–54.

18. Besides Jameson's *Political Unconscious* see Raymond Williams, *Marxism and Literature* (Oxford: Oxford University Press, 1977), 53–71 and 108–27, and Jorge Larrain, *The Concept of Ideology* (Athens: University of Georgia Press, 1979).

19. Karl Mannheim, *Ideology and Utopia: An Introduction to the Sociology of Knowledge*, trans. Louis Wirth and Edward Shils (1936; New York: Harcourt, Brace, n.d.).

20. Williams, *Marxism and Literature*, 70.

21. See *Writing Culture: The Poetics and Politics of Ethnography*, ed. James Clifford and George E. Marcus (Berkeley: University of California Press, 1986).

22. Clifford Geertz, "Ideology as a Cultural System," in his *The Interpretation of Cultures* (New York: Basic Books, 1973), 193–233.

23. Raymond Williams, *The Country and the City* (New York: Oxford University Press, 1973), 279.

24. Jomo Kenyatta, Facing Mount Kenya (London: Secker & Warburg, 1959), 317–18.

Chapter 1. From *Dawn Island* to *Heart of Darkness*

1. See A. G. L. Shaw, ed., *Great Britain and the Colonies, 1815–1865* (London: Methuen, 1970); Bernard Semmel, *The Rise of Free Trade Imperialism: Classical Political Economy, the Empire of Free Trade, and Imperialism, 1750–1850* (Cambridge: Cambridge University Press, 1970); and Donald Winch, *Classical Political Economy and Colonies* (London: G. Bell, 1965). The older book by Klaus E. Knorr, *British Colonial Theories, 1570–1850* (Toronto: University of Toronto Press, 1944), is still useful.

2. John Gallagher and Ronald Robinson, "The Imperialism of Free Trade," *Economic History Review*, 2d ser. 6:1 (1953), 1–15, reprinted in Shaw, *Great Britain and the Colonies*; Gallagher, Robinson, and Alice Denney, *Africa and the Victorians: The Climax of Imperialism in the Dark Continent* (London: Macmillan, 1961).

3. Gallagher and Robinson, "Imperialism of Free Trade," in Shaw, *Great Britain and the Colonies*, 144.

4. Goldwin Smith, *The Empire: A Series of Lectures Published in the "Daily News"* (London: Parker, 1863), 6.

5. Francis Hutchins, *The Illusion of Permanence: British Imperialism in India* (Princeton: Princeton University Press, 1967).

6. Richard Koebner and Helmut Dan Schmidt, *Imperialism: The Story and Significance of a Political Word, 1840–1960* (Cambridge: Cambridge University Press, 1964).

7. See A. G. L. Shaw, "British Attitudes to the Colonies, ca. 1820–1850," *Journal of British Studies* 9:1 (1969), 71–95.

8. See Christine Bolt, *Victorian Attitudes to Race* (London: Routledge & Kegan Paul, 1971), and Nancy Stepan, *The Idea of Race in Science: Great Britain, 1800–1960* (Hamden, Conn.: Archon, 1982).

9. Luke Owen Pike, *The English and Their Origin: A Prologue to Authentic English History* (London: Longman, Green, 1866), 15.

10. Robert Knox, *The Races of Men: A Fragment* (Philadelphia: Lea & Blanchard, 1850), 149–50.

11. James Mill, "Colony," Supplement to the *Encyclopaedia Britannica* (1824), excerpted in *The Concept of Empire: Burke to Attlee, 1774–1947*, ed. George Bennett (London: Adam & Charles Black, 1953), 84–87.

12. J. A. Roebuck, *The Colonies of England* (London: Parker, 1849), 138.

13. On Horton, Wakefield, and emigration, see H. J. M. Johnston, *British Emigration Policy 1815–1830* (Oxford: Clarendon Press, 1972).

14. Thomas Carlyle, *Chartism*, in *Works*, 30 vols. (London: Chapman & Hall, 1899), 29:204.

15. Samuel Taylor Coleridge, entry for 4 May 1833, in *Table Talk and Omniana*, ed. T. Ashe (London: George Bell, 1884), 216.

16. Robert Southey, "On the State of the Poor, the Principle of Mr. Malthus's Essay on Population, and the Manufacturing System" (1812), in his *Essays, Moral and Political*, 2 vols. (London: John Murray, 1832), 1:154.

17. Charles Kingsley, "Mansfield's *Paraguay, Brazil, and the Plate*," in his *Miscellanies*, 2 vols. (London: Parker, 1860), 2:21–22.

18. See Daniel R. Headrick, *The Tools of Empire: Technology and European Imperialism in the Nineteenth Century* (Oxford: Oxford University Press, 1981), 31–32. Felix Felton, *Thomas Love Peacock* (London: George Allen & Unwin, 1973), 229–38, describes Peacock's assignment in detail. He was to study both steam navigation and shortening the route to India, and he seems to have been the first to recommend traveling overland through the Near East and down the Euphrates to the Persian Gulf.

19. Thomas Love Peacock, "The Genius of the Thames—Analysis of the First Part," in *Works*, Halliford Edition, 10 vols. (London: Constable, 1927), 6:108.

20. Eric Stokes, *The English Utilitarians and India* (Oxford: Clarendon Press, 1959), xiv.

21. T. H. S. Escott, *Edward Bulwer, First Baron Lytton of Knebworth* (London: George Routledge, 1910), 273.

22. See John Lowe Duthie, "Lord Lytton and the Second Afghan War: A Psychohistorical Study," *Victorian Studies* 27 (Summer 1984), 461–75.

23. Cf. Coral Lansbury, *Arcady in Australia: The Evocation of Australia in Nineteenth-Century English Literature* (Melbourne: Melbourne University Press, 1970).

24. See Bernard Semmel, *Democracy versus Empire: The Jamaica Riots of 1865 and the Governor Eyre Controversy* (Garden City, N.Y.: Doubleday Anchor, 1965).

25. Captain Frederick Marryat, *Masterman Ready* (London: Nelson, n.d.), 140.

26. Thomas Babington Macaulay, "Speech on the Government of India" (1833), in *Macaulay: Prose and Poetry*, ed. G. M. Young (Cambridge: Harvard University Press, 1970), 718.

27. Harriet Martineau, *Dawn Island, A Tale* (Manchester: J. Gadsby, 1845), 22.

28. Semmel, *Rise of Free Trade Imperialism*, 4.

29. Noted in Ronald Hyam, *Britain's Imperial Century, 1815–1914* (London: Batsford, 1976), 95.

30. Lord Curzon, speech of 11 December 1907, in Bennett, *Concept of Empire*, 356–57.

31. Samuel Hynes, *The Edwardian Turn of Mind* (Princeton: Princeton University Press, 1968), 17.

32. Alfred, Lord Tennyson, "Locksley Hall Sixty Years After," in *The Poems of Tennyson*, ed. Christopher Ricks (London: Longman, 1969), 1362–63.

33. H. Rider Haggard, *Allan Quatermain*, in *She, King Solomon's Mines, Allan Quatermain: Three Adventure Novels* (New York: Dover 1951), 420.

34. Bernard Porter, *The Lion's Share: A Short History of British Imperialism, 1850–1983*, 2d ed. (London: Longman, 1984), xi.

35. George W. Steevens quoted by H. John Field, *Toward a Programme of Imperial Life: The British Empire at the Turn of the Century* (Westport, Conn.: Greenwood, 1982), 138–39.

36. J. A. Cramb, *The Origins and Destiny of Imperial Britain* (New York: Dutton, 1900), 154.

37. V. I. Lenin, *Imperialism: The Highest Stage of Capitalism* (Peking: Foreign Languages Press, 1975), 93.

38. J. A. Hobson, *Imperialism, A Study* (1902; Ann Arbor: University of Michigan Press, 1965), 142.

39. John M. MacKenzie, *Propaganda and Empire: The Manipulation of British Public Opinion, 1880–1960* (Manchester: Manchester University Press, 1984), 45.

40. "Rifle Clubs!!!" in *Poems of Tennyson*, 997.

41. Winston S. Churchill, *My Early Life: A Roving Commission* (New York: Scribner's 1958), 44–45.

42. James Anthony Froude, *Oceana; or, England and Her Colonies* (London: Longmans, Green, 1886), 78.

43. Arthur Conan Doyle, *The Lost World* (New York: Review of Reviews, 1912), 13.

44. Robert Louis Stevenson, *The Beach of Falesá*, in his *Island Nights' Entertainments* (1892; New York: Scribner's, 1925), 10.

45. Joseph Conrad, *An Outcast of the Islands* (1896; Harmondsworth: Penguin, 1975), 20.

46. Charles Kingsley, *Westward Ho!* (1853; New York: Dodd, Mead, 1941), 19–20. Kingsley dedicated his "epic" to George Selwyn, bishop of New Zealand, and Sir James ("Rajah") Brooke of Sarawak, one of Conrad's heroes, with this encomium: "That type of English virtue, at once manful and Godly, practical and enthusiastic, prudent and self-sacrificing, which [the author] has tried to depict in these pages, they have exhibited in a form even purer and more heroic than . . . that in which it was exhibited by the worthies whom Elizabeth . . . gathered around her in the ever glorious wars of her great reign."

47. Charles Kingsley, "Speech in Behalf of the Ladies' Sanitary Association, 1859," in *Miscellanies*, 2:310. There is a good treatment of Kingsley's racist thinking in Michael Banton, *The Idea of Race* (London: Tavistock, 1977), 63–88. Among much else, Banton notes that Kingsley even considered the serpent in the Garden of Eden to be of a lower race (Banton, 76).

Chapter 2. Bringing Up the Empire: Captain Marryat's Midshipmen

1. Florence Marryat, *The Life and Letters of Captain Marryat*, 2 vols. (New York: D. Appleton, 1872), 1:22. Hereafter volume and page numbers are given parenthetically in the text.

2. Frederick Marryat, *Masterman Ready* (London: Thomas Nelson, n.d.), 35, hereafter abbreviated *MR*. There is no authoritative edition of Marryat's novels; I have used accessible reprints.

3. Besides Florence Marryat's biography, sources for Marryat's life include Maurice-Paul Gautier, *Captain Frederick Marryat: L'homme et l'oeuvre* (Paris: Didier, 1973); Christopher Lloyd, *Captain Marryat and the Old Navy* (London: Longmans, Green, 1939); and Oliver Warner, *Captain Marryat: A Rediscovery* (London: Constable, 1953). See also Warren Tute, *Cochrane: A Life of Admiral the Earl of Dundonald* (London: Cassell, 1965).

4. Frederick Marryat, *The King's Own* (London: George Routledge, 1896), 361.

5. Frederick Marryat, *Peter Simple* (London: Gollancz, 1969), 377, hereafter abbreviated *PS*.

6. There is no adequate study of the maritime novelists of the 1830s as a school. Besides the works on Marryat cited here, see P. J. Van der Voort, *The Pen and the Quarterdeck: Life and Work of Captain Frederick Chamier, RN* (Leiden: Lieden University Press, 1972).

7. Frederick Marryat, *Mr. Midshipman Easy* (Harmondsworth: Penguin, 1982), 180, hereafter abbreviated *ME*.

8. Joseph Conrad, *Lord Jim* (Cambridge: Houghton Mifflin, 1958), 153.

9. Alfred, Lord Tennyson, "Locksley Hall," in *The Poems of Tennyson*, ed. Christopher Ricks (London: Longman, 1969), 694.

10. Frederick Marryat, *The Settlers in Canada* (London: Boy's Own Paper Office, n.d.), 19–20, hereafter abbreviated *SC*.

11. Frederick Marryat, *Frank Mildmay; or, The Naval Officer* (London: Dent, 1896), 20, hereafter abbreviated *FM*.

12. Michel Foucault, *Language, Counter-Memory, Practice: Selected Essays and Interviews* (Ithaca: Cornell University Press, 1977), 60–61.

13. For "altruistic suicide," see Emile Durkheim, *Suicide: A Study in Sociology* (New York: Free Press, 1966), 217–40.

14. George Cruikshank, *The Progress of a Midshipman, Exemplified in the Career of Master Blockhead* (London: G. Humphrey, 1829).

15. Thomas Dibdin, ed., *Songs Naval and National, of the Late Charles Dibdin, with a Memoir and Addenda* (London: John Murray, 1841), 118–20.

16. Joseph Conrad, "Tales of the Sea" (1898), in *Joseph Conrad on Fiction*, ed. Walter F. Wright (Lincoln: University of Nebraska Press, 1967), 48.

17. Maurice-Paul Gautier describes both Marryat's first unsuccessful election bid of 1820 and his second one of 1832, about which Gautier says: "Ses prises de position sur les brulants problèmes de l'actualité révélent, aux yeux des électeurs, un homme autoritaire, ce que l'un d'eux exprime non sans humeur: 'Well done, my old skipper, you have let the cat out of the bag with a vengeance'" (*Captain Frederick Marryat*, 89).

18. Edmund Burke, *Reflections on the Revolution in France* (Harmondsworth: Penguin, 1969), 160.

19. Michel Foucault, *Language, Counter-Memory, Practice*, 61.

20. See Leslie Fiedler's analysis of this pattern in *Love and Death in the American Novel* (New York: Stein & Day, 1966), especially 181–82.

21. See Aphra Behn, *Oroonoko; or, The Royal Slave* (New York: Norton, 1973). For abolitionist literature see Wylie Sypher, *Guinea's Captive Kings: British Anti-Slavery Literature of the XVIII Century* (Chapel Hill: University of North Carolina Press, 1942), and Eva Beatrice Dykes, *The Negro in English Romantic Thought* (Washington, D.C.: Associated Publishers, 1942).

22. Frederick Marryat, *Newton Forster; or, The Merchant Service* (London: George Routledge, 1897), 89, hereafter abbreviated *NF.*

23. Frederick Marryat, *Diary in America*, ed. Jules Zanger (Bloomington: Indiana University Press, 1969), 176, hereafter abbreviated *D.*

24. See Louise Barnett, *The Ignoble Savage: American Literary Racism, 1790–1890* (Westport, Conn.: Greenwood, 1975), 3–67, and *Captured by Indians: Fifteen First-Hand Accounts, 1750–1870*, ed. Frederick Drimmer (New York: Dover, 1961).

25. See Orlando Patterson, *Slavery and Social Death* (Cambridge: Harvard University Press, 1982).

26. Frederick Marryat, *The Mission; or, Scenes in Africa* (London: Rex Collings, 1970), 9, hereafter abbreviated *M.*

27. Frederick Marryat, *Diary on the Continent*, in *Olla Podrida* (London: George Routledge, 1897), 95, hereafter abbreviated *DC.*

28. *Life*, 2:299–300. See Virginia Woolf's interesting meditation on this passage and on Marryat's career in *The Captain's Death Bed, and Other Essays* (London: Hogarth, 1950), 39–48.

Chapter 3. Thackeray's India

1. William Makepeace Thackeray, "The Tremendous Adventures of Major Gahagan," in *The Yellowplush Papers and Early Miscellanies*, ed. George Saintsbury (Oxford: Oxford University Press, n.d.). Thackeray later named Major Gahagan as the learned translator of "Sultan Stork: Being the One Thousand and Second Night," a short parody of the *Arabian Nights* published in *Ainsworth's Magazine* in February and March 1842. "Sultan Stork," set partly in Persia and partly in India, is a minor exception to the generalization that Thackeray set no fictions other than "Major Gahagan" mainly in India.

2. George Levine, *The Realistic Imagination: English Fiction from Frankenstein to Lady Chatterley* (Chicago: University of Chicago Press, 1981), 132.

3. Gordon N. Ray, *The Buried Life: A Study of the Relation between Thackeray's Fiction and His Personal History* (Cambridge: Harvard University Press, 1952), 13.

4. Gordon N. Ray, *Thackeray: The Uses of Adversity, 1811–1846* (New York: McGraw-Hill, 1955), 67.

5. Henry James, untitled column in *Harper's Weekly* 41 (3 March 1897), 315.

6. Edmund Burke quoted by George R. Mellor, *British Imperial Trusteeship, 1783–1805* (London: Faber & Faber, 1951), 22. General accounts of the British in India include Percival Spear, *A History of India*, vol. 2 (Harmondsworth: Penguin, 1978), and M. E. Chamberlain, *Britain and India: The Interaction of Two Peoples* (Newton Abbott: David & Charles, 1974). See also George D. Bearce, *British Attitudes towards India, 1784–1858* (London: Oxford University Press, 1961).

7. Chamberlain, *Britain and India*, 70.

8. Charles Grant quoted by Eric Stokes, *The English Utilitarians and India* (Oxford: Clarendon Press, 1959), 31.

9. William Wilberforce quoted by Stokes, *English Utilitarians in India*, 31 and 35.

10. Reginald Heber, *Bishop Heber in Northern India: Selections from Heber's Journal*, ed. M. A. Laird (Cambridge: Cambridge University Press, 1971), 128.

11. James Mill, *The History of British India*, ed. William Thomas (Chicago: University of Chicago Press, 1975), 224.

12. Thomas Babington Macaulay, *Poetry and Prose*, ed. G. M. Young (Cambridge: Harvard University Press, 1970), 307. The essay on Clive appeared in the *Edinburgh Review* for January 1840; that on Hastings in the *Edinburgh Review* for October 1841.

13. Thomas Carlyle, *Chartism*, in *Works*, 30 vols. (London: Chapman & Hall, 1899), 29:184.

14. Sir John R. Seeley, *The Expansion of England*, ed. John Gross (Chicago: University of Chicago Press, 1971), 12. Seeley's series of lectures, originally delivered at Cambridge University in 1881–82, were published in 1883.

15. In *The Rise and Fall of British India: Imperialism as Inequality* (London: Methuen, 1983), 17, Karl de Schweinitz points to the contradiction in Victorian politics between "the democratization of political processes at home while abroad viceroys and district commissioners governed foreign populations who had little or no say in the matter. . . . [But the] incongruity of democracy at home and authoritarian rule abroad permeated the public mind slowly."

16. John Stuart Mill, *On Liberty* (Harmondsworth: Penguin, 1982), 136. See also Abram L. Harris, "John Stuart Mill: Servant of the East India Company," *Canadian Journal of Economics and Political Science* 30 (May 1964), 185–202. Harris offers perhaps the fullest answer to the question, "How did John Mill, the great exponent of nineteenth century liberalism, reconcile his employment as an official of a despotic government with his espousal of the principles of civil and political freedom?" (185).

17. John Stuart Mill, *Considerations on Representative Government*, ed. Currin V. Shields (New York: Liberal Arts, 1958), 261.

18. Macaulay, "Indian Education," in *Poetry and Prose*, 722. See also Gerald Sirkin and Natalie Robinson Sirkin, "The Battle of Indian Education: Macaulay's Opening Salvo Newly Rediscovered," *Victorian Studies* 14:4 (1970–71), 407–28.

19. See John Clive, *Macaulay: The Shaping of the Historian* (New York: Random House, 1973), 435. For Bentham's desire to be the Solon of India see Stokes, *English Utilitarians in India*, 51.

20. K. M. Panikkar, *Asia and Western Dominance: A Survey of the Vasco da Gama Epoch of Asian History, 1498–1945* (London: George Allen & Unwin, 1953), 497.

21. Jawaharlal Nehru, *The Discovery of India*, ed. Robert I. Crane (Garden City, N.Y.: Doubleday Anchor, 1960), 244.

22. Karl Marx, "The British Rule in India," *New York Daily Tribune*, 25 June 1853, in Marx and Frederick Engels, *On Colonialism* (New York: International Publishers, 1972), 36.

23. Marx, "British Rule in India," 41.

24. This suggestion is made by Chamberlain, *Britain and India*, 27. See also Robert Sencourt, *India in English Literature* (London: Simpkin, Marshall, Hamilton, Kent, 1923). The most significant eighteenth-century addition to Indian stereotypes is satiric portrayals of wealthy British "nabobs," as in Samuel Foote's 1772 play *The Nabob*; such satires inaugurated criticism in literature of the British presence in India.

25. Robert Southey, "Original Preface" to *The Curse of Kehama*, in *The Poetical Works of Robert Southey*, 5 vols. (Boston: Houghton, Osgood, 1878), 4:10.

26. *Curse of Kehana*, 126; Robert Southey, "Ode on the Portrait of Bishop Heber," *Poetical Works*, 3:241.

27. Philip Meadows Taylor, *The Story of My Life*, 2 vols. (Edinburgh: William Blackwood, 1877), 1:88.

28. Philip Meadows Taylor, *Confessions of a Thug* (London: Anthony Blond, 1967), 1. Taylor's dedication reads: "To the Right Honourable George, Lord Auckland, G.C.B., Governor-General of India, who is vigorously prosecuting those admirable measures for the suppression of Thuggee which were begun by the late Lord William Cavendish Bentinck, G.C.B. and G.C.H., his predecessor."

29. See Michel Foucault, *Discipline and Punish: The Birth of the Prison*, trans. Alan Sheridan (New York: Random House, 1979), especially 195–308.

30. Charles E. Trevelyan, "The Thugs; or, Secret Murders of India," *Quarterly Review* 64 (January 1837), 394. Several books and articles about Thuggee were published at this time, including Edward Thornton, *Illustrations of the History and Practice of the Thugs* (London: William H. Allen, 1837), and Sir William Sleeman, *The Thugs or Phansigars of India* (Philadelphia: Carey & Hart, 1839).

31. William Makepeace Thackeray, *The Newcomes*, 2 vols. (London: Everyman's Library, 1962), 1:301.

32. William Makepeace Thackeray, *Vanity Fair: A Novel without a Hero*, ed. Geoffrey and Kathleen Tillotson (Boston: Houghton Mifflin, 1963), 28.

33. Georg Lukács, *Writer and Critic, and Other Essays* (New York: Grosset & Dunlap, 1971).

34. William Makepeace Thackeray, *The History of Pendennis* (Harmondsworth: Penguin, 1972), 236.

35. Ray, *Thackeray: The Uses of Adversity*, 162. An account of the agency houses and their collapse appears in C. H. Philips, *The East India Company, 1784–1834* (Manchester: Manchester University Press, 1961), 277–80. According to Philips, "There were, by 1830, 7 principal and 3 secondary Houses of Agency and 20 smaller mercantile Houses at Calcutta, all of which were engaged in commerce; 3 of them also acted as banks and issued notes. The Government at Calcutta supported their efforts, and on various occasions between 1812 and 1828 loaned in all 88 lakhs [8.8 million] of rupees to the Houses. . . . Between 1825 and 1830, the House of John Palmer & Co. mismanaged its business, over-speculating in trade and over-issuing its money. It was hard hit by the reaction of the 1825–26 commercial crisis in England. In 1829, four of the chief partners simultaneously withdrew their money from the firm, on which a run at once began. The other six major Agency Houses selfishly, and, as it proved, unwisely, refused all help. The Government lent further sums of money to the firm, but in vain, and in January 1830, Palmer & Co. went bankrupt. Public confidence was shaken and a run began on the other Houses, most of which had also been over-speculating. Within a year, Alexander & Co. and Mackintosh & Co. ceased payment, and 16 of the smaller Houses became insolvent." It is worth noting that all of the names of companies and businessmen in Philips's account are British.

36. John Vernon, *Money and Fiction: Literary Realism in the Nineteenth and Early Twentieth Centuries* (Ithaca: Cornell University Press, 1982), 25. See also John R. Reed, "A Friend to Mammon: Speculation in Victorian Literature," *Victorian Studies* 27 (Winter 1984), 179–202.

37. J. Y. T. Greig, "The Social Critic," in *Thackeray: A Collection of Critical Essays*, ed. Alexander Welsh (Englewood Cliffs, N.J.: Prentice-Hall, 1968), 40.

38. If Thackeray wrote the essay in *Foreign and Quarterly Review*, April 1844, pp. 213–29, entitled "Problematic Invasion of British India," it was his only directly political statement about the land of his birth. Part of the author's purpose is to defend the British

presence in India by describing the many "benefits we have conferred on India," including the elimination of Thuggee and suttee. But the evidence that Thackeray wrote this piece is not compelling.

39. John Sutherland, "Thackeray as Victorian Racialist," *Essays in Criticism* 20 (1970), 441–45.

40. Thackeray's antisemitism is especially evident in his descriptions of the several rabbis and their families who made the voyage from Constantinople to Jaffa in *From Cornhill to Cairo* (1845), and his only explanation for the miseries of the peasants in *The Irish Sketchbook* (1842) is in racial terms.

Chapter 4. Black Swans; or, Botany Bay Eclogues

1. See Coral Lansbury, *Arcady in Australia: The Evocation of Australia in Nineteenth-Century English Literature* (Melbourne: Melbourne University Press, 1970), 132 and passim. See also Robert Hughes, *The Fatal Shore* (New York: Knopf, 1987).

2. See Keith Hollingsworth, *The Newgate Novel, 1830–1847: Bulwer, Ainsworth, Dickens, and Thackeray* (Detroit: Wayne State University Press, 1963).

3. Robert Southey, "Botany Bay Eclogues" (1794), in *The Poetical Works of Robert Southey*, 10 vols. (London: Longman, Orme, Brown, Green, & Longmans, 1837), 2:71–89.

4. Patrick Colquhoun, *A Treatise on the Police of the Metropolis* (London: C. Dilly, 1797), 321.

5. Quoted by A. G. L. Shaw, *Convicts and the Colonies: A Study of Penal Transportation from Great Britain and Ireland to Australia and Other Parts of the British Empire* (London: Faber & Faber, 1965), 103.

6. Alexander Dalrymple quoted by Shaw, *Convicts and the Colonies*, 50.

7. Eleanor Hodges, "The Bushman Legend," in *Intruders in the Bush: The Australian Quest for Identity*, ed. John Carroll (Melbourne: Oxford University Press, 1982), 4. 4.

8. Thomas Campbell, "Lines on the Departure of Emigrants for New South Wales" (1828), in *The Complete Poetical Works of Thomas Campbell* (New York: Haskell House, 1968), 281.

9. Thomas Malthus, *Principles of Political Economy*, 2d ed. (1820; New York: Augustus M. Kelley, 1951), 417.

10. Thomas Malthus, *On Population* (New York: Modern Library, 1960), 353.

11. Bentham quoted by Donald Winch, *Classical Political Economy and Colonies* (London: London School of Economics, 1965), 34.

12. Patrick Colquhoun, *A Treatise on the Wealth, Power, and Resources of the British Empire* (London: J. Mawman, 1814), 16.

13. Robert Torrens, "Paper on . . . Reducing the Poor Rates" (1817), quoted by Klaus E. Knorr, *British Colonial Theories, 1570–1850* (Toronto: University of Toronto Press, 1944), 279.

14. Robert Torrens, *The Budget* (London: Smith, Elder, 1844), 300, 177.

15. John Stuart Mill, *Principles of Political Economy* (Harmondsworth: Penguin, 1970), 337.

16. Oliver MacDonagh, "Introduction," in *Emigration in the Victorian Age: Debates on the Issue from 19th Century Critical Journals* (London: Gregg International, 1973), 9.

17. J. R. McCulloch, "Emigration," *Edinburgh Review* 45 (1826), 49–74, reprinted in MacDonagh, *Emigration in the Victorian Age*.

18. Sidney Godolphin Osborne, "Immortal Sewerage," in *Meliora; or, Better Times to Come*, ed. Viscount Ingestre, 1st ser. (1853; London: Frank Cass, 1971), 7–17.

19. Gertrude Himmelfarb, *The Idea of Poverty: England in the Early Industrial Age* (New York: Random House, 1983), 327.

20. Henry Mayhew, *London Labour and the London Poor*, 4 vols. (New York: Dover, 1968), 1:101, quoted by Himmelfarb, *Idea of Poverty*, 327.

21. Alexander Thomson, "Our Treatment of the Lower and Lowest Classes of Society," *Meliora*, 18–19.

22. H. J. M. Johnston, *British Emigration Policy, 1815–1830* (Oxford: Clarendon Press, 1972), 118.

23. Edward Gibbon Wakefield, *A View of the Art of Colonization, in Present Reference to the British Empire* (1849; New York: Augustus M. Kelley, 1969), 6.

24. On the concept of dangerous classes, see Himmelfarb, *Idea of Poverty*, 371–400.

25. Coleridge quoted by Harold A. Boner, *Hungry Generations: The Nineteenth-Century Case against Malthusianism* (New York: King's Crown Press, 1955), 123.

26. Lord Byron, *Don Juan*, canto 12, stanza 20, in *The Poetical Works of Lord Byron* (London: Oxford University Press, 1945), 801; William Wordsworth, *The Excursion*, book 9, lines 346–48, 363–82.

27. Thomas Carlyle, *Sartor Resartus*, in *Works*, 30 vols. (London: Chapman & Hall, 1896), 1:180–84.

28. Carlyle, *Past and Present*, in *Works* 10:266–68.

29. Charles Dickens, *The Posthumous Papers of the Pickwick Club* (London: New Oxford Illustrated Dickens, 1948), 74–81.

30. Samuel Sidney, "Three Colonial Epochs," *Household Words* 4 (31 January 1852), 435.

31. Edward Bulwer-Lytton, *The Caxtons, A Family Picture* (London: Routledge, 1849), 378.

32. Henry Kingsley quoted in J. S. D. Mellick, *The Passing Guest: A Life of Henry Kingsley* (New York: St. Martin's, 1983), 38.

33. Anthony Trollope quoted by Lansbury, *Arcady in Australia*, 130. For Charles Reade see Wayne Burns, *Charles Reade: A Study in Victorian Authorship* (New York: Bookman Associates, 1961).

34. "Two Letters from Australia," *Household Words* 1 (10 August 1850), 475–80. See also Samuel Sidney, "An Exploring Adventure," *Household Words* 1 (27 July 1850), 418–20.

35. Marcus Clarke, "Converting the Aborigines," in *A Colonial City: High and Low Life. Selected Journalism of Marcus Clarke*, ed. L. T. Hergenhan (St. Lucia: University of Queensland Press, 1972), 34. See also "Cui Bono," 214–15, and the editor's note, 446.

36. Marcus Clarke, "Port Arthur," in *The Portable Marcus Clarke*, ed. Michael Wilding (St. Lucia: University of Queensland Press, 1976), p. 512. This volume also contains the revised version of *For the Term of His Natural Life* (1874), cited parenthetically in the rest of the chapter. (The original version, with an opening that is quite different from the revision and other, less important differences throughout, appeared serially in the *Australian Journal* starting in March 1870, and is available in a Penguin edition, ed. Stephen Murray-Smith, 1970.) In several of his articles, Clarke exaggerated the effects of the "great round-up" of Tasmanian natives, during which only a few were killed or captured. But the process of extermination, spread over several decades, was relentless; from an original population of perhaps five thousand, there were only a few hundred left by 1830, and the last two Tasmans died in 1869. See C. M. H. Clark, *A History of Australia*, 4 vols. (Melbourne: Melbourne University Press, 1968), 2:146.

37. Clarke was thoroughly familiar with French literature and was influenced especially by Balzac and Hugo. Zola was just starting his Rougon-Macquart series in the early 1870s, but as many of the patterns and themes of *His Natural Life* are close to Zola's, it seems appropriate to call Clarke a "naturalist." Clarke was also familiar with the documentary techniques employed by Charles Reade in the prison and Australian scenes of *It Is Never Too Late to Mend*, but he dispensed with Reade's conversionist motifs.

38. Jeremy Bentham, *Panopticon versus New South Wales*, in *The Works of Jeremy Bentham*, ed. John Bowring, 11 vols. (New York: Russell & Russell, 1962), 4:176.

Chapter 5. The New Crusades

1. William Makepeace Thackeray, *Notes of a Journey from Cornhill to Grand Cairo*, Oxford Illustrated Thackeray vol. 9 (Oxford: Humphrey Milford, n.d.), 235.

2. R. K. Webb, *Harriet Martineau: A Radical Victorian* (London: Heinemann, 1960), 288.

3. For general surveys of the literature see Wallace Cable Brown, "The Popularity of English Travel Books about the Near East, 1775–1825," *Philological Quarterly* 15 (January 1936), 70–80; "Byron and English Interest in the Near East," *Studies in Philology* 34 (January 1937), 55–64; "English Travel Books and Minor Poetry about the Near East, 1775–1825," *Philological Quarterly* 16 (July 1937), 249–71; and also Yehoshua Ben-Arieh, *The Rediscovery of the Holy Land in the Nineteenth Century* (Jerusalem: Hebrew University, and Detroit: Wayne State University, 1979).

4. For the archaeological and religious rivalries see Neil Asher Silberman, *Digging for God and Country: Exploration, Archeology, and the Secret Struggle for the Holy Land, 1799–1917* (New York: Knopf, 1982), and Barbara W. Tuchman, *Bible and Sword: England and Palestine from the Bronze Age to Balfour* (New York: New York University Press, 1956). More general histories include David Gillard, *The Struggle for Asia, 1828–1914: A Study in British and Russian Imperialism* (London: Methuen, 1977); Harold Temperley, *England and the Near East: The Crimea* (London: Longmans, Green, 1936); and Sara Searight, *The British in the Middle East* (1969; London: East-West Publications, 1979).

5. For nineteenth-century medievalism generally, see Alice Chandler, *A Dream of Order: The Medieval Ideal in Nineteenth-Century English Literature* (Lincoln: University of Nebraska Press, 1970), and Mark Girouard, *The Return to Camelot: Chivalry and the English Gentleman* (New Haven: Yale University Press, 1981).

6. A. W. Kinglake, *Eothen* (London: Nelson, n.d.), 15. See also Gerald de Gaury, *Travelling Gent: The Life of Alexander Kinglake (1809–1891)* (London: Routledge & Kegan Paul, 1972), and Eliot Warburton, *The Crescent and the Cross; or, Romance and Realities of Eastern Travel* (1844; New York: George Putnam, 1852).

7. Lord Byron, "Childe Harold's Pilgrimage," in *The Poetical Works* (London: Oxford University Press, 1945), 2:45.

8. For Byron and the Near East, see William A. Borst, *Lord Byron's First Pilgrimage* (New Haven: Yale University Press, 1948), and Harold Nicolson, *Byron: The Last Journey, April 1823–April 1824* (1929; Hamden, Conn.: Archon, 1969).

9. Kenelm Henry Digby, *The Broad Stone of Honour; or, The True Sense and Practice of Chivalry*, 4 vols. (London: Bernard Quaritch, 1877), 2:24. See also, for instance, Charles Mills, *The History of Chivalry; or, Knighthood and Its Times*, 2 vols. (London: Longman, Rees, Orme, Brown & Green, 1825), 1:337–38. In 1910 Sir Charles Bruce named his study of imperial administration *The Broad Stone of Empire: Problems of Crown Colony Administration*, and began it with an epigraph from Digby's book.

10. A. Dwight Culler, *The Victorian Mirror of History* (New Haven: Yale University Press, 1985), 29.

11. Sir Walter Scott, *Ivanhoe* (Harmondsworth: Penguin, 1982), 318.

12. See Girouard, *Return to Camelot*, especially 163–76 and 220–48.

13. See J. W. Burrow, *A Liberal Descent: Victorian Historians and the English Past* (Cambridge: Cambridge University Press, 1981), and Christopher Hill, "The Norman Yoke," in *Democracy and the Labour Movement*, ed. John Saville (London: Lawrence & Wishart, 1954), 11–66.

14. Sir Walter Scott, *The Talisman* (London: Henry Frowde, 1905), ix.

15. Norman Daniel, *Islam, Europe and Empire* (Edinburgh: Edinburgh University Press, 1966), 59.

16. James Morier, *The Adventures of Hajji Baba of Ispahan* (New York: Modern Library, 1954), 283.

17. William F. Monypenny and George E. Buckle, *The Life of Benjamin Disraeli, Earl of Beaconsfield*, 2 vols. (1929; New York: Russell & Russell, 1968), 1:140. Hereafter volume and page numbers are given parenthetically in the text.

18. Robert Blake, *Disraeli's Grand Tour: Benjamin Disraeli and the Holy Land, 1830–31* (London: Weidenfeld & Nicolson, 1982), 30.

19. Benjamin Disraeli, *Alroy* (New York: Knopf, n.d.), 148.

20. Benjamin Disraeli, *Contarini Fleming: A Psychological Romance* (New York: Knopf, n.d.), 307.

21. Quoted in Robert Blake, *Disraeli* (Garden City, N.Y.: Doubleday Anchor, 1968), 186–87.

22. A perceptive reading of *Tancred* mainly in terms of religion is Richard Levine, "Disraeli's *Tancred* and 'The Great Asian Mystery,'" *Nineteenth-Century Fiction* 22 (1967), 71–85.

23. Benjamin Disraeli, *Tancred; or, The New Crusade* (1877; Westport, Conn.: Greenwood, 1970), 121–22.

24. Robert Knox, *The Races of Men: A Fragment* (Philadelphia: Lea & Blanchard, 1850), 90.

25. This is directly contrary to what Bronson Feldman claims Disraeli experienced at Jerusalem. See his psychohistorical essay "The Imperial Dreams of Disraeli," *Psychoanalytic Review* 54 (1966), 609–41.

26. Robert Blake points out that "all his life Disraeli was a convinced adherent of the conspiracy theory of history." *Disraeli's Grand Tour,* 56.

27. Here I agree with an excellent essay by Daniel Bivona on Disraeli's trilogy and imperialism, forthcoming in *NOVEL*. I am grateful to Bivona and to Roger Henkle, Editor of *NOVEL*, for sharing it with me.

28. In an 1850 polemic on the Holy Places the Frenchman Eugène Boré contended that "recurring to the traditional policy of the Crusades would serve the cause of the Church and increase [French] preponderance in the world." Quoted by Robert C. Binkley, *Realism and Nationalism, 1852–1871* (New York: Harper & Row, 1963), 169.

29. Edward Said, *Orientalism* (New York: Vintage, 1979), 190.

30. See Joseph Campbell, "Editor's Introduction," *The Portable Arabian Nights* (New York: Viking, 1952), 31–32.

31. See the next chapter for Burton's attitudes toward Africans and slavery.

32. Richard F. Burton, *Personal Narrative of a Pilgrimage to Al-Madinah and Meccah,* 2 vols. (New York: Dover, 1964), 1:40. Hereafter volume and page numbers are given parenthetically in the text.

33. Isabel Burton, *The Life of Sir Richard F. Burton*, 2 vols. (1893; Boston: Milford House, 1973), 2:269.

34. See the section on Doughty in Thomas J. Assad, *Three Victorian Travelers: Burton, Blunt, Doughty* (London: Routledge & Kegan Paul, 1964).

35. See *Anthropology and the Colonial Encounter*, ed. Talal Asad (New York: Humanities, 1973), and *The Politics of Anthropology: From Colonialism and Sexism toward a View from Below*, ed. Gerrit Huizer and Bruce Mannheim (The Hague: Mouton, 1979).

36. Richard F. Burton, *Sindh and the Races That Inhabit the Valley of the Indus*, introd. by H. T. Lambrick (London: Oxford University Press, 1973), xiii.

37. Richard F. Burton, *The Book of the Thousand Nights and a Night*, 10 vols. (London: Burton Club, 1886), 10:205.

38. Burton, *Book of the Thousand Nights*, 10:205–54.

39. Burton uses the phrase "anthropological notes" throughout his edition of the *Arabian Nights*; he indexes the notes in the last volume of *Supplemental Nights to the Book of the Thousand Nights and a Night*, 7 vols. (London: Burton Club, 1888).

40. See Ronald Rainger, "Race, Politics, and Science: The Anthropological Society of London in the 1860s," *Victorian Studies* 22 (Autumn 1978), 51–70.

41. See the papers on racial extinction by Richard Lee and T. Bendyshe in *Journal of the Anthropological Society* 2 (1864), xcv–cii.

42. James Hunt, "Presidential Address," *Journal of the Anthropological Society* 2 (1864), xciii.

43. Rev. Dunbar J. Heath, "Anniversary Address," *Journal of the Anthropological Society* 6 (1868), lxxxvi.

44. Burton, *Book of the Thousand Nights*, 10:301.

45. Richard F. Burton, *First Footsteps in East Africa; or, An Exploration of Harar*, 2 vols. (1856; London: Tylston & Edwards, 1894), 1:xxx–xxxi.

46. Richard F. Burton, *The Sentiment of the Sword: A Country-House Dialogue* (London: Horace Cox, 1911), 6.

47. See Girouard, *Return to Camelot*, 229.

Chapter 6. The Genealogy of the Myth of the "Dark Continent"

1. Joseph Conrad, *Heart of Darkness* (New York: Norton, 1963), 8. In *The Image of Africa: British Ideas and Action, 1780–1850* (Madison: University of Wisconsin Press, 1964), Philip D. Curtin writes that "the image of 'darkest Africa,' either as an expression of geographical ignorance, or as one of cultural arrogance, was a nineteenth-century invention" (9). See also Dorothy Hammond and Alta Jablow, *The Africa That Never Was: Four Centuries of British Writing about Africa* (New York: Twayne, 1970), especially 49–113.

2. Edward Said, *Orientalism* (New York: Vintage, 1979); the quotations are from Said, *The World, the Text, and the Critic* (Cambridge: Harvard University Press, 1983), 9 and 53, and Michel Foucault, *Language, Counter-Memory, Practice*, ed. Donald F. Bouchard (Ithaca: Cornell University Press, 1977), 148.

3. See especially Eric Williams, *Capitalism and Slavery* (Chapel Hill: University of North Carolina Press, 1944). Williams's theory has been often criticized, but not his general thesis of some sort of correlation between abolitionism and industrialization. See Roger T. Anstey, "Capitalism and Slavery: A Critique," *Economic History Review* 21 (1968), 307–20, but also David Brion Davis, *The Problem of Slavery in the Age of Revolution, 1770–1823* (Ithaca: Cornell University Press, 1975), 346–52. Other accounts

include Michael Craton, *Sinews of Empire: A Short History of British Slavery* (Garden City, N.Y.: Doubleday Anchor, 1974); Jack Gratus, *The Great White Lie: Slavery, Emancipation and Changing Racial Attitudes* (New York: Monthly Review Press, 1973); and Howard Temperley, *British Antislavery, 1833–1870* (London: Longman, 1972).

4. See Ralph A. Austen and Woodruff D. Smith, "Images of Africa and British Slave-Trade Abolition: The Transition to an Imperialist Ideology, 1787–1807," *African Historical Studies* 2:1 (1969), 69–83. The classic work on motives for expansion is Ronald Robinson, John Gallagher, and Alice Denney, *Africa and the Victorians: The Climax of Imperialism in the Dark Continent* (New York: St. Martin's, 1961).

5. Nancy Stepan, *The Idea of Race in Science: Great Britain, 1800–1960* (Hamden, Conn.: Archon, 1982), 1. See also Christine Bolt, *Victorian Attitudes to Race* (Toronto: University of Toronto Press, 1971).

6. William Blake, "The Little Black Boy," in *The Poetry and Prose of William Blake*, ed. David V. Erdman (Garden City, N.Y.: Doubleday, 1970), 9.

7. Robert Southey, *Poetical Works*, 10 vols. (London: Longman, Orme, Brown, Green, & Longmans, 1838), 2:129.

8. See Eva Beatrice Dykes, *The Negro in English Romantic Thought* (Washington, D.C.: Associated Publishers, 1942), and Wylie Sypher, *Guinea's Captive Kings: British Anti-Slavery Literature of the XVIIIth Century* (Chapel Hill: University of North Carolina Press, 1942).

9. Southey, "Poems Concerning the Slave Trade," *Poetical Works*, 2:57.

10. James Grahame, "Africa Delivered; or, The Slave Trade Abolished," in James Montgomery, Grahame, and E. Benger, *Poems on the Abolition of the Slave Trade* (1809; Freeport, N.Y.: Books for Libraries Press, 1971), 58.

11. Katherine George, "The Civilized West Looks at Primitive Africa: 1400–1800," *ISIS* 49 (1958), 62–72. Winthrop D. Jordan reaches a similar conclusion in *White Over Black: American Attitudes toward the Negro, 1550–1812* (Chapel Hill: University of North Carolina Press, 1968), 269–311. And see Curtin, *Image of Africa*, 9.

12. Thomas Edward Bowdich, *Mission from Cape Coast Castle to Ashantee* (1819; London: Frank Cass, 1966). Curtin calls Bowdich one of a group of "enlightened travellers" between 1795 and the 1820s, and his book "a glowing description of Ashanti society" (*Image of Africa*, 211, 169).

13. Curtin, *Image of Africa*, 298.

14. Thomas Fowell Buxton, *The African Slave Trade and Its Remedy* (1840; London: Frank Cass, 1967), 342. See also John Gallagher, "Fowell Buxton and the New African Policy, 1838–1842," *Cambridge Historical Journal* 10 (1950), 36–58.

15. Charles Dickens, "The Niger Expedition," *The Examiner*, 19 August 1848, reprinted in *Miscellaneous Papers*, National Library Edition of Dickens's Works, 20 vols. (New York: Bigelow, Brown, 1903), 18:64.

16. Dickens quoted by Donald H. Simpson, "Charles Dickens and the Empire," *Library Notes of the Royal Commonwealth Society*, n.s. 162 (June 1970), 15. See also Dickens, "The Noble Savage," *Household Words* 7 (11 June 1853), 337–39.

17. Mrs. R. Lee (Sarah Wallis), *The African Wanderers; or, The Adventures of Carlos and Antonio* (London: Grant & Griffith, 1847), 230 and 126, and Curtin, *Image of Africa*, 328.

18. Alan Moorehead, *The White Nile*, rev. ed. (New York: Harper & Row, 1971), likens the great Victorian explorers to astronauts. See also *Africa and Its Explorers: Motives, Methods, and Impact*, ed. Robert I. Rotberg (Cambridge: Harvard University Press, 1970).

19. William Somerset Maugham, *The Explorer* (1907; New York: Baker & Taylor,

1909), 45 and 175–76. Compare Joseph Conrad, "Geography and Some Explorers," *Last Essays* (1926; Freeport, N.Y.: Books for Libraries Press, 1970), 14.

20. Dickens quoted by Simpson, "Charles Dickens and Empire," 15.

21. Quoted by M. E. Chamberlain, *The Scramble for Africa* (London: Longman, 1974), 28.

22. Michel Foucault, "The Discourse on Language," appendix to *The Archaeology of Knowledge*, trans. A. M. Sheridan Smith (New York: Pantheon, 1972), 229.

23. Livingstone, quoted by Tim Jeal, *Livingstone* (New York: Putnam's, 1973), 146, 124; Jeal, *Livingstone*, 4.

24. See Philip Curtin and Paul Bohannan, *Africa and Africans* (Garden City, N.Y.: Natural History Press, 1971), 8.

25. May Crawford, *By the Equator's Snowy Peak: A Record of Medical Missionary Work and Travel in British East Africa* (London: Church Missionary Society, 1913), 29, 56.

26. On missionary attitudes see H. A. C. Cairns, *Prelude to Imperialism: British Reactions to Central African Society, 1840–1890* (London: Routledge & Kegan Paul, 1965).

27. Anthony Hope, *The God in the Car* (1895; New York: Appleton, 1896), 19.

28. Sir Richard Burton, *The Lake Regions of Central Africa*, 2 vols. (1861; New York: Horizon, 1961), 2:326.

29. Ibid., 2:347–48.

30. Sir Richard Burton, *Two Trips to Gorilla Land and the Cataracts of the Congo* (1876; New York: Johnson, 1967), 311.

31. Samuel White Baker, *The Albert N'yanza, Great Basin of the Nile and Exploration of the Nile Sources*, 2 vols. (1866; London: Sidgwick & Jackson, 1962), 1:211.

32. Henry S. Merriman [Hugh Stowell Scott], *With Edged Tools* (1894; London: Smith, Elder, 1909), 321–22.

33. The stamp design is reproduced in Roland Oliver, *Sir Harry Johnston and the Scramble for Africa* (London: Chatto & Windus, 1957). On racism and class see *Racism and Colonialism: Essays on Ideology and Social Structure*, ed. Robert Ross (The Hague: Martinus Nijhoff, 1982), and Douglas A. Lorimer, *Colour, Class and the Victorians: English Attitudes to the Negro in the Mid-Nineteenth Century* (Leicester: Leicester University Press, 1978).

34. See Ronald Rainger, "Race, Politics, and Science: The Anthropological Society of London in the 1860s," *Victorian Studies* 22 (Autumn 1978), 51–70.

35. Thomas Henry Huxley, *Man's Place in Nature* (Ann Arbor: University of Michigan Press, 1959), 58, 69–70. Huxley acknowledges that the "human butcher shop" is "irrelevant" to his argument. Nancy Stepan notes that in the nineteenth century, "textbook after textbook compared the Negro to the ape" (*Idea of Race*, 18).

36. Hammond and Jablow, *Africa That Never Was*, 94.

37. Winwood Reade, *Savage Africa; Being the Narrative of a Tour in Equatorial, Southwestern, and Northwestern Africa* (New York: Harper, 1864), 54.

38. Sir John Lubbock, *The Origin of Civilisation and the Primitive Condition of Man: Mental and Social Condition of Savages* (1870; London: Longmans, Green, 1912), 1–2.

39. George Romanes, *Mental Evolution in Man: Origin of Human Faculty* (New York: D. Appleton, 1893), 439.

40. Benjamin Kidd, *Social Evolution* (New York: Macmillan, 1894), 49–50.

41. Karl Pearson, *National Life from the Standpoint of Science* (London: Adam & Charles Black, 1901), 47–48.

42. Charles Darwin, *The Descent of Man, and Selection in Relation to Sex*, 2d ed.

(New York and London: Merrill & Baker, 1874), 613. See especially chap. 7, "On the Races of Man," 162–202. On racial extinction see also Sir Charles Wentworth Dilke, *Greater Britain: A Record of Travel in English-Speaking Countries during 1866 and 1867* (New York: Harper, 1869), 90–100, 221, 250, and 273.

43. Cf. George Stocking, Jr., *Race, Culture, and Evolution: Essays in the History of Anthropology* (New York: Free Press, 1968), 229: "Once the 'one grand scheme' of evolutionism was rejected, the multiplicity of *cultures* which took the place of the cultural *stages* of savagery, barbarism, and civilization were no more easily brought within one standard of evaluation than they were within one system of explanation."

44. Claude Lévi-Strauss, *Tristes tropiques*, trans. John and Doreen Weightman (New York: Atheneum, 1974), 123.

45. William Makepeace Thackeray, "Timbuctoo," in *Early Miscellanies* (London: Oxford University Press, n.d.), 2.

46. Henry M. Stanley, *My Kalulu: Prince, King, and Slave* (London: Sampson, Low, Marston, Searle, & Rivington, 1889), viii.

47. Joseph Thomson and E. Harriet-Smith, *Ulu: An African Romance*, 3 vols. (London: Sampson, Low, Marston, Searle, & Rivington, 1888), 2:18–19.

48. R. M. Ballantyne, *Black Ivory: A Tale of Adventure among the Slaves of East Africa* (1873; Chicago: Afro-American Press, 1969), v.

49. Similar messages appear in Ballantyne's other novels, including *The Gorilla Hunters* (1861). See Eric Quayle, *Ballantyne the Brave: A Victorian Writer and His Family* (London: Rupert Hart-Davis, 1967), 146.

50. Sir Harry H. Johnston, *The History of a Slave* (London: Kegan Paul, Trench, 1889), 6.

51. H. Rider Haggard, *King Solomon's Mines* (Harmondsworth: Penguin, 1965), 241.

52. John Buchan, *Prester John* (New York: Doran, 1910), 211, 148.

53. See S. J. Cookey, *Britain and the Congo Question, 1885–1913* (London: Longmans, 1968).

54. "Tropenkollered" was the term used by the Dutch naval captain Otto Lütken, quoted by Ian Watt, *Conrad in the Nineteenth Century* (Berkeley: University of California Press, 1979), 145.

55. Watt, *Conrad*, 141–46.

56. Sir Harry H. Johnston, *British Central Africa: An Attempt to Give Some Account of a Portion of the Territories under British Influence North of the Zambesi*, 3d ed. (London: Methuen, 1906), 68.

57. Charles Reade, *A Simpleton: A Story of the Day* (London: Chatto & Windus, 1873), 250–51.

58. Moffat and Pruen quoted by Cairns, *Prelude to Imperialism*, 68.

59. Dominique O. Mannoni, *Prospero and Caliban: The Psychology of Colonization* (London: Methuen, 1956), 21.

60. As well as Lévi-Strauss see Stanley Diamond, *In Search of the Primitive* (New Brunswick, N.J.: Transaction, 1974).

61. Karl Peters, *King Solomon's Golden Ophir: A Research into the Most Ancient Gold Production in History* (1899; New York: Negro Universities Press, 1969), is an example of the speculation about the Zimbabwe ruins that underlies Haggard's stories. The first scientific work demonstrating that the ruins had been built by Africans was David Randall-MacIver, *Mediaeval Rhodesia* (London: Macmillan, 1906). As late as the 1960s works published in Rhodesia and South Africa were still insisting that the builders of the ruins were non-African.

62. Frantz Fanon, *Black Skin, White Masks*, trans. Charles Markmann (New York: Grove, 1968), 18.

63. For nineteenth-century African responses to the European invasion see *Africa and the West: Intellectual Responses to European Culture*, ed. Philip D. Curtin (Madison: University of Wisconsin Press, 1972); *Protest and Power in Black Africa* ed. Robert I. Rotberg and Ali A. Mazrui (New York: Oxford University Press, 1970); and *Aspects of Central African History*, ed. Terence Ranger (Evanston: Northwestern University Press, 1968).

64. Kwame Nkrumah, *Neo-Colonialism: The Last Stage of Imperialism* (London: Nelson, 1965), 246.

65. Chinua Achebe, "An Image of Africa," *Research in African Literature* 9 (Spring 1978), 2 and 12. See also Ezekiel Mphahlele, *The African Image* (New York: Praeger, 1962) and Abdul R. JanMohamed, *Manichean Aesthetics: The Politics of Literature in Colonial Africa* (Amherst: University of Massachusetts Press, 1983).

Chapter 7. The Well at Cawnpore: Literary Representations of the Indian Mutiny of 1857

1. Hilda Gregg, "The Indian Mutiny in Fiction," *Blackwood's Magazine* 161 (February 1897), 218–31.

2. These figures are based on the titles listed in Brijen Kishore Gupta, *India in English Fiction, 1800–1970: An Annotated Bibliography* (Metuchen, N.J.: Scarecrow, 1973). There is also a useful survey in Shailendra Dhari Singh, *Novels on the Indian Mutiny* (New Delhi: Arnold-Heinemann, 1973).

3. Edward W. Said, *Orientalism* (New York: Vintage, 1979), 45, 26. The best account of the British response to the Mutiny is Thomas Metcalf, *The Aftermath of Revolt: India, 1857–1870* (Princeton: Princeton University Press, 1964). See also Francis G. Hutchins, *The Illusion of Permanence: British Imperialism in India* (Princeton: Princeton University Press, 1967), and Lewis D. Wurgaft, *The Imperial Imagination: Magic and Myth in Kipling's India* (Middletown: Wesleyan University Press, 1983).

4. On extropunitive projection see the classic study of the psychology of racism, Gordon W. Allport, *The Nature of Prejudice* (Reading, Mass.: Addison-Wesley, 1954), 349, 382–92. See also William Ryan, *Blaming the Victim* (New York: Pantheon, 1971), and Sander Gilman, *Difference and Pathology: Stereotypes of Sexuality, Race, and Madness* (Ithaca: Cornell University Press, 1985).

5. A readable, Eurocentric narrative history of the Mutiny is Christopher Hibbert, *The Great Mutiny: India in 1857* (New York: Viking, 1978). For Indian perspectives see Surendra Nath Sen, *Eighteen Fifty-Seven* (Calcutta: Ministry of Information, 1957), probably the most balanced history; Sashi Bhussan Chaudhuri, *Theories of the Indian Mutiny (1857–59)* (Calcutta: World Press, 1968); and Pratul Chandra Gupta, *Nana Sahib and the Rising at Cawnpore* (Oxford: Clarendon Press, 1963).

6. See Sen, *Eighteen Fifty-Seven*, 150–61; P. C. Gupta, *Nana Sahib*, 118. In *The Other Side of the Medal* (London: Hogarth, 1925), Edward Thompson pointed out that the massacres of Indians at Benares and Allahabad took place "long before the Cawnpore massacre" (70), but he did not speculate about the motives of the Cawnpore rebels. Thompson showed how throughout northern India "government by gallows . . . was supplemented by government by massacre" (74). He also criticized British writing about India for a general "misrepresentation of Indian history and character" (123).

7. Modern accounts that fail to perceive a connection between Neill's Bloody Assizes

and the Cawnpore massacres include Hibbert and Wurgaft, who both mention Benares and Allahabad only after the Cawnpore massacres. In *The Indian Mutiny: A Centenary History* (London: Hollis & Carter, 1957), Richard Hilton writes of Neill's actions in terms of "striking terror into the hearts of the disloyal and the looters." Although "some have accused Neill of undue severity," Hilton will have none of it, and of course he sees no link with Cawnpore (75). In *The Sound of Fury: An Account of the Indian Mutiny* (London: Collins, 1963), Richard Collier speaks of Neill's "reign of terror," but its salutary purpose was "to restore order," and again no connection is made with Cawnpore. Better is Michael Edwardes, *Red Year: The Indian Rebellion of 1857* (London: Hamish Hamilton, 1973). His chapter "The Madness of Colonel Neill" comes after a chapter on Cawnpore, but he describes Neill's Bloody Assizes in some detail and acknowledges, though without explanation, that "they had . . . led to the massacre of [Neill's] countrywomen at Cawnpore" (84). In contrast, see Vinayak Savarkar, *The Indian War of Independence, 1857* (Bombay: Phoenix, 1947), 205: "Neill's barbarities were not a revenge of Cawnpore, but the Cawnpore bloodshed was the result of and revenge of Neill's inhuman brutalities." Savarkar's book, written in 1909, was itself repressed until 1947.

8. Benjamin Disraeli in U.K. *Hansard Parliamentary Debates*, 3d. ser., vol. 147 (27 July 1857), 475.

9. Marx's writings on India are collected in Karl Marx and Friedrich Engels, *On Colonialism: Articles from the New York Tribune and Other Writings* (New York: International Publishers, 1972).

10. S. N. Sen, "Writings on the Mutiny," in *Historians of India, Pakistan and Ceylon*, ed. C. H. Philips (London: Oxford University Press, 1961), 383. See also Salahuddin Malik, "Nineteenth Century Approaches to the Indian 'Mutiny,'" *Journal of Asian History* 7 (1973), 95–127, and its companion, Michael Adas, "Twentieth Century Approaches to the Indian Mutiny of 1857–58," *Journal of Asian History* 5 (1971), 1–19.

11. G. O. Trevelyan, *Cawnpore* (London: Macmillan, 1865), 69–70.

12. When Victorian writers contend that the rebellion was fomented by a conspiracy, they sometimes also attribute it to Russian agents, a fantasy apparent in the Great Game in Kipling's *Kim*, though the events in that novel are set much later than the Mutiny.

13. Charles Ball, *History of the Indian Mutiny*, 2 vols. (London: London Printing & Publishing Co., 1858), 1:376. Ball retails atrocity and rape rumors, which were exposed as groundless in the various inquiries conducted at the end of the Mutiny, as recorded in Edward Lecky, *Fictions Connected with the Indian Outbreak of 1857 Exposed* (Bombay: Chesson & Woodhall, 1859). Trevelyan may spin his horror story out of flimsy sources, but at least he rejects the worst atrocity fantasies. See also Sen, *Eighteen Fifty-Seven*, 414–16.

14. William Henry Fitchett, *The Tale of the Great Mutiny* (London: Smith, Elder, 1901), 11.

15. Alfred, Lord Tennyson, "Havelock" and "The Defence of Lucknow," in *The Poems of Tennyson*, ed. Christopher Ricks (London: Longman, 1969), 1105, 1251–53. For examples by other poets, see "The Poetry of the Rebellion," *Calcutta Review* 31 (December 1858), 349–67.

16. See Allardyce Nicoll, *A History of Late Nineteenth-Century Drama, 1850–1900*, 2 vols. (Cambridge: Cambridge University Press, 1949), vol. 2, and also Richard Fawkes, *Dion Boucicault: A Biography* (London: Quartet, 1979), 98–101. The script of *Jessie Brown; or, The Relief of Lucknow* is reproduced in *Dick's Standard Plays* no. 473 (London: John Dicks, n.d.).

17. Charles Dickens, *Letters*, ed. Walter Dexter, 3 vols. (Bloomsbury: Nonesuch Press, 1937–38), 2:889.

18. Charles Dickens, "The Perils of Certain English Prisoners," in *Works*, National Library Edition, 22 vols. (New York: Bigelow, Brown, n.d.), 13:207–68.

19. Cf. William Odie, "Dickens and the Indian Mutiny," *The Dickensian* 68 (1972), 3–15. *The Moonstone* (1868), by the co-author of "Perils," Wilkie Collins, also distantly reflects the Mutiny, perhaps in an anti-imperialist way. See John R. Reed, "English Imperialism and the Unacknowledged Crime of *The Moonstone*," *Clio* 2(June 1973), 281–90.

20. G. A. Lawrence, *Maurice Dering; or, The Quadrilateral* (London: Tinsley, 1865), 454.

21. James Grant, *First Love and Last Love: A Tale of the Indian Mutiny*, 3 vols. (London: Routledge, 1868), 2:3–4.

22. In *Prospero and Caliban: The Psychology of Colonization* (London: Methuen, 1956), Dominique O. Mannoni writes: "The 'Prospero complex' . . . draws from the inside . . . a picture of the paternalist colonial, with his pride, his neurotic impatience, and his desire to dominate, [and] at the same time portrays the racialist whose daughter has suffered an attempted rape at the hands of an inferior being. . . . These rapes allegedly perpetrated by members of one race on those of another are pure projections of the unconscious" (110). See also Joel Kovel, *White Racism: A Psychohistory* (New York: Pantheon, 1970), 67–79.

23. Henry Kingsley, *Stretton*, 3 vols. (London: Tinsley, 1869), 3:279.

24. Mrs. Everard Cotes (Sarah Jeannette Duncan), *The Story of Sonny Sahib* (New York: Appleton, 1895), and Rudyard Kipling, "The Man Who Would Be King," in *Works*, Pocket Edition, 34 vols. (London: Macmillan, 1924), 5:205.

25. Sir George Chesney, *The Dilemma*, 3 vols. (Edinburgh: Blackwood, 1876).

26. Philip Meadows Taylor, *The Story of My Life* (London: Oxford University Press, 1920), 460–61.

27. Philip Meadows Taylor, *Seeta* (1872; London: C. Kegan Paul, 1881), 147–48.

28. G. A. Henty, *In Times of Peril: A Tale of India* (London: Griffith & Farran, 1881), 169.

29. G. A. Henty, *Rujub, the Juggler*, 3 vols. (London: Chatto & Windus, 1893), 3:33.

30. Miss Wheeler, racially mixed daughter of Major-General Wheeler, was apparently abducted at the time of the riverside massacre. It was later rumored that she killed her captor and his family and then committed suicide by throwing herself down a well. As Trevelyan complains, her story was made the subject of "a series of prurient and ghastly fictions. Under one shape or another the incident long went the round of provincial theatres, and sensation magazines, and popular lectures illustrated with dissolving views" (254). But Miss Wheeler did not kill her abductor and commit suicide. Instead, she converted to Islam and married her captor (or was he her rescuer?). The last word on her came many years later from a Catholic priest who discovered her just before her death in Cawnpore. On her deathbed she told him that she had been well-treated by her husband and that she had no wish to make contact with British officials (reported in Hibbert, *Great Mutiny*, 194–95).

31. Henry Seton Merriman (Hugh Stowell Scott), *Flotsam, The Study of a Life* (1896; London: Smith, Elder, 1909), 127.

32. Hume Nisbet, *The Queen's Desire: A Romance of the Indian Mutiny* (London: F. V. White, 1893), 185–86.

33. Flora Annie Steel, *On the Face of the Waters* (1896; New York: Macmillan, 1911), 38.

34. Flora Annie Steel, *The Garden of Fidelity, Being the Autobiography of Flora Annie Steel, 1847–1929* (London: Macmillan, 1930), 226.

35. There was little Indian writing about the Mutiny before World War I, a fact that itself testifies to British repression. The main historiographical exception is Sir Syed Ahmad Khan, *The Causes of the Indian Revolt* (Benares: Medical Hill Press, 1873), a sensible but pro-British account. Vinayak Savarkar's *The Indian War of Independence, 1857,* first published in 1909 but banned until independence, is a nationalist classic with Nana Sahib as one of its heroes. For nineteenth-century fiction by Indians in English, I have seen only S. C. Dutt, *Shunkur: A Tale of the Indian Mutiny of 1857,* in *Bengaliana: A Dish of Rice and Curry, and Other Indigestible Ingredients* (Calcutta: Thacker, Spink, 1885). In *Nationalism in Indo-Anglian Fiction* (New Delhi: Sterling, 1978), Gobinda Prasad Sarma makes a case for Dutt's story as nationalist (152–59), but, although *Shunkur* concerns an Indian who joins the Mutineers because his wife has been raped by British soldiers, it merely balances this atrocity against the lurid details of Cawnpore: "Great was the pleasure of Nana Sahib at the success of his treacherous and cowardly enterprise" (107). The point that betrayal and villainy occurred on both sides is valid but not by itself nationalist, while Dutt's portrayal of Nana Sahib as deceitful and murderous follows the British stereotype. Singh, *Novels on the Indian Mutiny,* 46, mentions also Hafiz Allard, *Nirgis: A Tale of the Indian Mutiny* (1860?), but I have been unable to obtain a copy. A recent novel by Manohar Malgonkar, *The Devil's Wind, Nana Sahib's Story* (New York: Viking, 1972), presents Nana Sahib as hero rather than villain.

36. E. M. Forster, *A Passage to India* (Harmondsworth: Penguin, 1961), 166.

37. John Masters, *Nightrunners of Bengal* (New York: Viking, 1961), vii.

Chapter 8. Imperial Gothic: Atavism and the Occult in the British Adventure Novel, 1880–1914

1. Bithia M. Croker, *The Old Cantonment; with Other Stories of India and Elsewhere* (London: Methuen, 1905), 48–63.

2. See Brooks Wright, *Interpreter of Buddhism to the West: Sir Edwin Arnold* (New York: Bookman Associates, 1957).

3. A brief account of the development of late-Victorian romanticism in conjunction with occultism appears in Tom Gibbons, *Rooms in the Darwin Hotel: Studies in English Literary Criticism and Ideas, 1880–1920* (Nedlands: University of Western Australia Press, 1973), 1–24. See also Ruth Brandon, *The Spiritualists: The Passion for the Occult in the Nineteenth and Twentieth Centuries* (New York: Knopf, 1983); Janet Oppenheim, *The Other World: Spiritualism and Psychical Research in England, 1850–1914* (Cambridge, Cambridge University Press, 1985); and Frank M. Turner, *Between Science and Religion: The Reaction to Scientific Naturalism in Late Victorian England* (New Haven: Yale Univeristy Press, 1974).

4. Oppenheim, *Other World,* 160.

5. J. A. Cramb, *The Origins and Destiny of Imperial Britain* (New York: Dutton, 1900), 230.

6. Carroll V. Peterson, *John Davidson* (New York: Twayne, 1972), 82.

7. John Davidson, "St. George's Day," in *The Poems of John Davidson,* ed. Andrew Turnbull, 2 vols. (Edinburgh: Scottish Academic Press, 1973), 1:228.

8. Rudyard Kipling, "Recessional," in *Works,* 36 vols., Pocket Edition (London: Methuen, 1923), 34:186.

9. Jerome Hamilton Buckley, *William Ernest Henley: A Study in the "Counter-Decadence" of the 'Nineties* (Princeton: Princeton University Press, 1945), 134. See also John Lester, *Journey through Despair, 1880–1914: Transformations in British Literary Culture* (Princeton: Princeton University Press, 1968), 9: both the imperialism and the

socialism of the turn of the century "became charged with an overplus of fervor which exalted each at times almost to religion."

10. Erskine Childers, *The Riddle of the Sands: A Record of Secret Service* (1903; New York: Dover, 1976), 15.

11. Both White and Shaw are quoted by Lester, *Journey through Despair*, 50n and 5.

12. Lester (*Journey through Despair*, 3) notes that this quotation from 1 Corinthians 10:11 "crops up recurrently in the literature of the time."

13. Lewis S. Wurgaft, *The Imperial Imagination: Magic and Myth in Kipling's India* (Middletown: Wesleyan University Press, 1983), 57.

14. Edgar Wallace, *Sanders of the River* (1909; Garden City, N.Y.: Doubleday, Doran, 1930), 277.

15. For these and other examples see *The Best Supernatural Tales of Arthur Conan Doyle*, ed. E. F. Bleiler (New York: Dover, 1979). An interesting variant is W. Somerset Maugham's *The Magician* (1908), based on the career of Aleister Crowley.

16. Andrew Lang, "Realism and Romance," *Contemporary Review* 52 (November 1887), 684. Page numbers are given parenthetically in the next two paragraphs of the text. See also Joseph Weintraub, "Andrew Lang: Critic of Romance," *English Literature in Transition* 18:1 (1975), 5–15.

17. Sir Edward Burnett Tylor, *Primitive Culture*, 2 vols. (1871; New York: Harper & Row, 1970), 1:155, 142.

18. Quoted by Wesley D. Sweetser, *Arthur Machen* (New York: Twayne, 1964), 116.

19. David Punter, *The Literature of Terror: A History of Gothic Fictions from 1765 to the Present Day* (London: Longman, 1980), 62, 241.

20. See Patrick Brantlinger and Richard Boyle, "The Education of Edward Hyde: Stevenson's 'Gothic Gnome' and the Mass Readership of Late-Victorian England," in *Jekyll and Hyde after 100 Years*, ed. William Veeder (Chicago: University of Chicago Press, 1987).

21. Judith Wilt, "The Imperial Mouth: Imperialism, the Gothic and Science Fiction," *Journal of Popular Culture* 14 (Spring 1981), 618–28.

22. Bram Stoker, *Dracula* (Harmondsworth: Penguin, 1979), 41. Punter (*Literature of Terror*, 257) calls Dracula "the final aristocrat."

23. See Norman Etherington, *Rider Haggard* (Boston: Twayne, 1984), 47.

24. H. Rider Haggard, *Three Adventure Novels: She, King Solomon's Mines, Allan Quatermain* (New York: Dover, 1951), 192–93.

25. Nina Auerbach, *Woman and the Demon: The Life of a Victorian Myth* (Cambridge: Harvard University Press, 1982), 37. See also Sandra M. Gilbert, "Rider Haggard's Heart of Darkness," *Partisan Review* 50 (1983), 444–53, and Carol A. Senf, "*Dracula*: Stoker's Response to the New Woman," *Victorian Studies* 26 (Autumn 1982), 33–49.

26. Quoted by Brian Aldiss, *Billion Year Spree: The True History of Science Fiction* (New York: Schocken, 1976), 8–9.

27. See I. F. Clarke, *Voices Prophesying War, 1763–1984* (London: Oxford University Press, 1966), 227–39. See also Samuel Hynes, *The Edwardian Turn of Mind* (Princeton: Princeton University Press, 1968), 34–53.

28. P. G. Wodehouse, *The Swoop! and Other Stories*, ed. David A. Jasen (New York: Seabury, 1979).

29. See David A. T. Stafford, "Spies and Gentlemen: The Birth of the British Spy Novel, 1893–1914," *Victorian Studies* 24 (Summer 1981), 489–509.

30. Joseph Schumpeter, *Imperialism and Social Classes* (1919; New York: Augustus M. Kelley, 1951), 84.

31. J. A. Hobson, *The Psychology of Jingoism* (London: Grant Richards, 1901), 19, and *Imperialism: A Study* (1902; Ann Arbor: University of Michigan Press, 1965). See also John Allett, *New Liberalism: The Political Economy of J. A. Hobson* (Toronto: University of Toronto Press, 1981).

32. See J. A. Hobson, *John Ruskin: Social Reformer* (Boston: Dana Estes, 1898).

33. Hobson, *Psychology of Jingoism*, 13. Page numbers in parentheses refer to this volume.

34. Frederic Harrison, *Memories and Thoughts* (London: Macmillan, 1906), 233.

35. Robert M. Ballantyne, *The Coral Island* (London: Nelson, n.d.), 22.

36. Quoted by Etherington, *Rider Haggard*, 66.

37. Joseph Conrad, "Geography and Some Explorers," in *Last Essays* (London: Dent, 1926), 17.

38. Andrew Lang, "The Supernatural in Fiction," in *Adventures in Books* (1905; Freeport, N.Y.: Books for Libraries Press, 1970), 279–80.

39. Andrew Lang, *Cock Lane and Common Sense* (London: Longmans, Green, 1894), 2.

40. Andrew Lang, "Psychical Research," *Encyclopedia Britannica*, 11th ed., 22:544–47.

41. See L. S. Hearnshaw, *A Short History of British Psychology, 1840–1940* (New York: Barnes & Noble, 1964), especially chaps. 9 and 10, and Ed Block, Jr., "James Sully, Evolutionist Psychology, and Late Victorian Gothic Fiction," *Victorian Studies* 25 (Summer 1982), 443–67.

42. Sigmund Freud, *The Future of an Illusion*, trans. James Strachey (New York: Norton, 1961), 28.

43. Quoted by Oppenheim, *Other Worlds*, 132.

44. Rudyard Kipling, "The Sending of Dana Da," in *Works* 6:307.

45. Charles Carrington believes that "They" contains a warning against engaging in "psychical research," and J. M. S. Tompkins thinks Kipling grew less rather than more interested in the supernatural. But "They" clearly describes a supernatural experience. Perhaps all that Kipling quit doing was writing "ghost stories" of the skeptical, frivolous, "Phantom Rickshaw" variety. Carrington, *Rudyard Kipling, His Life and Work* (London: Macmillan, 1955), 373; Tompkins, *The Art of Rudyard Kipling* (Lincoln: University of Nebraska Press, 1965), 204. See also Elliot L. Gilbert, *The Good Kipling: Studies in the Short Story* (Manchester: Manchester University Press, 1972), 80.

46. See Sir H. Rider Haggard, *The Days of My Life: An Autobiography*, 2 vols. (London: Longmans, Green, 1926), 1:37–41. Hereafter volume and page numbers are given parenthetically in the text.

47. Saintsbury quoted in *Rudyard Kipling to Rider Haggard: The Record of a Friendship*, ed. Morton Cohen (London: Hutchinson, 1965), 4.

48. Alan Sandison's contention in *The Wheel of Empire: A Study of the Imperial Idea in Some Late Nineteenth and Early Twentieth-Century Fiction* (London: Macmillan, 1967) that Haggard in *King Solomon's Mines* "as in every other [book] he wrote on Africa . . . repudiates without fuss the whole arrogant notion of the white man's burden" (31) is misleading. Haggard's frequent criticisms of the behavior of white settlers—especially Boers—toward black Africans lead to arguments for strengthening rather than weakening imperial authority. Haggard was a keen admirer of Theophilus Shepstone and Sir Charles Buller, and he patterned his imperialist thinking after theirs.

49. Theodor Adorno, "Theses against Occultism," in *Minima Moralia: Reflections from Damaged Life*, trans. E. F. N. Jephcott (London: Verso, 1978), 240.

50. Graham Greene, *Journey without Maps* (1936; London: Heinemann, 1978), 104: "The method of psychoanalysis is to bring the patient back to the idea which he is repressing: a long journey backwards without maps. . . . This is what you have feared, Africa may be imagined as saying, you can't avoid it."

51. Joseph Conrad, *Heart of Darkness*, ed. Robert Kimbrough (New York: Norton, 1963), 58.

52. George Gissing, *The Whirlpool* (Hassocks: Harvester, 1977), 16.

53. *The Last Will and Testament of Cecil John Rhodes*, ed. W. T. Stead (London: Review of Reviews Office, 1902), 190.

54. W. T. Stead, *After Death: A Personal Narrative* (New York: George H. Doran, 1914), 50.

55. Sir Oliver Lodge, *Phantom Walls* (New York: Putnam's, 1930), xi; Sir Arthur Conan Doyle, *Memories and Adventures* (Boston: Little, Brown, 1924), 390.

56. Sir Arthur Conan Doyle, *The Lost World* (New York: Review of Reviews, 1912), 13.

57. Sir Arthur Conan Doyle, *The Land of Mist* (New York: Doran, 1926), 132.

58. Sir Arthur Conan Doyle, *Pheneas Speaks: Direct Spirit Communication in the Family Circle* (London: Psychic Press, n.d.), 10.

59. Sir Arthur Conan Doyle, *The History of Spiritualism*, 2 vols. (New York: Doran, 1926), 1:173.

Chapter 9. Kurtz's "Darkness" and Conrad's *Heart of Darkness*

1. Chinua Achebe, "An Image of Africa," *Research in African Literatures* 9 (Spring 1978), 1–15. See also Chinua Achebe, "Viewpoint," *Times Literary Supplement*, 1 February 1980, 113.

2. Cedric Watts, " 'A Bloody Racist': About Achebe's View of Conrad," *Yearbook of English Studies* 13 (1983), 196–209. For another defense see Hunt Hawkins, "The Issue of Racism in *Heart of Darkness*," *Conradiana* 14:3 (1982), 163–171. Among critics who support Achebe see Susan L. Blake, "Racism and the Classics: Teaching *Heart of Darkness*," *College Language Association Journal* 25 (1982), 396–404, and Eugene B. Redmond, "Racism, or Realism? Literary Apartheid, or Poetic License? Conrad's Burden in *The Nigger of the 'Narcissus*,' " in Joseph Conrad, *The Nigger of the "Narcissus*," ed. Robert Kimbrough (New York: Norton, 1979), 358–68. Achebe is, however, in a minority even among nonwestern writers; see Peter Nazareth, "Out of Darkness: Conrad and Other Third World Writers," *Conradiana* 14:3 (1982), 173–87.

3. Joseph Conrad, *Heart of Darkness*, ed. Robert Kimbrough (New York: Norton, 1963), 7. Page numbers from this edition are given parenthetically in the text.

4. Fredric Jameson, *The Political Unconscious: Narrative as a Socially Symbolic Act* (Ithaca: Cornell University Press, 1981), 206–80. See also Ian Watt's discussions of "impressionism" and "symbolism" in *Conrad in the Nineteenth Century* (Berkeley: University of California Press, 1979), 168–200.

5. Benita Parry, *Conrad and Imperialism* (London: Macmillan, 1983), 10.

6. See S. J. Cookey, *Britain and the Congo Question, 1885–1913* (London: Longmans, 1968). Cookey dates the beginning of British humanitarian protest against Leopold's policies as early as 1888 (35). Edmund D. Morel estimated the decline of the population of the Congo over a twenty-five-year period as eight million. See his *History of the Congo Reform Movement*, ed. W. R. Louis and Jean Stengers (Oxford: Clarendon Press, 1968), 7. In the appendix the editors cite the Commission for the Protection of

Natives formed by the Belgian government, which in 1919 declared that the population of the Congo may have declined by as much as one half over the same period. Exact figures are, of course, impossible to come by. Roger Casement offered the perhaps conservative estimate that Leopold's exploitation reduced the population by three million. See Colin Legum, *Congo Disaster* (Baltimore: Penguin, 1961), 35.

7. Conrad's letter is quoted in E. D. Morel, *King Leopold's Rule in Africa* (1904; Westport, Conn.: Negro Universities Press, 1970), 351–52.

8. See Hunt Hawkins, "Joseph Conrad, Roger Casement, and the Congo Reform Movement," *Journal of Modern Literature* 9 (1981), 65–80; "Conrad and Congolese Exploitation," *Conradiana* 13:2 (1981), 94–100; and "Conrad's Critique of Imperialism in *Heart of Darkness*," *PMLA* 94:2 (1979), 286–99. The Morel quotation appears in the last article, 293, and originally in Morel, *History of the Congo Reform Movement*, 205n.

9. See Hawkins, "Conrad's Critique of Imperialism," 292–93.

10. Joseph Conrad and Ford Madox Hueffer, *The Inheritors: An Extravagant Story* (New York: McLure, Phillips, 1901), 16. Page numbers are given parenthetically in the text. On the collaboration between Conrad and Hueffer see Thomas C. Moser, *The Life in the Fiction of Ford Madox Ford* (Princeton: Princeton University Press, 1980), 40–47.

11. Conrad to Roger Casement quoted in Morel, *King Leopold's Rule in Africa*, 117.

12. See M. M. Mahood, *The Colonial Encounter: A Reading of Six Novels* (London: Rex Collings, 1977), 12.

13. See Norman Sherry, *Conrad's Western World* (Cambridge: Cambridge University Press, 1971); Gerard Jean-Aubry, *Joseph Conrad in the Congo* (1926; New York: Haskell House, 1973); and Henryk Zins, *Joseph Conrad and Africa* (Nairobi: Kenya Literature Bureau, 1982).

14. Morel, *King Leopold's Rule in Africa*, 103.

15. Ibid., 23.

16. Watt, *Conrad in the Nineteenth Century*, 142.

17. Captain Sidney L. Hinde, *The Fall of the Congo Arabs* (London: Methuen, 1897), 124–25. Molly Mahood makes the case for Hinde's book as one of Conrad's sources, in *Colonial Encounter*, 12.

18. E. J. Glave, "Cruelty in the Congo Free State," *Century Magazine* 54 (1897), 706. See also Glave, "New Conditions in Central Africa," *Century Magazine* 53 (1896–97), 900–915.

19. E. D. Morel, *Red Rubber: The Story of the Rubber Slave Trade on the Congo* (London: T. F. Unwin, 1906), 77.

20. See Edward W. Said, *Joseph Conrad and the Fiction of Autobiography* (Cambridge: Harvard University Press, 1966), 142–43.

21. Parry, *Conrad and Imperialism*, 23. See also Abdul R. JanMohamed, *Manichean Aesthetics: The Politics of Literature in Colonial Africa* (Amherst: University of Massachusetts Press, 1983).

22. Achebe, "Image of Africa," 10.

23. Jameson, *Political Unconscious*, 219.

24. Martin Green, *Dreams of Adventure, Deeds of Empire* (New York: Basic Books, 1979), 313.

25. Raymond Williams, *The English Novel from Dickens to Lawrence* (New York: Oxford University Press, 1970), 145.

26. Albert Guerard, *Conrad the Novelist* (Oxford: Oxford University Press, 1958), 39. See also the essays in Kimbrough, ed., *Conrad's Heart of Darkness*; *Conrad's "Heart of Darkness" and the Critics*, ed. Bruce Harkness (Belmont, Calif.: Wadsworth, 1960); and

Conrad: A Collection of Critical Essays, ed. Marvin Mudrick (Englewood Cliffs, N.J.: Prentice-Hall, 1966).

27. Morel, *Red Rubber*, 49.

28. Watt, *Conrad in the Nineteenth Century*, 141–45. See also Cookey, *Britain and the Congo Question*, 31–34.

29. Hannah Arendt, *Imperialism* (New York: Harcourt, Brace & World, 1968), 70.

30. Sir Harry H. Johnston, *British Central Africa* (London: Methuen, 1897), 68.

31. Lionel Trilling, "On the Modern Element in Literature," in *Beyond Culture: Essays on Literature and Learning* (New York: Harcourt Brace Jovanovich, 1965), 17–18.

32. Lionel Trilling, *Sincerity and Authenticity* (Cambridge: Harvard University Press, 1972), 106.

33. Trilling, "On the Modern Element," 18.

34. Daniel R. Schwarz calls Kurtz a "demonic artist" but does not elaborate on the comparison between Kurtz and Conrad. See his *Conrad: "Almayer's Folly" to "Under Western Eyes"* (Ithaca: Cornell University Press, 1980), 72.

35. I owe this point and the quotations that illustrate it to John A. McLure, *Kipling and Conrad: The Colonial Fiction* (Cambridge: Harvard University Press, 1981), 89–90.

Index

Library of Congress Cataloging-in-Publication Data

Brantlinger, Patrick, 1941–
    Rule of darkness.

    Bibliography: p.
    Includes index.
    1. English literature—19th century—History and
criticism.   2. Imperialism in literature.   3. Colonies
in literature.   4. English literature—20th century—
History and criticism.   I. Title.
PR469.I52B73   1988   820'.9'358   87-47823
ISBN 0-8014-2090-3 (alk. paper)